OXFORD E

General Editor

Associate General Editors: P

A WOMAN KILLED WITH KINDNESS

AND OTHER DOMESTIC PLAYS

IN about 1590, an unknown dramatist had the idea of writing a tragedy about the lives of ordinary people, instead of the genre's usual complement of kings and queens and politicians. His play, *Arden of Faversham*, inaugurated a new genre of 'domestic' drama, set in near-contemporary England and concerned with issues of marriage, crime, and property rather than war and power. Some of the plays, such as *The Witch of Edmonton*, dramatized notorious capital cases, while others, including *A Woman Killed with Kindness* and *The English Traveller*, dealt with the consequences of adultery for society, the household, and the tragic individual.

MARTIN WIGGINS is a Fellow of the Shakespeare Institute and Senior Lecturer in English at the University of Birmingham. He is the author of *Shakespeare and the Drama of His Time* (Oxford Shakespeare Topics, 2000), and editor of *Edward II* (New Mermaids, 1997), *Four Jacobean Sex Tragedies* (Oxford English Drama, 1998), and *'Tis Pity She's a Whore* (New Mermaids, 2003). He is completing a descriptive catalogue of the entire corpus of drama written by English, Scottish, Welsh, and Irish authors between 1533 and 1642.

MICHAEL CORDNER is Ken Dixon Professor of Drama at the University of York. He has edited George Farquhar's *The Beaux' Stratagem*, the *Complete Plays* of Sir George Etherege, and, for Oxford English Drama, *Four Restoration Marriage Plays* and Sheridan's *The School for Scandal and Other Plays*.

PETER HOLLAND is McMeel Family Professor in Shakespeare Studies at the University of Notre Dame.

OXFORD ENGLISH DRAMA

J. M. Barrie
Peter Pan and Other Plays

Aphra Behn
The Rover and Other Plays

John Ford
'Tis Pity She's a Whore and Other Plays

Ben Jonson
The Alchemist and Other Plays

Ben Jonson
The Devil is an Ass and Other Plays

Christopher Marlowe
Doctor Faustus and Other Plays

John Marston
The Malcontent and Other Plays

Thomas Middleton
*Women Beware Women and
Other Plays*

*A Mad World, My Masters, and
Other Plays*

Richard Brinsley Sheridan
The School for Scandal and Other Plays

J. M. Synge
*The Playboy of the Western World and
Other Plays*

John Vanbrugh
The Relapse and Other Plays

John Webster
*The Duchess of Malfi and
Other Plays*

Oscar Wilde
*The Importance of Being Earnest and
Other Plays*

William Wycherley
The Country Wife and Other Plays

Court Masques
ed. David Lindley

Eighteenth-Century Women Dramatists
ed. Melinda Finberg

Four Jacobean Sex Tragedies
ed. Martin Wiggins

Four Restoration Marriage Plays
ed. Michael Cordner

Four Revenge Tragedies
ed. Katharine Maus

*London Assurance and Other
Victorian Comedies*
ed. Klaus Stierstorfer

*The Roaring Girl and Other City
Comedies*
ed. James Knowles and Eugene
Giddens

*She Stoops to Conquer and Other
Comedies*
ed. Nigel Wood

*A Woman Killed with Kindness and
Other Domestic Plays*
ed. Martin Wiggins

OXFORD WORLD'S CLASSICS

A Woman Killed with Kindness
and Other Domestic Plays

The Tragedy of Master Arden of Faversham

THOMAS HEYWOOD
A Woman Killed with Kindness

THOMAS DEKKER, WILLIAM ROWLEY, and
JOHN FORD
The Witch of Edmonton

THOMAS HEYWOOD
The English Traveller

Edited with an Introduction and Notes by
MARTIN WIGGINS

OXFORD
UNIVERSITY PRESS

PREFACE AND ACKNOWLEDGEMENTS

Five days before I was expecting to submit this edition to Judith Luna, my wonderful, patient, and supportive editor at Oxford World's Classics, a disc drive failed and all the files were lost. Worse, those files were then found not to have backed up correctly, leaving me like John Frankford in *A Woman Killed with Kindness* wishing I could call back yesterday. Paul Vanezis took away the recalcitrant hardware and made a sterling attempt to pull the relevant documents out of the electronic wreckage. Had he succeeded, I should not have been obliged, against the clock, to reconstruct the body of the edition from old files, nor to rewrite the introduction from scratch. My gratitude for his efforts is undiminished by the fact that they proved fruitless.

During its long gestation, this edition has benefited immeasurably from the proximity of my friend and colleague Catherine Richardson, who knows more than anyone else about the domestic world of the English Renaissance, and who has never been less than generous in sharing that knowledge and insight. I was fortunate to have the text checked by Eleanor Lowe, who is no mean editor herself, and to have enjoyed the company, intellectual rigour, and imaginative stimulation of Stephanie Gamble, Emma Harper, Marilyn Neal-Fisher, Heloïse Sénéchal, Christian van Nieuwerburgh, and all the other members of the Shakespeare Institute's Renaissance Drama Research Group. The Institute's play-reading group enabled me to hear all four plays read aloud several times, and effectively 'road-tested' the edition. Peter Malin offered experienced and informed advice on points of staging. Kelley Costigan held off innumerable men from Porlock and, when occasionally thrust into the role herself, bore it with good grace; she has been, in the final words of Old Thorney in *The Witch of Edmonton*, 'more kind than I have cause to hope or look for'.

M.J.W.

INTRODUCTION

Arden of Faversham (*c*.1590), the earliest of the four plays in this collection, was written at a time when English tragedy was systematically enriching itself by incorporating elements more usually associated with the opposite genre of comedy: narrative plotting based on intrigue in *The Spanish Tragedy* (1587), farcical episodes in *Doctor Faustus* (1588) and *The Jew of Malta* (1589), even a kind of happy ending, with a marriage, in *Tamburlaine the Great* (1587). *Arden*'s particular originality in this movement is memorialized in the fuller version of its title: *The Tragedy of Master Arden of Faversham in Kent*. Tragedy traditionally dealt with the falls of princes, but this play's protagonist is just plain Master Arden. Tragedies laid their action long ago and far away, but *Arden of Faversham* dramatizes a murder which took place in an English provincial town only forty years earlier. This is tragedy dressed down (the epilogue goes so far as to call it 'naked'), dealing with the domestic concerns of ordinary people who were more often deemed to belong in comedies. English drama had seen nothing like it ever before, and as late as 1603, when Thomas Heywood wrote *A Woman Killed with Kindness*, a tragedy without any high politics was still unusual enough to require specific acknowledgement in the prologue:

> Look for no glorious state, our Muse is bent
> Upon a barren subject, a bare scene.
>
> (3–4)

It is important to see such disavowals in that context because otherwise, at second glance, they can look disingenuous. *Arden*'s epilogue speaks of the play's stylistic simplicity, without any 'filèd points . . . foisted in | To make it gracious to the ear or eye' (15–16), and the audience of *A Woman Killed with Kindness* is told not to expect anything fancy. Yet the prologue which issues that warning is itself a piece of fancy-work: a sonnet, an overtly literary form which was particularly associated with complex love poetry. *Arden* too is not as unadorned as it claims to be. In the opening scene, for example, Arden describes his marriage in allusively classical terms to evoke a genuinely loving relationship of mutual sexual attraction:

> Sweet love, thou know'st that we two, Ovid-like,
> Have often chid the morning when it 'gan to peep,

And often wished that dark night's purblind steeds
Would pull her by the purple mantle back
And cast her in the Ocean to her love.

(1.60–4)

The plays are engaged in a delicate balancing act: tragedy's emotional intensity is relocated away from the genre's usual courtly setting, but the verbal sophistication which conveys the one must not be mistaken for the high style that customarily marks out the other. In terms of the dichotomy presented by Heywood's prologue, they have to be homespun russet on the outside but glorious tissue within, because everyone has the potential for tragic grandeur, no matter how ordinary they may be. It takes Shakespeare's Cleopatra almost the whole play to realize that, though Queen of Egypt, she is dominated by the same passions as those which drive a milkmaid. That realization, from the other end on, is the conceptual starting point for these domestic tragedies.

Even so, we should not underestimate the characters' rank and social standing. John Frankford, the hero of *A Woman Killed with Kindness*, is a gentleman 'possessed of many fair revenues' (4.5) and eligible to marry a knight's sister, who has a gentlewoman's accomplishments, able to speak foreign languages and play musical instruments; his new brother-in-law can himself afford to lay £100—around £15,000 at modern values—on a casual wager. If Arden of Faversham gives the impression of being less secure in his wealth, that is only because it is a fortune still in the process of being made:

My saving husband hoards up bags of gold
To make our children rich.

(1.220–1)

One of the play's latent ironies is that the money does not, as intended, pass down to the next generation, but is used instead to hire his own murderers: his wife Alice first lays out ten pounds to engage them, with the promise of twenty more after the deed is done, and later doubles it; the killer Black Will collects the cash himself from Arden's own counting-house before making his escape. Both plays depict comfortable environments moderately stocked with material possessions: Alice Arden owns silver dice and a prayer-book with a gilded cover, and when the adulterous Anne Frankford is banished to her husband's second manor house, he insists that she take everything with her, leaving behind not 'a bodkin or a cuff, | A bracelet, necklace, or rebato wire' (15.7–8) to remind him of her existence. Both households employ servants, though Frankford maintains a larger establishment and seems to enjoy more leisure time than Arden: Heywood's tragedy is full of sports and pastimes, whereas Arden is constantly rushing around on business, and, when finally able to relax and play some backgammon, gets murdered instead.

Arden claims gentle birth, and also appears to have bettered himself by marrying a wife 'descended of a noble house' (1.202). On the other hand, Frankford has already been there and done that: by virtue of his birth, he says, he was once 'Companion with a king' (4.4). Though the plays are not directly concerned with state power, save for its most terrible manifestations like the prison and the gallows, the characters do nevertheless exist in a continuum with it. This is especially important in *Arden of Faversham*, where many of them belong to the retinues of powerful men, and even someone of the lowliest rank, Black Will, turns out to be personally known to the highest, Lord Cheyne. Arden's business dealings operate at the level where large-scale political events trickle down into private enterprise.

Early audiences, attuned to references to the King after thirty-odd years of Queen Elizabeth I, would quickly have recognized the specific context in the upheaval following the English Reformation, when sequestered ecclesiastical land paid for political favours and enabled many a Protestant entrepreneur to get rich quick, until, in the reign of Edward VI when the play is set, demand had outstripped supply. In this competitive environment, Arden has the advantage of a close connection to the centre of national power, not directly but through his friend Franklin. The play begins with Franklin handing over the deeds conferring on him the lands of Faversham Abbey, and dispossessing everyone who thought they had benefited in an earlier round of distribution: 'all former grants | Are cut off' (1.461-2), says the infuriated Richard Greene, one of the losers by the new arrangement. Ultimately this is about the relative power of two statesmen, neither of whom appears in the play: Greene is Sir Anthony Aucher's man, but Aucher, though a favoured courtier, is trumped by Franklin's patron, the Lord Protector himself, so Arden gets the Abbey lands. What is probably a matter of marginal concern at court causes real resentment at the sharp end in Faversham: 'no revenge but death will serve the turn' (2.90), says Greene. And that means murder.

Murder is usually a lonely affair: when there are fellow conspirators, it is practical to keep their number to a minimum, for fear of discovery. So it is striking that so many people are implicated in Arden's murder: Alice, Mosby, Michael, Susan, Clarke, Greene, Black Will, and Shakebag. In part, this reflects the manic energy with which Alice tries to rid herself of her husband using the only method available in a society still encumbered with perilously restrictive divorce laws: with the possible exception of her lover Mosby, everyone else is brought into the plot by her, directly or indirectly. At the root there is a determination to maximize her options, coupled perhaps with a developing delight in the sheer dynamics of conspiracy: when scheme after scheme goes wrong, and Mosby is ready to give up and let Arden live, it is Alice who talks excitedly of her 'new device' (12.60). The result is that what should be a fairly simple scenario spreads outwards into a tangle of competing plots, all with the same objective, filling the entire tragedy. (*Arden of Faversham* is the only play in this volume without a secondary focus of narrative interest.) The corollary is the same kind of jockeying for position that informs the scramble for land grants: there is rivalry, notably between Black Will and Michael, about who will actually get to do the murder. Black Will in particular is paradoxically honest in his determination to fulfil his commission: he soon realizes he has undersold his services and wishes he could withdraw, but 'a bargain is a bargain' (3.68) and professional ethics force him to go through with it. This sets in relief the insouciance with which Alice, uninterested in the affair's contractual underpinnings, feels able to promise Susan Mosby in marriage to both Clarke and Michael as the price of their involvement. There is an irrational, blinkered attention to the only consequence that matters to her, without any sense that she may also be setting up collateral complications to interfere with it: two men cannot concurrently have the same wife, and every new person in a murder plot is another potential wagging tongue. Even so, it says something that the crime remains a secret throughout a long series of failed attempts, and only ultimately comes to light through an indelible bloodstain and an observant Mayor. The large number of co-conspirators means that there are a lot of people who would be happy to see Arden dead.

At one level, this is simply because Arden is a nasty piece of work, obsessively avaricious and short on social conscience:

> Desire of wealth is endless in his mind,
> And he is greedy-gaping still for gain;
> Nor cares he though young gentlemen do beg,
> So he may scrape and hoard up in his pouch.
>
> (1.474–7)

Greene, who says this, may not be the most reliable of witnesses even before he taints his moral judgement with complicity in Alice's plot;

but his observations are later objectively confirmed when Arden deals harshly with Dick Reede, who has a grievance comparable with Greene's but relieves it only with curses, not crime. Yet Arden is not an atypical figure who may easily be demonized, for almost everyone in the play strives to better themselves through money-making and frantic social climbing. If Greene is driven by resentment, others are in the murder plot primarily for gain: Clarke's main interest in Susan Mosby seems to be the fat dowry she brings with her, and Black Will and Shakebag treat it as an unorthodox but lucrative kind of trade; Will even indulges in fantasies of professional advancement to be the head of the guild. The trajectory of everyone's aspirations is upwards, and that sometimes entails shoving others down, whether into destitution or death: Arden's murder is only an extension of the kind of entrepreneurial competitiveness by which he has lived his life.

This is also a dimension of the conflict between Arden and Mosby. The sexual insult of being cuckolded is compounded by the fact that, by trade, Mosby is a botcher, a kind of inferior tailor—and according to the proverb, it took nine tailors to make a man. But part of Arden's bile is directed at the fact that he has not remained a lowly botcher, but 'Crept into service of a nobleman' (1.27), Lord Clifford, and flattered himself into promotion to the stewardship, a high office within the household. Alice Arden is not only his lover but his next rung on the social ladder: her friends are always telling her 'That Mosby loves me not but for my wealth' (8.108), and they have a point, however partial it may be. That is why the role can pay dividends when played by an overtly gay actor, such as the camp, feline Tony Beckley in 1962: a more conspicuously masculine portrayal risks tipping the balance too far towards sex. The play itself lays a subtle hint in the opposite direction, in the long-term repercussions of the moment when Arden takes Mosby's sword, the accoutrement of a gentleman, and tells him to go back to the humbler tools of his trade: 'Now use your bodkin, | Your Spanish needle, and your pressing-iron' (1.312–13). It is an act of open social aggression, but the substitution of needle and bodkin for sword also carries a clear sexual subtext. The insult stays long with Mosby, to re-emerge in the murder scene. As each blow is struck, the different killers pithily express their reasons: 'there's for the ten pound in my sleeve' (14.230), says Shakebag, while Alice sends her dying husband on his way with 'Take this for hind'ring Mosby's love and mine' (232). Mosby's contribution is, 'There's for the pressing-iron you told me of' (229). It seems that, of the three workman's implements Arden mentioned, the one which has most rankled is the one which has no secondary phallic implications. In the end, Mosby becomes a murderer primarily because he is a social climber, rather than because he is an adulterer.

Several factors combine to make the murder a shocking climax. One is simply that it has been such a long time coming. Among the play's most obvious debts to comedy is the element of farce which dogs Black Will and Shakebag as they bungle it time after time, always getting the worst of it themselves: in St Paul's churchyard, a shop awning is let down on Black Will's head as he is about to strike, and as they track their quarry across the Kentish marshes, Shakebag loses his footing and falls in the mud. With each successive failure there builds up a momentum until, near the end of the play, we may be inclined to share Mosby's conviction that 'These knaves will never do it' (12.59). Meanwhile, Arden walks through the action, innocently unaware of the peril at his heels. He survives through all the dangerous places, in lonely country roads and the bustling, anonymous city of London, only to be cut down in his own home, the one place where by rights he should be safest. And if it is his vicious acquisitiveness that marks him out for murder, it is quite another side of his character that actually gets him killed.

Arden of Faversham is tragic in rather the same way that *The Jew of Malta* is. Both plays are set in a world dominated by corrupt pragmatism, and centre on a protagonist who embodies some of that world's worst traits, but who meets his downfall when, just for once, he does something principled. Arden's most positive quality, established early on and reiterated through the play, is that, in spite of everything, he genuinely loves his wife: 'dear I hold her love, as dear as heaven' (1.39). This makes him manipulable, so that Alice can all too easily put him on the defensive after the penultimate murder attempt. The aim was to provoke a brawl in which he would be killed, but in the event it is Mosby who is wounded (along with, inevitably, Shakebag); Alice then recuperates this final failure by blaming the altercation on her husband's overreaction to a good-natured tease. This leaves him feeling responsible, unwontedly solicitous for the injured man, ready to make amends by inviting Mosby into his home and allowing him the place of honour in the only chair while he himself sits on a stool with his back unprotected. And so, at long last, down he goes. In *The Jew of Malta*, the principle is articulated in the prologue, spoken by the ghost of Machiavelli, the arch-philosopher of Renaissance secular pragmatism: those who rise by following his amoral precepts, but later abandon them, 'are poisoned by my climbing followers'. The pity of it is not simply that Arden dies, but that he dies through his own good nature at the hands of people who share his vices.

A Woman Killed with Kindness

Whereas the main action of *Arden of Faversham* takes place in a small provincial town, *A Woman Killed with Kindness* is a country tragedy. Frankford's home is an isolated grange in the vast open spaces of the pre-industrial north, about three hours' ride from York: to get there in time for an 8 a.m. appointment, he would have to get up at five-o'clock (11.68). Alice Arden worries that her 'marrow-prying neighbours' (1.135) might discover her affair with Mosby, but the Frankfords have no nearby neighbours: the action is conceived in terms of large manorial estates, like the 'lordship' which Shafton has acquired and wants to augment by swallowing up the 'goodly ground' (7.13–14) of Sir Charles Mountford's ancestral lands. When Frankford, having dissembled an overnight business trip, creeps back into the house to find his wife in bed with his resident friend Wendoll, Heywood's writing emphasizes the utter stillness of a country night, so unlike the nocturnal London familiar to the play's first audiences, where the bellman regularly broke the silence by calling out the hours:

FRANKFORD   Hear'st thou no noise?
NICHOLAS Hear? I hear nothing but the owl and you.
FRANKFORD So; now my watch's hand points upon twelve,
   And it is dead midnight.   (13.3–6)

The household is necessarily an inward-looking community, which makes much of its own entertainment and extends its guests, such as Cranwell, the hospitality of an overnight stay. This reflects the more introspective concerns of the play, in contrast with the social volatility that drives *Arden of Faversham*, and goes a long way to explaining the sexual obsession which Wendoll develops for the household's only woman of rank.

The sense of isolation is compounded in an odd, jarring juxtaposition of the two plots: first, in the already well advanced sub-plot, we see Sir Charles Mountford released from prison, his creditors paid off by his enemy Sir Francis Acton; then, in the very next scene, Cranwell encourages Frankford to broker a truce between the two feuding knights, and expresses pity for Sir Charles, who (so far as Cranwell knows) still 'lies in York Castle, needy | And in great want' (11.26–7). Evidently news travels slowly here. More broadly, it is relevant that the sub-plot of Mountford and Acton seems to develop faster than the Frankford story. Heywood would use the same structural device two decades later in the tighter confines of *The English Traveller*, but here it serves specifically to create a sense of the sleepiness, the slow pace of life in Frankford's household compared with the outside world: Mountford has already been in and out of prison twice by the time, more than two-thirds of the way through the play, that Frankford makes his crucial, life-changing discovery that his wife is an adulteress. The point is underlined by the unexpected introduction, as startling as a crash zoom in a film, of an objective measure of time: the play began in the immediate aftermath of Frankford's wedding, and now he confronts the errant Anne with the two infant children of their marriage. Evidently a lot of fictional time has passed, perhaps two years, in no more than seventy-five minutes of playing time.

It is worth remembering that the prologue paradoxically proclaims the play's rustic simplicity in sonnet form. There is a hidden artfulness to the overall construction which operates through meaningful juxtapositions of incident: the play begins with the Frankfords' marriage and ends with the reaffirmation of that marriage; Anne embraces Wendoll on a bed of adultery, but ends up embracing her husband on her deathbed; the focal point of the household is the dinner table, and when Anne is banished, she starves herself to death in remorse. The same is true of the relationship between the two plots. Sub-plots in English Renaissance drama are usually less important for their circumstantial connections with the main plot than for their thematic parallels: *The English Traveller* uses nothing more than geographical proximity to bring its two plots together in narrative terms. In *A Woman Killed with Kindness*, Mountford's story is tenuously linked to Frankford's through Sir Francis Acton, who is both Frankford's brother-in-law and Mountford's enemy; but its principal contribution to the play as a whole lies in its contrasts and continuities with the main plot.

Frankford's story is essentially an indoor one, and its turning point in Scene 13 is staged as a process of penetration deeper and deeper into the private space of the house, ending at the master bedroom. Except for the prison scene, however, the sub-plot takes place mainly outdoors: the principal recreation is falconry where in the main plot it is cards, and Mountford and his sister Susan are shown 'Plying [their] husbandry' (7.11), forced by economic distress to make their living tilling the soil. This is one reason why the sub-plot develops more rapidly: its crises are open, whereas the Frankford house becomes a place of festering secrets half-glimpsed in the suggestive, but potentially quite innocent, names of the card games mentioned by the adulterous couple.

Both plots are ultimately social, centrally concerned with relations between people and the way they create bonds of obligation between themselves which go beyond the merely economic and contractual associations which are at the root of *Arden of Faversham*; but both are also rooted in private space, kicked into action by the emergence of evil from the dark places inside human beings. When Sir Francis Acton loses his £100 wager and quibbles about it, Mountford loses his temper, draws his sword, and unthinkingly propels himself into criminality by killing two of Acton's retainers. All the different explanations for human wickedness current in the period agreed that its origins lay in some compulsive, dominating force prior to a person's will to action; so Mountford is not, as it may seem, attempting a sophistical evasion of personal responsibility when he comes to his senses and says,

> My God! What have I done? What have I done?
> My rage hath plunged into a sea of blood,
> In which my soul lies drowned.
>   .   .   .   .   .
> Forgive me, God: 'twas in the heat of blood,
> And anger quite removes me from myself:
> It was not I, but rage, did this vile murder; ·
> Yet I, and not my rage, must answer it.
>   (3.41–51)

He has been temporarily taken over by the commanding but evanescent passion of anger, since classical times a recognized cause of (as distinct from motive for) murder. (Technically, however, Sir Charles's crime was defined in Elizabethan law as chance-medley, a lesser form of homicide which did not necessarily carry the death penalty.) This explains his sense of divided identity, in saying he has been entirely 'removed from himself': an enraged man was thought to be literally not responsible for his actions; the irony is that, as Sir Charles realizes in the last line quoted, he might nevertheless be held legally responsible for them.

Sir Charles is tortured by the knowledge of what he has done, but Wendoll endures the even more terrible awareness of what he is going to do: he speaks of himself as 'hurried to my own destruction' (6.18), forced on as if by some other agency to an act his will rejects. The play here engages in the contemporary dramatic interest in the premeditating criminal consciousness and the psychology of evil, which Shakespeare addressed most powerfully in *Julius Caesar* (1599) and *Macbeth* (1606). Wendoll is presented as an obsessive cursed with the inability to be single-minded in his fixation: underpinning the whole seduction scene is an intense portrayal of a man powerlessly watching himself slide into something against his will, constantly aware of the ethical status of his future deeds, but unable to stop himself putting intention into commission.

The peculiar psychological torsion of his temptation arises from the collision of a mastering passion with a powerful social duty. Frankford is represented as a fundamentally kind, generous man: when Sir Francis Acton warns him that, if he allows his wedding guests to feel neglected, they might 'charge you with unkindness', he instantly drops everything 'To prevent it' (1.78). As well as giving Wendoll house-room, he indulges his wife 'With every pleasure, fashion, and new toy' (13.108), and nobody ever loses by doing him a good turn. Even when having himself called away from home on a pretext, he acts true to his liberal nature and has the fictitious bearer of the summons taken down to the cellar to 'taste | A cup of our March beer' (11.48–9) for his reward. All this is kindness, in the full sense of the word, because each act of generosity is only the material expression of his positive feelings towards its recipient.

Accordingly, Wendoll's sense of transgression and shame is at least as much social as it is moral, focusing not so much on adultery as ingratitude. He fully understands the force of his obligation to his benefactor Frankford, to whom he is 'a mere stranger, . . . | A man by whom in no kind he could gain' (6.35–6): his adoption into the household has been an unconstrained act of generosity which he is about to repay with a cuckold's horns. So his better nature tries to assert itself:

> I will forget her; I will arm myself
> Not to entertain a thought of love to her;
> And when I come by chance into her presence,
> I'll hale these balls until my eyestrings crack
> From being pulled and drawn to look that way.
> (12–16)

But, as he says, 'villains, when they would, cannot repent' (51). All he achieves with his attempt at self-restraint is to stimulate the original obsession: in deciding not to think lustful thoughts about Anne, he thinks them; trying to forget her only brings on the idea of coming into her presence. Nor is he able to frighten himself out of it. Betraying Frankford will make him morally a traitor, and throughout the scene he can never quite get out of his mind the horrible image of a legal execution for high treason: it invades his discourse with unintended secondary meanings. If he is found out, Frankford 'will turn me off' (129), he says: he means that he will be expelled from the household, but the phrase also referred to the push which the hangman gave to the condemned man on the gallows. And when he tells Anne that her husband's kindness is 'recorded | Within the red-leaved table of my heart' (124–5), he is using a standard metaphor for the things one holds dear; but the word 'red' gives it a horrid physical particularity which recalls the climax of a hanging, drawing, and quartering, when the executioner would pull out the victim's heart and show it to the crowd with the words, 'This is the heart of a traitor'. But when this imagery comes to the surface of his discourse, he adroitly slips out of the victim's role and assigns it instead to Frankford:

> Hast thou the power straight with thy gory hands
> To rip thy image from his bleeding heart?
>
> (44–5)

Recasting the scene like this keeps up the pressure of self-recrimination—his new role as public executioner was the most detested of legal occupations—but allows him to dodge the fundamental implications of the metaphor. There is the same evasion when he invokes an alternative mode of retribution:

> Thou God of thunder,
> Stay in thy thoughts of vengeance and of wrath
> Thy great almighty and all-judging hand
> From speedy execution on a villain,
> A villain and a traitor to his friend.
>
> (21–5)

Again, the tone of his words belies their content: he calls himself a villain, and speaks of wrath, vengeance, and judgement, but what he actually asks for is a stay of execution. It is as if, whenever he looks like winning his struggle for self-control, he is taken over by another, less persuasive voice which ventriloquizes the rhetoric of condemnation, but allows the trenchant moral awareness to be supplanted with mere name-calling.

Beyond its usual associations of personal sexual betrayal, adultery was despised in the seventeenth century because it interfered with the smooth transfer of property down the generations. The usual assumption was that a son would inherit from his father, and would have a continuing duty to maintain and develop the estate. That is why Mountford, already feeling guilty at having used up his patrimony to

procure a pardon, will not sell his house to Shafton even though it
means a return to prison for debt:

> My great-great-grandfather,
> He in whom first our gentle style began,
> Dwelt here, and in this ground increased this molehill
> Unto that mountain which my father left me.
>
> (7.18–21)

Adultery complicated this stable onward progression because, once
discovered, it meant that a father could not be sure whether his heir
was also his son. When Frankford produces his children and tells Anne
that she 'Hath stained their names with stripe of bastardy' (13.124), he
does not mean that he actually believes they are Wendoll's biological
offspring, only that he can no longer ever really know.

The sub-plot presents the same collocation of personal and social
betrayal in the way Mountford is repeatedly crossed in his struggle
against destitution. Shafton, an intruder from the heartless entrepreneurial world of *Arden of Faversham*, is an obvious threat in the way he
feigns a friendly kindness only in order to secure the power of recipro-
cal obligation: he presses money on Sir Charles, 'not for love . . . |
But for my gain and pleasure' (5.52–3), then unilaterally turns the gift
into a loan when Mountford decides to give priority to kinship, and
will not sell the last remaining fragment of his dead father's property.
The irony is that he cannot rely on anyone else in the same terms: he
is left to rot in prison because nobody close to him, neither friends,
former tenants, nor even his uncle, will offer so much as a penny in
charity; 'He lost my kindred when he fell to need' (9.17), says Old
Mountford, earning himself the epithet of 'Unkind uncle' (10.4). In
the end, it is his enemy, Acton, who pays his debts and procures his
release.

As the two plots move towards a resolution, in each case
re-establishing the social ethic of kindness, they flip over. The rage
which made Mountford a homicide ignites in Frankford when he
discovers the adultery: he chases Wendoll across the stage with his
sword, but is prevented from making 'a bloody sacrifice' (13.68) by the
physical intervention of a maid, and retires to decide on a more considered way of dealing with things. Conversely, Acton is deflected from
his persecution of Mountford by the emergence of feelings not dissimilar to those which turned Wendoll into an adulterer: initially intend-
ing to cap his revenge on Sir Charles by sexually dishonouring Susan
Mountford, he finds himself unexpectedly falling in love with her.

The oddity of Sir Francis as a character lies in a combination of social virtue with crude, unpleasant behaviour: he fully understands and obeys the bonds of social obligation which are under strain everywhere else, but what he actually does by way of fulfilment is often crass and unsophisticated. His unrelenting vendetta against Sir Charles is a case in point. There is a queasy petulance in the way he always wants to go one step further before being 'Throughly revenged' (7.80), yet it is not really vengeance on his own account. The familiarity of *Hamlet* has naturalized the concept of avenging a blood relation, but Sir Francis acts according to a wider, more inclusive duty to his entire household: the men whom Mountford killed in the brawl were Acton retainers, and he treats this as an absolute and continuing relationship, not a mere contract voided by death.

There is a similar excess of zeal and lack of human sensitivity in the way he gets Sir Charles out of jail for the love of Susan. He is attempting unilaterally to create another bond of obligation:

> Well, I will fasten such a kindness on her
> As shall o'ercome her hate and conquer it.
>
> (9.66–7)

It is another coercive act, different from Shafton's only in that there is no hidden agenda. What he has not considered is the effect upon the recipient, not least because Sir Charles himself is incidental in the transaction, objectified as the gift being proffered to Susan. On learning what has happened, he tells his jailer,

> By Acton freed! Not all thy manacles
> Could fetter so my heels as this one word
> Hath thralled my heart, and it must now lie bound
> In more strict prison than thy stony jail.
> I am not free: I go but under bail.
>
> (10.92–6)

The problem is that it is a gift which cannot be refused or returned: Acton has paid the debts, so the jailer can't and won't take his former prisoner back. All Mountford can do is repay the money in kind, clearing the obligation by unwillingly giving his sister to his enemy; all she can do is submit to rape and then play the Lucrece, assuaging her shame in suicide. Acton, finally put on the back foot by this 'honourable, wrested courtesy' (14.121), ends the feud and marries the girl even though by ordinary social standards she is 'too poor' (124) for such an alliance. 'Take her,' Sir Charles tells him, 'She's worth your money' (108–9); but the point is that she is worth more than money. Mountford's action decisively shifts the sub-plot's spiral of financial transactions back into human terms, re-establishing the ethic of kindness, so Susan does not need to ply her knife. Even so, it is worth registering her lack of enthusiasm when she says that now she will 'learn to love where I till now did hate' (148).

The shaming power of kindness is also the key factor in the main plot's conclusion, and again it is the woman who is the loser by it. The play's title says it all in a complex of double meanings. Proverbially, one killed a wife with kindness by spoiling her, as arguably Frankford has done; and criminal history is littered with cases of husbands who have literally killed their wives upon finding them in bed with other men. Frankford's more measured response to the situation is supremely magnanimous, yet also, ironically, a killing kindness.

Anne's own brother avers that she deserves to die for her adultery: 'Death to such deeds of shame is the due meed' (17.22). It was also the only way to dissolve most seventeenth-century marriages: divorce was a rare and costly phenomenon, and usually required humiliating evidence of non-consummation. In letting Anne live, banished from his home but maintained in her own separate establishment seven miles away, Frankford cuts out of his life not only her but every comfort that marriage can offer: he is, he says, 'a widower ere my wife be dead' (15.30). It is a great act of self-denial, but it also denies Anne the very thing which, in her guilt, she most wants, some form of condign punishment:

> O to redeem my honour
> I would have this hand cut off, these my breasts seared,
> Be racked, strappadoed, put to any torment;
>
> . . . . .
>
> He cannot be so base as to forgive me,
> Nor I so shameless to accept his pardon.
>
> (13.133–9)

And so she imposes that punishment on herself, through a slow, remorseful process of self-starvation. By the end of the play, Sir Francis Acton has come round to the view that it might not have been such a good idea for Frankford to kill her after all:

> Brother, had you with threats and usage bad
> Punished her sin, the grief of her offence
> Had not with such true sorrow touched her heart.
>
> (17.131–3)

It is a characteristically blunt statement of the process: Anne was well treated, and in consequence she died a penitent. But the starkness of the moral equation, the lack of human delicacy helps to crystallize a scintilla of unease: it is rather like the Vietnam War general who destroyed a village in order to 'save' it. Frankford proposes that Anne's epitaph shall read, 'Here lies she whom her husband's kindness killed' (138). If that last line of the play is to be more than a jingling, self-satisfied recapitulation of the title, it must carry the implication of a downside. If it was kindness that first brought Wendoll into the household, and kindness that killed Anne, then, for all the word's positive, virtuous connotations, there is nevertheless some small sense in which it is also cruel to be kind.

The Witch of Edmonton

By the early 1620s, when *The Witch of Edmonton* and *The English Traveller* were written, English drama had cultivated a less rhetorical style. With the 'domestic' genre more firmly established, these plays were able to achieve a sense of realism by eschewing verbal elaboration and embracing the 'nakedness' which *Arden*'s epilogue only asserts. In *The Witch of Edmonton*, the high style, when it is adopted, carries connotations of insincerity. For example, Frank Thorney sweet-talks his new wife Susan Carter in the play's only sustained passage of metaphysical conceits:

> Diana herself
> Swells in thy thoughts and moderates thy beauty.
> Within thy left eye amorous Cupid sits
> Feathering love-shafts, whose golden heads he dipped
> In thy chaste breast. In the other lies
> Blushing Adonis scarfed in modesties.
> And still as wanton Cupid blows love-fires,
> Adonis quenches out unchaste desires.
>
> (2.2.95–102)

Whereas Arden uses classical allusion to authenticate his private emotional experience, Frank's words are feigned love-talk, unconnected with internal reality: he is already secretly married to his fellow-servant Winifred, in order to save her good name after she was made pregnant by their master, and has entered his bigamous alliance with Susan only in deference to his father, and for the sake of her dowry. In contrast, we see what can be done with a rough simplicity of discourse later in the scene, when Frank is preparing to leave Susan. She assumes he is going to fight a duel with a rival, and reacts with a raw passion which communicates itself through the unpolished repetitiveness of her lines: 'Dissemble not, 'tis too apparent. Then in his look I read it. Deny it not, I see't apparent' (160–1). The writer's art here lies in her artlessness, an anxious woman with feelings more powerful than she has words to express them with.

Ironically, *The Witch of Edmonton*, with its demons, ghosts, and sorcery, takes place in a world more alien to our modern experience than any of the others. The supernatural plays no part at all in the two Heywood plays (the ghost in *The English Traveller* is known all along for the spectacular falsehood it is), and its presence in *Arden of Faversham* is at best ambiguous. Some fundamentalist Elizabethans tended to regard human affairs as the focus of a struggle between metaphysical forces of good and evil: crime was instigated by diabolical intervention and exposed through the workings of divine providence. Nothing in *Arden* denies this interpretation of the world, but nothing requires it either: Alice's inability to scrape her murdered husband's blood off the floor—'The more I strive, the more the blood appears!' (14.251)—is explicable in terms of physics or theology according to an individual audience member's preference and prejudices; and after Arden's murdered body is dumped in the disputed Abbey lands, we are only told about, and do not witness for ourselves, the mysterious two-year persistence of its outline in the grass. Only *The Witch of Edmonton* takes as an uncontestable starting point the reality and power of metaphysical evil, as incarnated in one of its most memorable characters, the devil-dog.

Whenever the action takes a turn for the worse, be it tragical or comical, the murder of Susan Carter or Cuddy Banks getting a ducking, the Dog is present. But, oddly, he is generally treated as almost, but not quite, superfluous to events. The characters tend to assume that their lives are routinely influenced by invisible supernatural agencies. When Old Thorney hears that his son has married Winifred against his wishes, for example, Frank infers that 'Some swift spirit | Has blown this news abroad' (1.2.160–1), and he later ascribes his second marriage to the inexorable operation of a punitive providence which he is powerless to resist:

> No man can hide his shame from heaven that views him.
> In vain he flees whose destiny pursues him.
>
> (225–6)

Afterwards, having learned of the bigamy, Susan even treats her own murder as 'some good spirit's motion' (3.3.42), the intervention of a benign spiritual force seeking to save her from the shame of adultery.

But these are explanations which proffer themselves in lieu of any other. Just as, in *Arden of Faversham*, Mosby will swear a lie on his own salvation when it suits him (1.326–9), superstition here comes and goes according to whether it is needed. Frank thinks he understands the murder adequately in terms of his own will to action: 'The devil did not prompt me' (38), he says, oblivious to the Dog whom, in this scene, only we can see. The point is reinforced with an awful pun when he goes on to tell Susan that, in following him, 'You have dogged your own death' (40), and dramatic irony continues to cut starkly against him when he plans to present himself and Susan as victims of a robbery: he thinks he is tying himself up, and is surprised by his own facility— 'I did not think I could | Have done so well behind me' (73–4)— whereas we can see the reality, that the Dog is doing it for him.

At one level, the play is engaging with the same dilemma about human responsibility that torments Sir Charles Mountford in *A Woman Killed with Kindness*. Like Mountford's rage, diabolic temptation was a familiar explanation for homicide, explicitly mentioned in the standard formula for murder indictments. The play, like the law, operates in terms of the key Christian paradox that, though temptation is not coercive, sin is unavoidable: there is nobody who will not at some time succumb to the devil's blandishments, but every individual temptation is nevertheless resistible. The Dog makes it clear that his power is 'circumscribed | And tied in limits' (2.1.162–3): he cannot kill Old Banks as Mother Sawyer asks, for example. When he rubs up against people, as he does to Frank just before the murder, it does not inculcate criminality, only helps to bring it out:

> The mind's about it now. One touch from me
> Soon sets the body forward.
>
> (3.3.2–3)

In his final scene, he presents himself to Cuddy Banks as a spiritual predator stalking human beings, drawn towards incipient moral corruption like a shark to blood:

> Thou never art so distant
> From an evil spirit but that thy oaths,
> Curses, and blasphemies pull him to thine elbow.
> Thou never tell'st a lie but that a devil
> Is within hearing it; thy evil purposes
> Are ever haunted. But when they come to act,
> As thy tongue slandering, bearing false witness,
> Thy hand stabbing, stealing, cozening, cheating,

He's then within thee. Thou play'st, he bets upon thy part.
Although you lose, yet he will gain by thee.

(5.1.127–36)

But there is a central vagueness here about the nature of the influence
once he is 'within' his victim, which corresponds with the curious mar-
ginality of his agency in the murder.

Frank Thorney is not presented as merely a deluded puppet of a
malign but unsuspected higher power. With the possible exception of
the self-tied bonds, nothing in the murder scene *requires* the Dog to be
present; yet he is present all the same. This is even more true in his
story's second crucial turning point, when Susan's sister Katherine
finds the murder weapon in Frank's coat. Everything makes its own
knotted sense in terms of human behaviour alone: food is brought to
Frank, who is convalescent in bed after the supposed robbery, but the
maid forgets to bring him any cutlery to eat it with; Katherine decides
to save time by looking out Frank's own knife, which will still have
Susan's blood on it, and Frank tries to stop her by pretending he isn't
hungry; Katherine won't be diverted (sick people must eat to keep
their strength up), and finds the incriminating blade. And yet, once
again, the Dog is there too, shrugging for joy and dancing. It is as if we
are given a full and sufficient causal explanation for events—Frank's
murderousness, Katherine's benign persistence—and then the devil
on top. He is a factor over and above what is necessary, yet cannot be
cut away by Occam's razor because he is stubbornly *there*, a supernatural being who cannot be fully accommodated within the play's material world, and who appears both responsible and not responsible for
what happens.

The Elizabeth Sawyer plot has a similar uneasy sense of things not
fitting together as neatly as they might. There is an important intervention some way into the play, when the Justice forestalls the locals'
attempt to lynch Mother Sawyer, and insists that any accusation of a
capital crime, as witchcraft was in the seventeenth century, needs to be
grounded in harder evidence than mere angry assertion: 'Unless your
proofs come better armed, instead of turning her into a witch, you'll
prove yourselves stark fools' (4.1.42–3). That might usefully have
been said much earlier. When she first appears, Mother Sawyer makes
it clear that she is scapegoated by Edmonton for no better reason than
that she is an ugly, uneducated old woman:

> 'Cause I am poor, deformed and ignorant,
> And like a bow buckled and bent together
> By some more strong in mischiefs than myself,

Must I for that be made a common sink
For all the filth and rubbish of men's tongues
To fall and run into?

(2.1.3–8)

Repeatedly through the play, the animus against her is shown to be insufficiently related to anything she might actually have done. 'What witch have we about us but Mother Sawyer?' (4.1.8–9) asks one of the countrymen. Quite a few, if we are to believe one of the morris dancers in an earlier scene: 'witches themselves are so common nowadays. . . . They say we have three or four in Edmonton, besides Mother Sawyer' (3.1.11–13). But nobody seems to consider the possibility that bad events, like cattle blight or sexual misbehaviour, might be ascribed to some other witch, let alone to a non-magical cause: Elizabeth Sawyer takes the blame for it all.

The irony is that the Justice's assessment of the situation as the ignorant baiting of a harmless crone would once have been true, but is now out of date. Her original maltreatment leads her to reason that she might as well be what she is said to be—' 'Tis all one | To be a witch as to be counted one' (2.1.116–17)—and her expressions of impotent vindictiveness are the scent of wickedness that first brings the Dog into the play: 'Have I found thee cursing?' he says, 'Now thou art mine own' (119). Elizabeth Sawyer is no witch until she is made one by society: again the issue of responsibility comes into focus.

Just before the Dog first appears, Mother Sawyer describes her principal persecutor, Old Banks, in a way that strikingly anticipates the turn her life is about to take: she says she wants

Revenge upon this miser, this black cur
That barks and bites, and sucks the very blood
Of me and of my credit.

(114–16)

The metaphor then swiftly becomes literal: before the scene is out, she has actually suckled a black dog with her own blood. The collocation of social and supernatural evil is pertinent because they both have a similar status in the play, as half-acknowledged phenomena which are not adequately assimilated into the crude simplicity of the play's penal conclusion. Just as Old Banks precipitates Elizabeth Sawyer's downfall with his abuse, so, in a sense, does the undisciplined sexual behaviour of Sir Arthur Clarington set Frank Thorney on the road to bigamy and then murder: 'you are worthier to be hanged of the two, all things considered' (5.2.7–8), Old Carter tells the promiscuous knight.

But all things never are considered. At points, the play touches on a broader society whose upper ranks are riddled with bribery and sexual misconduct like Sir Arthur's. Ultimately the Dog spares fat Cuddy Banks because he represents lean pickings compared with the 'corrupted greatness' (5.1.180) to be found at court, and Mother Sawyer defines witchcraft in terms of the abuses committed by the rich and powerful:

> These by enchantments can whole lordships change
> To trunks of rich attire, turn ploughs and teams
> To Flanders mares and coaches, and huge trains
> Of servitors to a French butterfly.
> Have you not city-witches who can turn
> Their husbands' wares, whole standing shops of wares,
> To sumptuous tables, gardens of stol'n sin;
> In one year wasting what scarce twenty win?
> Are not these witches?
>
> (4.1.111–19)

In a sense, she is doing the same as one of the countrymen earlier in the scene when he implies that only black magic could explain his wife's adultery with a servant: she is attempting to deflect attention away from her own evils. Yet, tellingly, the justice agrees with her ethical thrust, whilst also having to admit that none of this metaphorical witchcraft is against the law, only the literal variety of which she stands accused. Moral guilt seems to escalate as you ascend the social scale, but it is always the lower orders who are the more easily indictable: Sir Arthur is fined, but Frank Thorney goes to the gallows.

As condemned men were wont to do, Frank asserts that he has earned his fate: '' 'tis just | That law should purge the guilt of blood and lust' (5.3.141–2). If one accepts, as everyone did in the seventeenth century, that anyone ever deserves to be hanged for anything, then it is impossible to disagree with Frank's self-assessment: the only legally meaningful interpretation of events is tightly focused on the ascription of the play's two capital crimes of witchcraft and murder to their respective criminals. But the process of the play, introducing the wildcards of social and supernatural evil, opens out and complicates our sense of individual culpability. Frank is a murderer, but he is also a weak, foolish victim of those around him. And, if the Dog cannot make anything happen that was not on the brink of happening anyway, how much harm has Elizabeth Sawyer actually done, even in precipitating the madness and suicide of Anne Ratcliffe? Their tragedy is not that they die as criminals, but that they become criminals in the first place, and so find themselves in the power of a society which is habitually tougher on crime than it is on the causes of crime.

The English Traveller

Like *A Woman Killed with Kindness*, *The English Traveller* has two plots, one tragic and one comic. Both are predicated on the assumption that, while there is experience and profit to be gained from travel, it is always much safer to remain at home. The play is set in a strikingly stable version of contemporary English society, in which there are no obvious social fractures or avaricious land-grabbers to threaten the well-off, property-owning principal characters and their households. It is a mark of that stability that these people are usually terribly polite to one another.

A case in point is the scene in which Wincott and his family pay a visit to Old Geraldine's house, take a walk in the grounds, and return having picked some flowers without their host's permission. Old Wincott's self-deprecating words are telling:

> See, Master Geraldine,
> How bold we are; especially these ladies
> Play little better than the thieves with you,
> For they have robbed your garden.
> (3.1.100–3)

Here, naming the threat excludes it: Wincott can only say such a thing because there are no thieves in the garden, because he is totally confident that his words will be taken as playful metaphor, implying no scintilla of blame. If it is nevertheless a little tactless (and the ladies do seem taken aback), Old Geraldine defuses the situation by saying that they are welcome to the entire field of flowers, not just the ones they are wearing: 'These and the rest | Are, ladies, at your service' (108–9). The exchange is driven by the two old men's concern to identify and neutralize the slightest cause of offence: first Wincott ensures that Geraldine cannot possibly object to the picked flowers by overstating the infraction, and then Geraldine reciprocates by giving the ladies back their good character. It all takes place at a level of courtesy which is unrelated to actual behaviour: just as nobody has really stolen any-thing, so nobody is going to accept Geraldine's implied invitation to denude the garden of the rest of its blooms. And at the root of it is Geraldine's affluence: 'in full fields | The gleanings are allowed' (107–8), says Prudentilla; Geraldine owns enough that he has no need to be zealously parsimonious with his property. The prevailing tone of geniality rests on the characters' secure sense of their own material sufficiency.

Wincott's servant Roger shares his master's facility with language. Throughout the play, he elaborates situations into fanciful extended metaphors which stand out against the classical plainness of the play's dominant style: the preparation and consumption of a meal is figured as a military operation, for example, and taking a drink at a tavern becomes a friendly meeting with a family of personified drinking vessels. Again, this has virtually nothing to do with experienced reality: every such speech is a playful exercise of the imagination which grows, like a genie out of a bottle, along the lines of its own internal logic. At that level, they are self-contained acts, offering the theatre audience much the same pleasure as they do to the clown himself and his on-stage listeners. But in this they also establish something about a servant's lot in the play's society. Because everything in these verbal games ultimately depends upon an analogy, there is nothing romantic or escapist about them: the clown can never lose himself in his fantasies because they are always grounded in the real life to which he will return at the end. And if the audience has the leisure to enjoy this kind of witty elaboration, then so has Roger: a precondition for his playfulness is a degree of relaxed contentment.

Where the play's masters have the security of their affluence, the servants have the security of their place. The tension between Reignald and Robin, Old Lionel's town steward and country servant, seems at first to arise from an anxiety in this area: 'Shall I be beat out of my master's house thus?' asks Robin (1.2.2). But no such final ejection is ever contemplated: when Robin objects to the riotous goings-on at the town house in his master's absence, he is merely sent back to the country house where (as Reignald points out with no less managerial insight than asperity) he will be happier in his work. Even when problems emerge between characters of significantly different rank, they are handled with a striking mildness and leniency. When Bess, Mrs Wincott's chambermaid, tries to warn Young Geraldine that her mistress is sleeping with Dalavill, he supposes that she must be lying, but the harshest words he gives her are 'You're not a good girl' (3.3.88), followed, astonishingly, by a tip: 'I could chide you,' he says, 'But I'll forbear' (89–90). Servants are treated with consideration even when they appear to be doing wrong; and equally, the servants feel secure enough to try when they must to tell unwelcome truths.

The servant who least obviously fits this pattern is Reignald, who conceals Young Lionel's prodigality by denying Old Lionel access to his own house, and then has to construct a progressively more complex deception to justify it. This is comparable with Roger the clown's extended fantasies: both servants bring their transforming wit to bear upon reality, but where Roger juggles only with words and concepts, Reignald tries to do so with actual events and circumstances. Roger's pretence operates only within the boundaries of his own discourse, with an acceptance that it will soon evaporate; but Reignald seeks to impose an alternative, acceptable explanation of what Old Lionel finds upon his return, and he will need to make it stick if it is to do any good. Of course, that can never happen: Old Lionel will not be fooled for ever, especially after Reignald starts painting himself into such corners as the disputed ownership of Ricott's house, so there is never any question of a permanent disruption. Reignald belongs to a run of characters in literary tradition whose appeal centres on the inventiveness with which they manipulate situations from moment to moment, rather than any long-term achievements they may intend. He draws most directly on the witty slaves who drive the plots of many Roman comedies (one of which, Plautus' *Mostellaria*, was the source of his part of the play); but he is named after the wily Reynard the Fox in medieval beast fable, which helps to focus the subversively comical intelligence he shares with many a fox in English culture, from Volpone to Basil Brush. He is actuated, as one character puts it, by 'knavish cunning' (4.6.302), not malice, and his tricks may be taken 'Rather as sports of wit than injuries' (305). So even as we know he will not succeed, we want him to get away with it because we have enjoyed the process of his stratagems. He is finally forgiven, in part because he has done no real harm, but also because even he can be construed as a true and loyal servant using unorthodox methods: 'What he did | Was but for his young master' (303–4). There is no challenge to the social order, so the tone can remain benevolently genial.

Each plot turns on the fact that a character has left the safety of England to travel overseas. Young Geraldine returns full of the sights he has seen and the languages he has learned, and he is said to be 'bettered by travel' (1.1.86). But Old Lionel, who went abroad as a merchant rather than a tourist, underlines the other side of the experience when he declares,

> we will rest ourselves
> And bid farewell to travel; for I vow
> After this hour no more to trust the seas
> Nor throw me to such danger.
>
> (2.2.126–9)

It is significant that Geraldine's itinerary has taken him not only to France and Spain, Italy and Germany, but also outside Christendom: Greece and Palestine were part of the Ottoman Empire, and so were deemed especially risky visits for Westerners to undertake. Throughout the play, there is an emphasis on the perils of travel as well as its benefits: Young Lionel, playing at shipwreck while safely on dry land, imagines his father praying in earnest to the same sea-gods whom he and his drunken friends invoke in sport (2.2.13–14); Mrs Wincott worries about Geraldine's determination once again to 'cross . . . dangerous seas' (5.1.114); and Old Lionel is said to face 'the parching heat | And biting cold, the terrors of the lands | And fears at sea', not to mention 'gulfs, cross-tides, | Pirates, and storms' (2.1.93–8). In leaving the safety of England, these men have risked their lives. If each of them finds an unwelcome surprise awaiting him on his return, it is partly because there was a real chance that he might never have returned.

Geraldine seems faintly embarrassed by one of the questions put to him about his overseas experiences. Despite paying precise attention to other countries' buildings and languages, he sheepishly explains that he has pointedly avoided checking out the local women:

> These passed me but as common objects did,
> Seen, but not much regarded.
>
> (1.1.138–9)

After all, he had a childhood sweetheart back in England, whom he was widely expected to marry, and, unlike many another English tourist, he behaved punctiliously well while abroad. It is because he continues to behave well back at home that we can scarcely detect a ripple of the disappointment he must feel at finding his girlfriend recently married to a man old enough to be her father. Mrs Wincott's account of the situation only hints at its emotional complexity:

> It was once voiced that we two should have matched.
> The world so thought, and many tongues so spake.
> But heaven hath now disposed us otherways,
> And being as it is (a thing in me
> Which, I protest, was never wished nor sought)
> Now done, I not repent it.
>
> (2.1.227–32)

The last line, refusing to regret, almost elides the heartache; but even so, she speaks of a marriage not of her choosing, wished upon her in the absence of her preferred fiancé, and perhaps upon the presumption that he will never return. But when the old man is so kind, and evidently so happy in his young wife, English good manners prevail over emotional disinhibition.

Old Lionel's unpleasant surprise is more obvious, but of the same order: in effect, his son and heir takes early possession of the estate because he, having exposed himself to danger, may well be dead. In that respect, the comic plot addresses another foundation of the English sense of security and stability: the characters generally know what will happen after they die. 'O what a happiness your father hath,' Wincott tells Geraldine, 'Far above me, one to inherit after him' (1.1.96–7). The kind of financial crisis and sharkish entrepreneurship which lead to the alienation of the Mountford lands in *A Woman Killed with Kindness* has little place in Heywood's later play: Reignald may pretend that Ricott has been forced to sell his house, 'To part with that which he hath kept so long, | Especially his inheritance' (4.1.93–4), but the usual expectation is a smooth transfer of property down the family line. Young Lionel incurs criticism because his inheritance will not go forward like this, but instead be prodigally frittered away within his own generation: as Wincott puts it, what the father gets at sea, the son 'shipwrecks in the harbour' (2.1.99).

Much of the comic plot, driven by Reignald's deceptions, serves to protect Old Lionel from this premonition of posthumous bankruptcy: the awful truth is temporarily replaced with the more acceptable story of a murder, a haunting, and a son who, requiring alternative accommodation, astutely buys a desirable house next door. In stage-managing this, Reignald paradoxically does his old master the service of keeping back that truth until it can no longer do any harm. Young Lionel's very first scene establishes not only his riots but his repentance, in his soliloquy figuring himself as a house going to rack and ruin (1.2.93–130). The effect of the extended metaphor is to link the moral with the material, establishing a sense of his transgression as much in terms of the correct maintenance of property as in the degeneration of his personal character towards vice. That he can see it that way that early lends psychological credibility to his about-turn at the end. His interlude of spendthrift misbehaviour, he assures his father, was a good buy: 'You have but paid so much as I have wasted | To purchase to yourself a thrifty son' (4.6.266–7). In the end, the comedy of *The English Traveller* leaves society as stable and secure as it was at the start.

The tragedy of *The English Traveller* is another matter. Here, English courtesy and good behaviour abet the destructive processes which carry Mrs Wincott to her death. The crucial scene in which Dalavill sets Old Geraldine against his son shows a false tale believed because it is told in the right way, and by a gentleman. With the usual polite attention to others' thoughts and feelings, Dalavill astutely pins his slanders on something which the father has already noticed for himself: at the start of the scene, Old Geraldine thanks Wincott for 'The oft and frequent welcomes given my son', and his friendly tone moderates, but cannot entirely hide, his mild paternal jealousy as he continues,

> You have took him from me quite, and have, I think,
> Adopted him into your family,
> He stays with me so seldom.
>
> (3.1.6–9)

Dalavill is sure-footed in his exploitation of those feelings as he hints that there may be an ulterior reason why Geraldine is spending so much time at the Wincotts' home, and his indirectness in saying so—Old Geraldine has to ask him to 'be more open-languaged' (57)—suggests a reluctance which commands credence. The old man may be predisposed to swallow the story, but he is also not suspicious enough of the polite, socially acceptable teller. It is as if the characters have mentally located the world's dangers so comprehensively on the far side of the English Channel that they are unprepared for the deceits they may encounter at home.

Wrongly suspected, Young Geraldine writhes in his efforts to do the right thing. Earlier, when he and Mrs Wincott privately agree to marry in her eventual widowhood, he shows a simple candour in disavowing any wish for old Wincott to facilitate this by dying before his time, and readily accepts the corollary of his promise, that he will remain chaste and single in the interim. Disposing of his father's misconstructions is trickier, partly because the old man chooses to test his honesty by demanding that he should marry immediately, and partly because admitting the vows which prevent him from doing so would give offence: a father would usually expect to be consulted about his son's choice of wife. His only honourable option is to give up visiting the Wincotts for the time being, thereby cutting off the supply of raw material for scandal and misreport.

The problem is the way this redoubles the emotional pressure on Mrs Wincott. If the Wincotts enjoy a loving marriage, it also seems to be an entirely celibate one: even with a wife in her prime, Wincott entertains no expectation of fathering an heir at this late stage, and there is an early indication (later amply confirmed) that the couple sleep in separate rooms when he leaves her to sit up late with the other young people while he goes off to bed (2.1.174–9); she subsequently tells Geraldine of her own 'frozen, almost widowed bed, | Warmed only in that future stored in you' (5.1.98–9). Once deprived even of his sight and company, she is easy prey for Dalavill, who still has unquestioned access to the household as a suitor to her sister. When he next visits the house, at Wincott's invitation but secretly at night, Geraldine finds the guilty pair in bed together. His subsequent repudiation of her is the last straw of her mounting misery, shocking her not just into repentance but death.

It is easy, but misleading, to use Dalavill as a kind of lightning rod for our censure: as a false friend, a seducer, a cunning defamer patterned after one of the seventeenth-century archetypes of villainy, Iago in *Othello*, he is the most visible agent of Mrs Wincott's tragedy. She herself subscribes to this interpretation in her final letter to her husband:

> beyond pardon Dalavill
> Hath played the villain, but for Geraldine,
> He hath been each way noble.
>
> (5.1.229–31)

That is true, but not the whole truth. Dalavill is a sketchily conceived character compared with his Shakespearian prototype, or with his immediate source, Wendoll in *A Woman Killed with Kindness*, and his seduction scheme is not fully thought through: though he plays Old Geraldine skilfully in the slander scene, he cannot have known the full ramifications of Young Geraldine's dilemma, nor anticipated exactly how he would deal with it. The main dramatic interest lies not in Dalavill's villainy but Geraldine's nobility, which is itself an integral part of the problem: in setting and maintaining high standards of behaviour for himself, he makes too little allowance for the human frailty of the others who are affected. In that sense, it is his English social graces, his good manners and good behaviour, which unwittingly procure the circumstances that bring about his future fiancée's downfall.

All four plays ask difficult, uncomfortable questions about English values and practices which are more often taken for granted, from entrepreneurism to generosity, and from politeness to crime. Accordingly, it is misleading to represent them as 'homiletic tragedies', single-agenda plays which dramatize a secure lesson suitable for sermonizing. In the dreary homiletic literature of the sixteenth century, the world turns on a see-saw of sin and retribution which is almost Newtonian in its precision: providence ensures that the murderer always dies for his crime, sometimes perishing by the very same weapon. Not so in

Arden of Faversham: eight people are implicated in the murder and eight people come to sticky ends, but one of them is Bradshaw, who innocently carried Greene's letter back to Faversham. The play proper ends with Bradshaw's protest ringing in our ears: 'My blood be on his head that gave the sentence!' (18.38). Franklin, who kicked off the play by procuring the Abbey lands for Arden, then tries to impose a moral order on events in his epilogue, but is forced to admit, 'The painter fled, and how he died we know not' (8). The one thing which is essential in a homiletic story, showing how divine judgement always and inevitably overtakes the guilty, he cannot supply.

It is the same in the other plays: they resist easy moral classifications. In *A Woman Killed with Kindness*, Wendoll goes into temporary exile, hoping to learn the foreign languages that will get him a cushy position at court on his return, and his *English Traveller* counterpart, Dalavill, just takes himself off with the observation, 'The storm's coming, I must provide for harbour' (5.1.206). The neck-breaking justice at the end of *The Witch of Edmonton* may not have miscarried, but we are still left with a dreadful feeling that it is oversimplifying and short on equity. There is never an uncomplicated, all-inclusive moral ending in which the good end happily and the bad unhappily; that, after all, is what tragedy means.

NOTE ON THE TEXTS

All four plays in this volume have been freshly edited from the earliest surviving copies. The paramount concern, as with all editions in this series, is to transmit to a reader, as far as is possible, the experience of the plays in the theatres for which they were written. The early printed editions are treated not as authoritative documents whose every material feature must be punctiliously preserved, but as textual witnesses from which an editor attempts to reconstruct the plays as they were offered to the theatregoers of their time.

Accordingly, the most important components of any written play-text are the words of the dialogue, the part of the play which is identical in both media. The least important are bibliographical features such as title-pages or colophons, which have no bearing on any aspect of a performance and are not transcribed here. (The reader is, however, provided with the usual convenience of a list of the characters of each play, compiled afresh in every case whether or not such a list appeared in the early editions.) Somewhere in between are the stage directions, which represent but do not in themselves reproduce elements of the performed text.

In this edition I assume that, while stage directions are significant indicators of non-verbal action, their precise wording in the original editions is not textually substantive. Accordingly, the original stage directions are revised or expanded where necessary to clarify the action for a modern reader, without underestimating the texts' openness to interpretation; however, the original wording has not been altered without a positive reason for doing so. Minor adjustments of this kind have been made silently, but square brackets are used to indicate substantive, editorially introduced items of stage action.

There are several reasons why an editor might need to insert new stage directions. Where an action is mentioned in a simultaneously spoken line (such as when Susan draws her knife at *A Woman Killed with Kindness* 14.84), it is not usually necessary to clarify further: the dialogue is already doing the job of pulling focus onto the action. However, I have tried to avoid the inversion of the sequence of experience that can happen when a reader is left to infer a preceding action from a subsequent line of dialogue. In some cases, moreover, inserted stage directions help to bring out a significant series of actions which is obvious in performance, but potentially less so on the page. For example, there is an escalating sequence in Scene 17 of *A Woman Killed with Kindness*, concerning the way Frankford relates physically to his wife; some of these actions are implied in lines spoken beforehand, some afterwards, but to omit stage directions relating to any of them would be to risk obscuring the overall pattern.

Act divisions were not generally used in the commercial theatre at the time *Arden of Faversham* and *A Woman Killed with Kindness* were written, but had become standard by the 1620s. Accordingly, *The Witch of Edmonton* and *The English Traveller* are divided into the five acts marked in the first editions, but no attempt has been made to impose an alien five-act structure on the two earlier plays. Formal scene divisions had no place in Elizabethan and Jacobean theatre practice, but are included here for convenience (and are supplied silently when they are not present in the control texts).

Spelling and punctuation have been modernized according to the principles set out by Stanley Wells in *Modernizing Shakespeare's Spelling* (Oxford, 1979), using the lemma forms of the *Oxford English Dictionary* as standard. Contractions are represented by the equivalent modern contraction of the root words.

The textual apparatus is necessarily limited to emendations introduced in this edition; changes to the control text which are already part of the editorial tradition are generally adopted silently. However, emendations are always discussed where they are relevant to points of literary interpretation.

Arden of Faversham was entered in the Stationers' Register on 3 April 1592 and first appeared later that year in a Quarto edition sold by Edward White, and probably printed for him by Edward Allde. Two subsequent early editions survive, dating from 1599 and 1633 respectively; each was printed from its predecessor, and neither has any independent authority. Scholarly opinion can scarcely have been more polarized about the play's textual transmission: the 1592 Quarto represents either an exceptionally good text, printed from the author's own manuscript, or an exceptionally poor text vitiated by widespread corruption originating in memorial piracy. There is one point where oral transmission might account for an odd-sounding reading ('plot the news', in the last line of Scene 9, might better read 'plot anew'), but the case for memorial reconstruction has been wildly overstated. Ultimately a judgement on the nature of the text depends on the assumptions one makes about the origins of the play itself. The proponents of memorial corruption ascribe the intermittently rough metrics, reminiscences of other plays, and miscellaneous unconformities to negligent or illicit textual transmission, seeing these things as extraneous grime on the face of a masterpiece; but they are equally explicable as marks of authorial inexperience, a view argued at length in Appendix 1. Some of the evidence of inexperience (notably in respect of the role of Alice) seems to me fundamental, rooted in the very design of the play. Moreover, there is no sign that the text as printed has been transmitted through the theatre, which would be a sine qua non for a memorial reconstruction.

In several prefaces to his published plays, including *The English Traveller*, Thomas Heywood claimed to be hostile to their appearance in print, preferring them to be experienced in the medium for which they were written, the theatre. With perhaps suspicious frequency, he would assert that the play in question had come to the press without his knowledge, and by the time he found out, it was too late to stop publication; all he could do was contribute a modestly apologetic address to the reader. It is odd, then, that in many cases these prefaces were demonstrably the first part of the book to have been printed, and odder still that the printers often set the texts from Heywood's own authorial working manuscripts, or 'foul papers'.

A case in point is *A Woman Killed with Kindness*, which first appeared (without preface) in a Quarto edition printed in 1607 by William Jaggard for John Hodgets. The text shows ample indication of its derivation from authorial foul papers. Sir Charles Mountford's sister starts off the play as Jane, and the name is not always extirpated from later scenes after Heywood has decided to call her Susan instead. The speech prefixes for Spiggot alternate between his name and his function, sometimes 'Spiggot' and sometimes 'Butler', depending on the author's conception of him at any particular moment. There are intermittent vaguenesses about the precise numbers of characters required on stage: the opening stage direction of Scene 2 calls for 'two or three musicians', for example, and that of Scene 8 requires 'three or four servingmen'. All these are things which would need to have been ironed out in a working theatrical document. In the process, some of the minor roles may have become more substantial than they appear in the text as printed: the anonymous servingmen in the Frankford household could be coextensive with Jack Slime and Roger Brickbat, and the maidservant who prevents Frankford from killing Wendoll may actually be Sisly Milk-Pail (as she has been in some modern productions).

Heywood's handwriting is notoriously difficult to read, so perhaps it is understandable that the Quarto should contain a range of minor errors, which often happen close together in little clumps of compositorial carelessness: omitted words, wrongly assigned or misplaced speech prefixes, the transposition of a couplet (10.4–5); some of these errors are corrected in the next surviving edition, printed in 1617 by Isaac Jaggard. It is possible, however, that some of these 'corrections' (notably at 17.54) are in fact sophistications which smooth away deliberate discontinuities; accordingly I have been more cautious than some of my predecessors in adopting them into the text.

The only early edition of *The Witch of Edmonton* is a Quarto which appeared in 1658, thirty-seven years after the play was written. It was entered in the Stationers' Register on 21 May that year by the publisher Edward Blackmore, and he engaged James Cottrel to print the book. Cottrel's compositors worked from a manuscript which had been prepared for a stage revival by Queen Henrietta's Men in the mid-1630s, including a new prologue which had not been part of the original play as written in 1621, and which appears in this edition as an additional passage at the end of the text of the play. (The epilogue may also have been a late addition, but in the absence of strong evidence it has been given the benefit of the doubt and allowed to stand in the body of the text.)

In the text as it appeared in 1658, it is sometimes difficult to tell verse and prose apart: verse is sometimes set as prose and vice versa. In trying to differentiate between the two modes, one cannot assume that they divide along clear lines of rank and status, as is often proposed of English Renaissance drama: the lowliest character, Elizabeth Sawyer, often speaks in verse, from her opening soliloquy onwards (2.1.1–15). It would be truer to say that the distinction between prose and verse is a matter of casualness and seriousness—which makes it a matter of more than incidental concern. Some of the passages printed as prose have discernible rhythms to them, but they are not always regular pentameter rhythms (and in any event it is a mistake to assume that rhythm is necessarily absent from prose). Rather it is as if the speakers are sometimes struggling to attain a higher style only to be kept down by their clay feet of prose. With all this in mind, I have been more conservative than some previous editors in retaining Q's prose.

The first edition of *The English Traveller* was printed by Robert Raworth in 1633; the book may have been sold by Nicholas Okes, who registered his rights in the text on 15 July that year under the title *The Traveller*. The text appears to have been printed from a transcript with some theatrical annotation. It was not reprinted in the seventeenth century, although the rights remained in the Okes family until 1673, when they were bought by Thomas Vere and John Wright.

I am particularly indebted to the work of the following modern editors of the plays: for *Arden of Faversham*, M. L. Wine (Revels Plays, 1973) and Martin White (New Mermaids, 1982); for *A Woman Killed with Kindness*, R. W. van Fossen (Revels Plays, 1961) and Brian Scobie (New Mermaids, 1985); for *The Witch of Edmonton*, Fredson Bowers (in *The Dramatic Works of Thomas Dekker*, 1953–61), Peter Corbin and Douglas Sedge (in *Three Jacobean Witchcraft Plays*, 1986), and Arthur F. Kinney (New Mermaids, 1998); and for *The English Traveller*, Paul Merchant (in *Three Marriage Plays*, Revels Plays Companion Library, 1996).

SELECT BIBLIOGRAPHY

The first substantial study of these plays and their genre was *English Domestic, or Homiletic Tragedy*, written by Henry Hitch Adams in 1943. The book's central argument is apparent from the penultimate word of the title: Adams emphasized the plays' theological aspect and attempted to draw links with the Elizabethan homilies prescribed for regular reading in churches. The genre's subsequent critical history is one of a shift of attention from moral to sociological themes, starting with Peter Ure's 'Marriage and the Domestic Drama in Heywood and Ford', *English Studies* 32 (1951), 200–16. An extensive interim survey was undertaken by Andrew Clark in *Domestic Drama* (1975), and more recently a useful, general account of the genre is Vivian Comensoli's *'Household Business': Domestic Plays of Early Modern England* (1996).

Scholarship has enriched our understanding of domestic drama by the investigation of its various cultural and material contexts. One relevant body of literature is the conduct manuals which Laura G. Bromley brings into apposition with Heywood's first domestic tragedy in 'Domestic Conduct in *A Woman Killed with Kindness*', *Studies in English Literature* 26 (1986), 259–76. Lena Cowen Orlin's *Private Matters and Public Culture* (1994) argues for a domestic world dominated by patriarchal ideologies, while both Leanore Lieblein in 'The Context of Murder in English Domestic Plays, 1590–1610', *Studies in English Literature* 23 (1983), 181–96 and Frances E. Dolan in *Dangerous Familiars: Representations of Domestic Crime in England, 1550–1700* (1994) take for their focus the way crime makes private space a matter of public concern. *The Antichrist's Lewd Hat* (2002), by Peter Lake and Michael Questier, supplies an especially broad context in the popular criminal literature of the period, with some engaging ideas about the cultural and political ends which the material served.

Most recently, historically informed criticism has moved decisively inside the home itself. Wendy Wall's *Staging Domesticity: Household Work and English Identity in Early Modern Drama* (2002) examines the plays in terms of what actually happened in seventeenth-century households, with particular attention to the kitchen. Catherine Richardson's *Domestic Life and Domestic Tragedy in Early Modern England* (2006), based on unparalleled archival research into the actual material contents of people's homes, engagingly illuminates the way the characters' behaviour reflects actual domestic and social experience in English provincial towns. A specific case study is her essay, 'Properties of Domestic Life: The Table in Heywood's *A Woman Killed with Kindness*', in Jonathan Gil Harris and Natasha Korda (eds.), *Staged Properties in Early Modern English Drama* (2002), 129–52.

A great deal of thought about *Arden of Faversham* has been unhelpfully preoccupied with the question of its authorship, which is neither answerable nor particularly illuminating about the play. The essay which does most to bring out the tragedy's real interest and vitality is Alexander Leggatt's masterly '*Arden of Faversham*', *Shakespeare Survey* 36 (1983), 121–33. Catherine Belsey offers a stimulating feminist analysis of the play, and Alice in particular, in *The Subject of Tragedy* (1985). The play's hired killers and their broader place in dramatic history are studied in Martin Wiggins's *Journeymen in Murder: The Assassin in English Renaissance Drama* (1991). Marguerite A. Tassi examines the portrayal of Clarke the painter in the context of sixteenth-century attitudes to visual culture in *The Scandal of Images* (2005). Other useful essays include: Sarah Youngblood, 'Theme and Imagery in *Arden of Faversham*', *Studies in English Literature* 3 (1963), 207–18; Ian Ousby and Heather Dubrow Ousby, 'Art and Language in *Arden of Faversham*', *Durham University Journal* (1975–6), 47–54; David Attwell, 'Property, Status, and the Subject in a Middle-Class Tragedy: *Arden of Faversham*', *English Literary Renaissance* 21 (1991), 328–48; John M. Breen, 'The Carnival Body in *Arden of Faversham*', *Cahiers Élisabéthains* 45 (1994), 13–20. Patricia Hyde's *Thomas Arden in Faversham: The Man behind the Myth* (1996), published by the Faversham Society, assembles documents and records relating to the historical Ardern in exhaustive detail. (However, the book's appendix on the play is a less scholarly piece of work by a different author, based on out-of-date and untrustworthy speculation, and best avoided.)

Most commentary on *A Woman Killed with Kindness* concerns itself with aspects of either the play's ethical themes or its distinctive dramatic mode. Examples of the former are: Patricia Meyer Townsend, 'Honor and Perception in *A Woman Killed with Kindness*', *Modern Language Quarterly* 20 (1959), 321–32; John Canuteson, 'The Theme of Forgiveness in the Plot and Subplot of *A Woman Killed with Kindness*', *Renaissance Drama*, NS 2 (1969), 123–41; Frederick Kiefer, 'Heywood as Moralist in *A Woman Killed with Kindness*', *Medieval and Renaissance Drama in England* 3 (1986), 83–98; David Atkinson, 'An Approach to the Main Plot of Thomas Heywood's *A Woman Killed with Kindness*', *English Studies* 70 (1989), 15–27; and Jennifer Panek,

'Punishing Adultery in *A Woman Killed with Kindness*', *Studies in English Literature* 34 (1994), 357–78. Essays considering issues raised by the play viewed primarily as a work of art include: David Cook, '*A Woman Killed with Kindness*: An Unshakespearian Tragedy', *English Studies* 45 (1964), 353–72; Otto Rauchbaur, 'Visual and Rhetorical Imagery in Thomas Heywood's *A Woman Killed with Kindness*', *English Studies* 57 (1976), 200–10; and Rick Bowers, '*A Woman Killed with Kindness*: Plausibility on a Smaller Scale', *Studies in English Literature* 24 (1984), 293–306.

The *Witch of Edmonton* and *The English Traveller* have received significantly less critical attention than the other two plays. Useful essays on the former include: Leonora Leet Brodwin, 'The Domestic Tragedy of Frank Thorney in *The Witch of Edmonton*', *Studies in English Literature* 7 (1967), 311–38; David Atkinson, 'Moral Knowledge and the Double Action in *The Witch of Edmonton*', *Studies in English Literature* 25 (1985), 419–37; and Anthony B. Dawson, 'Witchcraft/Bigamy: Cultural Conflict in *The Witch of Edmonton*', *Renaissance Drama* 20 (1989), 77–98. Much of the small body of work on *The English Traveller* is (unlike this edition's introduction) predicated on the use to which Heywood put the play in 1633, when he published it as his contribution to an antitheatrical controversy. Two key essays offering different readings in 'meta-theatrical' terms are Norman Rabkin's 'Dramatic Deception in Heywood's *The English Traveller*', *Studies in English Literature* 1 (1961), 1–16, and Richard Rowland's 'Thomas Heywood's *The English Traveller*', in Michael Cordner, Peter Holland, and John Kerrigan (eds.), *English Comedy* (1994), 137–57. Readers of Rowland's critically acute essay should bear in mind that his speculations about the play's conception, original purpose, and place in dramatic history have been superseded by the emergence among the play's recent editors of a consensus that it was written in 1624, not 1627. The sub-plot's use of source materials is examined by Allan Gilbert in 'Thomas Heywood's Debt to Plautus', *Journal of English and Germanic Philology* 12 (1913), 593–611, and Michel Grivelet presents a sensitive reading of the relations between the two plots in 'The Simplicity of Thomas Heywood', *Shakespeare Survey* 14 (1961), 56–65.

A CHRONOLOGY OF THE PLAYS
AND THEIR GENRE

Domestic Plays, 1590–1642

*c.*1590 *Arden of Faversham*

*c.*1595 Robert Yarington, *Two Lamentable Tragedies*

*c.*1598 *A Warning for Fair Women*

1599 Ben Jonson and Thomas Dekker, *Padge of Plymouth* (lost)

1599 William Haughton and John Day, *Cox of Cullompton* (lost)

1600 William Haughton and John Day, *Beech's Tragedy* (lost)

1602 John Day, *A Bristol Tragedy* (lost)

1603 Thomas Heywood, *A Woman Killed with Kindness*

1605 Thomas Middleton (?), *A Yorkshire Tragedy*

1606 George Wilkins, *The Miseries of Enforced Marriage*

1621 Thomas Dekker, William Rowley, and John Ford, *The Witch of Edmonton*

1624 Thomas Heywood, *The English Traveller*

1624 Thomas Dekker, John Ford, William Rowley, and John Webster, *The Late Murder in Whitechapel* (lost)

*c.*1625 William Sampson, *The Vow-Breaker*

1634 Thomas Heywood and Richard Brome, *The Witches of Lancashire*

Arden of Faversham

1551 In Faversham, Thomas Ardern was murdered by his wife Anne and her lover Thomas Morsby, on Saturday, 14 February.

1577 Publication of Raphael Holinshed's *Chronicles of England, Scotland, and Ireland*, the source of the play (the dramatist probably used the second edition of 1587).

*c.*1590 *Arden of Faversham* written.

1592 Two printed editions published; one of them was illegal and all copies of it were confiscated by the Stationers' Company. Later editions appeared in 1599 and 1633. The 1633 edition added a woodcut showing the murder.

1633 The story was retold in an anonymous ballad, *The Complaint and Lamentation of Mistress Arden of Faversham in Kent*.

*c.*1650 An adaptation of the play was made, possibly for use by provincial or local players. In 1716 it was transcribed by the antiquarian Thomas Southouse.

1730 Performed by local amateurs at the Roebuck, Faversham, on 2 January. There are records of intermittent amateur performances in Faversham during the eighteenth century.

1736 An adaptation by Eliza Haywood performed at the Little Theatre, Haymarket.

1736 Adapted for puppets by Henry Collyer and performed in Faversham.

1759 An adaptation by George Lillo and John Hoadly (who completed the work after Lillo's death) produced at Drury Lane. The cast included: William Havard (Arden); Astley Bransby (Mosby); Mr Phillips (Black Will); Henry Scrase (Franklin); John Wignell (Michael).

1790 The Lillo/Hoadly adaptation produced at Covent Garden, in an abridged version by Joseph Holman, who played Arden. The cast also included: Elizabeth Pope (Alicia Arden); Mr Hartley (Mosby); William Cubitt (Black Will).

1799 Adapted as a 'serious ballet of action with songs' and performed at Sadler's Wells, produced by Richard Hughes and Sarah Siddons.

1897 Adapted by William Poel under the title *Lilies that Fester*, and produced for the English Stage Society at St George's Hall, Langham Place, London. The cast included: Alice Isaac (Alice); D. L. Mannering (Arden); Leonard Outram (Mosby); Arthur Broughton (Black Will).

1921 Produced at Cambridge by the Marlowe Society. The cast included George Rylands (Alice).

1925 Produced at the Scala, London, directed by William Poel. The cast included: Miriam Lewes (Alice); Ernest Milton (Arden); D. L. Mannering (Mosby); G. Melville-Cooper (Black Will).

1938 Produced at the Théâtre Montparnasse, Paris, directed by Gaston Baty. The cast included: Marguerite Jamois (Alice); Georges Vitray (Arden); Lucien Nat (Mosby).

1952 Radio production by H. A. L. Craig, 14 September, directed by Raymond Raikes.

1954 Produced by Theatre Workshop at the Theatre Royal, Stratford East, directed by Joan Littlewood. The cast included: Barbara Brown (Alice); Maxwell Shaw (Arden); Harry H. Corbett (Mosby); George Cooper (Black Will). The production was the English entry in the 1955 Paris International Festival of Theatre.

1955 Radio production, 21 March, directed by R. D. Smith.

1961 Produced at the Arts Theatre, Cambridge, directed by William Gaskill. The cast included: Susan Engel (Alice).

1962   Radio production, broadcast 29 January, directed by Raymond Raikes. The cast included: Hugh Burden, Valentine Dyall, Norman Shelley, Michael Spice, June Tobin.

1962   Produced at the Theatre Royal, Margate. The cast included: Zoe Randall (Alice); Patrick Crean (Arden); Tony Beckley (Mosby).

1967   Adapted as an opera by Alexander Goehr (music) and Erich Fried (libretto), *Arden muss sterben* (*Arden Must Die*), and produced at the Hamburg Opera, directed by Egon Monk. The cast included: Kerstin Meyer (Alice); Toni Blankenheim (Arden); Ronald Dowd (Mosby).

1968   Produced at the Library Theatre, Scarborough. The cast included Tom Baker (Black Will).

1970   Produced by the Royal Shakespeare Company at the Roundhouse, London, directed by Buzz Goodbody. The cast included: Dorothy Tutin (Alice); Emrys James (Arden); David Bailie (Mosby); Geoffrey Hutchings (Black Will); Morgan Sheppard (Shakebag); Pip Donaghy (Prentice); Christopher Biggins (Sailor).

1974   Produced at the Citizens' Theatre, Glasgow, directed by Steven Dartnell. The cast included: Suzanne Bertish, Sam Cox, Anita Dobson, David Yelland.

1978   Produced at Theatr Clwyd, Mold, directed by Jonathan Petherbridge.

1982   Produced by the Royal Shakespeare Company at The Other Place, Stratford-upon-Avon, directed by Terry Hands. The cast included: Jenny Agutter (Alice); Bruce Purchase (Arden; Christopher Benjamin later took over the part); Robert O'Mahoney (Mosby); John Bowe (Black Will); David Bradley (Shakebag); Jeffery Dench (Franklin); Mark Rylance (Michael).

1990   Produced at the Old Red Lion, directed by Katie Mitchell. The cast included: Valerie Gogan (Alice); Ian Reddington (Arden); Peter Lindford (Mosby); David Dixon (Black Will); Kenn Sabberton (Shakebag); Emma Rice (Susan).

1991   Produced at the Schauspielhaus, Zurich, directed by Terry Hands.

2004   Produced off-off-Broadway at the Metropolitan Playhouse, New York, directed by Alex Roe. The cast included: Teresa Kelsey (Alice); Tod Mason (Arden); Carter Jackson (Mosby); Chris Glenn (Black Will); Jason Alan Griffin (Franklin); Andrew Firda (Michael); Jim DiBasion (Greene).

2006   Produced by Skin and Bone Theatre at the White Bear, London, directed by Samantha Potter. The cast included: Zoe Simon (Alice); Nicholas Prideaux (Arden); Dominic Tighe (Franklin); Chris New (Mosby).

A Woman Killed with Kindness

1567 Publication of the second volume of William Painter's *Palace of Pleasure*; one of the stories (2.30) was the source of the play's sub-plot.

c.1574 Birth of Thomas Heywood, probably in Lincolnshire.

1596 Heywood began his career as a dramatist.

1603 In February and March, the theatre financier Philip Henslowe paid Heywood £6 for writing the play; in February he also made payments for costumes totalling £8.5s. The play was performed at the Rose by the Earl of Worcester's Men (subsequently known as Queen Anne's Men), and was a noted success by March 1604 (even though the London theatres had been officially closed for most of the year following March 1603).

1607 A printed edition published; another appeared, calling itself the third edition, in 1617 (but if a second appeared in the interim, no copies are known to survive).

1776 Adapted by Benjamin Victor as *The Fatal Error*.

1810 Adapted by Joseph Moser as *Ingratitude, or The Adulteress*.

1887 Produced by the Dramatic Students' Society at the Olympic Theatre.

1913 Produced at the Théâtre du Vieux-Colombier, Paris, translated and directed by Jacques Copeau, who also played Wendoll. Also in the cast was Blanche Albane (Anne).

1922 Produced at Birmingham Repertory Theatre.

1931 Produced at the Malvern Festival, directed by H. K. Ayliff. The cast included Ralph Richardson, Robert Donat (Wendoll), and Miriam Adams.

1947 Radio production, 13 April, directed by Felix Felton. The cast included Peter Ustinov and Griselda Hervey.

1955 Radio production by H. A. L. Craig, 28 February.

1959 Radio production, 1 February, adapted and produced by Raymond Raikes.

1971 Produced at the National Theatre, directed by John Dexter. The cast included: Anthony Hopkins (Frankford); Joan Plowright (Anne); Frank Barrie (Wendoll); Derek Jacobi (Sir Charles); Tom Baker (Sir Francis); Tom Georgeson (Roger Brickbat).

1985 Two separate radio productions were broadcast by the BBC: the first on 6 June, adapted and directed by Penny Gold (with a cast including Nigel Anthony, Paola Dionisotti, Edward Kelsey, Colin Jeavons, James Laurenson, and Tom Wilkinson); the other on 9 November (BBC World Service), adapted and directed by Enyd Williams.

1991 Produced at The Other Place, Stratford-upon-Avon, by the Royal Shakespeare Company, directed by Katie Mitchell. The cast included: Michael Maloney (Frankford); Saskia Reeves (Anne); Barry Lynch

(Wendoll); Jonathan Cullen (Sir Charles); Sylvestra le Touzel (Susan); Valentine Pelka (Sir Francis); Sean Murray (Nicholas); Kenn Sabberton (Jenkin).

2003 Produced by Northern Broadsides, directed by Barrie Rutter. The cast included: Richard Standing (Frankford); Maeve Larkin (Anne); John Gully (Wendoll); Adam Sunderland (Nicholas); Andrew Vincent (Sir Charles); Paul Barnhill (Sir Francis).

The Witch of Edmonton

c.1572 Birth of Thomas Dekker.

1585? Birth of William Rowley.

1586 Birth of John Ford at Ilsington, Devon.

1597 Dekker began his career as a dramatist with *The Triangle of Cuckolds* (lost).

1602 Ford admitted to the Middle Temple for legal training.

1606 Ford published his first literary works, the poems *Honour Triumphant* and *Fame's Memorial*.

1607 Rowley began his career as a dramatist, contributing to four scenes of *The Travels of the Three English Brothers*. (The play's other authors were George Wilkins and John Day.)

c.1619 Rowley wrote *All's Lost by Lust*, which may be the source of the Frank Thorney plot.

1621 Elizabeth Sawyer tried for witchcraft and executed on Thursday, 19 April. Henry Goodcole's *The Wonderful Discovery of Elizabeth Sawyer, a Witch*, a pamphlet account of the case, was published just over a week later; this was used by the dramatists as their principal source material.

1621 *The Witch of Edmonton* performed by the Prince's Men at the Cockpit, Drury Lane, and at court on 29 December. The cast probably included: William Rowley (Cuddy Banks).

c.1635 Revived, with a new prologue, by Queen Henrietta's Men at the Cockpit. The cast included: Theophilus Bird (Prologue); Ezekiel Fenn (Winifred).

1658 A printed edition published, with a woodcut on the title-page illustrating three characters: Mother Sawyer, the Dog, and Cuddy Banks (fallen into the pond in 3.1).

1921 Produced by the Phoenix Society at the Lyric, Hammersmith, directed by Montague Summers. The cast included: Sybil Thorndike (Mother Sawyer); Russell Thorndike (Dog); Ion Swinley (Frank Thorney); Frank Cochrane (Cuddy Banks); Joseph A. Dodd (Old Carter); and Edith Evans (Anne Ratcliffe).

1936 Produced at the Old Vic, London, directed by Michel St Denis. The cast included: Edith Evans (Mother Sawyer); Hedley Briggs (Dog); Marius Goring (Frank Thorney); Beatrix Lehmann (Winifred); Ian Mackenzie (Cuddy Banks); Alec Guinness (Old Thorney); Michael Redgrave (Warbeck).

1962 Produced at the Mermaid Theatre, London, directed by Bernard Miles. The cast included: Ruby Head (Mother Sawyer); Melvyn Hayes (Dog); William Lucas (Frank Thorney); Timothy Bateson (Cuddy Banks); Ann Lynn (Winifred); Olive McFarland (Susan).

1981 Produced by the Royal Shakespeare Company at The Other Place, directed by Barry Kyle. The cast included: Miriam Karlin (Mother Sawyer); Miles Anderson (Dog); Gerard Murphy (Frank Thorney); Harriet Walter (Winifred); Juliet Stevenson (Susan); Anthony O'Donnell (Cuddy Banks); Andrew Jarvis (Ratcliffe); Julia Hills (Ann Ratcliffe).

1992 Produced at the Hen and Chickens, London, directed by Helen Fry. The cast included: Joan Marlow (Mother Sawyer); Charlotte Knight (Dog); Christopher Helmsdale (Frank Thorney).

1993 Produced at the Harbourfront, Toronto, directed by Peter Hinton. The mainly female cast included: Greg Kramer (Dog); Sandra Oh (Cuddy Banks); Dragana Varagic (Ann Ratcliffe).

2000 Produced at Southwark Playhouse, directed by Simon Cox. The cast included: Deirdre Doone (Mother Sawyer); Paul Panting (Dog); Tom Foster (Frank Thorney); Chris Garner (Cuddy Banks).

The English Traveller

3rd century BC Plautus' *Mostellaria* (*The Haunting*) written, the source of *The English Traveller*'s sub-plot.

*c.*1574 Birth of Thomas Heywood.

1603 *A Woman Killed with Kindness* written, the source of the play's main plot.

1624 *The English Traveller* written, probably for Lady Elizabeth's Men at the Cockpit, Drury Lane; it later passed into the repertory of the company's successors, Queen Henrietta's Men.

1624 Publication of Heywood's *Gunaikeion*, an extensive but hurriedly compiled collection of narratives about women, which includes the short story, 'A Modern History of an Adulteress', adapted from the play's main plot.

1633 A printed edition published, with a preface commenting on the antitheatrical controversy of that year.

THE TRAGEDY OF
MASTER ARDEN OF FAVERSHAM

THE PERSONS OF THE PLAY

ARDEN, a gentleman of Faversham
ALICE ARDEN, Arden's wife
FRANKLIN, Arden's friend, the Lord Protector's man
MOSBY, Alice's lover, formerly a botcher, now Lord Clifford's
   steward
MICHAEL, the Ardens' servant
SUSAN MOSBY, Mosby's sister, Alice's waiting-maid
CLARKE, a painter, Mosby's neighbour
RICHARD GREENE, one of Sir Anthony Aucher's men
BLACK WILL, a murderer, formerly a corporal at Boulogne
GEORGE SHAKEBAG, a murderer

ADAM FOWLE of the Flower de Luce, Faversham
BRADSHAW, a goldsmith, formerly a soldier at Boulogne
LORD CHEYNE of Kent
LORD CHEYNE'S MEN
A FERRYMAN
DICK REEDE, former owner of the Faversham Abbey lands
A SAILOR, Reede's associate
THE MAYOR of Faversham
THE WATCH at Faversham

A PRENTICE at St Paul's, London
TRADESMEN at St Paul's

The Tragedy of Master Arden of Faversham

Scene 1

Enter Arden and Franklin [who is carrying documents]
FRANKLIN Arden, cheer up thy spirits and droop no more.
My gracious lord the Duke of Somerset°
Hath freely given to thee and to thy heirs,
By letters patents from his majesty,°
All the lands of the Abbey of Faversham.°   5
Here are the deeds,
    [*He gives Arden the documents*]
Sealed and subscribed with his name and the King's.
Read them, and leave this melancholy mood.
ARDEN Franklin, thy love prolongs my weary life;
And, but for thee, how odious were this life,   10
That shows me nothing but torments my soul°
And those foul objects that offend mine eyes,°
Which makes me wish that for this veil of heaven°
The earth hung over my head and covered me.
Love letters passed 'twixt Mosby and my wife,   15
And they have privy meetings in the town.
Nay, on his finger did I spy the ring°
Which at our marriage day the priest put on.
Can any grief be half so great as this?
FRANKLIN Comfort thyself, sweet friend: it is not strange   20
That women will be false and wavering.
ARDEN Ay, but to dote on such a one as he
Is monstrous, Franklin, and intolerable.
FRANKLIN Why, what is he?
ARDEN A botcher, and no better at the first,°   25
Who, by base brokage getting some small stock,
Crept into service of a nobleman,
And by his servile flattery and fawning
Is now become the steward of his house,
And bravely jets it in his silken gown.°   30
FRANKLIN No nobleman will count'nance such a peasant.

ARDEN Yes, the Lord Clifford, he that loves not me.°
  But through his favour let not him grow proud;
  For, were he by the Lord Protector backed,
  He should not make me to be pointed at.   35
  I am by birth a gentleman of blood,
  And that injurious ribald that attempts
  To violate my dear wife's chastity
  (For dear I hold her love, as dear as heaven)
  Shall on the bed which he thinks to defile   40
  See his dissevered joints and sinews torn
  Whilst on the planchers pants his weary body,
  Smeared in the channels of his lustful blood.°
FRANKLIN Be patient, gentle friend, and learn of me
  To ease thy grief and save her chastity.   45
  Entreat her fair; sweet words are fittest engines
  To race the flint walls of a woman's breast.°
  In any case be not too jealous,°
  Nor make no question of her love to thee;
  But as securely, presently take horse,   50
  And lie with me at London all this term;°
  For women, when they may, will not,°
  But, being kept back, straight grow outrageous.°
ARDEN Though this abhors from reason, yet I'll try it,°
  And call her forth, and presently take leave.   55
  How, Alice!
      Here enters Alice
ALICE Husband, what mean you to get up so early?
  Summer nights are short, and yet you rise ere day.
  Had I been 'wake, you had not rise so soon.°
ARDEN Sweet love, thou know'st that we two, Ovid-like,°   60
  Have often chid the morning when it 'gan to peep,
  And often wished that dark night's purblind steeds
  Would pull her by the purple mantle back
  And cast her in the Ocean to her love.°
  But this night, sweet Alice, thou hast killed my heart: 65
  I heard thee call on Mosby in thy sleep.
ALICE 'Tis like I was asleep when I named him,°
  For being awake he comes not in my thoughts.
ARDEN Ay, but you started up and suddenly,
  Instead of him, caught me about the neck.   70
ALICE 'Instead of him'? Why, who was there but you?
  And where but one is, how can I mistake?

4

FRANKLIN Arden, leave to urge her overfar.
ARDEN Nay, love, there is no credit in a dream.°
  Let it suffice I know thou lovest me well.   75
ALICE Now I remember whereupon it came:
  Had we no talk of Mosby yesternight?
FRANKLIN Mistress Alice, I heard you name him once or twice.
ALICE And thereof came it, and therefore blame not me.
ARDEN I know it did, and therefore let it pass.   80
  I must to London, sweet Alice, presently.°
ALICE But tell me, do you mean to stay there long?
ARDEN No longer than till my affairs be done.
FRANKLIN He will not stay above a month at most.
ALICE A month? Ay me! Sweet Arden, come again°   85
  Within a day or two or else I die.
ARDEN I cannot long be from thee, gentle Alice.
  Whilst Michael fetch our horses from the field,°
  Franklin and I will down unto the quay,°
  For I have certain goods there to unload.   90
  Meanwhile prepare our breakfast, gentle Alice,
  For yet ere noon we'll take horse and away.
        Exeunt Arden and Franklin
ALICE Ere noon he means to take horse and away!
  Sweet news is this. O, that some airy spirit
  Would in the shape and likeness of a horse   95
  Gallop with Arden 'cross the ocean
  And throw him from his back into the waves!
  Sweet Mosby is the man that hath my heart,
  And he usurps it, having nought but this,°
  That I am tied to him by marriage.   100
  Love is a god, and marriage is but words;
  And therefore Mosby's title is the best.°
  Tush! Whether it be or no, he shall be mine
  In spite of him, of Hymen, and of rites.
       Here enters Adam of the Flower-de-Luce°
  And here comes Adam of the Flower-de-Luce.   105
  I hope he brings me tidings of my love.
  How now, Adam, what is the news with you?
  Be not afraid; my husband is now from home.
ADAM He whom you wot of, Mosby, Mistress Alice,
  Is come to town and sends you word by me   110
  In any case you may not visit him.°
ALICE Not visit him?

ADAM   No, nor take no knowledge of his being here.°
ALICE   But tell me, is he angry or displeased?
ADAM   Should seem so, for he is wondrous sad.   115
ALICE   Were he as mad as raving Hercules,°
      I'll see him. Ay, and were thy house of force,°
      These hands of mine should raze it to the ground
      Unless that thou wouldst bring me to my love.
ADAM   Nay, an you be so impatient, I'll be gone.   120
ALICE   Stay, Adam, stay. Thou wert wont to be my friend.
      Ask Mosby how I have incurred his wrath.
      Bear him from me these pair of silver dice
      With which we played for kisses many a time,
      And when I lost I won, and so did he   125
      (Such winning and such losing Jove send me!)
      And bid him, if his love do not decline,
      To come this morning but along my door°
      And as a stranger but salute me there.
      This may he do without suspect or fear.   130
           [*Adam takes the dice*]
ADAM   I'll tell him what you say, and so farewell.
ALICE   Do, and one day I'll make amends for all.
           Exit Adam
      I know he loves me well but dares not come
      Because my husband is so jealous
      And these my marrow-prying neighbours blab,°   135
      Hinder our meetings when we would confer.
      But, if I live, that block shall be removed;
      And, Mosby, thou that comes to me by stealth,
      Shalt neither fear the biting speech of men
      Nor Arden's looks: as surely shall he die   140
      As I abhor him and love only thee.
           Here enters Michael
      How now, Michael, whither are you going?
MICHAEL   To fetch my master's nag. I hope you'll think on me.
ALICE   Ay, but, Michael, see you keep your oath
      And be as secret as you are resolute.   145
MICHAEL   I'll see he shall not live above a week.
ALICE   On that condition, Michael, here is my hand:
      None shall have Mosby's sister but thyself.
MICHAEL   I understand the painter here hard by
      Hath made report that he and Sue is sure.   150

6

ALICE There's no such matter, Michael; believe it not.

MICHAEL But he hath sent a dagger sticking in a heart,°
    With a verse or two stolen from a painted cloth,°
    The which I hear the wench keeps in her chest.
    Well, let her keep it! I shall find a fellow   155
    That can both write and read and make rhyme too;°
    And, if I do well, I say no more.
    I'll send from London such a taunting letter
    As she shall eat the heart he sent with salt
    And fling the dagger at the painter's head.°   160

ALICE What needs all this? I say that Susan's thine.

MICHAEL Why, then I say that I will kill my master
    Or anything that you will have me do.

ALICE But, Michael, see you do it cunningly.

MICHAEL Why, say I should be took, I'll ne'er confess°   165
    That you know anything; and Susan, being a maid,
    May beg me from the gallows of the shrieve.°

ALICE Trust not to that, Michael.

MICHAEL You cannot tell me: I have seen it, I.
    But, mistress, tell her whether I live or die   170
    I'll make her more worth than twenty painters can;
    For I will rid mine elder brother away,
    And then the farm of Boughton is mine own.°
    Who would not venture upon house and land
    When he may have it for a right-down blow?   175
        Here enters Mosby

ALICE Yonder comes Mosby. Michael, get thee gone,
    And let not him nor any know thy drifts.
        Exit Michael
    Mosby, my love!

MOSBY Away, I say, and talk not to me now.

ALICE A word or two, sweetheart, and then I will.   180
    'Tis yet but early days: thou needst not fear.°

MOSBY Where is your husband?

ALICE 'Tis now high water, and he is at the quay.

MOSBY There let him be. Henceforward know me not.

ALICE Is this the end of all thy solemn oaths?   185
    Is this the fruit thy reconcilement buds?
    Have I for this given thee so many favours,
    Incurred my husband's hate, and (out alas!)
    Made shipwreck of mine honour for thy sake?

And dost thou say, 'Henceforward know me not'?   190
Remember, when I locked thee in my closet,°
What were thy words and mine? Did we not both
Decree to murder Arden in the night?
The heavens can witness, and the world can tell,
Before I saw that falsehood look of thine,   195
'Fore I was tangled with thy 'ticing speech,
Arden to me was dearer than my soul,
And shall be still. Base peasant, get thee gone,
And boast not of thy conquest over me,
Gotten by witchcraft and mere sorcery.   200
For what hast thou to countenance my love,°
Being descended of a noble house
And matched already with a gentleman°
Whose servant thou may'st be? And so farewell.°
MOSBY Ungentle and unkind Alice, now I see   205
That which I ever feared and find too true:
A woman's love is as the lightning flame
Which even in bursting forth consumes itself.
To try thy constancy have I been strange.°
Would I had never tried but lived in hope!   210
ALICE What needs thou try me whom thou never found false?
MOSBY Yet pardon me, for love is jealous.
ALICE So lists the sailor to the mermaid's song;°
So looks the traveller to the basilisk.
I am content for to be reconciled,   215
And that I know will be mine overthrow.
MOSBY Thine overthrow? First let the world dissolve!
ALICE Nay, Mosby, let me still enjoy thy love;
And, happen what will, I am resolute.
My saving husband hoards up bags of gold   220
To make our children rich, and now is he°
Gone to unload the goods that shall be thine,
And he and Franklin will to London straight.
MOSBY To London, Alice? If thou'lt be ruled by me,
We'll make him sure enough for coming there.°   225
ALICE Ah, would we could!
MOSBY I happened on a painter yesternight,
The only cunning man of Christendom,
For he can temper poison with his oil°
That whoso looks upon the work he draws   230

Shall, with the beams that issue from his sight,°
Suck venom to his breast and slay himself.
Sweet Alice, he shall draw thy counterfeit,°
That Arden may, by gazing on it, perish.

ALICE Ay, but, Mosby, that is dangerous;   235
For thou or I or any other else,
Coming into the chamber where it hangs, may die.

MOSBY Ay, but we'll have it covered with a cloth
And hung up in the study for himself.

ALICE It may not be; for, when the picture's drawn,   240
Arden, I know, will come and show it me.

MOSBY Fear not. We'll have that shall serve the turn.°
This is the painter's house; I'll call him forth.

ALICE But, Mosby, I'll have no such picture, I.

MOSBY I pray thee leave it to my discretion.   245
How, Clarke!
            Here enters Clarke
O, you are an honest man of your word; you served me well.

CLARKE Why, sir, I'll do it for you at any time,
Provided, as you have given your word,
I may have Susan Mosby to my wife.   250
For, as sharp-witted poets, whose sweet verse
Make heavenly gods break off their nectar draughts
And lay their ears down to the lowly earth,
Use humble promise to their sacred Muse,
So we that are the poets' favourites   255
Must have a love. Ay, love is the painter's Muse,°
That makes him frame a speaking countenance,
A weeping eye that witnesses heart's grief.
Then tell me, Master Mosby, shall I have her?

ALICE 'Tis pity but he should; he'll use her well.°   260

MOSBY Clarke, here's my hand; my sister shall be thine.

CLARKE Then, brother, to requite this courtesy,
You shall command my life, my skill, and all.

ALICE Ah, that thou couldst be secret!

MOSBY Fear him not. Leave; I have talked sufficient.   265

CLARKE You know not me that ask such questions.
Let it suffice I know you love him well
And fain would have your husband made away,
Wherein, trust me, you show a noble mind,
That rather than you'll live with him you hate   270

You'll venture life and die with him you love.°
The like will I do for my Susan's sake.

ALICE Yet nothing could enforce me to the deed
But Mosby's love. [*To Mosby*] Might I without control°
Enjoy thee still, then Arden should not die;   275
But, seeing I cannot, therefore let him die.

MOSBY Enough, sweet Alice; thy kind words makes me melt.
[*To Clarke*] Your trick of poisoned pictures we dislike.
Some other poison would do better far.

ALICE Ay, such as might be put into his broth,   280
And yet in taste not to be found at all.

CLARKE I know your mind, and here I have it for you.
Put but a dram of this into his drink,
Or any kind of broth that he shall eat,
And he shall die within an hour after.   285
         [*He gives Alice the poison*]

ALICE As I am a gentlewoman, Clarke, next day
Thou and Susan shall be married.

MOSBY And I'll make her dowry more than I'll talk of, Clarke.

CLARKE Yonder's your husband. Mosby, I'll be gone.
         Here enters Arden and Franklin

ALICE In good time, see where my husband comes.   290
Master Mosby, ask him the question yourself.
         Exit Clarke

MOSBY Master Arden, being at London yesternight,
The Abbey lands whereof you are now possessed
Were offered me on some occasion
By Greene, one of Sir Anthony Aucher's men. °   295
I pray you, sir, tell me, are not the lands yours?
Hath any other interest herein?

ARDEN Mosby, that question we'll decide anon.
Alice, make ready my breakfast; I must hence.
         Exit Alice
As for the lands, Mosby, they are mine   300
By letters patents from his majesty.
But I must have a mandate for my wife:
They say you seek to rob me of her love.
Villain, what makes thou in her company?
She's no companion for so base a groom.   305

MOSBY Arden, I thought not on her. I came to thee,
But rather than I pocket up this wrong—°

FRANKLIN What will you do, sir?

MOSBY Revenge it on the proudest of you both.
   Then Arden draws forth Mosby's sword
ARDEN So, sirrah, you may not wear a sword!   310
  The statute makes against artificers.°
  I warrant that I do. Now use your bodkin,°
  Your Spanish needle, and your pressing-iron,°
  For this shall go with me. And mark my words
  (You, goodman botcher, 'tis to you I speak),°   315
  The next time that I take thee near my house,
  Instead of legs I'll make thee crawl on stumps.
MOSBY Ah, Master Arden, you have injured me;
  I do appeal to God and to the world.
FRANKLIN Why, canst thou deny thou wert a botcher once? 320
MOSBY Measure me what I am, not what I was.
ARDEN Why, what art thou now but a velvet drudge,
  A cheating steward, and base-minded peasant?
MOSBY Arden, now thou hast belched and vomited
  The rancorous venom of thy mis-swoll'n heart,   325
  Hear me but speak: as I intend to live
  With God and his elected saints in heaven,°
  I never meant more to solicit her;
  And that she knows, and all the world shall see.
  I loved her once (sweet Arden, pardon me);   330
  I could not choose; her beauty fired my heart.
  But time hath quenched these over-raging coals;
  And, Arden, though I now frequent thy house,
  'Tis for my sister's sake, her waiting-maid,
  And not for hers. Mayest thou enjoy her long! 335
  Hell-fire and wrathful vengeance light on me
  If I dishonour her or injure thee.
ARDEN Mosby, with these thy protestations
  The deadly hatred of my heart is appeased,
  And thou and I'll be friends if this prove true.° 340
  As for the base terms I gave thee late,°
  Forget them, Mosby. I had cause to speak
  When all the knights and gentlemen of Kent
  Make common table-talk of her and thee.
MOSBY Who lives that is not touched with slanderous tongues? 345
FRANKLIN Then, Mosby, to eschew the speech of men,
  Upon whose general bruit all honour hangs,
  Forbear his house.

ARDEN Forbear it! Nay, rather frequent it more.
  The world shall see that I distrust her not.   350
  To warn him on the sudden from my house
  Were to confirm the rumour that is grown.
MOSBY By my faith, sir, you say true.
  And therefore will I sojourn here awhile
  Until our enemies have talked their fill;   355
  And then, I hope, they'll cease and at last confess
  How causeless they have injured her and me.
ARDEN And I will lie at London all this term
  To let them see how light I weigh their words.°
      Here enters Alice [with a bowl of broth, and Michael, who sets
      out a table and chairs]
ALICE Husband, sit down: your breakfast will be cold.   360
ARDEN Come, Master Mosby, will you sit with us?°
MOSBY I cannot eat, but I'll sit for company.°
      [Arden, Franklin, and Mosby sit at the table]
ARDEN Sirrah Michael, see our horse be ready.
      [Exit Michael. Arden starts to eat his broth, then stops]
ALICE Husband, why pause ye? Why eat you not?
ARDEN I am not well. There's something in this broth   365
  That is not wholesome. Didst thou make it, Alice?
ALICE I did, and that's the cause it likes not you.
      Then she throws down the broth on the ground
  There's nothing that I do can please your taste.
  You were best to say I would have poisoned you.
  I cannot speak or cast aside my eye,   370
  But he imagines I have stepped awry.
  Here's he that you cast in my teeth so oft;
  Now will I be convinced or purge myself.°
  [To Mosby] I charge thee speak to this mistrustful man,
  Thou that wouldst see me hang, thou, Mosby, thou.°   375
  What favour hast thou had more than a kiss
  At coming or departing from the town?
MOSBY You wrong yourself and me to cast these doubts.°
  Your loving husband is not jealous.
ARDEN Why, gentle Mistress Alice, cannot I be ill   380
  But you'll accuse yourself?
  Franklin, thou hast a box of mithridate;
  I'll take a little to prevent the worst.

FRANKLIN Do so, and let us presently take horse.
  My life for yours, ye shall do well enough.   385
ALICE Give me a spoon; I'll eat of it myself.
  Would it were full of poison to the brim,
  Then should my cares and troubles have an end!
  Was ever silly woman so tormented?
ARDEN Be patient, sweet love: I mistrust not thee.   390
ALICE God will revenge it, Arden, if thou dost,
  For never woman loved her husband better
  Than I do thee.
ARDEN I know it, sweet Alice. Cease to complain,
  Lest that in tears I answer thee again.°   395
     [Enter Michael]°
FRANKLIN Come, leave this dallying, and let us away.
ALICE Forbear to wound me with that bitter word.
  Arden shall go to London in my arms.
     [She embraces Arden]
ARDEN Loath am I to depart, yet I must go.
ALICE Wilt thou to London then, and leave me here?   400
  Ah, if thou love me, gentle Arden, stay.
  Yet, if thy business be of great import,
  Go if thou wilt; I'll bear it as I may.
  But write from London to me every week,
  Nay, every day, and stay no longer there   405
  Than thou must needs, lest that I die for sorrow.
ARDEN I'll write unto thee every other tide,°
  And so farewell, sweet Alice, till we meet next.
ALICE Farewell, husband, seeing you'll have it so.
  And, Master Franklin, seeing you take him hence,   410
  In hope you'll hasten him home I'll give you this.
     And then she kisseth him
FRANKLIN And, if he stay, the fault shall not be mine.
  Mosby, farewell, and see you keep your oath.
MOSBY I hope he is not jealous of me now.
ARDEN No. Mosby, no. Hereafter think of me   415
  As of your dearest friend, and so farewell.
     Exeunt Arden, Franklin and Michael
ALICE I am glad he is gone. He was about to stay,
  But did you mark me then how I brake off?
MOSBY Ay, Alice, and it was cunningly performed.
  But what a villain is this painter Clarke!   420

ALICE Was it not a goodly poison that he gave!
  Why, he's as well now as he was before.°
  It should have been some fine confection
  That might have given the broth some dainty taste.
  This powder was too gross and populous.°   425
MOSBY But, had he eaten but three spoonfuls more,
  Then had he died and our love continued.
ALICE Why, so it shall, Mosby, albeit he live.
MOSBY It is unpossible, for I have sworn
  Never hereafter to solicit thee   430
  Or, whilst he lives, once more importune thee.
ALICE Thou shalt not need; I will importune thee.
  What? Shall an oath make thee forsake my love?
  As if I have not sworn as much myself
  And given my hand unto him in the church!   435
  Tush, Mosby, oaths are words, and words is wind,
  And wind is mutable. Then, I conclude,
  'Tis childishness to stand upon an oath.
MOSBY Well proved, Mistress Alice. Yet, by your leave,°
  I'll keep mine unbroken whilst he lives.   440
ALICE Ay, do, and spare not. His time is but short;
  For, if thou beest as resolute as I,
  We'll have him murdered as he walks the streets.
  In London many alehouse ruffians keep,
  Which, as I hear, will murder men for gold.   445
  They shall be soundly fee'd to pay him home.
     Here enters Greene
MOSBY Alice, what's he that comes yonder? Knowest thou him?
ALICE Mosby, begone; I hope 'tis one that comes
  To put in practice our intended drifts.
     Exit Mosby
GREENE Mistress Arden, you are well met.   450
  I am sorry that your husband is from home
  Whenas my purposed journey was to him.
  Yet all my labour is not spent in vain,
  For I suppose that you can full discourse
  And flat resolve me of the thing I seek.   455
ALICE What is it, Master Greene? If that I may
  Or can with safety, I will answer you.
GREENE I heard your husband hath the grant of late,
  Confirmed by letters patents from the King,
  Of all the lands of the Abbey of Faversham,   460

Generally intitled, so that all former grants°
Are cut off, whereof I myself had one;
But now my interest by that is void.
This is all, Mistress Arden: is it true or no?

ALICE True, Master Greene: the lands are his in state,°   465
And whatsoever leases were before
Are void for term of Master Arden's life.
He hath the grant under the Chancery seal.°

GREENE Pardon me, Mistress Arden; I must speak,
For I am touched. Your husband doth me wrong°   470
To wring me from the little land I have.
My living is my life; only that
Resteth remainder of my portion.°
Desire of wealth is endless in his mind,
And he is greedy-gaping still for gain;   475
Nor cares he though young gentlemen do beg,
So he may scrape and hoard up in his pouch.
But, seeing he hath taken my lands, I'll value life
As careless as he is careful for to get;
And, tell him this from me, I'll be revenged,   480
And so as he shall wish the Abbey lands°
Had rested still within their former state.

ALICE Alas, poor gentleman, I pity you,
And woe is me that any man should want.
God knows, 'tis not my fault. But wonder not   485
Though he be hard to others when to me—
Ah, Master Greene, God knows how I am used!

GREENE Why, Mistress Arden, can the crabbèd churl
Use you unkindly? Respects he not your birth,
Your honourable friends, nor what you brought?°   490
Why, all Kent knows your parentage and what you are.

ALICE Ah, Master Greene, be it spoken in secret here,
I never live good day with him alone.
When he is at home, then have I froward looks,
Hard words, and blows to mend the match withal.   495
And, though I might content as good a man,°
Yet doth he keep in every corner trulls;
And, weary with his trugs at home,°
Then rides he straight to London. There, forsooth,
He revels it among such filthy ones   500
As counsels him to make away his wife.
Thus live I daily in continual fear,

In sorrow, so despairing of redress
As every day I wish with hearty prayer
That he or I were taken forth the world.   505
GREENE Now trust me, Mistress Alice, it grieveth me
So fair a creature should be so abused.
Why, who would have thought the civil sir so sullen?
He looks so smoothly. Now, fie upon him, churl,
And if he live a day he lives too long.   510
But frolic, woman, I shall be the man
Shall set you free from all this discontent.
And if the churl deny my interest
And will not yield my lease into my hand,
I'll pay him home, whatever hap to me.   515
ALICE But speak you as you think?
GREENE Ay, God's my witness, I mean plain dealing,
For I had rather die than lose my land.
ALICE Then, Master Greene, be counsellèd by me:
Endanger not yourself for such a churl,   520
But hire some cutter for to cut him short;
And here's ten pound to wager then withal.°
      [*She gives Greene a bag of money*]
When he is dead, you shall have twenty more;°
And the lands whereof my husband is possessed
Shall be intitled as they were before.   525
GREENE Will you keep promise with me?
ALICE Or count me false and perjured whilst I live.
GREENE Then here's my hand: I'll have him so dispatched.
      [*They shake hands*]
I'll up to London straight; I'll thither post
And never rest till I have compassed it.   530
Till then, farewell.
ALICE Good fortune follow all your forward thoughts.
And whosoever doth attempt the deed,
A happy hand I wish; and so farewell.
      Exit Greene
All this goes well. Mosby, I long for thee   535
To let thee know all that I have contrived.
      Here enters Mosby and Clarke
MOSBY How now, Alice, what's the news?
ALICE Such as will content thee well, sweetheart.
MOSBY Well, let them pass awhile, and tell me, Alice,°

How have you dealt and tempered with my sister?°   540
What, will she have my neighbour Clarke or no?
ALICE What, Master Mosby? Let him woo himself.
Think you that maids look not for fair words?
Go to her, Clarke; she's all alone within.
Michael my man is clean out of her books.°   545
CLARKE I thank you, Mistress Arden. I will in,
And, if fair Susan and I can make a gree,°
You shall command me to the uttermost
As far as either goods or life may stretch.
          Exit Clarke
MOSBY Now, Alice, let's hear thy news!   550
ALICE They be so good that I must laugh for joy
Before I can begin to tell my tale.
MOSBY Let's hear them, that I may laugh for company.
ALICE This morning, Master Greene (Dick Greene, I mean,
From whom my husband had the Abbey land)   555
Came hither, railing for to know the truth
Whether my husband had the lands by grant.
I told him all, whereat he stormed amain
And swore he would cry quittance with the churl
And, if he did deny his interest,°   560
Stab him whatsoever did befall himself.
Whenas I saw his choler thus to rise,°
I whetted on the gentleman with words;
And, to conclude, Mosby, at last we grew
To composition for my husband's death.   565
I gave him ten pound to hire knaves,
By some device to make away the churl;
When he is dead, he should have twenty more
And repossess his former lands again.
On this we 'greed, and he is ridden straight   570
To London to bring his death about.
MOSBY But call you this good news?
ALICE Ay, sweetheart, be they not?
MOSBY 'Twere cheerful news to hear the churl were dead;
But trust me, Alice, I take it passing ill   575
You would be so forgetful of our state
To make recount of it to every groom.
What? To acquaint each stranger with our drifts,
Chiefly in case of murder? Why,'tis the way

To make it open unto Arden's self°   580
And bring thyself and me to ruin both.
Forewarned, forearmed: who threats his enemy°
Lends him a sword to guard himself withal.

ALICE I did it for the best.

MOSBY Well, seeing 'tis done, cheerly let it pass.   585
You know this Greene: is he not religious?
A man, I guess, of great devotion.

ALICE He is.

MOSBY Then, sweet Alice, let it pass. I have a drift
Will quiet all, whatever is amiss.   590
    Here enters Clarke and Susan

ALICE How now, Clarke? Have you found me false?
Did I not plead the matter hard for you?

CLARKE You did.

MOSBY And what? Will't be a match?

CLARKE A match i'faith, sir. Ay, the day is mine.   595
The painter lays his colours to the life;°
His pencil draws no shadows in his love;
Susan is mine.

ALICE You make her blush.

MOSBY What, sister, is it Clarke must be the man?   600

SUSAN It resteth in your grant. Some words are passed,°
And haply we be grown unto a match
If you be willing that it shall be so.

MOSBY Ah, Master Clarke, it resteth at my grant;
You see my sister's yet at my dispose;   605
But, so you'll grant me one thing I shall ask,
I am content my sister shall be yours.

CLARKE What is it, Master Mosby?

MOSBY I do remember once in secret talk
You told me how you could compound by art   610
A crucifix impoisonèd,
That whoso look upon it should wax blind
And with the scent be stifled, that ere long
He should die poisoned that did view it well.
I would have you make me such a crucifix,   615
And then I'll grant my sister shall be yours.

CLARKE Though I am loath, because it toucheth life,°
Yet, rather ere I'll leave sweet Susan's love,
I'll do it, and with all the haste I may.
But for whom is it?   620

18

ALICE Leave that to us. Why, Clarke, is it possible
　　That you should paint and draw it out yourself,°
　　The colours being baleful and impoisonèd,
　　And no ways prejudice yourself withal?
MOSBY Well questioned, Alice. Clarke, how answer you that?　　625
CLARKE Very easily. I'll tell you straight
　　How I do work of these impoisoned drugs:
　　I fasten on my spectacles so close
　　As nothing can any way offend my sight;°
　　Then, as I put a leaf within my nose,　　　　　　　　　630
　　So put I rhubarb to avoid the smell,
　　And softly as another work I paint.°
MOSBY 'Tis very well, but against when shall I have it?
CLARKE Within this ten days.
MOSBY 'Twill serve the turn.　　　　　　　　　　　　　635
　　Now, Alice, let's in and see what cheer you keep.
　　I hope, now Master Arden is from home,
　　You'll give me leave to play your husband's part.
ALICE Mosby, you know who's master of my heart
　　He well may be the master of the house.　　　　　　640
　　　　Exeunt

Scene 2

　　　Here enters Greene and Bradshaw
BRADSHAW See you them that comes yonder, Master Greene?
GREENE Ay, very well. Do you know them?
　　　Here enters Black Will and Shakebag
BRADSHAW The one I know not, but he seems a knave,
　　Chiefly for bearing the other company;
　　For such a slave, so vile a rogue as he,　　　　　　5
　　Lives not again upon the earth;
　　Black Will is his name. I tell you, Master Greene,
　　At Boulogne he and I were fellow soldiers,°
　　Where he played such pranks
　　As all the camp feared him for his villainy.　　　　10
　　I warrant you he bears so bad a mind
　　That for a crown he'll murder any man.°
　　　[Bradshaw makes to leave]

GREENE [*aside*] The fitter is he for my purpose, marry.

WILL How now, fellow Bradshaw? Whither away so early?

BRADSHAW O Will, times are changed: no fellows now,   15
Though we were once together in the field;
Yet thy friend to do thee any good I can.

WILL Why, Bradshaw, was not thou and I fellow soldiers at Boulogne,
where I was a corporal and thou but a base mercenary groom? 'No
fellows now' because you are a goldsmith and have a little plate in   20
your shop? You were glad to call me 'fellow Will' and, with a curtsy
to the earth, 'One snatch, good corporal' when I stole the half ox
from John the victualler and domineered with it amongst good
fellows in one night.

BRADSHAW Ay, Will, those days are past with me.   25

WILL Ay, but they be not past with me, for I keep that same honourable
mind still. Good neighbour Bradshaw, you are too proud to be my
fellow; but, were it not that I see more company coming down the
hill, I would be fellows with you once more, and share crowns
with° you too. But let that·pass, and tell me whither you go.   30

BRADSHAW To London, Will, about a piece of service
Wherein haply thou may'st pleasure me.

WILL What is it?

BRADSHAW Of late Lord Cheyne lost some plate,
Which one did bring and sold it at my shop,   35
Saying he served Sir Anthony Cooke.°
A search was made, the plate was found with me,
And I am bound to answer at the 'size.
Now Lord Cheyne solemnly vows,
If law will serve him, he'll hang me for his plate.   40
Now I am going to London upon hope
To find the fellow. Now, Will, I know,
Thou art acquainted with such companions.

WILL What manner of man was he?

BRADSHAW A lean-faced, writhen knave,   45
Hawk-nosed and very hollow-eyed,
With mighty furrows in his stormy brows,
Long hair down his shoulders curled;°
His chin was bare, but on his upper lip
A mustachio, which he wound about his ear.   50

WILL What apparel had he?

BRADSHAW A watchet satin doublet all to-torn
(The inner side did bear the greater show),°

A pair of threadbare velvet hose, seam rent,°
A worsted stocking rent above the shoe, 55
A livery cloak, but all the lace was off—
'Twas bad, but yet it served to hide the plate.

WILL [*aside to Shakebag*] Sirrah Shakebag, canst thou remember since
we trolled the bowl° at Sittingbourne, where I broke the tapster's
head of the Lion° with a cudgel-stick? 60

SHAKEBAG [*aside to Will*] Ay, very well, Will.

WILL [*aside to Shakebag*] Why, it was with the money that the plate
was sold for. [*Aloud*] Sirrah Bradshaw, what wilt thou give him that
can tell thee who sold thy plate?°

BRADSHAW Who, I pray thee, good Will? 65

WILL Why, 'twas one Jack Fitten. He's now in Newgate for stealing a
horse, and shall be arraigned the next 'size.

BRADSHAW Why then, let Lord Cheyne seek Jack Fitten forth,° for
I'll back and tell him who robbed him of his plate. This cheers my
heart. Master Greene, I'll leave you, for I must to the Isle of Sheppey° 70
with speed.

GREENE Before you go, let me entreat you to carry this letter to Mistress
Arden of Faversham and humbly recommend me to herself.
       [*He gives Bradshaw a letter*]

BRADSHAW That will I, Master Greene, and so farewell. [*He gives
Will money*] Here, Will, there's a crown for thy good news. 75

WILL Farewell, Bradshaw; I'll drink no water for thy sake whilst this
lasts.
       Exit Bradshaw
Now, gentleman, shall we have your company to London?

GREENE Nay, stay, sirs.
A little more I needs must use your help, 80
And in a matter of great consequence,
Wherein, if you'll be secret and profound,°
I'll give you twenty angels for your pains.

WILL How? Twenty angels? Give my fellow George Shakebag and
me twenty angels; and, if thou'lt have thy own father slain that 85
thou may'st inherit his land, we'll kill him.

SHAKEBAG Ay, thy mother, thy sister, thy brother, or all thy kin.

GREENE Well, this it is: Arden of Faversham
Hath highly wronged me about the Abbey land,
That no revenge but death will serve the turn.
Will you two kill him? Here's the angels down, 90
And I will lay the platform of his death.°

WILL Plat me no platforms! Give me the money, and I'll stab him as
he stands pissing against a wall,° but I'll kill him.

SHAKEBAG Where is he?   95

GREENE He is now at London, in Aldersgate Street.°

SHAKEBAG He's dead as if he had been condemned by an Act of
Parliament if once Black Will and I swear his death.

GREENE Here is ten pound; and, when he is dead, ye shall have twenty
more.   100

WILL My fingers itches to be at the peasant. Ah, that I might be set
awork thus through the year and that murder would grow to an
occupation,° that a man might, without danger of law—Zounds,
I warrant I should be warden of the company!° Come, let us be
going, and we'll bait at Rochester, where I'll give thee a gallon of sack   105
to handsel the match withal.

Exeunt

Scene 3

Here enters Michael [carrying a letter]

MICHAEL I have gotten such a letter as will touch the painter, and
thus it is:

Here enters Arden and Franklin and hears Michael read this letter
'My duty remembered, Mistress Susan, hoping in God you be in good
health as I, Michael, was at the making hereof. This is to certify you
that, as the turtle true, when she hath lost her mate, sitteth alone,°   5
so I, mourning for your absence, do walk up and down Paul's° till
one day I fell asleep and lost my master's pantofles. Ah, Mistress
Susan, abolish that paltry painter, cut him off by the shins with a
frowning look of your crabbed countenance, and think upon
Michael, who, drunk with the dregs of your favour, will cleave as   10
fast to your love as a plaster of pitch° to a galled horseback. Thus
hoping you will let my passions penetrate, or rather impetrate
mercy of your meek hands, I end.°
Yours,
Michael, or else not Michael.'   15

ARDEN Why, you paltry knave,
Stand you here loitering, knowing my affairs,
What haste my business craves to send to Kent?

FRANKLIN 'Faith, friend Michael, this is very ill,
  Knowing your master hath no more but you;   20
  And do ye slack his business for your own?
ARDEN Where is the letter, sirrah? Let me see it.
  Then [Michael] gives him the letter
  See, Master Franklin, here's proper stuff:
  Susan my maid, the painter, and my man,
  A crew of harlots, all in love, forsooth.   25
  [*To Michael*] Sirrah, let me hear no more of this.
  Now, for thy life, once write to her a word—
  Here enters Greene, Will, and Shakebag
  Wilt thou be married to so base a trull?
  'Tis Mosby's sister. Come I once at home,
  I'll rouse her from remaining in my house.°   30
  Now, Master Franklin, let us go walk in Paul's.
  Come but a turn or two, and then away.
  Exeunt [Arden, Franklin and Michael]
GREENE The first is Arden, and that's his man;
  The other is Franklin, Arden's dearest friend.
WILL Zounds, I'll kill them all three.   35
GREENE Nay, sirs, touch not his man in any case;
  But stand close, and take your fittest standing,
  And, at his coming forth, speed him.°
  To the Nag's Head; there is this coward's haunt.°
  But now I'll leave you till the deed be done.   40
  Exit Greene
SHAKEBAG If he be not paid his own, ne'er trust Shakebag.
WILL Sirrah Shakebag, at his coming forth I'll run him through, and
  then to the Blackfriars° and there take water and away.
SHAKEBAG Why, that's the best; but see thou miss him not.
WILL How can I miss him when I think on the forty angels I must   45
  have more?
  Here enters a Prentice
PRENTICE 'Tis very late; I were best shut up my stall, for here will be
  old filching° when the press° comes forth of Paul's.
  Then lets he down his window,°and it breaks Black Will's head
WILL Zounds, draw, Shakebag, draw! I am almost killed.
  [*Enter other tradesmen. There is a noisy brawl*]°
PRENTICE We'll tame you, I warrant.   50
WILL Zounds, I am tame enough already.
  Here enters Arden, Franklin, and Michael

ARDEN   What troublesome fray or mutiny is this?
FRANKLIN   'Tis nothing but some brabbling, paltry fray,
    Devised to pick men's pockets in the throng.
ARDEN   Is 't nothing else? Come, Franklin, let us away.   55
         Exeunt [*Arden, Franklin, and Michael*]
WILL   What 'mends shall I have for my broken head?
PRENTICE   Marry, this 'mends, that, if you get you not away all the
    sooner, you shall be well beaten and sent to the Counter.°
WILL   Well, I'll be gone; but look to your signs, for I'll pull them down all.
         Exit Prentice
    Shakebag, my broken head grieves me not so much as by this means   60
      Arden hath escaped.
         Here enters Greene
I had a glimpse of him and his companion.
GREENE   Why, sirs, Arden's as well as I. I met him and Franklin going
    merrily to the ordinary. What, dare you not do it?
WILL   Yes, sir, we dare do it; but, were my consent to give again, we   65
    would not do it under ten pound more. I value every drop of my
    blood at a French crown. I have had ten pound to steal a dog, and
    we have no more here to kill a man. But that a bargain is a bargain
    and so forth, you should do it yourself.
GREENE   I pray thee, how came thy head broke?   70
WILL   Why, thou seest it is broke, dost thou not?
SHAKEBAG   Standing against a stall, watching Arden's coming, a boy
    let down his shop window and broke his head; whereupon arose a
    brawl, and in the tumult Arden escaped us and passed by
    unthought on. But forbearance is no acquittance:° another time   75
    we'll do it, I warrant thee.
GREENE   I pray thee, Will, make clean thy bloody brow,
    And let us bethink us on some other place
    Where Arden may be met with handsomely.
    Remember how devoutly thou hast sworn   80
    To kill the villain: think upon thine oath.
WILL   Tush, I have broken five hundred oaths!
    But wouldst thou charm me to effect this deed,
    Tell me of gold, my resolution's fee;
    Say thou seest Mosby kneeling at my knees,   85
    Off'ring me service for my high attempt;
    And sweet Alice Arden, with a lap of crowns,°
    Comes with a lowly curtsy to the earth,
    Saying, 'Take this but for thy quarterage;

Such yearly tribute will I answer thee.'   90
Why, this would steel soft-mettled cowardice,
With which Black Will was never tainted with.
I tell thee, Greene, the forlorn traveller
Whose lips are glued with summer's parching heat
Ne'er longed so much to see a running brook   95
As I to finish Arden's tragedy.
Seest thou this gore that cleaveth to my face?
From hence ne'er will I wash this bloody stain
Till Arden's heart be panting in my hand.°
GREENE Why, that's well said; but what saith Shakebag?   100
SHAKEBAG I cannot paint my valour out with words;
    But, give me place and opportunity,
    Such mercy as the starven lioness,
    When she is dry-sucked of her eager young,
    Shows to the prey that next encounters her,   105
    On Arden so much pity would I take.
GREENE So should it fare with men of firm resolve.
    And now, sirs, seeing this accident
    Of meeting him in Paul's hath no success,
    Let us bethink us on some other place   110
    Whose earth may swallow up this Arden's blood.°
        Here enters Michael
    See, yonder comes his man. And wot you what?
    The foolish knave is in love with Mosby's sister;
    And for her sake, whose love he cannot get
    Unless Mosby solicit his suit,   115
    The villain hath sworn the slaughter of his master.
    We'll question him, for he may stead us much.
    How now, Michael, whither are you going?
MICHAEL My master hath new supped, and I am going to prepare his
    chamber.   120
GREENE Where supped Master Arden?
MICHAEL At the Nag's Head, at the eighteen-pence ordinary.° How
    now, Master Shakebag? What, Black Will! God's dear lady, how
    chance your face is so bloody?
WILL Go to, sirrah! There is a chance in it.° This sauciness in you will   125
    make you be knocked.
MICHAEL Nay, an you be offended, I'll be gone.
GREENE Stay, Michael; you may not 'scape us so.
    Michael, I know you love your master well.

MICHAEL Why, so I do; but wherefore urge you that?   130
GREENE Because I think you love your mistress better.
MICHAEL So think not I. But say, i'faith, what if I should?
SHAKEBAG Come to the purpose. Michael, we hear
    You have a pretty love in Faversham.
MICHAEL Why, have I two or three, what's that to thee?°   135
WILL You deal too mildly with the peasant. [*To Michael*] Thus it is:
    'Tis known to us you love Mosby's sister;
    We know besides that you have ta'en your oath
    To further Mosby to your mistress' bed
    And kill your master for his sister's sake.   140
    Now, sir, a poorer coward than yourself
    Was never fostered in the coast of Kent.
    How comes it then that such a knave as you
    Dare swear a matter of such consequence?
GREENE Ah, Will—   145
WILL Tush, give me leave. There's no more but this:
    Sith thou hast sworn, we dare discover all;
    And, hadst thou or shouldst thou utter it,
    We have devised a complot underhand,°
    Whatever shall betide to any of us,   150
    To send thee roundly to the devil of hell.
    And therefore thus: I am the very man,
    Marked in my birth-hour by the Destinies,
    To give an end to Arden's life on earth;
    Thou but a member but to whet the knife°   155
    Whose edge must search the closet of his breast.
    Thy office is but to appoint the place
    And train thy master to his tragedy;
    Mine to perform it when occasion serves.
    Then be not nice, but here devise with us   160
    How and what way we may conclude his death.
SHAKEBAG So shalt thou purchase Mosby for thy friend,
    And by his friendship gain his sister's love.
GREENE So shall thy mistress be thy favourer,
    And thou disburdened of the oath thou made.   165
MICHAEL Well, gentlemen, I cannot but confess,
    Sith you have urged me so apparently,
    That I have vowed my master Arden's death;
    And he whose kindly love and liberal hand
    Doth challenge nought but good deserts of me   170

I will deliver over to your hands.
This night come to his house at Aldersgate.
The doors I'll leave unlocked against you come.°
No sooner shall ye enter through the latch,
Over the threshold to the inner court,° 175
But on your left hand shall you see the stairs
That leads directly to my master's chamber.
There take him and dispose him as ye please.
Now it were good we parted company.
What I have promisèd I will perform. 180
WILL Should you deceive us, 'twould go wrong with you.°
MICHAEL I will accomplish all I have revealed.
WILL Come, let's go drink. Choler makes me as dry as a dog.
       Exeunt Will, Greene, and Shakebag. Michael remains
MICHAEL Thus feeds the lamb securely on the down
Whilst through the thicket of an arbour brake 185
The hunger-bitten wolf o'erpries his haunt
And takes advantage to eat him up.
Ah, harmless Arden, how, how hast thou misdone
That thus thy gentle life is levelled at?
The many good turns that thou hast done to me 190
Now must I quittance with betraying thee.
I, that should take the weapon in my hand
And buckler thee from ill-intending foes,
Do lead thee with a wicked, fraudful smile,
As unsuspected, to the slaughterhouse. 195
So have I sworn to Mosby and my mistress;
So have I promised to the slaughtermen;
And, should I not deal currently with them,°
Their lawless rage would take revenge on me.
Tush, I will spurn at mercy for this once. 200
Let pity lodge where feeble women lie;
I am resolved, and Arden needs must die.
       Exit Michael

Scene 4

Here enters Arden and Franklin

ARDEN No, Franklin, no. If fear or stormy threats,
　　If love of me or care of womanhood,
　　If fear of God or common speech of men,
　　Who mangle credit with their wounding words
　　And couch dishonour as dishonour buds,°　　　　　　　5
　　Might 'join repentance in her wanton thoughts,°
　　No question then but she would turn the leaf
　　And sorrow for her dissolution;
　　But she is rooted in her wickedness,
　　Perverse and stubborn, not to be reclaimed.　　　　10
　　Good counsel is to her as rain to weeds,
　　And reprehension makes her vice to grow
　　As Hydra's head that plenished by decay.°
　　Her faults, methink, are painted in my face
　　For every searching eye to over-read;　　　　　　　15
　　And Mosby's name, a scandal unto mine,
　　Is deeply trenchèd in my blushing brow.
　　Ah, Franklin, Franklin, when I think on this,
　　My heart's grief rends my other powers
　　Worse than the conflict at the hour of death.　　　20
FRANKLIN Gentle Arden, leave this sad lament.
　　She will amend, and so your griefs will cease;
　　Or else she'll die, and so your sorrows end.
　　If neither of these two do haply fall,°
　　Yet let your comfort be that others bear　　　　　　25
　　Your woes twice doubled all with patience.
ARDEN My house is irksome: there I cannot rest.
FRANKLIN Then stay with me in London; go not home.
ARDEN Then that base Mosby doth usurp my room°
　　And makes his triumph of my being thence.　　　　30
　　At home or not at home, where'er I be,
　　Here, here it lies, ah, Franklin, here it lies°
　　That will not out till wretched Arden dies.
　　　　Here enters Michael
FRANKLIN Forget your griefs awhile. Here comes your man.
ARDEN What o'clock is't, sirrah?　　　　　　　　　　35
MICHAEL Almost ten.

ARDEN See, see, how runs away the weary time!
  Come, Master Franklin, shall we go to bed?
FRANKLIN I pray you, go before; I'll follow you.
     Exeunt Arden and Michael. Franklin remains
  Ah, what a hell is fretful jealousy!   40
  What pity-moving words, what deep-fetched sighs,
  What grievous groans and overlading woes
  Accompanies this gentle gentleman!
  Now will he shake his care-oppressèd head,
  Then fix his sad eyes on the sullen earth,   45
  Ashamed to gaze upon the open world;
  Now will he cast his eyes up towards the heavens,
  Looking that ways for redress of wrong.
  Sometimes he seeketh to beguile his grief
  And tells a story with his careful tongue;   50
  Then comes his wife's dishonour in his thoughts
  And in the middle cutteth off his tale,
  Pouring fresh sorrow on his weary limbs.
  So woe-begone, so inly charged with woe,
  Was never any lived and bare it so.°   55
     Here enters Michael
MICHAEL My master would desire you come to bed.
FRANKLIN Is he himself already in his bed?
MICHAEL He is and fain would have the light away.
     Exit Franklin. Michael remains
  Conflicting thoughts encampèd in my breast
  Awake me with the echo of their strokes,   60
  And I, a judge to censure either side,
  Can give to neither wishèd victory.
  My master's kindness pleads to me for life
  With just demand, and I must grant it him;
  My mistress she hath forced me with an oath   65
  For Susan's sake, the which I may not break,
  For that is nearer than a master's love;
  That grim-faced fellow, pitiless Black Will,
  And Shakebag, stern in bloody stratagem
  (Two rougher ruffians never lived in Kent),   70
  Have sworn my death if I infringe my vow,
  A dreadful thing to be considered of.
  Methinks I see them with their bolstered hair,°
  Staring and grinning in thy gentle face,

And in their ruthless hands their daggers drawn,   75
Insulting o'er thee with a peck of oaths°
Whilst thou, submissive, pleading for relief,
Art mangled by their ireful instruments.
Methinks I hear them ask where Michael is,
And pitiless Black Will cries, 'Stab the slave!   80
The peasant will detect the tragedy.'
The wrinkles in his foul, death-threat'ning face
Gapes open wide, like graves to swallow men.
My death to him is but a merriment,
And he will murder me to make him sport.   85
He comes, he comes! Ah, Master Franklin, help!
Call up the neighbours, or we are but dead!
    Here enters Franklin and Arden
FRANKLIN What dismal outcry calls me from my rest?°
ARDEN What hath occasioned such a fearful cry?
Speak, Michael! Hath any injured thee?   90
MICHAEL Nothing, sir; but, as I fell asleep
Upon the threshold, leaning to the stairs,°
I had a fearful dream that troubled me,
And in my slumber thought I was beset
With murderer thieves that came to rifle me.   95
My trembling joints witness my inward fear.
I crave your pardons for disturbing you.
ARDEN So great a cry for nothing I ne'er heard.
What, are the doors fast locked and all things safe?
MICHAEL I cannot tell; I think I locked the doors.   100
ARDEN I like not this, but I'll go see myself.
    [*He checks the doors*]
Ne'er trust me but the doors were all unlocked.
This negligence not half contenteth me.°
Get you to bed; and, if you love my favour,
Let me have no more such pranks as these.   105
Come, Master Franklin, let us go to bed.
FRANKLIN Ay, by my faith: the air is very cold.
Michael, farewell. I pray thee dream no more.
    Exeunt

Scene 5

SHAKEBAG [*within*] Black night hath hid the pleasures of the day,
    Here enters Will, Greene and Shakebag°
  And sheeting darkness overhangs the earth
  And with the black fold of her cloudy robe
  Obscures us from the eyesight of the world,
  In which sweet silence such as we triumph.°   5
  The lazy minutes linger on their time,
  Loath to give due audit to the hour,
  Till in the watch our purpose be complete°
  And Arden sent to everlasting night.
  Greene, get you gone and linger here about,   10
  And at some hour hence come to us again,
  Where we will give you instance of his death.
GREENE Speed to my wish whose will soe'er says no;
  And so I'll leave you for an hour or two.
    Exit Greene
WILL I tell thee, Shakebag, would this thing were done.   15
  I am so heavy that I can scarce go.
  This drowsiness in me bodes little good.
SHAKEBAG How now, Will, become a precisian?
  Nay, then, let's go sleep when bugs and fears°
  Shall kill our courages with their fancy's work.°   20
WILL Why, Shakebag, thou mistakes me much
  And wrongs me too in telling me of fear.
  Were 't not a serious thing we go about,
  It should be slipped till I had fought with thee°
  To let thee know I am no coward, I.   25
  I tell thee, Shakebag, thou abusest me.
SHAKEBAG Why, thy speech bewrayed an inly kind of fear
  And savoured of a weak, relenting spirit.
  Go forward now in that we have begun,
  And afterwards attempt me when thou darest.   30
WILL And if I do not, heaven cut me off!
  But let that pass, and show me to this house,
  Where thou shalt see I'll do as much as Shakebag.
SHAKEBAG This is the door. [*He tries to open the door*] But soft,
  methinks 'tis shut.
  The villain Michael hath deceivèd us.   35

WILL   Soft, let me see. [*He tries the door*] Shakebag, 'tis shut indeed.
　　Knock with thy sword: perhaps the slave will hear.°
SHAKEBAG   It will not be: the white-livered peasant
　　Is gone to bed and laughs us both to scorn.
WILL   And he shall buy his merriment as dear   40
　　As ever coistrel bought so little sport.
　　Ne'er let this sword assist me when I need,
　　But rust and canker after I have sworn,
　　If I, the next time that I meet the hind,
　　Lop not away his leg, his arm, or both.   45
SHAKEBAG   And let me never draw a sword again,
　　Nor prosper in the twilight, cock-shut light,
　　When I would fleece the wealthy passenger,
　　But lie and languish in a loathsome den,
　　Hated and spit at by the goers-by,   50
　　And in that death may die unpitièd
　　If I, the next time that I meet the slave,
　　Cut not the nose from off the coward's face
　　And trample on it for this villainy.
WILL   Come, let's go seek out Greene; I know he'll swear.   55
SHAKEBAG   He were a villain an he would not swear.
　　'Twould make a peasant swear amongst his boys,
　　That ne'er durst say before but 'yea' and 'no',
　　To be thus flouted of a coisterel.
WILL   Shakebag, let's seek out Greene, and in the morning   60
　　At the alehouse 'butting Arden's house
　　Watch the outcoming of that prick-eared cur,
　　And then let me alone to handle him.
　　　　Exeunt

Scene 6

　　Here enters Arden, Franklin, and Michael
ARDEN [*to Michael*]   Sirrah, get you back to Billingsgate°
　　And learn what time the tide will serve our turn.
　　Come to us in Paul's. First go make the bed,
　　And afterwards go hearken for the flood.°
　　　　Exit Michael
　　Come, Master Franklin, you shall go with me.   5
　　This night I dreamed that, being in a park,

A toil was pitched to overthrow the deer,°
And I upon a little rising hill
Stood whistly watching for the herd's approach.
Even there methoughts a gentle slumber took me   10
And summoned all my parts to sweet repose;
But in the pleasure of this golden rest
An ill-thewed foster had removed the toil
And rounded me with that beguiling home
Which late, methought, was pitched to cast the deer.°   15
With that he blew an evil-sounding horn;
And at the noise another herdman came
With falchion drawn, and bent it at my breast,
Crying aloud, 'Thou art the game we seek.'
With this I waked and trembled every joint,   20
Like one obscurèd in a little bush
That sees a lion foraging about,
And, when the dreadful forest king is gone,
He pries about with timorous suspect
Throughout the thorny casements of the brake,   25
And will not think his person dangerless
But quakes and shivers though the cause be gone.
So, trust me, Franklin, when I did wake,
I stood in doubt whether I waked or no,
Such great impression took this fond surprise.   30
God grant this vision bedeem me any good!
FRANKLIN This fantasy doth rise from Michael's fear,
Who being awaked with the noise he made,
His troubled senses yet could take no rest;
And this, I warrant you, procured your dream.   35
ARDEN It may be so—God frame it to the best!—
But oftentimes my dreams presage too true.
FRANKLIN To such as note their nightly fantasies,°
Some one in twenty may incur belief.
But use it not: 'tis but a mockery.°   40
ARDEN Come, Master Franklin, we'll now walk in Paul's,
And dine together at the ordinary,
And by my man's direction draw to the quay,
And with the tide go down to Faversham.
Say, Master Franklin, shall it not be so?   45
FRANKLIN At your good pleasure, sir; I'll bear you company.
    Exeunt

Scene 7

Here enters Michael at one door. Here enters Greene, Will and
Shakebag at another door

WILL Draw, Shakebag, for here's that villain Michael.

GREENE First, Will, let's hear what he can say.

WILL Speak, milksop slave, and never after speak!

MICHAEL For God's sake, sirs, let me excuse myself,
For here I swear, by heaven and earth and all,   5
I did perform the outmost of my task
And left the doors unbolted and unlocked.
But see the chance: Franklin and my master
Were very late conferring in the porch,
And Franklin left his napkin where he sat,   10
With certain gold knit in it, as he said.
Being in bed, he did bethink himself,°
And coming down he found the doors unshut.
He locked the gates and brought away the keys,
For which offence my master rated me.   15
But now I am going to see what flood it is,
For with the tide my master will away,
Where you may front him well on Rainham Down,
A place well fitting such a stratagem.

WILL Your excuse hath somewhat mollified my choler.   20
Why now, Greene, 'tis better now nor e'er it was.

GREENE But, Michael, is this true?

MICHAEL As true as I report it to be true.°

SHAKEBAG Then, Michael, this shall be your penance: to feast us all
at the Salutation,° where we will plot our purpose thoroughly.   25

GREENE And, Michael, you shall bear no news of this tide because
they two may be in Rainham Down before your master.°

MICHAEL Why, I'll agree to anything you'll have me, so you will
except of° my company.

Exeunt

Scene 8

Here enters Mosby

MOSBY Disturbèd thoughts drives me from company
And dries my marrow with their watchfulness.
Continual trouble of my moody brain
Feebles my body by excess of drink
And nips me as the bitter northeast wind   5
Doth check the tender blossoms in the spring.
Well fares the man, howe'er his cates do taste,
That tables not with foul suspicion;
And he but pines amongst his delicates
Whose troubled mind is stuffed with discontent.   10
My golden time was when I had no gold:
Though then I wanted, yet I slept secure;
My daily toil begat me night's repose;
My night's repose made daylight fresh to me.
But, since I climbed the top bough of the tree   15
And sought to build my nest among the clouds,
Each gentle starry gale doth shake my bed°
And makes me dread my downfall to the earth.
But whither doth contemplation carry me?
The way I seek to find where pleasure dwells   20
Is hedged behind me that I cannot back
But needs must on although to danger's gate.
Then, Arden, perish thou by that decree,
For Greene doth ear the land and weed thee up
To make my harvest nothing but pure corn.   25
And for his pains I'll heave him up awhile
And, after, smother him to have his wax;
Such bees as Greene must never live to sting.
Then is there Michael and the painter too,
Chief actors to Arden's overthrow,   30
Who, when they shall see me sit in Arden's seat,
They will insult upon me for my meed
Or fright me by detecting of his end.
I'll none of that, for I can cast a bone
To make these curs pluck out each other's throat;   35
And then am I sole ruler of mine own.
Yet Mistress Arden lives; but she's myself,°

And holy church rites makes us two but one.°
But what for that I may not trust you, Alice?°
You have supplanted Arden for my sake   40
And will extirpen me to plant another.
'Tis fearful sleeping in a serpent's bed,
And I will cleanly rid my hands of her.
          Here enters Alice [carrying a prayerbook]
But here she comes, and I must flatter her.
How now, Alice! What, sad and passionate?   45
Make me partaker of thy pensiveness:
Fire divided burns with lesser force.
ALICE   But I will dam that fire in my breast
    Till by the force thereof my part consume.
    Ah, Mosby!   50
MOSBY   Such deep pathaires, like to a cannon's burst
    Discharged against a ruinated wall,
    Breaks my relenting heart in thousand pieces.
    Ungentle Alice, thy sorrow is my sore;
    Thou know'st it well, and 'tis thy policy   55
    To forge distressful looks to wound a breast
    Where lies a heart that dies when thou art sad.
    It is not love that loves to anger love.
ALICE   It is not love that loves to murder love.
MOSBY   How mean you that?   60
ALICE   Thou knowest how dearly Arden lovèd me.
MOSBY   And then?
ALICE   And then—conceal the rest, for 'tis too bad,
    Lest that my words be carried with the wind
    And published in the world to both our shames.   65
    I pray thee, Mosby, let our springtime wither;
    Our harvest else will yield but loathsome weeds.
    Forget, I pray thee, what hath passed betwixt us,
    For now I blush and tremble at the thoughts.
MOSBY   What, are you changed?   70
ALICE   Ay, to my former happy life again,
    From title of an odious strumpet's name
    To honest Arden's wife, not Arden's honest wife.°
    Ha, Mosby, 'tis thou hast rifled me of that
    And made me sland'rous to all my kin.   75
    Even in my forehead is thy name engraven,
    A mean artificer, that low-born name.

I was bewitched. Woe worth the hapless hour°
And all the causes that enchanted me!
MOSBY Nay, if thou ban, let me breathe curses forth;   80
And, if you stand so nicely at your fame,
Let me repent the credit I have lost.
I have neglected matters of import
That would have stated me above thy state,°
Forslowed advantages, and spurned at time.   85
Ay, Fortune's right hand Mosby hath forsook
To take a wanton giglot by the left.
I left the marriage of an honest maid
Whose dowry would have weighed down all thy wealth,
Whose beauty and demeanour far exceeded thee.   90
This certain good I lost for changing bad,°
And wrapped my credit in thy company.°
I was bewitched (that is no theme of thine!)°
And thou unhallowed hast enchanted me.
But I will break thy spells and exorcisms   95
And put another sight upon these eyes
That showed my heart a raven for a dove.°
Thou art not fair: I viewed thee not till now.°
Thou art not kind: till now I knew thee not.
And now the rain hath beaten off thy gilt   100
Thy worthless copper shows thee counterfeit.
It grieves me not to see how foul thou art
But mads me that ever I thought thee fair.
Go, get thee gone, a copesmate for thy hinds!
I am too good to be thy favourite.   105
ALICE Ay, now I see, and too soon find it true,
Which often hath been told me by my friends,
That Mosby loves me not but for my wealth,
Which, too incredulous, I ne'er believed.
Nay, hear me speak, Mosby, a word or two;   110
I'll bite my tongue if it speak bitterly.
Look on me, Mosby, or I'll kill myself;
Nothing shall hide me from thy stormy look.
If thou cry war, there is no peace for me.
I will do penance for offending thee   115
And burn this prayerbook, where I here use
The holy word that had converted me.
See, Mosby, I will tear away the leaves,

And all the leaves, and in this golden cover
Shall thy sweet phrases and thy letters dwell,   120
And thereon will I chiefly meditate
And hold no other sect but such devotion.°
Wilt thou not look? Is all thy love overwhelmed?
Wilt thou not hear? What malice stops thine ears?
Why speaks thou not? What silence ties thy tongue?   125
Thou hast been sighted as the eagle is,°
And heard as quickly as the fearful hare,°
And spoke as smoothly as an orator,
When I have bid thee hear or see or speak,
And art thou sensible in none of these?   130
Weigh all thy good turns with this little fault
And I deserve not Mosby's muddy looks.
A fount once troubled is not thickened still:°
Be clear again, I'll ne'er more trouble thee.
MOSBY   O, no, I am a base artificer;   135
My wings are feathered for a lowly flight.
Mosby? Fie, no! Not for a thousand pound.
Make love to you? Why, 'tis unpardonable;
We beggars must not breathe where gentles are.°
ALICE   Sweet Mosby is as gentle as a king,   140
And I too blind to judge him otherwise.
Flowers do sometimes spring in fallow lands;
Weeds in gardens, roses grow on thorns.
So, whatsoe'er my Mosby's father was,
Himself is valued gentle by his worth.   145
MOSBY   Ah, how you women can insinuate
And clear a trespass with your sweet-set tongue!
I will forget this quarrel, gentle Alice,
Provided I'll be tempted so no more.
        Here enters Bradshaw
ALICE   Then with thy lips seal up this new-made match.°   150
MOSBY   Soft, Alice, for here comes somebody.
ALICE   How now, Bradshaw, what's the news with you?
BRADSHAW   I have little news, but here's a letter
That Master Greene importuned me to give you.
ALICE   Go in, Bradshaw, call for a cup of beer.   155
'Tis almost supper time; thou shalt stay with us.
        Exit [Bradshaw]. Then she reads the letter

'We have missed of our purpose at London,° but shall perform it by
     the way. We thank our neighbour Bradshaw.
Yours,
Richard Greene.'   160
How likes my love the tenor of this letter?
MOSBY Well, were his date complete and expired!
ALICE Ah, would it were! Then comes my happy hour.
     Till then my bliss is mixed with bitter gall.
     Come, let us in to shun suspicion.   165
MOSBY I to the gates of death to follow thee.°
          Exeunt

Scene 9

Here enters Greene, Will, and Shakebag
SHAKEBAG Come, Will, see thy tools be in a readiness!
     Is not thy powder dank, or will thy flint strike fire?
WILL Then ask me if my nose be on my face,
     Or whether my tongue be frozen in my mouth.°
     Zounds, here's a coil! You were best swear me on the inter'gatories°   5
     How many pistols I have took in hand,°
     Or whether I love the smell of gunpowder,
     Or dare abide the noise the dag will make,
     Or will not wink at flashing of the fire.°
     I pray thee, Shakebag, let this answer thee,   10
     That I have took more purses in this down
     Than e'er thou handledst pistols in thy life.
SHAKEBAG Ay, haply thou hast picked more in a throng;
     But, should I brag what booties I have took,
     I think the overplus that's more than thine   15
     Would mount to a greater sum of money
     Than either thou or all thy kin are worth.
     Zounds, I hate them as I hate a toad
     That carry a muscado in their tongue
     And scarce a hurting weapon in their hand.   20
WILL O Greene, intolerable!
     It is not for mine honour to bear this.
     Why, Shakebag, I did serve the King at Boulogne,
     And thou canst brag of nothing that thou hast done.

SHAKEBAG Why, so can Jack of Faversham,   25
    That swoonèd for a fillip on the nose,°
    When he that gave it him hallowed in his ear,
    And he supposed a cannon-bullet hit him.
        Then they fight.
GREENE I pray you, sirs, list to Aesop's talk:°
    Whilst two stout dogs were striving for a bone,   30
    There comes a cur and stole it from them both;
    So, while you stand striving on these terms of manhood,°
    Arden escapes us and deceives us all.
SHAKEBAG Why, he begun.
WILL   And thou shalt find I'll end.
    I do but slip it until better time.   35
    But, if I do forget—
        Then he kneels down and holds up his hands to heaven°
GREENE Well, take your fittest standings, and once more°
    Lime your twigs to catch this weary bird.°
    I'll leave you, and at your dag's discharge
    Make towards, like the longing water-dog°   40
    That coucheth till the fowling-piece be off,°
    Then seizeth on the prey with eager mood.
    Ah, might I see him stretching forth his limbs
    As I have seen them beat their wings ere now.
SHAKEBAG Why, that thou shalt see if he come this way.   45
GREENE Yes, that he doth, Shakebag, I warrant thee.
    But brawl not when I am gone in any case,
    But, sirs, be sure to speed him when he comes;
    And in that hope I'll leave you for an hour.
        Exit Greene. [Will and Shakebag conceal themselves.] Here
        enters Arden, Franklin, and Michael
MICHAEL 'Twere best that I went back to Rochester.   50
    The horse halts downright; it were not good
    He travelled in such pain to Faversham.
    Removing of a shoe may haply help it.
ARDEN Well, get you back to Rochester; but, sirrah, see
    Ye overtake us ere we come to Rainham Down,°   55
    For it will be very late ere we get home.
MICHAEL [*aside*] Ay, God he knows, and so doth Will and Shakebag,
    That thou shalt never go further than that down;
    And therefore have I pricked the horse on purpose
    Because I would not view the massacre.   60
        Exit Michael

ARDEN Come, Master Franklin, onwards with your tale.°
FRANKLIN I assure you, sir, you task me much.
 A heavy blood is gathered at my heart,
 And on the sudden is my wind so short
 As hindereth the passage of my speech.   65
 So fierce a qualm yet ne'er assailèd me.
ARDEN Come, Master Franklin, let us go on softly.
 The annoyance of the dust or else some meat
 You ate at dinner cannot brook with you.°
 I have been often so and soon amended.   70
FRANKLIN Do you remember where my tale did leave?
ARDEN Ay, where the gentleman did check his wife.
FRANKLIN She being reprehended for the fact,
 Witness produced that took her with the deed,
 Her glove brought in which there she left behind,   75
 And many other assurèd arguments,
 Her husband asked her whether it were not so.
ARDEN Her answer then? I wonder how she looked,
 Having forsworn it with such vehement oaths,
 And at the instant so approved upon her.   80
FRANKLIN First did she cast her eyes down to the earth,
 Watching the drops that fell amain from thence;
 Then softly draws she forth her handkercher,
 And modestly she wipes her tear-stained face;
 Then hemmed she out, to clear her voice should seem,° 85
 And with a majesty addressed herself
 To encounter all their accusations.
 Pardon me, Master Arden, I can no more;
 This fighting at my heart makes short my wind.
ARDEN Come, we are almost now at Rainham Down.   90
 Your pretty tale beguiles the weary way;
 I would you were in state to tell it out.°
SHAKEBAG [*aside to Will*] Stand close, Will: I hear them coming.
  Here enters Lord Cheyne with his men
WILL [*aside to Shakebag*] Stand to it, Shakebag, and be resolute.°
LORD CHEYNE Is it so near night as it seems,   95
 Or will this black-faced evening have a shower?
 What, Master Arden, you are well met.
 I have longed this fortnight's day to speak with you.
 You are a stranger, man, in the Isle of Sheppey.
ARDEN Your honour's always, bound to do you service.   100

LORD CHEYNE Come you from London and ne'er a man with you?

ARDEN My man's coming after, but here's my honest friend that came
    along with me.

LORD CHEYNE [to Franklin] My Lord Protector's man, I take you
to be.   105

FRANKLIN Ay, my good lord, and highly bound to you.

LORD CHEYNE You and your friend come home and sup with me.

ARDEN I beseech your honour pardon me;
    I have made a promise to a gentleman,
    My honest friend, to meet him at my house.   110
    The occasion is great, or else would I wait on you.

LORD CHEYNE Will you come tomorrow and dine with me,
    And bring your honest friend along with you?
    I have divers matters to talk with you about.

ARDEN Tomorrow we'll wait upon your honour.   115

LORD CHEYNE [to his men] One of you stay my horse at the top of
    the hill.
        [Exit a man]
    What, Black Will, for whose purse wait you?
    Thou wilt be hanged in Kent when all is done.

WILL Not hanged, God save your honour.   120
    I am your beadsman, bound to pray for you.°

LORD CHEYNE I think thou ne'er saidest prayer in all thy life.
    [To his men] One of you give him a crown.
    [To Will] And, sirrah, leave this kind of life.
    If thou beest 'tainted for a penny matter   125
    And come in question, surely thou wilt truss.°
    Come, Master Arden, let us be going;
    Your way and mine lies four mile together.°
        Exeunt all but Black Will and Shakebag

WILL The devil break all your necks at four miles' end!
    Zounds, I could kill myself for very anger!   130
    His lordship chops me in even when°
    My dag was levelled at his heart.°
    I would his crown were molten down his throat.°

SHAKEBAG Arden, thou hast wondrous holy luck.
    Did ever man escape as thou hast done?   135
    Well, I'll discharge my pistol at the sky,
    For by this bullet Arden might not die.
        [Shakebag fires his gun.] Here enters Greene

GREENE What, is he down? Is he dispatched?!

SHAKEBAG Ay, in health towards Faversham to shame us all.
GREENE The devil he is! Why, sirs, how escaped he?   140
SHAKEBAG When we were ready to shoot, comes my Lord Cheyne to
    prevent his death.
GREENE The Lord of Heaven hath preservèd him.
WILL 'Preserved'—a fig! The Lord Cheyne hath preserved him,°
    And bids him to a feast to his house at Shurland.°   145
    But by the way once more I'll meet with him,°
    And if all the Cheynes in the world say no,
    I'll have a bullet in his breast tomorrow.
    Therefore come, Greene, and let us to Faversham.
GREENE Ay, and excuse ourselves to Mistress Arden.   150
    O, how she'll chafe when she hears of this!
SHAKEBAG Why, I'll warrant you she'll think we dare not do it.
WILL Why, then let us go, and tell her all the matter,
    And plot the news to cut him off tomorrow.°
    Exeunt

Scene 10

Here enters Arden and his wife, Franklin, and Michael
ARDEN See how the Hours, the guardant of heaven's gate,°
    Have by their toil removed the darksome clouds,
    That Sol may well discern the trampled pace
    Wherein he wont to guide his golden car.°
    The season fits. Come, Franklin, let's away.   5
ALICE I thought you did pretend some special hunt°
    That made you thus cut short the time of rest.
ARDEN It was no chase that made me rise so early
    But, as I told thee yesternight, to go to the Isle of Sheppey,
        there to dine with my Lord Cheyne;   10
    For so his honour late commanded me.
ALICE Ay, such kind husbands seldom want excuses;
    Home is a wild cat to a wand'ring wit.
    The time hath been (would God it were not past)
    That honour's title nor a lord's command   15
    Could once have drawn you from these arms of mine.
    But my deserts or your desires decay,
    Or both; yet if true love may seem desert,
    I merit still to have thy company.

FRANKLIN Why, I pray you, sir, let her go along with us.   20
   I am sure his honour will welcome her
   And us the more for bringing her along.
ARDEN Content. [*To Michael*] Sirrah, saddle your mistress' nag.
ALICE No, begged favour merits little thanks.
   If I should go, our house would run away   25
   Or else be stol'n; therefore I'll stay behind.
ARDEN Nay, see how mistaking you are. I pray thee, go.
ALICE No, no, not now.
ARDEN Then let me leave thee satisfied in this,
   That time, nor place, nor persons alter me   30
   But that I hold thee dearer than my life.
ALICE That will be seen by your quick return.
ARDEN And that shall be ere night an if I live.
   Farewell, sweet Alice. We mind to sup with thee.
      Exit Alice
FRANKLIN Come, Michael, are our horses ready?   35
MICHAEL Ay, your horse are ready, but I am not ready, for I have lost
   my purse with six-and-thirty shillings in it, with taking up of my
   master's nag.
FRANKLIN Why, I pray you, let us go before.
   Whilst he stays behind to seek his purse.   40
ARDEN Go to, sirrah!
   See you follow us to the Isle of Sheppey,
   To my Lord Cheyne's, where we mean to dine.
      Exeunt Arden and Franklin. Michael remains
MICHAEL So, fair weather after you, for before you lies Black Will and
   Shakebag in the broom close, too close for you. They'll be your   45
   ferrymen to long home.°
      Here enters [Clarke] the Painter
   But who is this? The painter, my corrival, that would needs win
   Mistress Susan.
CLARKE How now, Michael? How doth my mistress and all at home?
MICHAEL Who? Susan Mosby? She is your mistress, too?   50
CLARKE Ay, how doth she and all the rest?
MICHAEL All's well but Susan; she is sick.
CLARKE Sick? Of what disease?
MICHAEL Of a great fear.
CLARKE A fear of what?   55
MICHAEL A great fever.
CLARKE A fever? God forbid!

MICHAEL Yes, faith, and of a lurdan, too, as big as yourself.

CLARKE O Michael, the spleen prickles you. Go to; you carry an eye
over° Mistress Susan.   60

MICHAEL Ay, faith, to keep her from the painter.

CLARKE Why more from a painter than from a serving-creature like
yourself?

MICHAEL Because you painters make but a painting-table of a pretty
wench and spoil her beauty with blotting.   65

CLARKE What mean you by that?

MICHAEL Why, that you painters paint lambs in the lining of
wenches' petticoats, and we servingmen put horns to them to make
them become sheep.

CLARKE Such another word will cost you a cuff or a knock.   70

MICHAEL What, with a dagger made of a pencil? Faith, 'tis too weak,
and therefore thou too weak to win Susan.

CLARKE Would Susan's love lay upon this stroke!
        Then he breaks Michael's head. Here enters Mosby, Greene and Alice

ALICE I'll lay my life, this is for Susan's love.
        [*To Michael*] Stayed you behind your master to this end? 75
        Have you no other time to brabble in
        But now when serious matters are in hand?
        Say, Clarke, hast thou done the thing thou promised?

CLARKE Ay, here it is: the very touch is death.
        [*Clarke shows the poisoned crucifix*]

ALICE Then this, I hope, if all the rest do fail,   80
        Will catch Master Arden
        And make him wise in death that lived a fool.
        [*To Mosby*] Why should he thrust his sickle in our corn,
        Or what hath he to do with thee, my love,
        Or govern me that am to rule myself?   85
        Forsooth, for credit sake, I must leave thee.
        Nay, he must leave to live that we may love,
        May live, may love: for what is life but love?
        And love shall last as long as life remains,
        And life shall end before my love depart.   90

MOSBY Why, what's love without true constancy?
        Like to a pillar built of many stones,
        Yet neither with good mortar well compact
        Nor cement to fasten it in the joints
        But that it shakes with every blast of wind   95
        And, being touched, straight falls unto the earth

And buries all his haughty pride in dust.
No, let our love be rocks of adamant,
Which time nor place nor tempest can asunder.

GREENE Mosby, leave protestations now,   100
And let us bethink us what we have to do.
Black Will and Shakebag I have placed
In the broom close, watching Arden's coming.
Let's to them and see what they have done.
          Exeunt

Scene 11

          Here enters Arden and Franklin
ARDEN O ferryman, where art thou?
          Here enters the Ferryman°
FERRYMAN Here, here! Go before to the boat, and I will follow you.
ARDEN We have great haste; I pray thee come away.
FERRYMAN Fie, what a mist is here!°
ARDEN This mist, my friend, is mystical,°   5
Like to a good companion's smoky brain,
That was half-drowned with new ale overnight.
FERRYMAN 'Twere pity but his skull were opened to make more
chimney room.
FRANKLIN Friend, what's thy opinion of this mist?   10
FERRYMAN I think 'tis like to a curst wife in a little house, that never
leaves her husband till she have driven him out at doors with a wet
pair of eyes. Then looks he as if his house were afire, or some of his
friends dead.
ARDEN Speaks thou this of thine own experience?   15
FERRYMAN Perhaps ay, perhaps no; for my wife is as other women
are, that is to say, governed by the moon.°
FRANKLIN By the moon? How, I pray thee?
FERRYMAN Nay, thereby lies a bargain, and you shall not have it fresh
and fasting.   20
ARDEN Yes, I pray thee, good ferryman.
FERRYMAN Then for this once: let it be midsummer moon, but yet
my wife has another moon.
FRANKLIN Another moon?
FERRYMAN Ay, and it hath influences and eclipses.   25

ARDEN Why, then, by this reckoning you sometimes play the man in
the moon.°

FERRYMAN Ay, but you had not best to meddle with that moon lest
I scratch you by the face with my bramble-bush.°

ARDEN I am almost stifled with this fog. Come, let's away.   30

FRANKLIN And, sirrah, as we go, let us have some more of your bold
yeomanry.°

FERRYMAN Nay, by my troth, sir, but flat knavery.

      Exeunt

Scene 12

    Here enters Will at one door and Shakebag at another

SHAKEBAG O, Will, where art thou?

WILL Here, Shakebag, almost in hell's mouth, where I cannot see my
way for smoke.

SHAKEBAG I pray thee speak still that we may meet by the sound, for
I shall fall into some ditch or other unless my feet see better than   5
my eyes.

WILL Didst thou ever see better weather to run away with another
man's wife or play with a wench at pot-finger?°

SHAKEBAG No; this were a fine world for chandlers if this weather
would last, for then a man should never dine nor sup without candle-   10
light. But sirrah Will, what horses are those that passed?

WILL Why, didst thou hear any?

SHAKEBAG Ay, that I did.

WILL My life for thine, 'twas Arden and his companion, and then all
our labour's lost.   15

SHAKEBAG Nay, say not so, for, if it be they, they may haply lose their
way as we have done, and then we may chance meet with them.

WILL Come, let us go on like a couple of blind pilgrims.

Then Shakebag falls into a ditch°

SHAKEBAG Help, Will, help! I am almost drowned.

    Here enters the Ferryman

FERRYMAN Who's that that calls for help?   20

WILL 'Twas none here; 'twas thou thyself.

FERRYMAN I came to help him that called for help. Why, how now?
Who is this that's in the ditch? You are well enough served° to go
without a guide such weather as this!

[*Shakebag climbs out of the ditch with the Ferryman's help; his
    clothes are now muddy*]

WILL Sirrah, what companies hath passed your ferry this morning?   25

FERRYMAN None but a couple of gentlemen that went to dine at my
    Lord Cheyne's.

WILL Shakebag, did not I tell thee as much?

FERRYMAN Why, sir, will you have any letters carried to them?

WILL No, sir; get you gone.   30

FERRYMAN Did you ever see such a mist as this?

WILL No, nor such a fool as will rather be hocked than get his way.°

FERRYMAN Why, sir, this is no Hock Monday;° you are deceived.
    [*To Shakebag*] What's his name, I pray you, sir?

SHAKEBAG His name is Black Will.   35

FERRYMAN I hope to see him one day hanged upon a hill.
        Exit Ferryman

SHAKEBAG See how the sun hath cleared the foggy mist,
    Now we have missed the mark of our intent.
        Here enters Greene, Mosby, and Alice

MOSBY Black Will and Shakebag, what make you here?
    What, is the deed done? Is Arden dead?   40

WILL What could a blinded man perform in arms?
    Saw you not how till now the sky was dark,
    That neither horse nor man could be discerned?
    Yet did we hear their horses as they passed.

GREENE Have they escaped you then and passed the ferry?   45

SHAKEBAG Ay, for a while; but here we two will stay
    And at their coming back meet with them once more.
    Zounds, I was ne'er so toiled in all my life
    In following so slight a task as this.

MOSBY [*to Shakebag*] How cam'st thou so bewrayed?   50

WILL With making false footing in the dark.
    He needs would follow them without a guide.
        [*Alice gives money to Will and Shakebag*]

ALICE Here's to pay for a fire and good cheer.
    Get you to Faversham to the Flower-de-Luce
    And rest yourselves until some other time.   55

GREENE Let me alone; it most concerns my state.°

WILL Ay, Mistress Arden, this will serve the turn
    In case we fall into a second fog.
        Exeunt Greene, Will and Shakebag

MOSBY These knaves will never do it; let us give it over.

48

ALICE First tell me how you like my new device: 60
　　Soon, when my husband is returning back,
　　You and I, both marching arm in arm
　　Like loving friends, we'll meet him on the way
　　And boldly beard and brave him to his teeth.
　　When words grow hot and blows begin to rise,   65
　　I'll call those cutters forth your tenement,°
　　Who, in a manner to take up the fray,
　　Shall wound my husband Hornsby to the death.°
MOSBY Ah, fine device! Why, this deserves a kiss.
　　[*He kisses her.*] *Exeunt*

Scene 13

Here enters Dick Reede and a Sailor

SAILOR Faith, Dick Reede, it is to little end.°
　　His conscience is too liberal and he too niggardly
　　To part from anything may do thee good.
REEDE He is coming from Shurland as I understand.
　　Here I'll intercept him, for at his house   5
　　He never will vouchsafe to speak with me.
　　If prayers and fair entreaties will not serve
　　Or make no batt'ry in his flinty breast,
　　　　Here enters Franklin, Arden, and Michael
　　I'll curse the carl and see what that will do.
　　See where he comes to further my intent.   10
　　Master Arden, I am now bound to the sea.
　　My coming to you was about the plot of ground
　　Which wrongfully you detain from me.
　　Although the rent of it be very small,
　　Yet will it help my wife and children,   15
　　Which here I leave in Faversham, God knows,
　　Needy and bare. For Christ's sake, let them have it.
ARDEN Franklin, hearest thou this fellow speak?
　　That which he craves I dearly bought of him
　　Although the rent of it was ever mine.   20
　　[*To Reede*] Sirrah, you that ask these questions,
　　If with thy clamorous impeaching tongue
　　Thou rail on me, as I have heard thou dost,

I'll lay thee up so close a twelvemonth's day
As thou shalt neither see the sun nor moon.   25
Look to it, for, as surely as I live,
I'll banish pity if thou use me thus.

REEDE What, wilt thou do me wrong and threat me too?
Nay, then, I'll tempt thee, Arden, do thy worst.
God, I beseech thee, show some miracle   30
On thee or thine in plaguing thee for this.
That plot of ground which thou detains from me
(I speak it in an agony of spirit)
Be ruinous and fatal unto thee!
Either there be butchered by thy dearest friends,   35
Or else be brought for men to wonder at,
Or thou or thine miscarry in that place,
Or there run mad and end thy cursèd days.

FRANKLIN Fie, bitter knave, bridle thine envious tongue;
For curses are like arrows shot upright,   40
Which, falling down, light on the shooter's head.

REEDE Light where they will! Were I upon the sea,
As oft I have in many a bitter storm,
And saw a dreadful southern flaw at hand,
The pilot quaking at the doubtful storm,   45
And all the sailors praying on their knees,
Even in that fearful time would I fall down
And ask of God, whate'er betide of me,
Vengeance on Arden or some misevent
To show the world what wrong the carl hath done.   50
This charge I'll leave with my distressful wife;
My children shall be taught such prayers as these.
And thus I go, but leave my curse with thee.
        Exeunt Reede and Sailor

ARDEN It is the railingest knave in Christendom,
And oftentimes the villain will be mad.   55
It greatly matters not what he says,
But I assure you I ne'er did him wrong.

FRANKLIN I think so, Master Arden.

ARDEN Now that our horses are gone home before,
My wife may haply meet me on the way;   60
For God knows she is grown passing kind of late
And greatly changèd from the old humour
Of her wonted frowardness,
And seeks by fair means to redeem old faults.

FRANKLIN Happy the change that alters for the best!   65
　　But see in any case you make no speech
　　Of the cheer we had at my Lord Cheyne's
　　Although most bounteous and liberal,
　　For that will make her think herself more wronged
　　In that we did not carry her along;   70
　　For sure she grieved that she was left behind.
ARDEN Come, Franklin, let us strain to mend our pace
　　And take her unawares playing the cook;
　　　　Here enters Alice and Mosby [arm in arm]
　　For I believe she'll strive to mend our cheer.
FRANKLIN Why, there's no better creatures in the world   75
　　Than women are when they are in good humours.
ARDEN Who is that? Mosby? What, so familiar?
　　Injurious strumpet and thou ribald knave,
　　Untwine those arms.
ALICE Ay, with a sugared kiss let them untwine.   80
　　　　[She kisses Mosby]
ARDEN Ah, Mosby! perjured beast! Bear this and all!
MOSBY And yet no hornèd beast: the horns are thine.
FRANKLIN O monstrous! Nay, then, 'tis time to draw.
　　　　[Arden and Franklin draw their swords]
ALICE Help! help! They murder my husband.
　　　　Here enters Will and Shakebag
SHAKEBAG Zounds, who injures Master Mosby?   85
　　　　[They fight.° Shakebag and Mosby are wounded]
　　Help, Will! I am hurt.
MOSBY I may thank you, Mistress Arden, for this wound.
　　　　Exeunt Mosby, Will and Shakebag
ALICE Ah, Arden, what folly blinded thee?
　　Ah, jealous harebrain man, what hast thou done?
　　When we, to welcome thee, intended sport,   90
　　Came lovingly to meet thee on thy way,
　　Thou drew'st thy sword, enraged with jealousy,
　　And hurt thy friend whose thoughts were free from harm,
　　All for a worthless kiss and joining arms,
　　(Both done but merrily to try thy patience);   95
　　And me unhappy that devised the jest,
　　Which, though begun in sport, yet ends in blood.
FRANKLIN Marry, God defend me from such a jest!
ALICE Couldst thou not see us friendly smile on thee
　　When we joined arms and when I kissed his cheek?   100

Hast thou not lately found me overkind?
Didst thou not hear me cry they murder thee?
Called I not help to set my husband free?
No, ears and all were witched. Ah me accursed,
To link in liking with a frantic man!   105
Henceforth I'll be thy slave, no more thy wife;
For with that name I never shall content thee.
If I be merry, thou straightways thinks me light;
If sad, thou sayest the sullens trouble me;
If well attired, thou thinks I will be gadding;   110
If homely, I seem sluttish in thine eye.
Thus am I still, and shall be while I die,
Poor wench abused by thy misgovernment.

ARDEN   But is it for truth that neither thou nor he
Intendedst malice in your misdemeanour?   115

ALICE   The heavens can witness of our harmless thoughts.

ARDEN   Then pardon me, sweet Alice, and forgive this fault.
Forget but this and never see the like.
Impose me penance, and I will perform it;
For in thy discontent I find a death,   120
A death tormenting more than death itself.

ALICE   Nay, hadst thou loved me as thou dost pretend,
Thou wouldst have marked the speeches of thy friend,
Who going wounded from the place, he said
His skin was pierced only through my device.   125
And if sad sorrow taint thee for this fault,
Thou wouldst have followed him, and seen him dressed,
And cried him mercy whom thou hast misdone;°
Ne'er shall my heart be eased till this be done.

ARDEN   Content thee, sweet Alice, thou shalt have thy will, 130
Whate'er it be. For that I injured thee
And wronged my friend, shame scourgeth my offence.
Come thou thyself, and go along with me,
And be a mediator 'twixt us two.

FRANKLIN   Why, Master Arden, know you what you do?   135
Will you follow him that hath dishonoured you?

ALICE   Why, canst thou prove I have been disloyal?

FRANKLIN   Why, Mosby taunts your husband with the horn.

ALICE   Ay, after he had reviled him
By the injurious name of perjured beast.   140

He knew no wrong could spite a jealous man
More than the hateful naming of the horn.
FRANKLIN Suppose 'tis true, yet is it dangerous
    To follow him whom he hath lately hurt.
ALICE A fault confessed is more than half amends,   145
    But men of such ill spirit as yourself
    Work crosses and debates 'twixt man and wife.°
ARDEN I pray thee, gentle Franklin, hold thy peace;
    I know my wife counsels me for the best.
    I'll seek out Mosby where his wound is dressed.   150
    And salve his hapless quarrel if I may
        Exeunt Arden and Alice
FRANKLIN He whom the devil drives must go perforce.
    Poor gentleman, how soon he is bewitched!
    And yet, because his wife is the instrument,
    His friends must not be lavish in their speech.   155
    Exit Franklin

Scene 14

Here enters Will, Shakebag, and Greene

WILL Sirrah Greene, when was I so long in killing a man?
GREENE I think we shall never do it. Let us give it over.
SHAKEBAG Nay. Zounds, we'll kill him though we be hanged at his
    door° for our labour.
WILL Thou knowest, Greene, that I have lived in London this twelve   5
    years, where I have made some go upon wooden legs for taking the
    wall° on me, divers with silver noses° for saying, 'There goes Black
    Will.' I have cracked as many blades as thou hast done nuts.°
GREENE O monstrous lie!
WILL Faith, in a manner I have. The bawdy-houses have paid me   10
    tribute: there durst not a whore set up unless she have agreed with
    me first for opening her shop windows. For a cross word of a tapster
    I have pierced one barrel after another with my dagger and held
    him by the ears till all his beer hath run out. In Thames Street° a
    brewer's cart was like to have run over me; I made no more ado but   15
    went to the clerk and cut all the notches off his tallies° and beat
    them about his head. I and my company have taken the constable
    from his watch and carried him about the fields on a cowl-staff.

I have broken a sergeant's head with his own mace, and bailed
whom I list with my sword and buckler. All the tenpenny alehouses   20
would stand every morning with a quart pot in his hand,° saying,
'Will it please your worship drink?' He that had not done so had
been sure to have had his sign pulled down and his lattice° borne
away the next night. To conclude, what have I not done? Yet cannot
do this! Doubtless he is preserved by miracle.   25

Here enters Alice and Michael

GREENE Hence, Will! Here comes Mistress Arden.

ALICE Ah, gentle Michael, art thou sure they're friends?

MICHAEL Why, I saw them when they both shook hands.
When Mosby bled, he even wept for sorrow°
And railed on Franklin that was cause of all.   30
No sooner came the surgeon in at doors,
But my master took to his purse and gave him money,
And, to conclude, sent me to bring you word
That Mosby, Franklin, Bradshaw, Adam Fowle,
With divers of his neighbours and his friends,   35
Will come and sup with you at our house this night.

ALICE Ah, gentle Michael, run thou back again,
And, when my husband walks into the fair,°
Bid Mosby steal from him and come to me;°
And this night shall thou and Susan be made sure.   40

MICHAEL I'll go tell him.

ALICE And, as thou goest, tell John cook of our guests,
And bid him lay it on; spare for no cost.°

Exit Michael

WILL Nay, an there be such cheer, we will bid ourselves. Mistress
Arden, Dick Greene and I do mean to sup with you.   45

ALICE And welcome shall you be. Ah, gentlemen,
How missed you of your purpose yesternight?

GREENE 'Twas long of Shakebag, that unlucky villain.

SHAKEBAG Thou dost me wrong: I did as much as any.

WILL Nay, then Mistress Alice, I'll tell you how it was. When he should   50
have locked with both his hilts, he in a bravery flourished over his
head. With that comes Franklin at him lustily and hurts the slave.
With that he slinks away. Now, his way had been to have come
in hand and feet, one and two round at his costard. He like a
fool bears his sword-point half a yard out of danger. I lie here for my   55
life. If the devil come and he have no more strength than fence, he
shall never beat me from this ward. I'll stand to it, a buckler in a

skilful hand is as good as a castle—nay, 'tis better than a sconce, for
I have tried it. Mosby, perceiving this, began to faint. With that
comes Arden with his arming-sword and thrust him through the 60
shoulder in a trice.

ALICE Ay, but I wonder why you both stood still.

WILL Faith, I was so amazed I could not strike.

ALICE Ah, sirs, had he yesternight been slain,
For every drop of his detested blood 65
I would have crammed in angels in thy fist,
And kissed thee, too, and hugged thee in my arms.

WILL Patient yourself. We cannot help it now.
Greene and we two will dog him through the fair,
And stab him in the crowd, and steal away. 70

Here enters Mosby [with his arm bandaged]

ALICE It is unpossible. But here comes he
That will, I hope, invent some surer means.
Sweet Mosby, hide thy arm: it kills my heart.

MOSBY Ay, Mistress Arden, this is your favour.°

ALICE Ah, say not so, for when I saw thee hurt, 75
I could have took the weapon thou lett'st fall
And run at Arden, for I have sworn
That these mine eyes, offended with his sight,
Shall never close till Arden's be shut up.
This night I rose and walked about the chamber, 80
And twice or thrice I thought to have murdered him.

MOSBY What, in the night? Then had we been undone.

ALICE Why, how long shall he live?

MOSBY Faith, Alice, no longer than this night.
Black Will and Shakebag, will you two 85
Perform the complot that I have laid?

WILL Ay, or else think me as a villain.

GREENE And rather than you shall want, I'll help myself.

MOSBY You, Master Greene, shall single Franklin forth
And hold him with a long tale of strange news, 90
That he may not come home till supper time.
I'll fetch Master Arden home; and we, like friends,
Will play a game or two at tables here.

ALICE But what of all this? How shall he be slain?

MOSBY Why, Black Will and Shakebag, locked within the counting 95
house,
Shall, at a certain watchword given, rush forth.

WILL   What shall the watchword be?
MOSBY   'Now I take you'—that shall be the word.
    But come not forth before in any case.
WILL   I warrant you. But who shall lock me in?   100
ALICE   That will I do. Thou'st keep the key thyself.
MOSBY   Come, Master Greene, go you along with me.
    See all things ready, Alice, against we come.
ALICE   Take no care for that; send you him home.
    And, if he e'er go forth again, blame me.   105
        Exeunt Mosby and Greene
    Come, Black Will, that in mine eyes art fair;
    Next unto Mosby do I honour thee.
    Instead of fair words and large promises
    My hands shall play you golden harmony.
    How like you this? Say, will you do it, sirs?   110
WILL   Ay, and that bravely, too. Mark my device:
    Place Mosby, being a stranger, in a chair,
    And let your husband sit upon a stool,°
    That I may come behind him cunningly
    And with a towel pull him to the ground,   115
    Then stab him till his flesh be as a sieve.
    That done, bear him behind the Abbey,
    That those that find him murdered may suppose
    Some slave or other killed him for his gold.
ALICE   A fine device! You shall have twenty pound,   120
    And, when he is dead, you shall have forty more;
    And, lest you might be suspected staying here,
    Michael shall saddle you two lusty geldings.
    Ride whither you will, to Scotland or to Wales,
    I'll see you shall not lack wher'er you be.   125
WILL   Such words would make one kill a thousand men!
    Give me the key. Which is the counting house?
        [*Alice hands over the key and points out the counting house door*]
ALICE   Here would I stay and still encourage you,
    But that I know how resolute you are.
SHAKEBAG   Tush! You are too faint-hearted; we must do it.   130
ALICE   But Mosby will be there, whose very looks
    Will add unwonted courage to my thought
    And make me the first that shall adventure on him.°
WILL   Tush, get you gone! 'Tis we must do the deed.
    When this door opens next, look for his death.°   135
        [*Exeunt Will and Shakebag through the counting house door*]

ALICE   Ah, would he now were here, that it might open!
   I shall no more be closed in Arden's arms,
   That like the snakes of black Tisiphone°
   Sting me with their embracings. Mosby's arms
   Shall compass me, and, were I made a star,   140
   I would have none other spheres but those.°
   There is no nectar but in Mosby's lips!
   Had chaste Diana kissed him, she like me
   Would grow lovesick and from her wat'ry bower
   Fling down Endymion and snatch him up.°   145
   Then blame not me that slay a silly man°
   Not half so lovely as Endymion.
       Here enters Michael

MICHAEL   Mistress, my master is coming hard by.

ALICE   Who comes with him?

MICHAEL   Nobody but Mosby.   150

ALICE   That's well, Michael. Fetch in the tables,° and, when thou hast
   done, stand before the counting house door.

MICHAEL   Why so?

ALICE   Black Will is locked within to do the deed.

MICHAEL   What? Shall he die tonight?   155

ALICE   Ay, Michael.

MICHAEL   But shall not Susan know it?

ALICE   Yes, for she'll be as secret as ourselves.

MICHAEL   That's brave! I'll go fetch the tables.

ALICE   But, Michael, hark to me a word or two: 160
   When my husband is come in, lock the street door;
   He shall be murdered or the guests come in.°
       Exit Michael. Here enters Arden and Mosby [through the
       street door. In the background, enter Michael, who sets out
       a table, a chair, stools, and a set of tables, and locks the
       street door]
   Husband, what mean you to bring Mosby home?
   Although I wished you to be reconciled,
   'Twas more for fear of you than love of him.   165
   Black Will and Greene are his companions,
   And they are cutters and may cut you short;
   Therefore I thought it good to make you friends.
   But wherefore do you bring him hither now?
   You have given me my supper with his sight.°   170

MOSBY   Master Arden, methinks your wife would have me gone.

ARDEN No, good Master Mosby, women will be prating.
  Alice, bid him welcome; he and I are friends.
ALICE You may enforce me to it if you will,
  But I had rather die than bid him welcome.   175
  His company hath purchased me ill friends,
  And therefore will I ne'er frequent it more.
MOSBY [aside] O, how cunningly she can dissemble!
ARDEN Now he is here, you will not serve me so.
ALICE I pray you be not angry or displeased;   180
  I'll bid him welcome, seeing you'll have it so.
  You are welcome, Master Mosby. Will you sit down?
     [Mosby sits in the chair]
MOSBY I know I am welcome to your loving husband,
  But for yourself you speak not from your heart.
ALICE And if I do not, sir, think I have cause.   185
MOSBY Pardon me, Master Arden, I'll away.
ARDEN No, good Master Mosby.
ALICE We shall have guests enough though you go hence.
MOSBY I pray you, Master Arden, let me go.
ARDEN I pray thee, Mosby, let her prate her fill.   190
ALICE The doors are open, sir, you may be gone.
MICHAEL [aside] Nay, that's a lie, for I have locked the doors.
ARDEN Sirrah, fetch me a cup of wine; I'll make them friends.
     [Exit Michael]
  And, gentle Mistress Alice, seeing you are so stout,
  You shall begin. Frown not; I'll have it so.   195
ALICE I pray you meddle with that you have to do.
ARDEN Why, Alice, how can I do too much for him
  Whose life I have endangered without cause?
     [Enter Michael with wine]
ALICE 'Tis true; and, seeing 'twas partly through my means,
  I am content to drink to him for this once.   200
  Here, Master Mosby! [Drinks] And, I pray you, henceforth
  Be you as strange to me as I to you.
  Your company hath purchased me ill friends,
  And I for you, God knows, have undeserved
  Been ill spoken of in every place;   205
  Therefore, henceforth frequent my house no more.
MOSBY I'll see your husband in despite of you.
  Yet, Arden, I protest to thee by heaven,

Thou ne'er shalt see me more after this night.
I'll go to Rome rather than be forsworn.   210
ARDEN   Tush, I'll have no such vows made in my house.
ALICE   Yes, I pray you, husband, let him swear;
And, on that condition, Mosby, pledge me here.°
MOSBY   Ay, as willingly as I mean to live.
      [*Alice hands Mosby the cup of wine and he drinks*]
ARDEN   Come, Alice, is our supper ready yet?   215
ALICE   It will by then you have played a game at tables.
ARDEN   Come, Master Mosby, what shall we play for?
MOSBY   Three games for a French crown, sir, an 't please you.
ARDEN   Content.
      [*He sits down.*] *Then they play at the tables.* [*Enter Will and
      Shakebag from the counting house*]
WILL   [*whispers*] Can he not take him yet? What a spite is that!   220
ALICE   [*whispers*] Not yet, Will. Take heed he see thee not.
WILL   [*whispers*] I fear he will spy me as I am coming.
MICHAEL   [*whispers*] To prevent that, creep betwixt my legs.°
MOSBY   One ace, or else I lose the game.
      [*He throws the dice*]
ARDEN   Marry, sir, there's two for failing.   225
MOSBY   Ah, Master Arden, 'Now I can take you.'
      Then Will pulls him down with a towel
ARDEN   Mosby! Michael! Alice! What will you do?
WILL   Nothing but take you up, sir, nothing else.°
      [*Mosby stabs Arden*]
MOSBY   There's for the pressing-iron you told me of.°
      [*Shakebag stabs Arden*]
SHAKEBAG   And there's for the ten pound in my sleeve.   230
      [*Arden moans*]
ALICE   What, groans thou? [*To Mosby*] Nay, then give me the weapon!
Take this for hind'ring Mosby's love and mine.
      [*Alice stabs Arden, and he dies*]
MICHAEL   O, mistress!
WILL   Ah, that villain will betray us all.
MOSBY   Tush, fear him not: he will be secret.   235
MICHAEL   Why, dost thou think I will betray myself?
SHAKEBAG   In Southwark dwells a bonny northern lass,°
The widow Chambley. I'll to her house now;
And, if she will not give me harbour,
I'll make booty of the quean even to her smock.   240

WILL   Shift for yourselves: we two will leave you now.
ALICE   First lay the body in the counting house.
          Then [Black Will and Shakebag] lay the body in the counting house
WILL   We have our gold. Mistress Alice, adieu;
     Mosby, farewell; and, Michael, farewell too.
          *Exeunt [Will and Shakebag. There is knocking at the street
          door.] Enter Susan*
SUSAN   Mistress, the guests are at the doors.   245
     Hearken! They knock. What, shall I let them in?
ALICE   Mosby, go thou and bear them company.
          Exit Mosby
     And, Susan, fetch water and wash away this blood.
          *[Exit Susan. She returns with cleaning materials and starts
          washing the floor]*
SUSAN   The blood cleaveth to the ground and will not out.°
ALICE   But with my nails I'll scrape away the blood.   250
          [She scratches at the floor]
     The more I strive, the more the blood appears!
SUSAN   What's the reason, Mistress, can you tell?
ALICE   Because I blush not at my husband's death.
          Here enters Mosby
MOSBY   How now, what's the matter? Is all well?
ALICE   Ay, well, if Arden were alive again!   255
     In vain we strive, for here his blood remains.
MOSBY   Why, strew rushes on it, can you not?
     This wench doth nothing. [*To Susan*] Fall unto the work.
ALICE   'Twas thou that made me murder him.
MOSBY   What of that?   260
ALICE   Nay, nothing, Mosby, so it be not known.
MOSBY   Keep thou it close, and 'tis unpossible.
ALICE   Ah, but I cannot. Was he not slain by me?
     My husband's death torments me at the heart.
MOSBY   It shall not long torment thee, gentle Alice.   265
     I am thy husband: think no more of him.
          Here enters Adam Fowle and Bradshaw [through the street door]
BRADSHAW   How now, Mistress Arden? What ail you weep?°
MOSBY   Because her husband is abroad so late.
     A couple of ruffians threat'ned him yesternight,
     And she, poor soul, is afraid he should be hurt.   270
ADAM   Is't nothing else? Tush, he'll be here anon.
          Here enters Greene [through the street door]

GREENE Now, Mistress Arden, lack you any guests?

ALICE Ah, Master Greene, did you see my husband lately?

GREENE I saw him walking behind the Abbey even now.

Here enters Franklin [through the street door]

ALICE I do not like this being out so late.   275

Master Franklin, where did you leave my husband?

FRANKLIN Believe me, I saw him not since morning.

Fear you not: he'll come anon. Meantime,

You may do well to bid his guests sit down.

ALICE Ay, so they shall. Master Bradshaw, sit you there.   280

I pray you be content, I'll have my will.

Master Mosby, sit you in my husband's seat.

[Mosby and the guests sit down]

MICHAEL *[aside to Susan]* Susan, shall thou and I wait on them?

Or, an thou say'st the word, let us sit down too.

SUSAN *[aside to Michael]* Peace, we have other matters now in hand. 285

I fear me, Michael, all will be bewrayed.

MICHAEL *[aside to Susan]* Tush, so it be known that I shall marry thee

in the morning, I care not though I be hanged ere night. But to

prevent the worst I'll buy some ratsbane.

SUSAN *[aside to Michael]* Why, Michael, wilt thou poison thyself?   290

MICHAEL *[aside to Susan]* No, but my mistress, for I fear she'll tell.

SUSAN *[aside to Michael]* Tush, Michael, fear not her; she's wise

enough.

MOSBY Sirrah Michael, give's a cup of beer.

[Michael fetches drink]

Mistress Arden, here's to your husband.   295

[Mosby drinks]

ALICE My husband!

FRANKLIN What ails you, woman, to cry so suddenly?

ALICE Ah, neighbours, a sudden qualm came over my heart;

My husband's being forth torments my mind.

I know something's amiss; he is not well,   300

Or else I should have heard of him ere now.

MOSBY *[aside]* She will undo us through her foolishness.

GREENE Fear not, Mistress Arden, he's well enough.

ALICE Tell not me: I know he is not well.

He was not wont for to stay thus late.   305

Good Master Franklin, go and seek him forth,

And, if you find him, send him home to me,

And tell him what a fear he hath put me in.

FRANKLIN [*aside*] I like not this; I pray God all be well.
  [*Aloud*] I'll seek him out and find him if I can.   310
      Exeunt Franklin, Mosby, and Greene [*through the street door*]
ALICE [*aside*] Michael, how shall I do to rid the rest away?
MICHAEL [*aside*] Leave that to my charge; let me alone.
  'Tis very late, Master Bradshaw,
  And there are many false knaves abroad,
  And you have many narrow lanes to pass.   315
BRADSHAW Faith, friend Michael, and thou sayest true.
  Therefore I pray thee light's forth and lend's a link.
ALICE Michael, bring them to the doors, but do not stay.°
  You know I do not love to be alone.
      Exeunt Bradshaw, Adam, and Michael [*through the street door*]
  Go, Susan, and bid thy brother come.   320
  But wherefore should he come? Here is nought but fear.
  Stay, Susan, stay, and help to counsel me.
SUSAN Alas, I counsel! Fear frights away my wits.°
      Then [*Alice and Susan*] *open the counting house door and look*
      upon Arden
ALICE See, Susan, where thy *quondam* master lies:
  Sweet Arden, smeared in blood and filthy gore.   325
SUSAN My brother, you, and I shall rue this deed.
ALICE Come, Susan, help to lift his body forth,
  And let our salt tears be his obsequies.
      [*They drag the corpse onto the stage.*] *Here enters Mosby and*
      Greene [*through the street door*]
MOSBY How now, Alice, whither will you bear him?
ALICE Sweet Mosby, art thou come? Then weep that will;°   330
  I have my wish in that I 'joy thy sight.
GREENE Well, it 'hoves us to be circumspect.
MOSBY Ay, for Franklin thinks that we have murdered him.
ALICE Ay, but he cannot prove it for his life.
  We'll spend this night in dalliance and in sport.   335
      Here enters Michael [*through the street door*]
MICHAEL O mistress, the Mayor and all the watch°
  Are coming towards our house with glaives and bills.
ALICE Make the door fast; let them not come in.
      [*Michael locks the street door*]
MOSBY Tell me, sweet Alice, how shall I escape?
ALICE Out at the back door, over the pile of wood,   340
  And for one night lie at the Flower-de-Luce.

MOSBY That is the next way to betray myself.

GREENE Alas, Mistress Arden, the watch will take me here
 And cause suspicion where else would be none.

ALICE Why, take that way that Master Mosby doth;   345
 But first convey the body to the fields.
  *Then [Mosby, Greene, Susan, and Michael] bear the body
  into the fields. [Alice is left alone on stage.° Enter Mosby,
  Greene, Susan, and Michael]*

MOSBY Until tomorrow, sweet Alice, now farewell,
 And see you confess nothing in any case.

GREENE Be resolute, Mistress Alice; betray us not,
 But cleave to us as we will stick to you.   350
  Exeunt Mosby and Greene

ALICE Now let the judge and juries do their worst;
 My house is clear, and now I fear them not.

SUSAN As we went, it snowèd all the way,
 Which makes me fear our footsteps will be spied.

ALICE Peace, fool! The snow will cover them again.   355

SUSAN But it had done before we came back again.
  [There is knocking at the street door]

ALICE Hark, hark, they knock! Go, Michael, let them in.
  *[Michael opens the street door.] Here enters the Mayor
  and the Watch*

How now, Master Mayor, have you brought my husband home?

MAYOR I saw him come into your house an hour ago.

ALICE You are deceived: it was a Londoner.   360

MAYOR Mistress Arden, know you not one that is called Black Will?

ALICE I know none such. What mean these questions?

MAYOR I have the Council's warrant to apprehend him.

ALICE *[aside]* I am glad it is no worse.

 [Aloud] Why, Master Mayor, think you I harbour any such?   365

MAYOR We are informed that here he is;
 And, therefore, pardon us, for we must search.

ALICE Ay, search, and spare you not, through every room.
 Were my husband at home, you would not offer this.
  Here enters Franklin [through the street door]

Master Franklin, what mean you come so sad?   370

FRANKLIN Arden, thy husband and my friend, is slain.

ALICE Ah, by whom? Master Franklin, can you tell?

FRANKLIN I know not, but behind the Abbey
 There he lies murdered in most piteous case.

MAYOR But, Master Franklin, are you sure 'tis he?   375
FRANKLIN I am too sure. Would God I were deceived!
ALICE Find out the murderers, let them be known.
FRANKLIN Ay, so they shall. Come you along with us.
ALICE Wherefore?
FRANKLIN Know you this hand-towel and this knife?   380
SUSAN [*aside*] Ah, Michael, through this thy negligence thou hast
    betrayed and undone us all.
MICHAEL [*aside*] I was so afraid I knew not what I did. I thought I had
    thrown them both into the well.
ALICE [*to Franklin*] It is the pig's blood we had to supper.   385
    But wherefore stay you? Find out the murderers.
MAYOR I fear me you'll prove one of them yourself.
ALICE I one of them? What mean such questions?
FRANKLIN I fear me he was murdered in this house
    And carried to the fields, for from that place   390
    Backwards and forwards may you see
    The print of many feet within the snow.
    And look about this chamber where we are,
    And you shall find part of his guiltless blood;
    For in his slipshoe did I find some rushes,°   395
    Which argueth he was murdered in this room.
MAYOR Look in the place where he was wont to sit.
    See, see! His blood! It is too manifest.
ALICE It is a cup of wine that Michael shed.
MICHAEL Ay, truly.   400
FRANKLIN It is his blood, which, strumpet, thou hast shed.
    But, if I live, thou and thy complices
    Which have conspired and wrought his death shall rue it.
ALICE Ah, Master Franklin, God and heaven can tell
    I loved him more than all the world beside.   405
    But bring me to him, let me see his body.
FRANKLIN [*pointing to Michael*] Bring that villain and Mosby's
        sister too;
    And one of you go to the Flower-de-Luce,
    And seek for Mosby, and apprehend him too.   395
        Exeunt

Scene 15

Here enters Shakebag alone
SHAKEBAG The widow Chambley in her husband's days I kept;°
  And, now he's dead, she is grown so stout
  She will not know her old companions.
  I came thither, thinking to have had harbour as I was wont, and she
    was ready to thrust me out at doors. But, whether she would or no,   5
    I got me up; and, as she followed me, I spurned her down the
    stairs, and broke her neck, and cut her tapster's throat; and now
    I am going to fling them in the Thames. I have the gold: what
    care I though it be known? I'll cross the water and take sanctuary.°
  Exit Shakebag

Scene 16

*Here enters the Mayor, Mosby, Alice, Franklin, Michael,
  and Susan. [Arden's body is discovered]°*
MAYOR See, Mistress Arden, where your husband lies.
  Confess this foul fault and be penitent.
ALICE Arden, sweet husband, what shall I say?
  The more I sound his name, the more he bleeds.
  This blood condemns me and in gushing forth   5
  Speaks as it falls and asks me why I did it.°
  Forgive me, Arden; I repent me now,
  And, would my death save thine, thou shouldst not die.
  Rise up, sweet Arden, and enjoy thy love,
  And frown not on me when we meet in heaven: 10
  In heaven I love thee though on earth I did not.
MAYOR Say, Mosby, what made thee murder him?
FRANKLIN Study not for an answer; look not down.
  His purse and girdle found at thy bed's head
  Witness sufficiently thou didst the deed.   15
  It bootless is to swear thou didst it not.
MOSBY I hired Black Will and Shakebag, ruffians both,
  And they and I have done this murd'rous deed.
  But wherefore stay we? Come and bear me hence.

FRANKLIN Those ruffians shall not escape. I will up to London and   20
get the Council's warrant to apprehend them.
    Exeunt

Scene 17

    Here enters Will
WILL Shakebag, I hear, hath taken sanctuary,
   But I am so pursued with hues and cries°
   For petty robberies that I have done
   That I can come unto no sanctuary.
   Therefore must I in some oyster-boat at last be fain to go aboard some   5
      hoy, and so to Flushing:° there is no staying here. At Sittingbourne
      the watch was like to take me, and, had I not with my buckler
      covered my head and run full blank at all adventures,° I am sure
      I had ne'er gone further than that place, for the constable had twenty
      warrants to apprehend me. Besides that, I robbed him and his man   10
      once at Gads Hill.° Farewell, England; I'll to Flushing now.
    Exit Will

Scene 18

    Here enters the Mayor, Mosby, Alice, Michael, Susan, and
    Bradshaw [*with the Watch*]
MAYOR [*to the Watch*] Come, make haste, and bring away the prisoners.
BRADSHAW Mistress Arden, you are now going to God,
   And I am by the law condemned to die
   About a letter I brought from Master Greene.
   I pray you, Mistress Arden, speak the truth: 5
   Was I ever privy to your intent or no?
ALICE What should I say? You brought me such a letter,
   But I dare swear thou knewest not the contents.
   Leave now to trouble me with worldly things,
   And let me meditate upon my saviour Christ,   10
   Whose blood must save me for the blood I shed.
MOSBY How long shall I live in this hell of grief?
   Convey me from the presence of that strumpet.

ALICE Ah, but for thee I had never been strumpet.
 What cannot oaths and protestations do   15
 When men have opportunity to woo?
 I was too young to sound thy villainies,
 But now I find it and repent too late.
SUSAN *[to Mosby]* Ah, gentle brother, wherefore should I die?
 I knew not of it till the deed was done.   20
MOSBY For thee I mourn more than for myself,
 But let it suffice I cannot save thee now.
MICHAEL *[to Susan]* And if your brother and my mistress had not
 promised me you in marriage, I had ne'er given consent to° this foul
 deed.   25
MAYOR Leave to accuse each other now,
 And listen to the sentence I shall give.
 Bear Mosby and his sister to London straight,
 Where they in Smithfield must be executed.°
 Bear Mistress Arden unto Canterbury,   30
 Where her sentence is she must be burnt.°
 Michael and Bradshaw in Faversham must suffer death.
ALICE Let my death make amends for all my sins.
MOSBY Fie upon women: this shall be my song.
 But bear me hence, for I have lived too long.   35
SUSAN Seeing no hope on earth, in heaven is my hope.
MICHAEL Faith, I care not, seeing I die with Susan.°
BRADSHAW My blood be on his head that gave the sentence!
MAYOR To speedy execution with them all!
 Exeunt

Epilogue

Here enters Franklin

FRANKLIN Thus have you seen the truth of Arden's death.
 As for the ruffians, Shakebag and Black Will,
 The one took sanctuary and, being sent for out,
 Was murderèd in Southwark as he passed
 To Greenwich, where the Lord Protector lay.   5
 Black Will was burnt in Flushing on a stage.
 Greene was hanged at Ospringe in Kent.°
 The painter fled, and how he died we know not.

But this above the rest is to be noted:
Arden lay murdered in that plot of ground   10
Which he by force and violence held from Reede,
And in the grass his body's print was seen
Two years and more after the deed was done.
Gentlemen, we hope you'll pardon this naked tragedy°
Wherein no filèd points are foisted in°   15
To make it gracious to the ear or eye;
For simple truth is gracious enough
And needs no other points of glozing stuff.
    [*Exit*]

A WOMAN KILLED WITH KINDNESS

THOMAS HEYWOOD

THE PERSONS OF THE PLAY

PROLOGUE

JOHN FRANKFORD, a young gentleman of noble descent; Anne's husband

ANNE FRANKFORD, Frankford's young wife

WENDOLL, a young gentleman of a good, but poor, family

NICHOLAS, Frankford's servant

JENKIN, a servant in Frankford's household

SISLY MILK-PAIL, the cook in Frankford's household

SPIGGOT, Frankford's butler

ANNE'S COACHMAN

THREE CARTERS, Frankford's tenants

A MAID in Frankford's household

SERVINGMEN of Frankford's household

WEDDING GUESTS of the lower orders, including JACK SLIME, ROGER BRICKBAT, JOAN MINIVER, JANE TRUBKIN, and ISBEL MOTLEY

MUSICIANS at the Frankfords' wedding

SIR FRANCIS ACTON, a knight, Anne's elder brother

SIR CHARLES MOUNTFORD, a young knight

SUSAN MOUNTFORD, Sir Charles's sister

MALBY, a friend of Sir Francis

CRANWELL, a friend of Sir Charles and Frankford

TWO FALCONERS and TWO HUNTSMEN serving Sir Charles and Sir Francis respectively

THE SHERIFF

THE SHERIFF'S OFFICERS

THE KEEPER of York Castle prison

SHAFTON

A SERGEANT

OLD MOUNTFORD, uncle of Sir Charles and Susan

SANDY, a former friend of the Mountfords

RODER, formerly Sir Charles's tenant

TYDY, an older kinsman of Sir Charles and Susan

EPILOGUE

A Woman Killed with Kindness

Prologue

[*Enter the Prologue*]
PROLOGUE I come but like a harbinger, being sent
To tell you what these preparations mean.°
Look for no glorious state, our Muse is bent°
Upon a barren subject, a bare scene.
We could afford this twig a timber-tree,°   5
Whose strength might boldly on your favours build;
Our russet, tissue; drone, a honey-bee;°
Our barren plot, a large and spacious field;
Our coarse fare, banquets; our thin water, wine;
Our brook, a sea; our bat's eyes, eagle's sight;°   10
Our poet's dull and earthy Muse, divine;
Our ravens, doves; our crow's black feathers, white.
But gentle thoughts, when they may give the foil,°
Save them that yield, and spare where they may spoil.°
    [*Exit*]

Scene 1

Enter Master John Frankford, Sir Francis Acton,
Mistress Anne, Sir Charles Mountford, Master Malby,
Master Wendoll, and Master Cranwell
SIR FRANCIS Some music there! None lead the bride a dance?
SIR CHARLES Yes, would she dance 'The Shaking of the Sheets'! °
    But that's the dance her husband means to lead her!
WENDOLL That's not the dance that every man must dance,°
    According to the ballad.   5
SIR FRANCIS Music, ho!°
    [*To Mistress Anne*] By your leave, sister—by your
        husband's leave
    I should have said—the hand that but this day
    Was given you in the church I'll borrow. Sound!

[*Music is played*]
This marriage music hoists me from the ground.   10
[*Sir Francis and Mistress Anne dance*]
FRANKFORD Ay, you may caper, you are light and free;
Marriage hath yoked my heels—pray then pardon me.
SIR FRANCIS I'll have you dance too, brother.
SIR CHARLES   Master Frankford,
You are a happy man, sir; and much joy
Succeed your marriage mirth, you have a wife   15
So qualified and with such ornaments°
Both of the mind and body. First, her birth
Is noble, and her education such
As might become the daughter of a prince.
Her own tongue speaks all tongues, and her own hand   20
Can teach all strings to speak in their best grace,
From the shrill treble to the hoarsest bass.
To end her many praises in one word,
She's Beauty and Perfection's eldest daughter,
Only found by yours, though many a heart hath sought her.°   25
FRANKFORD But that I know your virtues and chaste thoughts,
I should be jealous of your praise, Sir Charles.
CRANWELL He speaks no more than you approve.°
MALBY Nor flatters he that gives to her her due.
ANNE I would your praise could find a fitter theme   30
Than my imperfect beauty to speak on.
Such as they be, if they my husband please,°
They suffice me now I am marrièd.
His sweet content is like a flattering glass,
To make my face seem fairer to mine eye: 35
But the least wrinkle from his stormy brow
Will blast the roses in my cheeks that grow.
SIR FRANCIS A perfect wife already, meek and patient.
How strangely the word 'husband' fits your mouth,
Not married three hours since. Sister, 'tis good;   40
You that begin betimes thus, must needs prove
Pliant and duteous in your husband's love.
Godamercies, brother, wrought her to it already?
'Sweet husband' and a curtsey the first day.
Mark this, mark this, you that are bachelors,   45
And never took the grace of honest man,
Mark this against you marry, this one phrase:°

In a good time that man both wins and woos
That takes his wife down in her wedding shoes.°

FRANKFORD Your sister takes not after you, Sir Francis.   50
All his wild blood your father spent on you;
He got her in his age when he grew civil.
All his mad tricks were to his land entailed,°
And you are heir to all. Your sister, she
Hath to her dower her mother's modesty.   55

SIR CHARLES Lord, sir, in what a happy state live you!
This morning, which to many seems a burden
Too heavy to bear, is unto you a pleasure.
This lady is no clog, as many are;
She doth become you like a well-made suit   60
In which the tailor hath used all his art,
Not like a thick coat of unseasoned frieze,°
Forced on your back in summer. She's no chain
To tie your neck and curb you to the yoke,
But she's a chain of gold to adorn your neck.   65
You both adorn each other, and your hands
Methinks are matches. There's equality
In this fair combination: you are both scholars,
Both young, both being descended nobly.
There's music in this sympathy: it carries   70
Consort and expectation of much joy,
Which God bestow on you from this first day,
Until your dissolution—that's for aye.

SIR FRANCIS We keep you here too long, good brother Frankford.
Into the hall! Away, go, cheer your guests!   75
What, bride and bridegroom both withdrawn at once?
If you be missed, the guests will doubt their welcome,
And charge you with unkindness.

FRANKFORD   To prevent it,
I'll leave you here, to see the dance within.

ANNE And so will I.
          [*Exeunt Frankford and Anne*]

SIR FRANCIS   To part you it were sin.   80
          [*Sounds of merriment can be heard off stage*]
Now gallants, while the town musicians
Finger their frets within, and the mad lads
And country lasses, every mother's child
With nosegays and bride-laces in their hats,°

Dance all their country measures, rounds, and jigs,   85
What shall we do? Hark, they are all on the hoigh,°
They toil like mill-horses, and turn as round—°
Marry, not on the toe. Ay, and they caper,
But without cutting. You shall see tomorrow°
The hall floor pecked and dinted like millstone,   90
Made with their high shoes: though their skill be small,
Yet they tread heavy where their hobnails fall.

SIR CHARLES   Well, leave them to their sports. Sir Francis Acton,
I'll make a match with you: meet me tomorrow
At chevy chase, I'll fly my hawk with yours.°   95

SIR FRANCIS   For what? for what?

SIR CHARLES   Why, for a hundred pound.

SIR FRANCIS   Pawn me some gold of that.
          [Sir Charles gives him money]

SIR CHARLES   Here are ten angels;
I'll make them good a hundred pound tomorrow
Upon my hawk's wing.

SIR FRANCIS   'Tis a match, 'tis done.
Another hundred pound upon your dogs,   100
Dare you, Sir Charles?

SIR CHARLES   I dare. Were I sure to lose
I durst do more than that. Here's my hand,
The first course for a hundred pound.

SIR FRANCIS   A match.

WENDOLL   Ten angels on Sir Francis Acton's hawk;
As much upon his dogs.   105

CRANWELL   I am for Sir Charles Mountford: I have seen
His hawk and dog both tried! What, clap you hands,
Or is't no bargain!

WENDOLL   Yes, and stake them down.°
Were they five hundred they were all my own.

SIR FRANCIS   Be stirring early with the lark tomorrow;   110
I'll rise into my saddle ere the sun
Rise from his bed.

SIR CHARLES   If there you miss me, say
I am no gentleman; I'll hold my day.

SIR FRANCIS   It holds on all sides; come, tonight let's dance.
Early tomorrow let's prepare to ride;   115
We had need be three hours up before the bride.
          [Exeunt]

Scene 2

Enter Nick and Jenkin, Jack Slime, Roger Brickbat, with
[four] country Wenches, and two or three Musicians

JENKIN Come, Nick, take you Joan Miniver to trace withal; Jack Slime, traverse you with Sisly Milk-pail, I will take Jane Trubkin, and Roger Brickbat shall have Isbel Motley; and now that they are busy in the parlour, come, strike up, we'll have a crash here in the yard.

NICHOLAS My humour is not compendious: dancing I possess not,   5
though I can foot it;° yet since I am fallen into the hands of Sisly Milk-pail,° I assent.

JACK Truly, Nick, though we were never brought up like serving courtiers,° yet we have been brought up with serving creatures, ay, and God's creatures too, for we have been brought up to serve sheep,   10
oxen, horses, and hogs, and such like; and though we be but country fellows, it may be in the way of dancing we can do the horse-trick as well as servingmen.

ROGER Ay, and the cross-point, too.

JENKIN O Slime, O Brickbat, do not you know that comparisons are   15
odious?° Now we are odious ourselves, too; therefore there are no comparisons to be made betwixt us.

NICHOLAS I am sudden, and not superfluous;
I am quarrelsome, and not seditious;
I am peaceable, and not contentious;   20
I am brief, and not compendious;
Slime, foot it quickly. If the music overcome not my melancholy, I shall quarrel; and if they suddenly do not strike up, I shall presently strike thee down.

JENKIN No quarrelling, for God's sake! Truly, if you do, I shall set a   25
knave between you.

JACK I come to dance, not to quarrel. Come, what shall it be? 'Rogero'?

JENKIN 'Rogero' No. We will dance 'The Beginning of the World'.

SISLY I love no dance so well as 'John, Come Kiss Me Now'.   30

NICHOLAS I, that have ere now deserved a cushion,° call for the cushion dance.°

ROGER For my part, I like nothing so well as 'Tom Tyler'.

JENKIN No, we'll have 'The Hunting of the Fox'.

JACK The hay, the hay, there's nothing like the hay.   35

NICHOLAS I have said, I do say, and I will say again—

JENKIN Every man agree to have it as Nick says.

ALL Content.

NICHOLAS It hath been, it now is, and it shall be—

SISLY What, Master Nicholas, what?   40

NICHOLAS 'Put on Your Smock o' Monday'.

JENKIN So the dance will come cleanly off.° Come, for God's sake
    agree of something. If you like not that, put it to the musicians,° or
    let me speak for all, and we'll have 'Sellenger's Round'.°

ALL That, that, that!   45

NICHOLAS No, I am resolved thus it shall be: first take hands, then
    take you to your heels.

JENKIN Why, would you have us run away?

NICHOLAS No, but I would have you shake your heels. Music, strike up.
    [*The musicians play.*] *The servants dance; Nicholas, dancing,*
    speaks stately and scurvily, the rest after the country fashion°

JENKIN Hey! lively, my lasses! Here's a turn for thee!   50
    [*Exeunt*]

Scene 3

Horns are sounded. Enter Sir Charles, Sir Francis, Malby,°
Cranwell, Wendoll, Falconers,° *and Huntsmen*

SIR CHARLES So, well cast off. Aloft, aloft! Well flown!
    O now she takes her at the souse, and strikes her
    Down to the earth, like a swift thunderclap.°

WENDOLL She hath struck ten angels out of my way.

SIR FRANCIS A hundred pound from me.

SIR CHARLES   What, falconer?   5

FALCONER At hand, sir.

SIR CHARLES Now she hath seized the fowl, and 'gins to plume her.
    Rebeck her not: rather stand still and chirk her,
    So; seize her gets, her jesses, and her bells.°
    Away!   10
    [*Exit Sir Charles's Falconer*]

SIR FRANCIS My hawk killed, too.

SIR CHARLES   Ay, but 'twas at the querre,
    Not at the mount like mine.

SIR FRANCIS   Judgement, my masters.

CRANWELL Yours missed her at the ferre.°

WENDOLL Ay, but our merlin first had plumed the fowl,
    And twice renewed her from the river, too.   15
    Her bells, Sir Francis, had not both one weight,
    Nor was one semitune above the other.
    Methinks these Milan bells do sound too full,
    And spoil the mounting of your hawk.
SIR CHARLES   'Tis lost.°
SIR FRANCIS I grant it not. Mine likewise seized a fowl   20
    Within her talons, and you saw her paws
    Full of the feathers; both her petty singles
    And her long singles gripped her more than other.°
    The terrials of her legs were stained with blood:
    Not of the fowl only she did discomfit   25
    Some of her feathers, but she brake away.°
    Come, come, your hawk is but a rifler.°
        [Enter Sir Charles's Falconer]°
SIR CHARLES   How?
SIR FRANCIS Ay, and your dogs are trundle-tails and curs.
SIR CHARLES You stir my blood.
    You keep not a good hound in all your kennel,   30
    Nor one good hawk upon your perch.
SIR FRANCIS   How, knight?
SIR CHARLES So, knight? You will not swagger, sir?
SIR FRANCIS   Why, say I did?
SIR CHARLES Why, sir, I say you would gain as much by swagg'ring
    As you have got by wagers on your dogs;
    You will come short in all things.   35
SIR FRANCIS Not in this! Now I'll strike home.°
SIR CHARLES Thou shalt to thy long home, or I will want my will.°
SIR FRANCIS All they that love Sir Francis follow me.
SIR CHARLES All that affect Sir Charles draw on my part.
CRANWELL On this side heaves my hand.
WENDOLL   Here goes my heart.   40
        They divide themselves [and draw their weapons]. Sir Charles,
        Cranwell, Falconer, and Huntsman fight° against Sir Francis,
        Wendoll, his Falconer, and Huntsman. [Sir Charles and others
        are wounded.]° Sir Charles hath the better, and beats them
        away, killing Sir Francis's [Falconer and Huntsman. Exeunt
        all except Sir Charles and the dead bodies]
SIR CHARLES My God! What have I done? What have I done?
    My rage hath plunged into a sea of blood,

In which my soul lies drowned. Poor innocents,
For whom we are to answer. Well, 'tis done,
And I remain the victor. A great conquest,   45
When I would give this right hand, nay this head,
To breathe in them new life whom I have slain.
Forgive me, God: 'twas in the heat of blood,
And anger quite removes me from myself:
It was not I, but rage, did this vile murder;   50
Yet I, and not my rage, must answer it.
Sir Francis Acton he is fled the field,
With him, all those that did partake his quarrel,
And I am left alone, with sorrow dumb,
And in my height of conquest, overcome.   55
          Enter Susan
SUSAN O God, my brother wounded among the dead!
    Unhappy jest that in such earnest ends.
    The rumour of this fear stretched to my ears,°
    And I am come to know if you be wounded.
SIR CHARLES O sister, sister, wounded at the heart.   60
SUSAN My God forbid!
SIR CHARLES In doing that thing which he forbade,
    I am wounded, sister.
SUSAN   I hope not at the heart.
SIR CHARLES Yes, at the heart.°
SUSAN O God! A surgeon there!   65
SIR CHARLES Call me a surgeon, sister, for my soul;
    The sin of murder it hath pierced my heart,
    And made a wide wound there, but for these scratches,
    They are nothing, nothing.
SUSAN   Charles, what have you done?
    Sir Francis hath great friends, and will pursue you°   70
    Unto the utmost danger of the law.°
SIR CHARLES My conscience is become my enemy,
    And will pursue me more than Acton can.
SUSAN O fly, sweet brother.
SIR CHARLES   Shall I fly from thee?
    What, Sue, art weary of my company?   75
SUSAN Fly from your foe.
SIR CHARLES   You, sister, are my friend,
    And flying you, I shall pursue my end.

SUSAN Your company is as my eyeball dear;
  Being far from you, no comfort can be near.
  Yet fly to save your life: what would I care   80
  To spend my future age in black despair,
  So you were safe? And yet to live one week°
  Without my brother Charles, through every cheek
  My streaming tears would downwards run so rank°
  Till they could set on either side a bank,   85
  And in the midst a channel; so my face
  For two salt-water brooks shall still find place.
SIR CHARLES Thou shalt not weep so much, for I will stay
  In spite of danger's teeth. I'll live with thee,
  Or I'll not live at all. I will not sell   90
  My country and my father's patrimony,
  No, thy sweet sight, for a vain hope of life.
      Enter Sheriff with [armed] Officers
SHERIFF Sir Charles, I am made the unwilling instrument
  Of your attach and apprehension.
  I am sorry that the blood of innocent men   95
  Should be of you exacted. It was told me
  That you were guarded with a troop of friends,
  And therefore I come armed.
SIR CHARLES   O master Sheriff,
  I came into the field with many friends,
  But, see, they all have left me. Only one   100
  Clings to my sad misfortune, my dear sister.
  I know you for an honest gentleman;
  I yield my weapons and submit to you.
      [The Officers disarm him]
  Convey me where you please.
SHERIFF   To prison then,
  To answer for the lives of these dead men.   105
SUSAN O God! O God!
SIR CHARLES   Sweet sister, every strain
  Of sorrow from your heart augments my pain.
  Your grief abounds and hits against my breast.
SHERIFF Sir, will you go?
SIR CHARLES   Even where it likes you best.
      [Exeunt with the bodies]°

Scene 4

Enter Master Frankford in a study°
FRANKFORD How happy am I amongst other men
That in my mean estate embrace content.
I am a gentleman, and by my birth
Companion with a king. A king's no more,
I am possessed of many fair revenues,   5
Sufficient to maintain a gentleman.°
Touching my mind, I am studied in all arts,
The riches of my thoughts, and of my time
Have been a good proficient. But the chief°
Of all the sweet felicities on earth,   10
I have a fair, a chaste, and loving wife,
Perfection all, all truth, all ornament.
If man on earth may truly happy be,
Of these at once possessed, sure I am he.
     Enter Nicholas
NICHOLAS Sir, there's a gentleman attends without to speak with you.   15
FRANKFORD On horseback?
NICHOLAS Ay, on horseback.
FRANKFORD Entreat him to alight; I will attend him.
Knowest thou him, Nick?
NICHOLAS   I know him. His name's Wendoll.
It seems he comes in haste: his horse is booted   20
Up to the flank in mire, himself all spotted
And stained with plashing. Sure he rid in fear
Or for a wager: horse and man both sweat.
I ne'er saw two in such a smoking heat.
FRANKFORD Entreat him in. About it instantly.   25
     [*Exit Nicholas*]
This Wendoll I have noted, and his carriage
Hath pleased me much by observation.°
I have noted many good deserts in him:
He's affable and seen in many things,°
Discourses well, a good companion,   30
And though of small means, yet a gentleman
Of a good house, somewhat pressed by want.°
I have preferred him to a second place°
In my opinion and my best regard.
     Enter Wendoll, Mistress Anne, and Nicholas

ANNE O Master Frankford, Master Wendoll here   35
    Brings you the strangest news that e'er you heard.
FRANKFORD What news, sweet wife? What news, good Master
    Wendoll?
WENDOLL You knew the match made 'twixt Sir Francis Acton
    And Sir Charles Mountford.
FRANKFORD   True, with their hounds and hawks.
WENDOLL The matches were both played.
FRANKFORD   Ha, and which won?   40
WENDOLL Sir Francis, your wife's brother, had the worst
    And lost the wager.
FRANKFORD   Why, the worse his chance.
    Perhaps the fortune of some other day
    Will change his luck.
ANNE   O, but you hear not all!
    Sir Francis lost, and yet was loath to yield.   45
    In brief the two knights grew to difference,
    From words to blows, and so to banding sides,°
    Where valorous Sir Charles slew in his spleen°
    Two of your brother's men: his falconer
    And his good huntsman, whom he loved so well.   50
    More men were wounded, no more slain outright.
FRANKFORD Now trust me I am sorry for the knight;
    But is my brother safe?
WENDOLL   All whole and sound,°
    His body not being blemished with one wound.
    But poor Sir Charles is to the prison led,   55
    To answer at th' assize for them that's dead.
FRANKFORD I thank your pains, sir. Had the news been better,
    Your will was to have brought it, Master Wendoll.°
    Sir Charles will find hard friends: his case is heinous,°
    And will be most severely censured on.   60
    I am sorry for him. Sir, a word with you:
    I know you, sir, to be a gentleman
    In all things, your possibilities but mean.
    Please you to use my table and my purse:
    They are yours.
WENDOLL   O Lord, sir, I shall never deserve it!   65
FRANKFORD O sir, disparage not your worth too much;
    You are full of quality and fair desert.
    Choose of my men which shall attend on you,
    And he is yours. I will allow you, sir,

Your man, your gelding, and your table, all°   70
   At my own charge. Be my companion.
WENDOLL Master Frankford, I have oft been bound to you
   By many favours. This exceeds them all
   That I shall never merit your least favour:
   But when your last remembrance I forget,°   75
   Heaven at my soul exact that weighty debt.
FRANKFORD There needs no protestation, for I know you
   Virtuous, and therefore grateful. Prithee, Nan,
   Use him with all thy loving'st courtesy.
ANNE As far as modesty may well extend,   80
   It is my duty to receive your friend.
FRANKFORD To dinner. Come, sir, from this present day
   Welcome to me for ever. Come away.
      [*Exeunt Master Frankford, Wendoll, and Mistress Anne*]
NICHOLAS I do not like this fellow by no means;
   I never see him but my heart still earns.°   85
   Zounds! I could fight with him, yet know not why;
   The Devil and he are all one in my eye.
      Enter Jenkin
JENKIN O Nick, what gentleman is that comes to lie° at our house?
   My master allows him one to wait on him, and I believe it will fall
      to thy lot.   90
NICHOLAS I love my master (by these hilts I do),
   But rather than I'll ever come to serve him,°
   I'll turn away my master.
      Enter Sisly
SISLY Nicholas, where are you, Nicholas? You must come in, Nicholas,
   and help the young gentleman off with his boots.   95
NICHOLAS If I pluck off his boots, I'll eat the spurs,
   And they shall stick fast in my throat like burrs.
      Exit Nicholas
SISLY Then, Jenkin, come you.
JENKIN 'Tis no boot° for me to deny° it. My master hath given me a
   coat° here, but he takes pain himself to brush it once or twice a day 100
   with a holly wand.°
SISLY Come, come, make haste, that you may wash your hands again
   and help to serve in dinner.
      Exit Sisly
JENKIN [*to the audience*] You may see, my masters, though it be
   afternoon with you, 'tis but early days with us, for we have not   105

dined yet.° Stay but a little: I'll but go in and help to bear up the first
course and come to you again presently.

Exit

Scene 5

Enter Malby and Cranwell

MALBY This is the sessions day; pray, can you tell me
How young Sir Charles hath sped? Is he acquit,
Or must he try the law's strict penalty?°

CRANWELL He's cleared of all, spite of his enemies,
Whose earnest labours was to take his life;   5
But in this suit of pardon he hath spent
All the revenues that his father left him,
And he is now turned a plain countryman,
Reformed in all things. See, sir, here he comes.

Enter Sir Charles and his Keeper

KEEPER Discharge your fees, and you are then at freedom!°   10

SIR CHARLES Here, master keeper, take the poor remainder
Of all the wealth I have. My heavy foes
Have made my purse light, but alas, to me,
'Tis wealth enough that you have set me free.

[*The Keeper takes Sir Charles's money*]

MALBY God give you joy of your delivery.   15
I am glad to see you abroad, Sir Charles.

SIR CHARLES The poorest knight in England, Master Malby.
My life hath cost me all the patrimony
My father left his son. Well, God forgive them
That are the authors of my penury.   20

Enter Shafton

SHAFTON Sir Charles, a hand, a hand—at liberty.
Now by the faith I owe, I am glad to see it.°
What want you? Wherein may I pleasure you?

SIR CHARLES O me! O most unhappy gentleman!
I am not worthy to have friends stirred up   25
Whose hands may help me in this plunge of want.°
I would I were in heaven, to inherit there
Th'immortal birthright which my saviour keeps,
And by no unthrift can be bought and sold;

For here on earth, what pleasures should we trust?   30
SHAFTON To rid you from these contemplations,
      Three hundred pounds you shall receive of me—
      Nay, five for fail. Come, sir, the sight of gold°
      Is the most sweet receipt for melancholy
      And will revive your spirits. You shall hold law°   35
      With your proud adversaries. Tush, let Frank Acton
      Wage with knighthood-like expense with me,
      And he will sink, he will. Nay, good Sir Charles,
      Applaud your fortune, and your fair escape
      From all these perils.
SIR CHARLES   O sir, they have undone me.   40
      Two thousand and five hundred pound a year
      My father at his death possessed me of,
      All which the envious Acton made me spend,
      And notwithstanding all this large expense,
      I had much ado to gain my liberty;   45
      And I have now only a house of pleasure,°
      With some five hundred pounds, reserved
      Both to maintain me and my loving sister.
SHAFTON [aside] That must I have: it lies convenient for me.°
      If I can fasten but one finger on him,   50
      With my full hand I'll grip him to the heart.
      'Tis not for love I proffered him this coin,
      But for my gain and pleasure. [To Sir Charles] Come, Sir Charles,
      I know you have need of money: take my offer.
SIR CHARLES Sir, I accept it, and remain indebted   55
      Even to the best of my unable power.
      Come, gentlemen, and see it tendered down.
            Exeunt

Scene 6

      Enter Wendoll melancholy
WENDOLL I am a villain if I apprehend
      But such a thought; then to attempt the deed—
      Slave, thou art damned without redemption.
      I'll drive away this passion with a song.
      A song! Ha, ha! A song, as if, fond man,   5

Thy eyes could swim in laughter, when thy soul
Lies drenched and drowned in red tears of blood.
I'll pray, and see if God within thy heart
Plant better thoughts! Why, prayers are meditations,
And when I meditate (O God, forgive me!)   10
It is on her divine perfections.
I will forget her; I will arm myself
Not to entertain a thought of love to her;
And when I come by chance into her presence,
I'll hale these balls until my eyestrings crack°   15
From being pulled and drawn to look that way.
      Enter Frankford, Anne, and Nicholas; they pass over the stage
      [and exeunt]
O God! O God! with what a violence
I am hurried to my own destruction.
There goest thou the most perfect'st man
That ever England bred a gentleman;   20
And shall I wrong his bed? Thou God of thunder,
Stay in thy thoughts of vengeance and of wrath
Thy great almighty and all-judging hand
From speedy execution on a villain,
A villain and a traitor to his friend.   25
      Enter Jenkin. [Wendoll does not notice him]
JENKIN Did your worship call?
WENDOLL He doth maintain me, he allows me largely
  Money to spend—
JENKIN *[aside]* By my faith, so do not you me; I cannot get a cross of
  you.   30
WENDOLL   My gelding and my man.
JENKIN *[aside]* That's Sorrel and I.
WENDOLL This kindness grows of no alliance 'twixt us—°
JENKIN *[aside]* Nor is my service of any great acquaintance.
WENDOLL I never bound him to me by desert.
  Of a mere stranger, a poor gentleman,°   35
  A man by whom in no kind he could gain,
  He hath placed me in the height of all his thoughts,
  Made me companion with the best and chiefest
  In Yorkshire. He cannot eat without me,
  Nor laugh without me. I am to his body   40
  As necessary as his digestion,
  And equally do make him whole or sick.

And shall I wrong this man? Base man, ingrate!
Hast thou the power straight with thy gory hands
To rip thy image from his bleeding heart?   45
To scratch thy name from out the holy book
Of his remembrance, and to wound his name°
That holds thy name so dear, or rend his heart
To whom thy heart was joined and knit together?
And yet I must. Then, Wendoll, be content;   50
Thus villains, when they would, cannot repent.

JENKIN [aside] What a strange humour is my new master in. Pray
  God he be not mad; if he should be so, I should never have any
  mind to serve him in Bedlam. It may be he is mad for missing of
  me.   55

WENDOLL [seeing Jenkin] What, Jenkin? Where's your mistress?

JENKIN Is your worship married?

WENDOLL Why dost thou ask?

JENKIN Because you are my master, and if I have a mistress, I would
  be glad like a good servant to do my duty to her.   60

WENDOLL I mean where's Mistress Frankford?

JENKIN Marry, sir, her husband is riding out of town, and she went
  very lovingly to bring him on his way to horse. Do you see, sir, here
  she comes, and here I go.

WENDOLL Vanish.   65

   [Exit Jenkin.] Enter Anne

ANNE You are well met, sir. Now in troth my husband
  Before he took horse had a great desire
  To speak with you. We sought about the house,
  Hallowed into the fields, sent every way,
  But could not meet you; therefore he enjoined me   70
  To do unto you his most kind commends.
  Nay, more, he wills you, as you prize his love
  Or hold in estimation his kind friendship,
  To make bold in his absence and command
  Even as himself were present in the house;   75
  For you must keep his table, use his servants,
  And be a present Frankford in his absence.

WENDOLL I thank him for his love.
  [Aside] Give me a name, you whose infectious tongues
  Are tipped with gall and poison, as you would   80
  Think on a man that had your father slain,
  Murdered thy children, made your wives base strumpets:

86

So call me, call me so! Print in my face
The most stigmatic title of a villain
For hatching treason to so true a friend.   85
ANNE Sir, you are much beholding to my husband.
    You are a man most dear in his regard.
WENDOLL I am bound unto your husband and you too.
    [*Aside*] I will not speak to wrong a gentleman
    Of that good estimation, my kind friend.   90
    I will not! Zounds, I will not! I may choose,
    And I will choose! Shall I be so misled?
    Or shall I purchase to my father's crest
    The motto of a villain? If I say
    I will not do it, what thing can enforce me?   95
    Who can compel me? What sad destiny
    Hath such command upon my yielding thoughts?
    I will not. Ha! Some fury pricks me on;
    The swift Fates drag me at their chariot wheel
    And hurry me to mischief. Speak I must: 100
    Injure myself, wrong her, deceive his trust.
ANNE Are you not well, sir, that you seem thus troubled?
    There is sedition in your countenance!
WENDOLL And in my heart, fair angel, chaste and wise.
    I love you. Start not, speak not, answer not.   105
    I love you. Nay, let me speak the rest.
    Bid me to swear, and I will call to record
    The host of Heaven.
ANNE   The host of Heaven forbid
Wendoll should hatch such a disloyal thought.
WENDOLL Such is my fate; to this suit I was born,   110
    To wear rich pleasure's crown, or fortune's scorn.
ANNE My husband loves you.
WENDOLL   I know it.
ANNE   He esteems you
    Even as his brain, his eyeball, or his heart.
WENDOLL I have tried it.°
ANNE His purse is your exchequer, and his table   115
    Doth freely serve you.
WENDOLL   So I have found it.
ANNE O with what face of brass, what brow of steel,
    Can you unblushing speak this to the face
    Of the espoused wife of so dear a friend?

It is my husband that maintains your state.   120
Will you dishonour him? I am his wife
That in your power hath left his whole affairs.
It is to me you speak?
WENDOLL   O speak no more,
For more than this I know and have recorded
Within the red-leaved table of my heart.°   125
Fair, and of all beloved, I was not fearful
Bluntly to give my life into your hand,
And at one hazard all my earthly means.
Go, tell your husband: he will turn me off,
And I am then undone. I care not, I: 130
'Twas for your sake. Perchance in rage he'll kill me.
I care not: 'twas for you. Say I incur
The general name of villain through the world,
Of traitor to my friend: I care not, I.
Beggary, shame, death, scandal, and reproach: 135
For you I'll hazard all. What care I?
For you I'll live, and in your love I'll die.
ANNE You move me, sir, to passion and to pity;
The love I bear my husband is as precious
As my soul's health.
WENDOLL   I love your husband too,   140
And for his love I will engage my life.
Mistake me not, the augmentation
Of my sincere affection borne to you
Doth no whit lessen my regard of him.
I will be secret, lady, close as night,   145
And not the light of one small glorious star
Shall shine here in my forehead to bewray
That act of night.
ANNE [aside]   What shall I say?
My soul is wandering and hath lost her way.
[Aloud] O Master Wendoll, O.
WENDOLL   Sigh not, sweet saint,   150
For every sigh you breathe draws from my heart
A drop of blood.
ANNE [aside]   I ne'er offended yet.
My fault, I fear, will in my brow be writ.
Women that fall not quite bereft of grace

Have their offences noted in their face.   155
I blush and am ashamed. [*Aloud*] O Master Wendoll,
Pray God I be not born to curse your tongue,
That hath enchanted me. This maze I am in
I fear will prove the labyrinth of sin.
          Enter Nicholas. [Anne and Wendoll do not see him]
WENDOLL The path of pleasure and the gate to bliss,   160
Which on your lips I knock at with a kiss.
          [*Wendoll kisses Anne*]
NICHOLAS [*aside*] I'll kill the rogue.
WENDOLL Your husband is from home, your bed's no blab.
Nay, look not down and blush.
          [*Exeunt Wendoll and Anne*]
NICHOLAS   Zounds, I'll stab!
Ay, Nick, was it thy chance to come just in the nick?°   165
I love my master, and I hate that slave;
I love my mistress, but these tricks I like not.
My master shall not pocket up this wrong;°
I'll eat my fingers first. [*He draws his dagger*] What say'st thou, metal?
Does not the rascal Wendoll go on legs   170
That thou must cut off? Hath he not hamstrings
That thou must hock? Nay, metal, thou shalt stand
To all I say. I'll henceforth turn a spy,°
And watch them in their close conveyances.
I never looked for better of that rascal   175
Since he came miching first into our house.
It is that Satan hath corrupted her,
For she was fair and chaste. I'll have an eye
In all their gestures. Thus I think of them:
If they proceed as they have done before,   180
Wendoll's a knave, my mistress is a . . .°
          Exit

Scene 7

          Enter Sir Charles and Susan [in poor clothes]
SIR CHARLES Sister, you see we are driven to hard shift
To keep this poor house we have left unsold.°

I am now enforced to follow husbandry,
And you to milk, and do we not live well?
Well, I thank God.

SUSAN   O brother, here's a change,   5
Since old Sir Charles died, in our father's house.°

SIR CHARLES All things on earth thus change, some up, some down.
Content's a kingdom, and I wear that crown.
          Enter Shafton with a Sergeant°

SHAFTON Good morrow,
Good morrow, Sir Charles. What, with your sister   10
Plying your husbandry? (Sergeant, stand off.)
You have a pretty house here, and a garden,
And goodly ground about it. Since it lies
So near a lordship that I lately bought,°
I would fain buy it of you. I will give you—   15

SIR CHARLES O pardon me; this house successively°
Hath 'longed to me and my progenitors
Three hundred year. My great-great-grandfather,
He in whom first our gentle style began,°
Dwelt here, and in this ground increased this molehill   20
Unto that mountain which my father left me.
Where he the first of all our house begun,
I, now the last, will end and keep this house,
This virgin title never yet deflowered
By any unthrift of the Mountfords' line.   25
In brief, I will not sell it for more gold
Than you could hide or pave the ground withal.

SHAFTON Ha, ha! A proud mind and a beggar's purse.
Where's my three hundred pounds, beside the use?
I have brought it to an execution°   30
By course of law. What, is my money ready?

SIR CHARLES An execution, sir, and never tell me
You put my bond in suit? You deal extremely.

SHAFTON Sell me the land and I'll acquit you straight.

SIR CHARLES Alas, alas! 'Tis all trouble hath left me°   35
To cherish me and my poor sister's life.
If this were sold, our names should then be quite
Razed from the bead-roll of gentility.
You see what hard shift we have made to keep it
Allied still to our own name. This palm you see   40
Labour hath glowed within. Her silver brow,

That never tasted a rough winter's blast
Without a mask or fan, doth with a grace
Defy cold winter and his storms outface.
SUSAN Sir, we feed sparing, and we labour hard,   45
  We lie uneasy, to reserve to us
  And our succession this small plot of ground.
SIR CHARLES I have so bent my thoughts to husbandry
  That I protest I scarcely can remember
  What a new fashion is, how silk or satin   50
  Feels in my hand. Why, pride is grown to us
  A mere, mere stranger. I have quite forgot
  The names of all that ever waited on me;
  I cannot name ye any of my hounds,
  Once from whose echoing mouths I heard all the music   55
  That e'er my heart desired. What should I say?
  To keep this place I have changed myself away.°
SHAFTON [*to the Sergeant*] Arrest him at my suit. [*To Sir Charles*]
  Actions and actions°
  Shall keep thee in perpetual bondage fast.
  Nay, more, I'll sue thee by a late appeal   60
  And call thy former life in question.°
  The keeper is my friend: thou shalt have irons,
  And usage such as I'll deny to dogs.
  Away with him!
SIR CHARLES You are too timorous; but trouble is my master,   65
  And I will serve him truly. My kind sister,
  Thy tears are of no force to mollify
  This flinty man. Go to my father's brother,
  My kinsmen and allies; entreat them from me
  To ransom me from this injurious man   70
  That seeks my ruin.
SHAFTON   Come, irons, irons, away!°
  I'll see thee lodged far from the sight of day.
      Exeunt [*Shafton, the Sergeant, and Sir Charles*]. *Enter*
      Sir Francis and Malby. [*They do not notice Susan, nor she them*]
SUSAN My heart's so hardened with the frost of grief
  Death cannot pierce it through. Tyrant too fell!
  So lead the fiends condemnèd souls to hell.   75
SIR FRANCIS Again to prison! Malby, hast thou seen
  A poor slave better tortured? Shall we hear
  The music of his voice cry from the grate

'Meat for the Lord's sake'? No, no, yet I am not°
Throughly revenged. They say he hath a pretty wench   80
Unto his sister. Shall I, in mercy sake
To him and to his kindred, bribe the fool
To shame herself by lewd, dishonest lust?
I'll proffer largely, but, the deed being done,
I'll smile to see her base confusion.   85

MALBY Methinks, Sir Francis, you are full revenged
For greater wrongs than he can proffer you.
See where the poor sad gentlewoman stands.

SIR FRANCIS Ha, ha! now I will flout her poverty,
Deride her fortunes, scoff her base estate.   90
My very soul the name of Mountford hates.
But stay, my heart, O what a look did fly
To strike my soul through with thy piercing eye.
I am enchanted, all my spirits are fled,
And with one glance my envious spleen struck dead.   95

SUSAN [seeing them] Acton, that seeks our blood!
          Exit Susan, running away

SIR FRANCIS   O chaste and fair!

MALBY Sir Francis, why, Sir Francis! Zounds, in a trance?
Sir Francis, what cheer, man? Come, come, how is't?°

SIR FRANCIS Was she not fair? Or else this judging eye
Cannot distinguish beauty.

MALBY   She was fair.   100

SIR FRANCIS She was an angel in a mortal's shape,
And ne'er descended from old Mountford's line.
But soft, soft, let me call my wits together.
A poor, poor wench, to my great adversary
Sister, whose very souls denounce stern war   105
One against other. How now, Frank, turned fool
Or madman, whether? But no, master of°
My perfect senses and directest wits.
Then why should I be in this violent humour
Of passion and of love, and with a person   110
So different every way, and so opposed
In all contractions and still-warring actions?
Fie, fie, how I dispute against my soul!
Come, come, I'll gain her, or in her fair quest
Purchase my soul free and immortal rest.   115
          Exeunt

Scene 8

*Enter three or four Servingmen [including Spiggot the butler and
Nicholas], one with a voider° and a wooden knife to take away all,
another the salt and bread, another the tablecloth and napkins,
another the carpet.° Jenkin with two lights after them*

JENKIN So, march in order and retire in battle 'ray. My master and
the guests have supped already: all's taken away. Here, now spread
for the servingmen in the hall.° Butler, it belongs to your office.

SPIGGOT I know it, Jenkin. What do you call the gentleman that
supped here tonight?   5

JENKIN Who, my master?

SPIGGOT No, no, Master Wendoll, he is a daily° guest. I mean the
gentleman that came but this afternoon.

JENKIN His name is Master Cranwell. [*There is a call off stage*] God's
light! Hark, within there, my master calls to lay more billets on the   10
fire. Come, come! Lord, how we that are in office here in the house
are troubled. One spread the carpet in the parlour and stand ready
to snuff the lights; the rest be ready to prepare their stomachs.
More lights in the hall there. Come, Nicholas.
  [*Exeunt all but Nicholas*]

NICHOLAS I cannot eat, but had I Wendoll's heart   15
I would eat that. The rogue grows impudent:
O I have seen such vile, notorious tricks,
Ready to make my eyes dart from my head.
I'll tell my master, by this air I will;
Fall what may fall, I'll tell him. Here he comes.°   20
  *Enter Frankford, as it were brushing the crumbs from his clothes
  with a napkin, and newly risen from supper*

FRANKFORD Nich'las, what make you here? Why are not you
At supper in the hall there with your fellows?

NICHOLAS Master, I stayed your rising from the board°
To speak with you.

FRANKFORD   Be brief, then, gentle Nich'las,
My wife and guests attend me in the parlour.   25
  [*Nicholas says nothing*]
Why dost thou pause? Now, Nich'las, you want money,
And unthrift-like would eat into your wages
Ere you have earned it. [*Offers money*] Here's, sir, half a crown;
Play the good husband, and away to supper.°

NICHOLAS [*aside*] By this hand, an honourable gentleman. I will not   30
   see him wronged. [*Aloud*] Sir, I have served you long; you
   entertained me seven years before your beard. You knew me, sir,
   before you knew my mistress.
FRANKFORD   What of this, good Nich'las?
NICHOLAS   I never was a makebate or a knave.   35
   I have not fault but one: I am given to quarrel,
   But not with women. I will tell you, master,
   That which will make your heart leap from your breast,
   Your hair to startle from your head, your ears to tingle.
FRANKFORD   What preparation's this to dismal news?   40
NICHOLAS   'Sblood, sir, I love you better than your wife:
   I'll make it good.°
FRANKFORD   Thou art a knave, and I have much ado
   With wonted patience to contain my rage
   And not to break thy pate. Thou art a knave!   45
   I'll turn you with your base comparisons°
   Out of my doors.
NICHOLAS   Do, do. There's not room for Wendoll and me too both in
   one house. O master, master, that Wendoll is a villain.
FRANKFORD   Ay, saucy!   50
         [*Frankford threatens to strike Nicholas*]
NICHOLAS   Strike, strike, do strike; yet hear me: I am no fool;
   I know a villain when I see him act
   Deeds of a villain. Master, master, that base slave
   Enjoys my mistress and dishonours you.
FRANKFORD   Thou hast killed me with a weapon whose sharp'ned point   55
   Hath pricked quite through and through my shivering heart.
   Drops of cold sweat sit dangling on my hairs
   Like morning's dew upon the golden flowers,
   And I am plunged into a strange agony.
   What didst thou say? If any word that touched   60
   His credit or her reputation,
   It is as hard to enter my belief
   As Dives into Heaven.
NICHOLAS   I can gain nothing;°
   They are two that never wronged me. I knew before
   'Twas but a thankless office, and perhaps   65
   As much as my service or my life is worth.
   All this I know, but this and more,
   More by a thousand dangers could not hire me

To smother such a heinous wrong from you.
I saw, and I have said.   70
FRANKFORD [aside] 'Tis probable: though blunt, yet he is honest;
  Though I durst pawn my life, and on their faith
  Hazard the dear salvation of my soul,
  Yet in my trust I may be too secure.
  May this be true? O may it? Can it be?   75
  Is it by any wonder possible?
  Man, woman, what thing mortal may we trust
  When friends and bosom wives prove so unjust?
  [To Nicholas] What instance hast thou of this strange report?
NICHOLAS Eyes, eyes.   80
FRANKFORD Thy eyes may be deceived I tell thee,
  For should an angel from the heavens drop down
  And preach this to me that thyself hast told,
  He should have much ado to win belief,
  In both their loves I am so confident.   85
NICHOLAS Shall I discourse the same by circumstance?°
FRANKFORD No more; to supper, and command your fellows
  To attend us and the strangers. Not a word:°
  I charge thee on thy life be secret then,
  For I know nothing.   90
NICHOLAS I am dumb, and now that I have eased my stomach,
  I will go fill my stomach.
FRANKFORD   Away, begone.
      Exit Nicholas
  She is well born, descended nobly;
  Virtuous her education; her repute
  Is in the general voice of all the country   95
  Honest and fair; her carriage, her demeanour
  In all her actions that concern the love
  To me her husband, modest, chaste, and godly.
  Is all this seeming gold plain copper?
  But he, that Judas that hath borne my purse,°   100
  And sold me for a sin—O God, O God,
  Shall I put up these wrongs? No, shall I trust
  The base report of this suspicious groom
  Before the double gilt, the well-hatched ore
  Of their two hearts? No, I will loose these thoughts;   105
  Distraction I will banish from my brow
  And from my looks exile sad discontent;

Their wonted favours in my tongue shall flow.
Till I know all, I'll nothing seem to know.
[*Calls*] Lights and a table there! Wife, Master Wendoll, and gentle   110
    Master Cranwell!

> *Enter Mistress Anne, Master Wendoll, Master Cranwell,*
> *Nicholas, and Jenkin, with cards, carpet, stools, and other*
> *necessaries*

O you are a stranger, Master Cranwell, you,
And often balk my house; faith, you are a churl.
Now we have supped, a table and to cards.

> [*Nicholas and Jenkin set out a table*]

JENKIN A pair° of cards, Nich'las, and a carpet to cover the table.   115
    Where's Sisly with her counters° and her box? Candles and
    candlestick there!

> [*Enter Servants with counters and candles*]

Fie, we have such a household of serving creatures! Unless it be Nick
and I, there's not one amongst them all can say boo to a goose.° [*To*
Nicholas] Well said, Nick.   120

> *The servants spread a carpet* [*on the table*], *and set down lights*
> *and cards.* [*Exeunt all servants except Nicholas and Jenkin*]

ANNE Come, Master Frankford, who shall take my part?°
FRANKFORD Marry, that will I, sweet wife.
WENDOLL No, by my faith, sir, when you are together I sit out:° it
    must be Mistress Frankford and I, or else it is no match.
FRANKFORD I do not like that match.°   125
NICHOLAS [*aside*] You have no reason, marry, knowing all.
FRANKFORD 'Tis no great matter, neither. Come, Master Cranwell,
    shall you and I take them up?°
CRANWELL At your pleasure, sir.
FRANKFORD I must look to you, Master Wendoll, for you will be   130
    playing false;° nay, so will my wife, too.
NICHOLAS [*aside*] Ay, I will be sworn she will.
ANNE Let them that are taken playing false forfeit the set.°
FRANKFORD Content. It shall go hard but I'll take you.°
CRANWELL Gentlemen, what shall our game be?   135
WENDOLL Master Frankford, you play best at noddy.°
FRANKFORD You shall not find it so, indeed you shall not!
ANNE I can play at nothing so well as double-ruff.°
FRANKFORD If Master Wendoll and my wife be together,° there's no
    playing against them at double hand.°   140
NICHOLAS I can tell you, sir, the game that Master Wendoll is best at.

WENDOLL What game is that, Nick?

NICHOLAS Marry, sir, knave out of doors.°

WENDOLL She and I will take you at loadum.°

ANNE Husband, shall we play at saint?°   145

FRANKFORD [*aside*] My saint's turned devil. [*Aloud*] No, we'll none
　of saint. You're best at new-cut, wife, you'll play at that.

WENDOLL If you play at new-cut,° I am soonest hitter° of any here,
　for a wager.

FRANKFORD [*aside*] 'Tis me they play on. Well, you may draw out°   150
　For all your cunning. 'Twill be to your shame.
　I'll teach you at your new-cut a new game.
　[*Aloud*] Come, come.

CRANWELL If you cannot agree upon the game, to post and pair.°

WENDOLL We shall be soonest pairs, and my good host,   155
　When he comes late home, he must kiss the post.°

FRANKFORD Whoever wins, it shall be to thy cost.°

CRANWELL Faith, let it be vied-ruff, and let's make honours.°

FRANKFORD If you make honours, one thing let me crave:
　Honour the king and queen; except the knave.°   160

WENDOLL Well, as you please for that. Lift who shall deal.°

ANNE The least in sight. What are you, Master Wendoll?
　　　[*Wendoll cuts the cards*]

WENDOLL I am a knave.

NICHOLAS [*aside*]　　　　　I'll swear it.
　　　[*Anne cuts the cards*]

ANNE　　　　　　　　　　　　I a queen.

FRANKFORD [*aside*] A quean thou should'st say.
　　　[*Frankford cuts the cards*]
　　　[*Aloud*]　　　　　　　　　Well, the cards are mine.
　　　[*Frankford takes the pack and shuffles it*]
　They are the grossest pair that e'er I felt.°   165

ANNE Shuffle, I'll cut. [*Aside*] Would I had never dealt!
　　　[*Frankford deals the cards*]

FRANKFORD I have lost my dealing.

WENDOLL　　　　　　　　Sir, the fault's in me.°
　This queen I have more than my own, you see.
　Give me the stock.
　　　[*Frankford gives Wendoll the cards and he deals*]

FRANKFORD　　　　　My mind's not on my game.
　[*Aside*] Many a deal I have lost, the more's your shame.   170
　[*Aloud*] You have served me a bad trick, Master Wendoll!

WENDOLL Sir, you must take your lot. To end this strife,
  I know I have dealt better with your wife.
FRANKFORD [*aside*] Thou hast dealt falsely, then.
ANNE What's trumps?   175
WENDOLL Hearts. Partner, I rub.
FRANKFORD [*aside*] Thou robbest me of my soul, of her chaste love.
  In thy false dealing thou hast robbed my heart.
  Booty you play; I like a loser stand,°
  Having no heart, or here or in my hand.   180
  [*Aloud*] I will give o'er the set. I am not well.
  Come, who will hold my cards?
ANNE Not well, sweet Master Frankford?
  Alas, what ail you? 'Tis some sudden qualm.
WENDOLL How long have you been so, Master Frankford?   185
FRANKFORD Sir, I was lusty and I had my health,
  But I grew ill when you began to deal.°
  Take hence this table.
      [*Nicholas and Jenkin remove the table*]
                Gentle Master Cranwell,
  You are welcome; see your chamber at your pleasure.°
  I am sorry that this megrim takes me so   190
  I cannot sit and bear you company.
  Jenkin, some lights, and show him to his chamber.
      [*Exeunt Cranwell and Jenkin*]
ANNE A night gown for my husband, quickly there.
      [*Nicholas fetches a gown*]
  It is some rheum or cold!
WENDOLL Now, in good faith, this illness you have got   195
  By sitting late without your gown.
FRANKFORD I know it, Master Wendoll.
  Go, go, to bed, lest you complain like me.
  Wife, prithee wife, into my bedchamber.
  The night is raw and cold and rheumatic.   200
  Leave me my gown and light; I'll walk away my fit.
WENDOLL Sweet sir, good night.
FRANKFORD My self, good night.
    [*Exit Wendoll*]
ANNE   Shall I attend you, husband?°
FRANKFORD No, gentle wife, thou'lt catch cold in thy head;
  Prithee, begone, sweet, I'll make haste to bed.   205

ANNE No sleep will fasten on mine eyes, you know,
　　Until you come.
FRANKFORD　　　　Sweet Nan, I prithee, go.
　　　　[*Exit Anne*]
　　　　[*To Nicholas*] I have bethought me; get me by degrees
　　The keys of all my doors, which I will mould
　　In wax, and take their fair impression,　　　　　　　　　210
　　To have by them new keys. This being compassed,
　　At a set hour a letter shall be brought me,°
　　And when they think they may securely play,°
　　They are nearest to danger. Nick, I must rely
　　Upon thy trust and faithful secrecy.　　　　　　　　　215
NICHOLAS Build on my faith.
FRANKFORD　　　　　　　　To bed then, not to rest;
　　Care lodges in my brain, grief in my breast.
　　　　Exeunt

Scene 9

　　　　Enter Susan, Old Mountford, Sandy, Roder, and Tydy
OLD MOUNTFORD You say my nephew is in great distress:
　　Who brought it to him but his own lewd life?
　　I cannot spare a cross. I must confess
　　He was my brother's son; why, niece, what then?
　　This is no world in which to pity men.　　　　　　　　　5
SUSAN I was not born a beggar. Though his extremes
　　Enforce this language from me, I protest
　　No fortune of mine own could lead my tongue
　　To this base key. I do beseech you, uncle,
　　For the name's sake, for Christianity°　　　　　　　　　10
　　Nay, for God's sake to pity his distress.
　　He is denied the freedom of the prison,
　　And in the hole is laid with men condemned.°
　　Plenty he hath of nothing but of irons,
　　And it remains in you to free him thence.°　　　　　　　15
OLD MOUNTFORD Money I cannot spare. Men should take heed.
　　He lost my kindred when he fell to need.
　　　　Exit Old Mountford

SUSAN Gold is but earth; thou earth enough shalt have
  When thou hast once took measure of thy grave.°
  You know me, Master Sandy, and my suit.   20
SANDY I knew you, lady, when the old man lived;
  I knew you ere your brother sold his land.
  Then you were Mistress Sue, tricked up in jewels;
  Then you sung well, played sweetly on the flute;
  But now I neither know you nor your suit.   25
      [*Exit Sandy*]
SUSAN You, Master Roder, was my brother's tenant.
  Rent-free he placed you in that wealthy farm
  Of which you are possessed.
RODER   True, he did,
  And have I not there dwelt still for his sake?
  I have some business now, but without doubt   30
  They that have hurled him in will help him out.
      Exit Roder
SUSAN Cold comfort still. What say you, cousin Tydy?
TYDY I say this comes of roisting, swaggering.
  Call me not cousin: each man for himself.
  Some men are born to mirth and some to sorrow.   35
  I am no cousin unto them that borrow.
      Exit Tydy
SUSAN O Charity, why art thou fled to heaven,°
  And left all things on this earth uneven?
  Their scoffing answers I will ne'er return,
  But to myself his grief in silence mourn.   40
      Enter Sir Francis and Malby
SIR FRANCIS She is poor. I'll therefore tempt her with this gold.
      [*He gives Malby a bag of gold*]
  Go, Malby, in my name deliver it,
  And I will stay thy answer.
MALBY Fair mistress, as I understand your grief
  Doth grow from want, so I have here in store   45
  A means to furnish you, a bag of gold
  Which to your hands I freely tender you.
      [*Malby gives Susan the gold*]
SUSAN I thank you, heavens, I thank you, gentle sir!
  God make me able to requite this favour.
MALBY This gold Sir Francis Acton sends by me,   50
  And prays you—°

SUSAN Acton! O God, that name I am born to curse.
    Hence, bawd! Hence, broker! See, I spurn his gold!
        [*She throws away the bag of gold*]
    My honour never shall for gain be sold.
SIR FRANCIS Stay, lady, stay!
SUSAN   From you I'll posting hie,   55
    Even as the doves from feathered eagles fly.
        [*Exit Susan*]
SIR FRANCIS She hates my name, my face; how should I woo?
    I am disgraced in everything I do.
    The more she hates me and disdains my love,
    The more I am rapt in admiration   60
    Of her divine and chaste perfections.
    Woo her with gifts I cannot, for all gifts
    Sent in my name she spurns; with looks I cannot,
    For she abhors my sight; nor yet with letters,
    For none will she receive. How then? How then?   65
    Well, I will fasten such a kindness on her
    As shall o'ercome her hate and conquer it.
    Sir Charles, her brother, lies in execution°
    For a great sum of money; and, besides,
    The appeal is sued still for my huntsman's death,°   70
    Which only I have power to reverse.
    In her I'll bury all my hate of him.
    Go seek the keeper, Malby, bring me to him.
    To save his body, I his debts will pay;
    To save his life, I his appeal will stay.   75
        Exeunt

Scene 10

*Enter Sir Charles in prison, with irons; his feet° bare, his
garments all ragged and torn*

SIR CHARLES Of all on the earth's face most miserable,°
    Breathe in the hellish dungeon thy laments.
    Thus like a slave ragg'd, like a felon gyved!
    O unkind uncle! O my friends ingrate,
    That hurls thee headlong to this base estate!   5
    Unthankful kinsmen! Mountfords all too base,

To let thy name lie fettered in disgrace.
A thousand deaths here in this grave I die:
Fear, hunger, sorrow, cold, all threat my death
And join together to deprive my breath.   10
But that which most torments me, my dear sister
Hath left to visit me, and from my friends°
Hath brought no hopeful answer; therefore I
Divine they will not help my misery.
If it be so, shame, scandal, and contempt   15
Attend their covetous thoughts, need make their graves.
Usurers they live, and may they die like slaves.
      Enter Keeper
KEEPER Knight, be of comfort, for I bring thee freedom
From all thy troubles.
SIR CHARLES   Then I am doomed to die;
Death is th'end of all calamity.   20
KEEPER Live, your appeal is stayed, the execution
Of all your debts discharged, your creditors
Even to the utmost penny satisfied,
In sign whereof your shackles I knock off.
      [*He removes Sir Charles's irons*]
You are not left so much indebted to us   25
As for your fees: all is discharged, all paid.
Go freely to your house or where you please;
After long miseries embrace your ease.
SIR CHARLES Thou grumblest out the sweetest music to me
That ever organ played. Is this a dream   30
Or do my waking senses apprehend
The pleasing taste of these applausive news?
Slave that I was to wrong such honest friends,
My loving kinsmen and my near allies.
Tongue, I will bite thee for the scandal breath   35
Against such faithful kinsmen: they are all
Composed of pity and compassion,
Of melting charity, and of moving ruth.
That which I spake before was in my rage;
They are my friends, the mirrors of this age,   40
Bounteous and free. The noble Mountfords' race
Ne'er bred a covetous thought or humour base.
      Enter Susan

SUSAN I can no longer stay from visiting
    My woeful brother. While I could I kept
    My hapless tidings from his hopeful ear.   45
SIR CHARLES Sister, how much am I indebted to thee
    And to thy travail!
SUSAN   What, at liberty?
SIR CHARLES Thou seest I am, thanks to thy industry.
    O unto which of all my courteous friends
    Am I thus bound? My uncle Mountford, he   50
    Even of an infant loved me; was it he?
    So did my cousin Tydy; was it he?
    So Master Roder, Master Sandy too.
    Which of all these did this high kindness do?
SUSAN Charles, can you mock me in your poverty,   55
    Knowing your friends deride your misery?
    Now I protest I stand so much amazed
    To see your bonds free and your irons knocked off
    That I am rapt into a maze of wonder,
    The rather for I know not by what means   60
    This happiness hath chanced.
SIR CHARLES   Why, by my uncle,
    My cousins, and my friends; who else, I pray,
    Would take upon them all my debts to pay?
SUSAN O brother, they are men all of flint,
    Pictures of marble, and as void of pity   65
    As chased bears. I begged, I sued, I kneeled,°
    Laid open all your griefs and miseries,
    Which they derided; more than that, denied us
    A part in their alliance, but in pride°
    Said that our kindred with our plenty died.   70
SIR CHARLES Drudges too much! What, did they? O known evil:°
    Rich fly the poor as good men shun the devil.
    Whence should my freedom come? Of whom alive,
    Saving of those, have I deserved so well?
    Guess, sister, call to mind, remember me.°   75
    These I have raised, these follow the world's guise,
    When, rich in honour, they in woe despise.
SUSAN My wits have lost themselves. Let's ask the keeper.
SIR CHARLES Jailer!
KEEPER At hand, sir.   80

103

SIR CHARLES Of courtesy resolve me one demand:
    What was he took the burden of my debts
    From off my back, stayed my appeal to death,
    Discharged my fees, and brought me liberty?
KEEPER A courteous knight, one called Sir Francis Acton.   85
SUSAN Acton!
SIR CHARLES Ha! Acton! O me, more distressed in this
    Than all my troubles. Hale me back,
    Double my irons, and my sparing meals
    Put into halves, and lodge me in a dungeon   90
    More deep, more dark, more cold, more comfortless.
    By Acton freed! Not all thy manacles
    Could fetter so my heels as this one word
    Hath thralled my heart, and it must now lie bound
    In more strict prison than thy stony jail.   95
    I am not free: I go but under bail.
KEEPER My charge is done, sir, now I have my fees.
    As we get little, we will nothing leese.
       Exit Keeper
SIR CHARLES By Acton freed, my dangerous opposite.
    Why, to what end, or what occasion? Ha!   100
    Let me forget the name of enemy
    And with indifference balance this high favour. Ha!°
SUSAN [*aside*] His love to me, upon my soul 'tis so;
    That is the root from whence these strange things grow.
SIR CHARLES [*aside*] Had this proceeded from my father, he   105
    That by the law of nature is most bound
    In offices of love, it had deserved
    My best employment to requite that grace!
    Had it proceeded from my friends, or him,
    From them this action had deserved my life;   110
    And from a stranger more, because from such
    There is less execution of good deeds.°
    But he, nor father, nor ally, nor friend,
    More than a stranger, both remote in blood
    And in his heart opposed my enemy: 115
    That this high bounty should proceed from him!
    O there I lose myself. What should I say,
    What think, what do, his bounty to repay?
SUSAN You wonder, I am sure, whence this strange kindness
    Proceeds in Acton. I will tell you, brother: 120

He dotes on me and oft hath sent me gifts,
Letters, and tokens. I refused them all.
SIR CHARLES I have enough; though poor, my heart is set
In one rich gift to pay back all my debt.
      Exeunt

Scene 11

    Enter Frankford with a letter in his hand, and Nicholas with keys
FRANKFORD This is the night, and I must play the touch,°
To try two seeming angels. Where's my keys?
NICHOLAS They are made according to your mould in wax.
I bade the smith be secret, gave him money,
And there they are. The letter, sir.   5
FRANKFORD True, take it: there it is;
    [*They exchange keys and letter*]
And when thou seest me in my pleasant'st vein
Ready to sit to supper, bring it me.
NICHOLAS I'll do 't; make no more question but I'll do 't.
    Exit Nicholas. Enter Mistress Anne, Cranwell, Wendoll, and
    Jenkin
ANNE [*to Jenkin*] Sirrah, 'tis six o'clock already struck.   10
Go bid them spread the cloth and serve in supper.
JENKIN It shall be done forsooth, mistress. Where is Spiggot the
butler to give us out salt and trenchers?
    [*Exit Jenkin*]
WENDOLL We that have been a-hunting all the day
Come with prepared stomachs, Master Frankford;   15
We wished you at our sport.
FRANKFORD My heart was with you, and my mind was on you.
Fie, Master Cranwell, you are still thus sad.
[*Calls*] A stool, a stool! Where's Jenkin, and where's Nick?
    [*Enter Servingmen and set out the table and stools*]
'Tis supper time at least an hour ago.   20
[*To his guests*] What's the best news abroad?
WENDOLL   I know none good.
FRANKFORD [*aside*] But I know too much bad.
    Enter Spiggot the Butler and Jenkin with a tablecloth,
    bread, trenchers, and salt. [*They set the table and exeunt*]

CRANWELL Methinks, sir, you might have that interest
  In your wife's brother to be more remiss
  In this hard dealing against poor Sir Charles,°   25
  Who, as I hear, lies in York Castle, needy
  And in great want.
FRANKFORD Did not more weighty business of my own
  Hold me away, I would have laboured peace
  Betwixt them with all care, indeed I would, sir.   30
ANNE I'll write unto my brother earnestly
  In that behalf.
WENDOLL   A charitable deed,
  And will beget the good opinion
  Of all your friends that love you, Mistress Frankford.
FRANKFORD That's you for one: I know you love Sir Charles.   35
  [Aside] And my wife too well.
WENDOLL   He deserves the love
  Of all true gentlemen. Be yourselves judge.
FRANKFORD [calls] But supper, ho! Now as thou lovest me, Wendoll,
  Which I am sure thou dost, be merry, pleasant,
  And frolic it tonight. Sweet Master Cranwell,   40
  Do you the like. Wife, I protest, my heart
  Was ne'er more bent on sweet alacrity.°
  Where be those lazy knaves to serve in supper?
     Enter Nicholas
NICHOLAS Sir, here's a letter.
FRANKFORD Whence comes it, and who brought it?   45
NICHOLAS A stripling that below attends your answer,°
  And, as he tells me, it is sent from York.
FRANKFORD Have him into the cellar; let him taste
  A cup of our March beer. Go, make him drink.°
NICHOLAS I'll make him drunk, if he be a Trojan.°   50
     [Exit Nicholas. Frankford opens and reads the letter]
FRANKFORD [calls] My boots and spurs! Where's Jenkin? God forgive
  me,
  How I neglect my business. Wife, look here:
  I have a matter to be tried tomorrow
  By eight o'clock, and my attorney writes me
  I must be there betimes with evidence,   55
  Or it will go against me. Where's my boots?
     Enter Jenkin with boots and spurs

ANNE I hope your business craves no such dispatch
  That you must ride tonight.
WENDOLL [*aside*]   I hope it doth.
FRANKFORD God's me! No such dispatch?
  Jenkin, my boots.
        [*Frankford starts to put on his boots*]
                        Where's Nick? Saddle my roan,   60
  And the grey dapple for himself.
        [*Exit Jenkin*]
  [*To Cranwell*]   Content ye,°
  It much concerns me, gentle Master Cranwell;
  And, Master Wendoll, in my absence use
  The very ripest pleasure of my house.
WENDOLL Lord, Master Frankford, will you ride tonight?   65
  The ways are dangerous.
FRANKFORD   Therefore will I ride
  Appointed well, and so shall Nick, my man.°
ANNE I'll call you up by five o'clock tomorrow.
FRANKFORD No, by my faith, wife, I'll not trust to that:
  'Tis not such easy rising in a morning   70
  From one I love so dearly. No, by my faith,
  I shall not leave so sweet a bedfellow
  But with much pain. You have made me a sluggard
  Since I first knew you.
ANNE   Then if you needs will go
  This dangerous evening, Master Wendoll,   75
  Let me entreat you bear him company.
WENDOLL With all my heart, sweet mistress. [*Calls*] My boots there!
FRANKFORD Fie, fie, that for my private business
  I should disease my friend and be a trouble
  To the whole house. [*Calls*] Nick!   80
NICHOLAS [*within*] Anon, sir.
FRANKFORD [*calls*] Bring forth my gelding. [*To Wendoll*] As you love
  me, sir,
  Use no more words. A hand, good Master Cranwell.
CRANWELL [*shaking Frankford's hand*] Sir, God be your good speed.
FRANKFORD Good night, sweet Nan. Nay, nay, a kiss and part   85
        [*Anne kisses Frankford*]
  [*Aside*] Dissembling lips, you suit not with my heart.°
        [*Exit Frankford*]

WENDOLL [*aside*] How business, time, and hours all gracious proves
    And are the furtherers to my new-born love.
    I am husband now in Master Frankford's place
    And must command the house. [*Aloud, to Anne*] My pleasure is   90
    We will not sup abroad so publicly,°
    But in your private chamber, Mistress Frankford.
ANNE [*aside to Wendoll*] O sir, you are too public in your love,
    And Master Frankford's wife —
CRANWELL   Might I crave favour,
    I would entreat you I might see my chamber.   95
    I am on the sudden grown exceeding ill
    And would be spared from supper.
WENDOLL [*calls*]   Light there, ho!°
    [*To Cranwell*] See you want nothing, sir, for if you do,
    You injure that good man, and wrong me too.
CRANWELL I will make bold. Good night.
        [*Exit Cranwell*]
WENDOLL   How all conspire   100
    To make our bosom sweet and full entire.
    Come, Nan, I prithee let us sup within.
ANNE O what a clog unto the soul is sin.
    We pale offenders are still full of fear;°
    Every suspicious eye brings danger near,   105
    When they whose clear heart from offence are free,
    Despise report, base scandals to outface,
    And stand at mere defiance with disgrace.
WENDOLL Fie, fie, you talk too like a puritan.°
ANNE You have tempted me to mischief, Master Wendoll;   110
    I have done I know not what. Well, you plead custom;°
    That which for want of wit I granted erst
    I now must yield through fear. Come, come, let's in.
    Once o'er shoes, we are straight o'er head in sin.°
WENDOLL My jocund soul is joyful above measure;   115
    I'll be profuse in Frankford's richest treasure.
        Exeunt

Scene 12

Enter Sisly, Jenkin, Spiggot the Butler, and other Servingmen°

JENKIN My mistress and Master Wendoll, my master, sup in her
chamber tonight. Sisly, you are preferred from being the cook to be
chambermaid. Of all the loves betwixt thee and me, tell me what
thou thinkest of this.

SISLY Mum.° There's an old proverb, 'When the cat's away the   5
mouse may play'.°

JENKIN Now you talk of a cat, Sisly, I smell a rat.°

SISLY Good words, Jenkin, lest you be called to answer° them.

JENKIN Why, 'God make my mistress an honest woman'. Are not
these good words? 'Pray God my new master play not the knave   10
with my old master'. Is there any hurt in this? 'God send no villainy
intended, and if they do sup together, pray God they do not lie
together. God keep my mistress chaste and make us all his
servants'. What harm is there in all this? Nay, more, here is my
hand; thou shalt never have my heart unless thou say 'Amen'.   15

SISLY 'Amen, I pray God', I say.

Enter Servingmen

SERVINGMAN My mistress sends that you should make less noise, to
lock up the doors, and see the household all got to bed. You, Jenkin,
for this night° are made the porter, to see the gates shut in.

JENKIN Thus by little and little I creep into office. Come to kennel,   20
my masters, to kennel: 'tis eleven o'clock already.

SERVINGMAN When you have locked the gates in, you must send up
the keys to my mistress.

SISLY Quickly, for God's sake, Jenkin, for I must carry them. I am
neither pillow nor bolster, but I know more than both.   25

JENKIN To bed, good Spiggot; to bed, good honest serving creatures,
and let us sleep as snug as pigs in pease-straw.°

Exeunt

Scene 13

Enter Frankford and Nicholas [carrying a dark lantern]°

FRANKFORD Soft, soft. We have tied our geldings to a tree
Two flight-shot off, lest by their thund'ring hooves
They blab our coming back. Hear'st thou no noise?

NICHOLAS Hear? I hear nothing but the owl and you.
FRANKFORD So; now my watch's hand points upon twelve,   5
    And it is dead midnight. Where are my keys?
NICHOLAS [*handing them over*] Here, sir.
FRANKFORD This is the key that opes my outward gate,°
    This is the hall door, this my withdrawing chamber.°
    But this, that door that's bawd unto my shame,   10
    Fountain and spring of all my bleeding thoughts,°
    Where the most hallowed order and true knot
    Of nuptial sanctity hath been profaned.
    It leads to my polluted bedchamber,
    Once my terrestrial heaven, now my earth's hell,   15
    The place where sins in all their ripeness dwell—
    But I forget myself. Now to my gate.°
NICHOLAS It must ope with far less noise than Cripplegate,° or your
    plot's dashed.
FRANKFORDçSo, reach me my dark lantern to the rest.°   20
    Tread softly, softly.
NICHOLAS   I will walk on eggs this pace.
FRANKFORD A general silence hath surprised the house,°
    And this is the last door. Astonishment,
    Fear, and amazement play against my heart,
    Even as a madman beats upon a drum.   25
    O keep my eyes, you heavens, before I enter,
    From any sight that may transfix my soul;
    Or if there be so black a spectacle,
    O strike mine eyes stark blind; or if not so,
    Lend me such patience to digest my grief   30
    That I may keep this white and virgin hand
    From any violent outrage or red murder.
    And with that prayer I enter.
        [*Exit Frankford*]
NICHOLAS   Here's a circumstance!°
    A man may be made cuckold in the time
    That he's about it. An the case were mine   35
    As 'tis my master's—'sblood, that he makes me swear—
    I would have placed his action, ent'red there,°
    I would, I would—
        [*Enter Frankford*]
FRANKFORD O, O!
NICHOLAS Master, 'sblood, master, master!   40

FRANKFORD   O me unhappy, I have found them lying
    Close in each other's arms, and fast asleep.
    But that I would not damn two precious souls
    Bought with my saviour's blood and send them laden
    With all their scarlet sins upon their backs   45
    Unto a fearful judgement, their two lives°
    Had met upon my rapier.°
NICHOLAS   'Sblood, master, have you left them sleeping still? Let me
    go wake them.
FRANKFORD   Stay, let me pause awhile.   50
    O God, O God, that it were possible
    To undo things done, to call back yesterday;
    That Time could turn up his swift, sandy glass,°
    To untell the days, and to redeem these hours;
    Or that the sun   55
    Could, rising from the west, draw his coach backward,
    Take from the account of time so many minutes,
    Till he had all these seasons called again,
    Those minutes and those actions done in them,
    Even from her first offence; that I might take her   60
    As spotless as an angel in my arms.
    But O! I talk of things impossible,
    And cast beyond the moon. God give me patience,°
    For I will in to wake them.
       Exit Frankford
NICHOLAS   Here's patience perforce;   65
    He needs must trot afoot that tires his horse.
       Enter Wendoll, running over the stage in a night-gown,°
       Frankford after him with his sword drawn; the maid in her smock°
       stays his hand and clasps hold on him. He pauses a while
FRANKFORD   I thank thee, maid: thou like the angel's hand
    Hast stayed me from a bloody sacrifice.
    Go, villain, and my wrongs sit on thy soul
    As heavy as this grief doth upon mine.   70
    When thou record'st my many courtesies
    And shalt compare them with thy treacherous heart,
    Lay them together, weigh them equally,
    'Twill be revenge enough. Go, to thy friend
    A Judas; pray, pray, lest I live to see   75
    Thee Judas-like, hanged on an elder tree.°
       Enter Mistress Anne in her smock, night-gown, and night attire

ANNE O by what word, what title, or what name
    Shall I entreat your pardon? Pardon! O,
    I am as far from hoping such sweet grace,
    As Lucifer from heaven, to call you husband.°   80
    O me most wretched, I have lost that name:
    I am no more your wife.
        [*Anne collapses to the floor*]
NICHOLAS   'Sblood, sir, she swoons.
FRANKFORD Spare thou thy tears, for I will weep for thee;
    And keep thy countenance, for I'll blush for thee.
    Now, I protest, I think 'tis I am tainted   85
    For I am most ashamed, and 'tis more hard
    For me to look upon thy guilty face
    Than on the sun's clear brow. What wouldst thou speak?
ANNE I would I had no tongue, no ears, no eyes,
    No apprehension, no capacity.   90
    When do you spurn me like a dog? When tread me
    Under your feet? When drag me by the hair?
    Though I deserve a thousand thousand fold
    More than you can inflict, yet, once my husband,
    For womanhood (to which I am a shame,   95
    Though once an ornament) even for his sake
    That hath redeemed our souls, mark not my face°
    Nor hack me with your sword, but let me go
    Perfect and undeformèd to my tomb.
    I am not worthy that I should prevail   100
    In the least suit, no, not to speak to you,
    Nor look on you, nor to be in your presence;
    Yet as an abject this one suit I crave.
    This granted, I am ready for my grave.
FRANKFORD My God, with patience arm me. Rise: nay, rise,   105
    And I'll debate with thee.
        [*Anne stands up*]
                    Was it for want
    Thou playedst the strumpet? Was thou not supplied
    With every pleasure, fashion, and new toy—
    Nay, even beyond my calling?
ANNE   I was.°
FRANKFORD Was it then disability in me,   110
    Or in thine eye seemed he a properer man?
ANNE O no.

FRANKFORD Did I not lodge thee in my bosom?
  Wear thee here in my heart?
ANNE   You did.
FRANKFORD I did indeed; witness my tears I did.
  [*To the maid*] Go bring my infants hither.
          [*Exit maid. She returns with two infant children*]°
                                O Nan, O Nan,   115
  If either fear of shame, regard of honour,
  The blemish of my house, nor my dear love
  Could have withheld thee from so lewd a fact,
  Yet for these infants, these young harmless souls,
  On whose white brows thy shame is charactered,   120
  And grows in greatness as they wax in years—
  Look but on them, and melt away in tears.
  Away with them, lest as her spotted body
  Hath stained their names with stripe of bastardy,°
  So her adult'rous breath may blast their spirits   125
  With her infectious thoughts. Away with them!
          [*Exit maid with the children*]
ANNE In this one life I die ten thousand deaths.
FRANKFORD Stand up, stand up: I will do nothing rashly.
  I will retire awhile into my study,
  And thou shalt hear thy sentence presently.   130
          Exit Frankford
ANNE 'Tis welcome, be it death. O me, base strumpet,
  That having such a husband, such sweet children,
  Must enjoy neither. O to redeem my honour
  I would have this hand cut off, these my breasts seared,
  Be racked, strappadoed, put to any torment;°   135
  Nay, to whip but this scandal out, I would hazard
  The rich and dear redemption of my soul.
  He cannot be so base as to forgive me,
  Nor I so shameless to accept his pardon.
  [*To the audience*] O women, women, you that have yet kept   140
  Your holy matrimonial vow unstained,
  Make me your instance: when you tread awry,
  Your sins like mine will on your conscience lie.
          *Enter Sisly, Spiggot, all the servingmen, and Jenkin, as newly
          come out of bed*
ALL O mistress, mistress, what have you done, mistress?
NICHOLAS 'Sblood, what a caterwauling keep you here!   145

JENKIN O Lord, mistress, how comes this to pass? My master is run
    away in his shirt,° and never so much as called me to bring his
    clothes after him.

ANNE See what guilt is: here stand I in this place,
    Ashamed to look my servants in the face.   150
        Enter Master Frankford and Cranwell, whom seeing, she falls
        on her knees

FRANKFORD My words are registered in heaven already;
    With patience hear me: I'll not martyr thee
    Nor mark thee for a strumpet, but with usage
    Of more humility torment thy soul
    And kill thee even with kindness.

CRANWELL   Master Frankford—   155

FRANKFORD Good Master Cranwell. Woman, hear thy judgement:°
    Go make thee ready in thy best attire;
    Take with thee all thy gowns, all thy apparel;
    Leave nothing that did ever call thee mistress,°
    Or by whose sight being left here in the house   160
    I may remember such a woman by.
    Choose thee a bed and hangings for a chamber,°
    Take with thee everything that hath thy mark,
    And get thee to my manor seven mile off,
    Where live. 'Tis thine: I freely give it thee.   165
    My tenants by shall furnish thee with wains°
    To carry all thy stuff within two hours;
    No longer will I limit thee my sight.°
    Choose which of all my servants thou likest best,
    And they are thine to attend thee.

ANNE   A mild sentence.   170

FRANKFORD But as thou hopest for heaven, as thou believest
    Thy name's recorded in the book of life,°
    I charge thee never after this sad day
    To see me, or to meet me, or to send
    By word, or writing, gift, or otherwise   175
    To move me, by thyself or by thy friends,
    Nor challenge any part in my two children.
    So farewell, Nan, for we will henceforth be
    As we had never seen, ne'er more shall see.

ANNE [*weeping*] How full my heart is in my eyes appears;   180
    What wants in words, I will supply in tears.

FRANKFORD Come, take your coach, your stuff: all must along.
Servants and all make ready, all be gone.
It was thy hand cut two hearts out of one.°
    [*Exeunt*]

Scene 14

*Enter Sir Charles, gentlemanlike, and Susan
his sister, gentlewomanlike*

SUSAN Brother, why have you tricked me like a bride?°
Bought me this gay attire, these ornaments?
Forget you our estate, our poverty?°
SIR CHARLES Call me not brother, but imagine me
Some barbarous outlaw or uncivil kern,°   5
For if thou shut'st thy eye and only hear'st
The words that I shall utter, thou shalt judge me
Some staring ruffian, not thy brother Charles.°
O Susan!
SUSAN O brother, what doth this strange language mean?   10
SIR CHARLES Dost love me, sister? Wouldst thou see me live
A bankrupt beggar in the world's disgrace
And die indebted to my enemies?
Wouldst thou behold me stand like a huge beam°
In the world's eye, a byword and a scorn?   15
It lies in thee of these to acquit me free,
And all my debt I may outstrip by thee.
SUSAN By me? Why, I have nothing, nothing left;
I owe even for the clothes upon my back;
I am not worthy—
SIR CHARLES   O sister, say not so.   20
It lies in you my downcast state to raise,
To make me stand on even points with the world.
Come, sister, you are rich! Indeed you are,
And in your power you have without delay
Acton's five hundred pound back to repay.   25
SUSAN Till now I had thought you loved me. By mine honour,
Which I had kept as spotless as the moon,

I ne'er was mistress of a single doit
Which I reserved not to supply your wants;
And do you think that I would hoard from you?   30
Now by my hopes in heaven, knew I the means
To buy you from the slavery of your debts,
Especially from Acton, whom I hate,
I would redeem it with my life or blood.

SIR CHARLES I challenge it, and kindred set apart.°   35
Thus ruffian-like I lay siege to your heart.
What do I owe to Acton?

SUSAN Why, some five hundred pounds, toward which I swear
In all the world I have not one denier.

SIR CHARLES It will not prove so. Sister, now resolve me: 40
What do you think (and speak your conscience!)
Would Acton give might he enjoy your bed?

SUSAN He would not shrink to spend a thousand pound
To give the Mountfords' name so deep a wound.

SIR CHARLES A thousand pound! I but five hundred owe;   45
Grant him your bed, he's paid with interest so.

SUSAN O brother!

SIR CHARLES   O sister, only this one way,
With that rich jewel you my debts may pay.°
In speaking this my cold heart shakes with shame,
Nor do I woo you in a brother's name,   50
But in a stranger's. Shall I die in debt
To Acton, my grand foe, and you still wear
The precious jewel that he holds so dear?

SUSAN My honour I esteem as dear and precious
As my redemption.

SIR CHARLES   I esteem you, sister,   55
As dear for so dear prizing it.

SUSAN   Will Charles
Have me cut off my hands and send them Acton?
Rip up my breast, and with my bleeding heart
Present him as a token?

SIR CHARLES   Neither, Sue,°
But hear me in my strange assertion: 60
Thy honour and my soul are equal in my regard,
Nor will thy brother Charles survive thy shame.
His kindness like a burden hath surcharged me,
And under his good deeds I stooping go,

Not with an upright soul. Had I remained   65
In prison still, there doubtless I had died;
Then unto him that freed me from that prison
Still do I owe that life. What moved my foe
To enfranchise me? 'Twas, sister, for your love!
With full five hundred pounds he bought your love,   70
And shall he not enjoy it? Shall the weight
Of all this heavy burden lean on me,
And will not you bear part? You did partake
The joy of my release; will you not stand
In joint bond bound to satisfy the debt?   75
Shall I be only charged?
SUSAN   But that I know
These arguments come from an honoured mind
(As in your most extremity of need,
Scorning to stand in debt to one you hate;
Nay, rather would engage your unstained honour   80
Than to be held ingrate), I should condemn you.
I see your resolution, and assent.
So Charles will have me, and I am content.
SIR CHARLES For this I tricked you up.
SUSAN   But here's a knife,
To save mine honour, shall slice out my life.°   85
SIR CHARLES I know thou pleasest me a thousand times
More in that resolution than thy grant.°
[*Aside*] Observe her love: to soothe them in my suit°
Her honour she will hazard, though not lose;
To bring me out of debt, her rigorous hand   90
Will pierce her heart. O wonder, that will choose,
Rather than stain her blood, her life to lose.
[*Aloud*] Come, you sad sister to a woeful brother.
      [*He takes her hand*]
This is the gate; I'll bear him such a present,
Such an acquittance for the knight to seal,   95
As will amaze his senses and surprise
With admiration all his fantasies.
      Enter Sir Francis and Malby
SUSAN Before his unchaste thoughts shall seize on me,
'Tis here shall my imprisoned soul set free.
SIR FRANCIS How, Mountford with his sister hand in hand.   100
What miracle's afoot?

MALBY   It is a sight
   Begets in me much admiration.
SIR CHARLES Stand not amazed to see me thus attended.
   Acton, I owe thee money, and being unable
   To bring thee the full sum in ready coin,   105
   Lo, for thy more assurance, here's a pawn:
   My sister, my dear sister, whose chaste honour
   I prize above a million. Here. Nay, take her:
   She's worth your money, man; do not forsake her.
SIR FRANCIS I would he were in earnest.°   110
SUSAN Impute it not to my immodesty.
   My brother being rich in nothing else
   But in his interest that he hath in me,°
   According to his poverty hath bought you
   Me, all his store, whom howsoe'er you prize   115
   As forfeit to your hand, he values highly,
   And would not sell, but to acquit your debt,
   For any emperor's ransom.
SIR FRANCIS [aside]   Stern heart, relent;
   Thy former cruelty at length repent.
   Was ever known in any former age   120
   Such honourable, wrested courtesy?
   Lands, honours, lives, and all the world forgo
   Rather than stand engaged to such a foe.°
SIR CHARLES Acton, she is too poor to be thy bride,
   And I too much opposed to be thy brother.   125
   There, take her to thee. If thou hast the heart
   To seize her as a rape or lustful prey,
   To blur our house that never yet was stained,
   To murder her that never meant thee harm,
   To kill me now whom once thou savedst from death,   130
   Do them at once on her. All these rely°
   And perish with her spotted chastity.
SIR FRANCIS You overcome me in your love, Sir Charles.
   I cannot be so cruel to a lady
   I love so dearly. Since you have not spared   135
   To engage your reputation to the world,°
   Your sister's honour which you prize so dear,
   Nay, all the comforts which you hold on earth,
   To grow out of my debt, being your foe,
   Your honoured thoughts, lo, thus I recompense: 140
   Your metamorphosed foe receives your gift

In satisfaction of all former wrongs.
This jewel I will wear here in my heart,
And where before I thought her for her wants
Too base to be my bride, to end all strife   145
I seal you my dear brother, her my wife.

SUSAN You still exceed us. I will yield to fate
And learn to love where I till now did hate.

SIR CHARLES With that enchantment you have charmed my soul
And made me rich even in those very words.   150
I pay no debt but am indebted more;
Rich in your love I never can be poor.

SIR FRANCIS All's mine is yours; we are alike in state.
Let's knit in love what was opposed in hate.
Come, for our nuptials we will straight provide,   155
Blessed only in our brother and fair bride.
            Exeunt

Scene 15

Enter Cranwell, Frankford, and Nicholas

CRANWELL Why do you search each room about your house,
Now that you have dispatched your wife away?

FRANKFORD O sir, to see that nothing may be left
That ever was my wife's. I loved her dearly,
And when I do but think of her unkindness,   5
My thoughts are all in hell, to avoid which torment,
I would not have a bodkin or a cuff,
A bracelet, necklace, or rebato wire,
Nor anything that ever was called hers
Left me, by which I might remember her.   10
Seek round about!

NICHOLAS 'Sblood, master, here's her lute flung in a corner.

FRANKFORD Her lute! O God, upon this instrument
Her fingers have run quick division,°
Sweeter than that which now divides our hearts.   15
These frets have made me pleasant, that have now
Frets of my heartstrings made. O Master Cranwell,
Oft hath she made this melancholy wood,
Now mute and dumb for her disastrous chance,
Speak sweetly many a note, sound many a strain   20

To her own ravishing voice, which, being well strung,
What pleasant, strange airs have they jointly sung.
[*To Nicholas*] Post with it after her. [*To Cranwell*] Now nothing's left;
Of her and hers I am at once bereft.

NICHOLAS I'll ride and overtake her, do my message,   25
And come back again.
        [*Exit Nicholas with the lute*]

CRANWELL   Meantime, sir, if you please,
I'll to Sir Francis Acton and inform him
Of what hath passed betwixt you and his sister.

FRANKFORD Do as you please. How ill am I bestead
To be a widower ere my wife be dead.   30
        [*Exeunt*]

Scene 16

*Enter Anne, with Jenkin, her maid Sisly, her Coachman, and
three carters*

ANNE Bid my coach stay. Why should I ride in state,
Being hurled so low down by the hand of fate?
A seat like to my fortunes let me have,
Earth for my chair, and for my bed a grave.

JENKIN Comfort, good mistress; you have watered your coach with tears   5
already. You have but two mile now to go to your manor. A man
cannot say by my old Master Frankford as he may say by° me, that
he wants manners,° for he hath three or four, of which this is one
that we are going to.

SISLY Good mistress, be of good cheer. Sorrow you see hurts you, but   10
helps you not. We all mourn to see you so sad.

CARTER Mistress, I spy one of my landlord's men
Comes riding post. 'Tis like he brings some news.

ANNE Comes he from Master Frankford, he is welcome;
So are his news, because they come from him.   15
        Enter Nicholas. [He gives Anne the lute]

NICHOLAS There.

ANNE I know the lute. Oft have I sung to thee;
We both are out of tune, both out of time.°

NICHOLAS Would that had been the worst instrument that e'er you
played on. My master commends him to ye; there's all he can find that   20

was ever yours. He hath nothing left that ever you could lay claim
to but his own heart, and he could afford you that.° All that I have
to deliver you is this. He prays you to forget him, and so he
bids you farewell.

ANNE I thank him; he is kind and ever was.   25
All you that have true feeling of my grief,
That know my loss, and have relenting hearts,
Gird me about, and help me with your tears
To wash my spotted sins. My lute shall groan;
It cannot weep, but shall lament my moan.   30
        [*She plays the lute.*] *Enter Wendoll.* [*He does not see Anne
        and her group, nor do they see him*]

WENDOLL Pursued with horror of a guilty soul
And with the sharp scourge of repentance lashed,
I fly from my own shadow. O my stars,
What have my parents in their lives deserved
That you should lay this penance on their son?   35
When I but think of Master Frankford's love
And lay it to my treason, or compare°
My murdering him for his relieving me,
It strikes a terror like a lightning's flash
To scorch my blood up. Thus I, like the owl,   40
Ashamed of day, live in these shadowy woods
Afraid of every leaf or murmuring blast,
Yet longing to receive some perfect knowledge
How he hath dealt with her. [*He notices Anne*] O my sad fate!
Here, and so far from home, and thus attended.   45
O God, I have divorced the truest turtles°
That ever lived together, and being divided
In several places, make their several moan;°
She in the fields laments and he at home.
So poets write that Orpheus made the trees°   50
And stones to dance to his melodious harp,
Meaning the rustic and the barbarous hinds,
That had no understanding part in them;
So she from these rude carters tears extracts,
Making their flinty hearts with grief to rise   55
And draw down rivers from their rocky eyes.

ANNE [*to Nicholas*] If you return unto your master, say
(Though not from me, for I am all unworthy
To blast his name so with a strumpet's tongue)

That you have seen me weep, wish myself dead.   60
Nay, you may say too, for my vow is passed,
Last night you saw me eat and drink my last.
This to your master you may say and swear,
For it is writ in heaven and decreed here.
NICHOLAS I'll say you wept; I'll swear you made me sad.   65
Why how now, eyes, what now, what's here to do?°
I am gone, or I shall straight turn baby too.
WENDOLL [aside] I cannot weep; my heart is all on fire.
Cursed be the fruits of my unchaste desire.
        [Anne gives the lute to the Coachman]
ANNE Go break this lute upon my coach's wheel,°   70
As the last music that I e'er shall make,
Not as my husband's gift, but my farewell
To earth's joy; [to Nicholas] and so your master tell.
        [Exit the Coachman with the lute]
NICHOLAS If I can for crying.
WENDOLL [aside]   Grief, have done,
Or like a madman I shall frantic run.   75
ANNE You have beheld the woefullest wretch on earth,
A woman made of tears. Would you had words
To express but what you see. My inward grief
No tongue can utter, yet unto your power
You may describe my sorrow and disclose   80
To thy sad master my abundant woes.
NICHOLAS I'll do your commendations.
ANNE   O no,
I dare not so presume, nor to my children.
I am disclaimed in both. Alas, I am.
O never teach them when they come to speak   85
To name the name of Mother. Chide their tongue
If they by chance light on that hated word.
Tell them 'tis naught, for when that word they name,
Poor pretty souls, they harp on their own shame.
WENDOLL [aside] To recompense her wrongs, what canst thou do? 90
Thou hast made her husbandless and childless too.
ANNE I have no more to say. Speak not for me,
Yet you may tell your master what you see!
NICHOLAS I'll do't.
        Exit Nicholas

WENDOLL [*aside*] I'll speak to her and comfort her in grief.   95
    O, but her wound cannot be cured with words.
    No matter though, I'll do my best good will
    To work a cure on her whom I did kill.
ANNE So, now unto my coach, then to my home,
    So to my deathbed, for from this sad hour   100
    I never will nor eat, nor drink, nor taste
    Of any cates that may preserve my life.
    I never will nor smile, nor sleep, nor rest,
    But when my tears have washed my black soul white,
    Sweet saviour, to thy hands I yield my sprite.   105
       [*Wendoll approaches Anne*]
WENDOLL O Mistress Frankford!
ANNE   O for God's sake fly:
    The devil doth come to tempt me ere I die!
    My coach! This sin that with an angel's face
    Courted mine honour till he sought my wrack,
    In my repentant eyes seems ugly black.   110
      Exeunt [*Anne, Sisly, and carters*], *the carters whistling*
JENKIN What, my young master that fled in his shirt! How come you
    by your clothes again? You have made our house in a sweet pickle,
    have you not, think you? What, shall I serve you still or cleave to
    the old house?
WENDOLL Hence, slave, away with thy unseasoned mirth!°   115
    Unless thou canst shed tears, and sigh, and howl,
    Curse thy sad fortunes, and exclaim on fate,
    Thou art not for my turn.
JENKIN Marry, an you will not, another will. Farewell and be
    hanged.° Would you had never come to have kept this coil° within   120
    our doors. We shall ha' you run away like a sprite again.
      Exit Jenkin
WENDOLL She's gone to death, I live to want and woe,
    Her life, her sins, and all upon my head,
    And I must now go wander like a Cain°
    In foreign countries and remoted climes,   125
    Where the report of my ingratitude
    Cannot be heard. I'll over, first to France,
    And so to Germany, and Italy,
    Where, when I have recovered, and by travel°
    Gotten those perfect tongues, and that these rumours°   130

May in their height abate, I will return;°
And I divine, however now dejected,°
My worth and parts being by some great man praised,
At my return I may in court be raised.
    Exit

Scene 17

    Enter Sir Francis, Sir Charles, Cranwell, [Malby,] and Susan
SIR FRANCIS Brother, and now my wife, I think these troubles°
  Fall on my head by justice of the heavens,
  For being so strict to you in your extremities;
  But we are now atoned. I would my sister°
  Could with like happiness o'ercome her griefs   5
  As we have ours.°
SUSAN You tell us, Master Cranwell, wondrous things
  Touching the patience of that gentleman,
  With what strange virtue he demeans his grief.°
CRANWELL I told you what I was witness of;   10
  It was my fortune to lodge there that night.
SIR FRANCIS O that same villain Wendoll, 'twas his tongue
  That did corrupt her. She was of herself
  Chaste and devoted well. Is this the house?°
CRANWELL Yes sir, I take it here your sister lies.   15
SIR FRANCIS My brother Frankford showed too mild a spirit
  In the revenge of such a loathèd crime;
  Less than he did, no man of spirit could do.
  I am so far from blaming his revenge
  That I commend it. Had it been my case,   20
  Their souls at once had from their breasts been freed:
  Death to such deeds of shame is the due meed.
    Enter Jenkin and Sisly
JENKIN O my mistress, my mistress, my poor mistress!
SISLY Alas that ever I was born! What shall I do for my poor mistress?
SIR CHARLES Why, what of her?   25
JENKIN O Lord, sir, she no sooner heard that her brother and his
  friends were come to see how she did, but she for very shame of her
  guilty conscience fell into a swoon, and we had much ado to get life
  into her.

SUSAN Alas that she should bear so hard a fate;   30
    Pity it is repentance comes too late.
SIR FRANCIS Is she so weak in body?
JENKIN O sir, I can assure you there's no help of life in her, for she
    will take no sustenance. She hath plainly starved herself, and now
    she is as lean as a lath. She ever looks for the good hour.° Many   35
    gentlemen and gentlewomen of the country are come to comfort
    her.
        Enter Anne in her bed°
MALBY How fare you, Mistress Frankford?
ANNE Sick, sick, O sick! Give me some air I pray you.
    Tell me, O tell me, where's Master Frankford?   40
    Will not he deign to see me ere I die?
MALBY Yes, Mistress Frankford: divers gentlemen,
    Your loving neighbours, with that just request
    Have moved and told him of your weak estate,
    Who, though with much ado to get belief,   45
    Examining of the general circumstance,
    Seeing your sorrow and your penitence,
    And hearing therewithal the great desire
    You have to see him ere you left the world,
    He gave to us his faith to follow us,   50
    And sure he will be here immediately.
ANNE You half revived me with those pleasing news.
    Raise me a little higher in my bed.
    Blush I not, Master Frankford? Blush I not, Sir Charles?°
    Can you not read my fault writ in my cheek?   55
    Is not my crime there? Tell me, gentlemen!
SIR CHARLES Alas, good mistress, sickness hath not left you
    Blood in your face enough to make you blush.
ANNE Then sickness like a friend my fault would hide.
    Is my husband come? My soul but tarries   60
    His arrive and I am fit for heaven.
SIR FRANCIS I came to chide you, but my words of hate
    Are turned to pity and compassionate grief;
    I came to rate you, but my brawls, you see,°
    Melt into tears, and I must weep by thee.   65
        Enter Frankford
    Here's Master Frankford now.
FRANKFORD Good morrow, brother; good morrow, gentlemen.
    God, that hath laid this cross upon our heads,°
    Might, had he pleased, have made our cause of meeting

On a more fair and a more contented ground;   70
But he that made us, made us to this woe.°
ANNE And is he come? Methinks that voice I know.
FRANKFORD How do you, woman?
ANNE Well, Master Frankford, well; but shall be better
I hope within this hour. Will you vouchsafe,   75
Out of your grace and your humanity,
To take a spotted strumpet by the hand?°
        [*Frankford takes her hand*]
FRANKFORD That hand once held my heart in faster bonds
Than now 'tis gripped by me. God pardon them
That made us first break hold.
ANNE   Amen, amen.   80
Out of my zeal to heaven, whither I am now bound,
I was so impudent to wish you here,
And once more beg your pardon. O good man,
And father to my children, pardon me.
Pardon, O pardon me! My fault so heinous is   85
That if you in this world forgive it not,
Heaven will not clear it in the world to come.
Faintness hath so usurped upon my knees°
That kneel I cannot; but on my heart's knees
My prostrate soul lies thrown down at your feet   90
To beg your gracious pardon. Pardon, O pardon me!
FRANKFORD As freely from the low depth of my soul
As my redeemer hath forgiven his death,°
I pardon thee. I will shed tears for thee,
Pray with thee, and in mere pity   95
Of thy weak state I'll wish to die with thee.
ALL So do we all.
NICHOLAS [*aside*] So will not I;
I'll sigh and sob, but, by my faith, not die.
SIR FRANCIS O Master Frankford, all the near alliance
I lose by her shall be supplied in thee.   100
You are my brother by the nearest way;
Her kindred hath fallen off, but yours doth stay.°
FRANKFORD [*to Anne*] Even as I hope for pardon at that day
When the great judge of heaven in scarlet sits°
So be thou pardoned. Though thy rash offence   105
Divorced our bodies, thy repentant tears
Unite our souls.

SIR CHARLES   Then comfort, Mistress Frankford:
    You see your husband hath forgiven your fall;
    Then rouse your spirits and cheer your fainting soul.
SUSAN How is it with you?
SIR FRANCIS   How do you feel yourself?   110
ANNE Not of this world.
FRANKFORD I see you are not, and I weep to see it.
    My wife, the mother to my pretty babes,
    Both those lost names I do restore thee back,
    And with this kiss I wed thee once again.   115
        [*Frankford kisses Anne*]
    Though thou art wounded in thy honoured name,
    And with that grief upon thy death-bed liest,
    Honest in heart, upon my soul, thou diest.
        [*Frankford and Anne embrace*]
ANNE Pardoned on earth, soul, thou in heaven art free.
    Once more thy wife dies thus embracing thee.°   120
        [*Anne dies*]
FRANKFORD New married and new widowed. O, she's dead,
    And a cold grave must be our nuptial bed.
SIR CHARLES Sir, be of good comfort, and your heavy sorrow
    Part equally amongst us: storms divided
    Abate their force, and with less rage are guided.   125
CRANWELL Do, Master Frankford. He that hath least part
    Will find enough to drown one troubled heart.
SIR FRANCIS Peace with thee, Nan. Brothers and gentlemen,
    All we that can plead interest in her grief,
    Bestow upon her body funeral tears.   130
    Brother, had you with threats and usage bad
    Punished her sin, the grief of her offence
    Had not with such true sorrow touched her heart.
FRANKFORD I see it had not; therefore on her grave
    I will bestow this funeral epitaph,   135
    Which on her marble tomb shall be engraved.
    In golden letters shall these words be filled:
    'Here lies she whom her husband's kindness killed.'
        [*Exeunt*]

Epilogue

[*Enter the Epilogue*]

EPILOGUE   An honest crew, disposèd to be merry,
　　Came to a tavern by and called for wine.
　　The drawer brought it, smiling like a cherry,°
　　And told them it was pleasant, neat, and fine.°
　　　'Taste it,' quoth one. He did so. 'Fie!' quoth he,   5
　　　'This wine was good; now't runs too near the lee'.°

　　Another sipped, to give the wine his due,
　　And said unto the rest it drunk too flat.°
　　The third said it was old, the fourth too new.
　　'Nay', quoth the fifth, 'the sharpness likes me not'.   10
　　　Thus, gentlemen, you see how in one hour
　　　The wine was new, old, flat, sharp, sweet, and sour.

　　Unto this wine we do allude our play,°
　　Which some will judge too trivial, some too grave.
　　You as our guests we entertain this day   15
　　And bid you welcome to the best we have.
　　　Excuse us, then: good wine may be disgraced
　　　When every several mouth hath sundry taste.
　　　　[*Exit*]

THE WITCH OF EDMONTON

THOMAS DEKKER, JOHN FORD, *and*
WILLIAM ROWLEY

ELIZABETH SAWYER, a crook-backed old witch
A DOG, the devil

FRANK THORNEY, a gentleman, Sir Arthur's servingman
WINIFRED, Sir Arthur's maid, Frank's wife
SIR ARTHUR CLARINGTON, a knight
OLD THORNEY, Frank's father
JOHN CARTER of Cheshunt, a wealthy old Hertfordshire yeoman
SUSAN, Carter's daughter
KATHERINE, Carter's daughter, Susan's sister
WARBECK, a young wastrel ruffian, Susan's suitor
SOMERTON, Katherine's suitor
A SPIRIT in Katherine's shape
JANE, a maidservant in Carter's household
SERVANTS of Sir Arthur
A CONSTABLE
OFFICERS
COFFIN-BEARERS
OFFICERS and SPECTATORS at the execution
OLD BANKS, a miserly landowner
CUDDY BANKS, a young man, Old Banks's son
FOUR MORRIS DANCERS accompanying Cuddy Banks; one is named
    ROWLAND and another JACK
FATHER SAWGUT, an old fiddler
THREE COUNTRYMEN
W. HAMLUC,° a countryman
A JUSTICE

ANNE RATCLIFFE
RATCLIFFE, Anne's husband

The Witch of Edmonton

1.1

Enter Frank Thorney and Winifred with child°
FRANK THORNEY Come, wench. Why, here's a business soon
    dispatched.
  Thy heart, I know, is now at ease. Thou needst not
  Fear what the tattling gossips in their cups°
  Can speak against thy fame. Thy child shall know
  Who to call dad now. 5
WINIFRED You have discharged the true part of an honest man.
  I cannot request a fuller satisfaction
  Than you have freely granted. Yet methinks
  'Tis a hard case, being lawful man and wife,
  We should not live together.
FRANK THORNEY   Had I failed 10
  In promise of my truth to thee, we must
  Have then been ever sundered. Now the longest
  Of our forbearing either's company
  Is only but to gain a little time
  For our continuing thrift, that so hereafter° 15
  The heir that shall be born may not have cause
  To curse his hour of birth, which made him feel
  The misery of beggary and want,
  Two devils that are occasions to enforce°
  A shameful end. My plots aim but to keep 20
  My father's love.
WINIFRED   And that will be as difficult
  To be preserved when he shall understand
  How you are married, as it will be now
  Should you confess it to him.
FRANK THORNEY   Fathers are
  Won by degrees, not bluntly, as our masters 25
  Or wrongèd friends are; and besides, I'll use
  Such dutiful and ready means, that ere
  He can have notice of what's past, th'inheritance

To which I am born heir shall be assured.
That done, why, let him know it. If he like it not,   30
Yet he shall have no power in him left
To cross the thriving of it.
WINIFRED   You, who had
The conquest of my maiden-love, may easily
Conquer the fears of my distrust. And whither
Must I be hurried?
FRANK THORNEY   Prithee do not use   35
A word so much unsuitable to the constant
Affections of thy husband. Thou shalt live
Near Waltham Abbey with thy uncle Selman.°
I have acquainted him with all at large.
He'll use thee kindly: thou shalt want no pleasures,   40
Nor any other fit supplies whatever
Thou canst in heart desire.
WINIFRED   All these are nothing
Without your company.
FRANK THORNEY   Which thou shalt have
Once every month at least.
WINIFRED   Once every month!
Is this to have a husband?
FRANK THORNEY   Perhaps oftener;   45
That's as occasion serves.
WINIFRED   Ay, ay; in case
No other beauty tempt your eye whom you
Like better, I may chance to be remembered,
And see you now and then. Faith, I did hope
You'd not have used me so. 'Tis but my fortune.   50
And yet, if not for my sake, have some pity
Upon the child I go with that's your own.
And, 'less you'll be a cruel-hearted father,°
You cannot but remember that.
Heaven knows how—
FRANK THORNEY   To quit which fear at once,   55
As by the ceremony late performed,
I plighted thee a faith as free from challenge
As any double thought, once more, in hearing
Of heaven and thee, I vow that never henceforth
Disgrace, reproof, lawless affections, threats,   60

Or what can be suggested 'gainst our marriage
Shall cause me falsify that bridal oath
That binds me thine. And, Winifred, whenever
The wanton heat of youth, by subtle baits
Of beauty or what woman's art can practise,   65
Draw me from only loving thee, let heaven
Inflict upon my life some fearful ruin.
I hope thou dost believe me.
WINIFRED   Swear no more.
I am confirmed, and will resolve to do
What you think most behoveful for us.   70
FRANK THORNEY Thus then: make thyself ready at the furthest house
Upon the green without the town. Your uncle
Expects you. For a little time, farewell.
WINIFRED   Sweet,
We shall meet again as soon as thou canst possibly?
FRANK THORNEY We shall. One kiss. [*They kiss*] Away.   75
   [*Exit Winifred.*] *Enter Sir Arthur Clarington*
SIR ARTHUR Frank Thorney.
FRANK THORNEY Here, sir.
SIR ARTHUR Alone? Then must I tell thee in plain terms thou hast
   wronged thy master's house basely and lewdly.
FRANK THORNEY Your house, sir?
SIR ARTHUR   Yes, sir. If the nimble devil 80
That wantoned in your blood rebelled against
All rules of honest duty, you might, sir,
Have found out some more fitting place than here
To have built a stews in. All the country whispers
How shamefully thou hast undone a maid   85
Approved for modest life, for civil carriage,
Till thy prevailing perjuries enticed her
To forfeit shame. Will you be honest yet,°
Make her amends and marry her?
FRANK THORNEY   So, sir,
I might bring both myself and her to beggary,   90
And that would be a shame worse than the other.
SIR ARTHUR You should have thought on this before, and then
Your reason would have overswayed the passion
Of your unruly lust. But that you may
Be left without excuse, to salve the infamy   95

133

Of my disgracèd house, and 'cause you are
A gentleman, and both of you my servants,
I'll make the maid a portion.

FRANK THORNEY   So you promised me
Before, in case I married her. I know
Sir Arthur Clarington deserves the credit   100
Report hath lent him, and presume you are
A debtor to your promise. But upon
What certainty shall I resolve? Excuse me
For being somewhat rude.

SIR ARTHUR   'Tis but reason.
Well, Frank, what thinkst thou of two hundred pounds   105
And a continual friend?

FRANK THORNEY   Though my poor fortunes°
Might happily prefer me to a choice
Of a far greater portion, yet, to right
A wrongèd maid and to preserve your favour,
I am content to accept your proffer.

SIR ARTHUR   Art thou?   110

FRANK THORNEY Sir, we shall every day have need to employ
The use of what you please to give.

SIR ARTHUR   Thou shalt have't.

FRANK THORNEY Then I claim your promise. We are man and wife.

SIR ARTHUR Already?

FRANK THORNEY   And more than so; I have promised her
Free entertainment in her uncle's house   115
Near Waltham Abbey, where she may securely
Sojourn, till time and my endeavours work
My father's love and liking.

SIR ARTHUR   Honest Frank!

FRANK THORNEY I hope, sir, you will think I cannot keep her
Without a daily charge.

SIR ARTHUR   As for the money,   120
'Tis all thine own, and though I cannot make thee
A present payment, yet thou shalt be sure
I will not fail thee.

FRANK THORNEY   But our occasions—°

SIR ARTHUR Nay, nay, talk not of your occasions. Trust my bounty:
it shall not sleep. Hast married her, i'faith, Frank?   125
'Tis well, 'tis passing well. Then, Winifred,
Once more thou art an honest woman. Frank,°

Thou hast a jewel. Love her, she'll deserve it.
And when to Waltham?
FRANK THORNEY   She is making ready.
Her uncle stays for her.
SIR ARTHUR   Most provident speed.   130
Frank, I will be thy friend, and such a friend!
Thou'lt bring her thither?
FRANK THORNEY   Sir, I cannot. Newly°
My father sent me word I should come to him.
SIR ARTHUR Marry, and do. I know thou hast a wit
To handle him.   135
FRANK THORNEY I have a suit t'ye.
SIR ARTHUR   What is't?
Anything, Frank, command it.
FRANK THORNEY   That you'll please
By letters to assure my father that
I am not married.
SIR ARTHUR   How?
FRANK THORNEY   Someone or other
Hath certainly informed him that I purposed   140
To marry Winifred, on which he threatened
To disinherit me. To prevent it,
Lowly I crave your letters, which he seeing°
Will credit; and I hope ere I return,
On such conditions as I'll frame, his lands   145
Shall be assured.
SIR ARTHUR   But what is there to quit
My knowledge of the marriage?
FRANK THORNEY   Why, you were not
A witness to it.
SIR ARTHUR   I conceive; and then,
His land confirmed, thou wilt acquaint him throughly
With all that's passed.
FRANK THORNEY   I mean no less.
SIR ARTHUR   Provided   150
I never was made privy to it.
FRANK THORNEY   Alas, sir,
Am I a talker?
SIR ARTHUR   Draw thyself the letter,°
I'll put my hand to it. I commend thy policy.
Thou'rt witty, witty Frank. Nay, nay, 'tis fit,
Dispatch it.

FRANK THORNEY I shall write effectually.   155
    Exit
SIR ARTHUR Go thy way, cuckoo. Have I caught the young man?°
    One trouble then is freed. He that will feast
    At others' cost must be a bold-faced guest.
    Enter Winifred in a riding suit
WINIFRED I have heard the news: all now is safe;
    The worst is past.
SIR ARTHUR　　　　　　Thy lip, wench. [*He kisses her*] I must bid   160
    Farewell for fashion's sake, but I will visit thee
    Suddenly girl. This was cleanly carried,
    Ha, was't not, Win?
WINIFRED　　　　　　Then were my happiness
    That I in heart repent I did not bring him
    The dower of a virginity. Sir, forgive me;   165
    I have been much to blame. Had not my lewdness
    Given way to your immoderate waste of virtue,
    You had not with such eagerness pursued
    The error of your goodness.
SIR ARTHUR　　　　　　Dear, dear Win,
    I hug this art of thine. It shows how cleanly   170
    Thou canst beguile, in case occasion serve
    To practice. It becomes thee. Now we share°
    Free scope enough, without control or fear,
    To interchange our pleasures. We will surfeit
    In our embraces, wench. Come, tell me, when   175
    Wilt thou appoint a meeting?
WINIFRED　　　　　　What to do?
SIR ARTHUR Good, good, to con the lesson of our loves,
    Our secret game.
WINIFRED　　　　　O blush to speak it further!
    As you're a noble gentleman, forget
    A sin so monstrous. 'Tis not gently done   180
    To open a cured wound. I know you speak
    For trial. Troth, you need not.
SIR ARTHUR　　　　　　I for trial?°
    Not I, by this good sunshine!
WINIFRED　　　　　　Can you name
    That syllable of good and yet not tremble
    To think to what a foul and black intent   185

You use it for an oath? Let me resolve you:
If you appear in any visitation
That brings not with it pity for the wrongs
Done to abusèd Thorney, my kind husband;
If you infect mine ear with any breath   190
That is not throughly perfumèd with sighs
For former deeds of lust, may I be cursed,
Even in my prayers, when I vouchsafe
To see or hear you. I will change my life
From a loose whore to a repentant wife.   195

SIR ARTHUR Wilt thou turn monster now? Art not ashamed
    After so many months to be honest at last?
    Away, away! Fie on't!

WINIFRED   My resolution
    Is built upon a rock. This very day°
    Young Thorney vowed, with oaths not to be doubted,   200
    That never any change of love should cancel
    The bonds in which we are to either bound°
    Of lasting truth. And shall I then, for my part,
    Unfile the sacred oath set on record
    In heaven's book? Sir Arthur, do not study   205
    To add to your lascivious lust the sin
    Of sacrilege; for if you but endeavour
    By any unchaste word to tempt my constancy
    You strive, as much as in you lies, to ruin°
    A temple hallowed to the purity   210
    Of holy marriage. I have said enough:
    You may believe me.

SIR ARTHUR   Get you to your nunnery,°
    There freeze in your cold cloister. This is fine!

WINIFRED Good angels guide me. Sir, you'll give me leave
    To weep and pray for your conversion?   215

SIR ARTHUR Yes. Away to Waltham! Pox on your honesty!°
    Had you no other trick to fool me? Well,
    You may want money yet.

WINIFRED   None that I'll send for°
    To you for hire of a damnation.
    When I am gone, think on my just complaint: 220
    I was your devil; O be you my saint!
        Exit

SIR ARTHUR Go, go thy ways, as changeable a baggage
  As ever cozened knight. I'm glad I'm rid of her.
  Honest? Marry, hang her! Thorney is my debtor;
  I thought to have paid him too, but fools have fortune.°   225
    Exit

1.2

  Enter Old Thorney and Old Carter
OLD THORNEY You offer, Master Carter, like a gentleman;
  I cannot find fault with it, 'tis so fair.
OLD CARTER No gentleman I, Master Thorney; spare the Mastership,
  call me by my name, John Carter. Master is a title my father, nor his
  before him, were acquainted with. Honest Hertfordshire yeomen,   5
  such an one am I. My word and my deed shall be proved one° at
  all times. I mean to give you no security for the marriage-
  money.
OLD THORNEY How! No security?
  Although it need not so long as you live,   10
  Yet who is he has surety of his life one hour?
  Men, the proverb says, are mortal, else, for my part,°
  I distrust you not, were the sum double.
OLD CARTER Double, treble, more or less, I tell you, Master Thorney,
  I'll give no security. Bonds and bills are but tarriers° to catch fools 15
  and keep lazy knaves busy. My security shall be present° payment.
  And we here about Edmonton hold present payment as sure as an
  alderman's bond in London, Master Thorney.
OLD THORNEY I cry you mercy, sir, I understood you not.
OLD CARTER I like young Frank well, so does my Susan too. The girl   20
  has a fancy to him, which makes me ready in my purse. There be
  other suitors within, that make much noise to little purpose. If Frank
  love Sue, Sue shall have none but Frank. 'Tis a mannerly girl,
  Master Thorney, though but a homely man's daughter. There have
  worse faces looked out of black bags,° man.   25
OLD THORNEY You speak your mind freely and honestly. I marvel
  my son comes not. I am sure he will be here sometime today.
OLD CARTER Today or tomorrow, when he comes he shall be welcome
  to bread, beer and beef: yeoman's fare, we have no kickshaws.

Full dishes, whole bellyfuls. Should I diet three days at one of   30
the slender city suppers, you might send me to Barber-Surgeons'
Hall° the fourth day to hang up for an anatomy. Here come they
that—

    Enter Warbeck with Susan, Somerton with Katherine

How now, girls! Every day play-day with you? Valentine's day
too, all by couples? Thus will young folks do when we are laid   35
in our graves, Master Thorney. Here's all the care they take. And
how do you find the wenches, gentlemen? Have they any mind
to a loose gown° and a straight shoe? Win 'em and wear 'em. They
shall choose for themselves by my consent.

WARBECK You speak like a kind father. Sue, thou hearest the liberty   40
  that's granted thee. What sayest thou? Wilt thou be mine?

SUSAN Your what, sir? I dare swear, never your wife.

WARBECK Canst thou be so unkind, considering how dearly I affect
  thee, nay, dote on thy perfections?

SUSAN You are studied too scholar-like in words I understand not.   45
  I am too coarse for such a gallant's love as you are.

WARBECK By the honour of gentility—

SUSAN Good sir, no swearing. Yea and nay with us°
  Prevails above all oaths you can invent.

WARBECK By this white hand of thine—

SUSAN   Take a false oath?   50
  Fie, fie! Flatter the wise, fools not regard it,
  And one of these am I.

WARBECK   Dost thou despise me?

OLD CARTER Let 'em talk on, Master Thorney. I know Sue's mind.
  The fly may buzz about the candle; he shall but singe his wings when
  all's done. Frank, Frank is he has her heart.   55

SOMERTON But shall I live in hope, Kate?

KATHERINE Better so than a desperate man.

SOMERTON Perhaps thou thinkst it is thy portion
  I level at. Wert thou as poor in fortunes
  As thou art rich in goodness, I would rather   60
  Be suitor for the dower of thy virtues
  Than twice thy father's whole estate. And, prithee,
  Be thou resolvèd so.

KATHERINE   Master Somerton,
  It is an easy labour to deceive   65

A maid that will believe men's subtle promises;
Yet I conceive of you as worthily
As I presume you do deserve.

SOMERTON   Which is
As worthily in loving thee sincerely
As thou art worthy to be so beloved.   70

KATHERINE I shall find time to try you.

SOMERTON   Do, Kate, do.
And when I fail, may all my joys forsake me.

OLD CARTER Warbeck and Sue are at it still. I laugh to myself, Master
Thorney, to see how earnestly he beats the bush while the bird is
flown into another's bosom. A very unthrift, Master Thorney, one   75
of the country roaring lads.° We have such as well as the city, and as
arrant rakehells as they are, though not so nimble at their prizes of wit.
Sue knows the rascal to a hair's breadth, and will fit him accordingly.

OLD THORNEY What is the other gentleman?

OLD CARTER One Somerton, the honester man of the two by five pound   80
in every stone-weight.° A civil fellow. He has a fine convenient
estate of land in West Ham, by Essex. Master Ranges, that dwells
by Enfield, sent him hither. He likes Kate well. I may tell you, I
think she likes him as well. If they agree, I'll not hinder the match
for my part. But that Warbeck is such another——°I use him   85
kindly for Master Somerton's sake, for he came hither first as a
companion of his. Honest men, Master Thorney, may fall into
knaves' company now and then.

WARBECK Three hundred a year jointure,° Sue.

SUSAN Where lies it, by sea or by land? I think by sea.°   90

WARBECK Do I look like a captain?

SUSAN   Not a whit, sir.
Should all that use the seas be reckoned captains,
There's not a ship should have a scullion in her
To keep her clean.

WARBECK   Do you scorn me, Mistress Susan?
Am I a subject to be jeered at?

SUSAN   Neither   95
Am I a property for you to use
As stale to your fond, wanton, loose discourse.
Pray, sir, be civil.

WARBECK   Wilt be angry, wasp?

OLD CARTER God-a-mercy, Sue! She'll firk him, on my life, if he
fumble with her.   100

     Enter Frank

Master Francis Thorney, you are welcome indeed. Your father
expected your coming. How does the right worshipful knight, Sir
Arthur Clarington, your master?

FRANK THORNEY
In health this morning. [*To Old Thorney*] Sir, my duty.

OLD THORNEY   Now
You come as I could wish.

WARBECK   Frank Thorney, ha!   105

SUSAN You must excuse me.

FRANK THORNEY   Virtuous Mistress Susan.
Kind Mistress Katherine.
     Salutes them

                  Gentlemen, to both
Good time o'th'day.

SOMERTON   The like to you.

WARBECK   'Tis he.
[*To Somerton*] A word, friend. On my life, this is the man
Stands fair in crossing Susan's love to me.   110

SOMERTON [*to Warbeck*] I think no less. Be wise, and take no
    notice on't.
He that can win her, best deserves her.

WARBECK [*to Somerton*]   Marry
A servingman? Mew!

SOMERTON [*to Warbeck*] Prithee, friend, no more.

OLD CARTER Gentlemen all, there's within a slight dinner ready, if you
please to taste of it. Master Thorney, Master Francis, Master   115
—Why girls! What, hussies, will you spend all your forenoon in tittle-
tattles? Away! It's well, i'faith. Will you go in, gentlemen?

OLD THORNEY We'll follow presently. My son and I
Have a few words of business.

OLD CARTER   At your pleasure.
    Exeunt Carter, Somerton, Warbeck, Susan, Katherine

OLD THORNEY I think you guess the reason, Frank, for which I sent   120
for you.

FRANK THORNEY
        Yes, sir.

OLD THORNEY   I need not tell you
With what a labyrinth of dangers daily
The best part of my whole estate's encumbered.
Nor have I any clew to wind it out°
But what occasion proffers me. Wherein   125

If you should falter, I shall have the shame,
And you the loss. On these two points rely
Our happiness or ruin. If you marry
With wealthy Carter's daughter there's a portion
Will free my land, all which I will instate   130
Upon the marriage to you. Otherwise
I must be of necessity enforced
To make a present sale of all; and yet,
For aught I know, live in as poor distress,
Or worse, than now I do. You hear the sum: 135
I told you thus before. Have you considered on't?

FRANK THORNEY I have, sir. And however I could wish
To enjoy the benefit of single freedom
For that I find no disposition in me
To undergo the burden of that care   140
That marriage brings with it; yet to secure
And settle the continuance of your credit,
I humbly yield to be directed by you
In all commands.

OLD THORNEY   You have already used
Such thriving protestations to the maid   145
That she is wholly yours. And, speak the truth,
You love her, do you not?

FRANK THORNEY   'Twere pity, sir,
I should deceive her.

OLD THORNEY   Better you'd been unborn.
But is your love so steady that you mean,
Nay, more, desire to make her your wife?

FRANK THORNEY   Else, sir,   150
It were a wrong not to be righted.

OLD THORNEY   True,
It were. And you will marry her?

FRANK THORNEY   Heaven prosper it,°
I do intend it.

OLD THORNEY O thou art a villain!
A devil like a man! Wherein have I
Offended all the powers so much, to be   155
Father to such a graceless, godless son?

FRANK THORNEY To me, sir, this? O my cleft heart!

OLD THORNEY   To thee,
Son of my curse. Speak truth and blush, thou monster.

Hast thou not married Winifred, a maid
Was fellow-servant with thee?

FRANK THORNEY [*aside*]   Some swift spirit   160
Has blown this news abroad. I must outface it.

OLD THORNEY D'you study for excuse? Why all the country
is full on't.

FRANK THORNEY With your licence, 'tis not charitable,
I am sure it is not fatherly, so much
To be o'erswayed with credulous conceit   165
Of mere impossibilities. But fathers
Are privileged to think and talk at pleasure.

OLD THORNEY Why, canst thou yet deny thou hast no wife?

FRANK THORNEY What do you take me for? An atheist?
One that nor hopes the blessedness of life   170
Hereafter, neither fears the vengeance due
To such as make the marriage-bed an inn
Which travellers day and night,
After a toilsome lodging, leave at pleasure?
Am I become so insensible of losing   175
The glory of creation's work, my soul?
O I have lived too long!

OLD THORNEY   Thou hast, dissembler.
Darest thou persever yet, and pull down wrath
As hot as flames of hell to strike thee quick
Into the grave of horror? I believe thee not.   180
Get from my sight!

FRANK THORNEY   Sir, though mine innocence
Needs not a stronger witness than the clearness
Of an unperished conscience, yet, for that
I was informed how mainly you had been
Possessed of this untruth, to quit all scruple
Please you peruse this letter. 'Tis to you.   185

OLD THORNEY From whom?

FRANK THORNEY   Sir Arthur Clarington, my master.

OLD THORNEY Well, sir.

          [*Frank gives Old Thorney the letter, and he reads it*]

FRANK THORNEY [*aside*] On every side I am distracted, am waded
deeper into mischief than virtue can avoid. But on I must. Fate   190
leads me; I will follow. [*To Old Thorney*] There you read what may
confirm you.

OLD THORNEY Yes, and wonder at it. Forgive me, Frank. Credulity
abused me. My tears express my joy, and I am sorry I injured
innocence.   195

FRANK THORNEY Alas! I knew your rage and grief proceeded from
your love to me. So I conceived it.

OLD THORNEY My good son, I'll bear with many faults in thee hereafter;
bear thou with mine.

FRANK THORNEY The peace is soon concluded.   200
          Enter Old Carter [and Susan]

OLD CARTER Why, Master Thorney, d'ye mean to talk out your dinner?
The company attends your coming. What must it be: Master Frank,
or son Frank? I am plain Dunstable.°

OLD THORNEY Son, brother, if your daughter like to have it so.

FRANK THORNEY I dare be confident she's not altered   205
From what I left her at our parting last.
Are you, fair maid?

SUSAN   You took too sure possession
Of an engaged heart.

FRANK THORNEY   Which now I challenge.°

OLD CARTER Marry, and much good may it do thee, son. Take her to
thee. Get me a brace of boys at a burden,° Frank. The nursing shall   210
not stand thee in a pennyworth of milk. Reach her home and spare
not. When's the day?

OLD THORNEY Tomorrow, if you please. To use ceremony
Of charge and custom were to little purpose:
Their loves are married fast enough already.   215

OLD CARTER A good motion. We'll e'en have a household dinner,
and let the fiddlers go scrape.° Let the bride and bridegroom dance
at night° together, no matter for the guests. Tomorrow, Sue,
tomorrow.—Shall's to dinner now?

OLD THORNEY We are on all sides pleased, I hope.   220

SUSAN Pray heaven I may deserve the blessing sent me.
Now my heart is settled.

FRANK THORNEY   So is mine.

OLD CARTER Your marriage-money shall be received before your
wedding-shoes can be pulled on. Blessing on you both!

FRANK THORNEY [*aside*] No man can hide his shame from heaven that
views him.   225
In vain he flees whose destiny pursues him.
          Exeunt

2.1

Enter Elizabeth Sawyer gathering sticks

ELIZABETH SAWYER And why on me? Why should the envious world
    Throw all their scandalous malice upon me?
    'Cause I am poor, deformed and ignorant,
    And like a bow buckled and bent together
    By some more strong in mischiefs than myself,   5
    Must I for that be made a common sink
    For all the filth and rubbish of men's tongues
    To fall and run into? Some call me witch,
    And, being ignorant of myself, they go°
    About to teach me how to be one, urging   10
    That my bad tongue, by their bad usage made so,
    Forspeaks their cattle, doth bewitch their corn,
    Themselves, their servants and their babes at nurse.
    This they enforce upon me, and in part
        Enter Old Banks
    Make me to credit it. And here comes one   15
    Of my chief adversaries.
OLD BANKS Out, out upon thee, witch!
ELIZABETH SAWYER   Dost call me witch?
OLD BANKS I do, witch, I do; and worse I would, knew I a name
    more hateful. What makest thou upon my ground?
ELIZABETH SAWYER Gather a few rotten sticks to warm me.   20
OLD BANKS Down with them when I bid thee, quickly. I'll make
    thy bones rattle in thy skin else.
ELIZABETH SAWYER You won't, churl, cut-throat, miser! [*Puts down*
    the sticks] There they be. Would they stuck 'cross thy throat, thy
    bowels, thy maw, thy midriff.   25
OLD BANKS Sayest thou me so? Hag, out of my ground.
    [*He hits her*]
ELIZABETH SAWYER Dost strike me, slave? Curmudgeon, now thy
    bones aches, thy joints cramps, and convulsions stretch and crack
    thy sinews.
OLD BANKS Cursing, thou hag? [*He beats her*] Take that, and that!   30
    Exit Old Banks
ELIZABETH SAWYER Strike, do, and withered may that hand and arm
    Whose blows have lamed me, drop from the rotten trunk.
    Abuse me! Beat me! Call me hag and witch!

What is the name? Where and by what art learned?
What spells, what charms or invocations   35
May the thing called familiar be purchased?
>   *Enter Cuddy Banks and* [*Morris Dancers*]°

CUDDY BANKS A new head for the tabor, and silver tipping for the pipe.
Remember that, and forget not five leash of new bells.

FIRST DANCER Double bells! Crooked Lane,° ye shall have 'em straight
in Crooked Lane. Double bells all if it be possible.   40

CUDDY BANKS Double bells? Double coxcombs! Trebles,° buy me
trebles, all trebles, for our purpose is to be in the altitudes.

SECOND DANCER All trebles? Not a mean?

CUDDY BANKS Not one. The morris is so cast we'll have neither mean
nor base in our company, fellow Rowland.°   45

THIRD DANCER What! Nor a counter?

CUDDY BANKS By no means, no hunting counter.° Leave that to Enfield
Chase° men. All trebles, all in the altitudes. Now for the disposing
of parts in the morris, little or no labour will serve.°

SECOND DANCER If you that be minded to follow your leader, know   50
me, an ancient honour belonging to our house, for a fore-horse in a
team and fore-gallant in a morris. My father's stable is not
unfurnished.

THIRD DANCER So much for the fore-horse, but how for a good
hobby-horse?°   55

CUDDY BANKS For a hobby-horse? Let me see an almanac. [*A dancer
passes him a book*] Midsummer-moon, let me see ye. 'When the
moon's in the full, then's wit in the wane.' No more. Use your best
skill; your morris will suffer an eclipse.

FIRST DANCER An eclipse?   60

CUDDY BANKS A strange one.

SECOND DANCER Strange?

CUDDY BANKS Yes, and most sudden. Remember the fore-gallant and
forget the hobby-horse.° The whole body of your morris will be
darkened. There be of us—but 'tis no matter. Forget the hobby-horse.   65

FIRST DANCER Cuddy Banks, have you forgot since he paced it from
Enfield Chase to Edmonton? Cuddy, honest Cuddy, cast thy stuff.

CUDDY BANKS Suffer may ye all. It shall be known I can take mine
ease as well as another man. Seek your hobby-horse where you can
get him.   70

FIRST DANCER Cuddy, honest Cuddy, we confess, and are sorry for
our neglect.

SECOND DANCER The old horse shall have a new bridle,—

THIRD DANCER The caparisons new painted,—

FOURTH DANCER The tail repaired,— 75

FIRST DANCER The snaffle and the bosses new saffroned o'er. Kind,—

SECOND DANCER Honest,—

THIRD DANCER Loving, ingenious,—

FOURTH DANCER Affable Cuddy.

CUDDY BANKS To show I am not flint but affable, as you say, very 80
    well stuffed, a kind of warm dough or puff-paste, I relent, I connive,
    most affable Jack. Let the hobby-horse provide a strong back;° he
    shall not want a belly when I am in 'im.
        [*Cuddy sees Elizabeth Sawyer*]
    But 'uds me, Mother Sawyer!

FIRST DANCER The old Witch of Edmonton! If our mirth be not 85
    crossed—

SECOND DANCER Bless us, Cuddy, and let her curse her tother eye
    out.° What dost now?

CUDDY BANKS Ungirt,° unblessed, says the proverb; but my girdle
    shall serve a riding knot, and a fig for all the witches in Christendom! 90
    What wouldst thou?

FIRST DANCER The devil cannot abide to be crossed.

SECOND DANCER And scorns to come at any man's whistle.

THIRD DANCER Away—

FOURTH DANCER—with the witch! 95

ALL Away with the Witch of Edmonton!
        Exeunt Cuddy Banks and Morris Dancers in strange postures

ELIZABETH SAWYER Still vexed! Still tortured! That curmudgeon
    Banks
    Is ground of all my scandal. I am shunned°
    And hated like a sickness, made a scorn
    To all degrees and sexes. I have heard old beldams 100
    Talk of familiars in the shape of mice,
    Rats, ferrets, weasels and I wot not what,
    That have appeared and sucked, some say, their blood.
    But by what means they came acquainted with them
    I'm now ignorant. Would some power, good or bad, 105
    Instruct me which way I might be revenged
    Upon this churl, I'd go out of myself
    And give this fury leave to dwell within
    This ruined cottage ready to fall with age;
    Abjure all goodness, be at hate with prayer, 110
    And study curses, imprecations,

Blasphemous speeches, oaths, detested oaths,
Or anything that's ill, so I might work
Revenge upon this miser, this black cur
That barks and bites, and sucks the very blood   115
Of me and of my credit. 'Tis all one
To be a witch as to be counted one.
Vengeance, shame, ruin light upon that canker!
　　　Enter Dog
DOG Ho! Have I found thee cursing? Now thou art mine own.
ELIZABETH SAWYER Thine? What art thou?   120
DOG He thou hast so often importuned to appear to thee, the devil.
ELIZABETH SAWYER Bless me! The devil?
DOG Come, do not fear, I love thee much too well
　　To hurt or fright thee. If I seem terrible,
　　It is to such as hate me. I have found   125
　　Thy love unfeigned, have seen and pitied
　　Thy open wrongs, and come, out of my love,
　　To give thee just revenge against thy foes.
ELIZABETH SAWYER May I believe thee?
DOG　　　　　　　　　　　　　　To confirm't, command me
　　Do any mischief unto man or beast,   130
　　And I'll effect it, on condition
　　That, uncompelled, thou make a deed of gift°
　　Of soul and body to me.
ELIZABETH SAWYER　　　　　Out, alas!
　　My soul and body?
DOG　　　　　　　　And that instantly,
　　And seal it with thy blood. If thou deniest   135
　　I'll tear thy body in a thousand pieces.°
ELIZABETH SAWYER I know not where to seek relief. But shall I,
　　After such covenants sealed, see full revenge
　　On all that wrong me?
DOG　　　　　　　　Ha, ha! Silly woman!
　　The devil is no liar to such as he loves.   140
　　Didst ever know or hear the devil a liar
　　To such as he affects?
ELIZABETH SAWYER Then I am thine, at least so much of me
　　As I can call mine own.
DOG　　　　　　　　　Equivocations?
　　Art mine or no? Speak or I'll tear!
ELIZABETH SAWYER　　　　　　All thine.   145

DOG Seal't with thy blood.
    Sucks her arm. Thunder and lightning
                See, now I dare call thee mine.
  For proof, command me. Instantly I'll run
  To any mischief; goodness can I none.
ELIZABETH SAWYER And I desire as little. There's an old churl, one
  Banks—   150
DOG That wronged thee. He lamed thee, called thee witch.
ELIZABETH SAWYER The same; first upon him I'd be revenged.
DOG Thou shalt. Do but name how.
ELIZABETH SAWYER Go touch his life.
DOG I cannot.   155
ELIZABETH SAWYER Hast thou not vowed? Go kill the slave.
DOG I wonnot.
ELIZABETH SAWYER I'll cancel then my gift.
DOG Ha, ha!
ELIZABETH SAWYER Dost laugh?   160
  Why wilt not kill him?
DOG   Fool, because I cannot.
  Though we have power, know it is circumscribed
  And tied in limits. Though he be curst to thee,
  Yet of himself he is loving to the world
  And charitable to the poor. Now men   165
  That, as he, love goodness, though in smallest measure,
  Live without compass of our reach. His cattle
  And corn I'll kill and mildew, but his life
  (Until I take him as I late found thee,
  Cursing and swearing) I have no power to touch.   170
ELIZABETH SAWYER Work on his corn and cattle then.
DOG   I shall.
  The witch of Edmonton shall see his fall
  If she at least put credit in my power,
  And in mine only, make orisons to me,
  And none but me.°
ELIZABETH SAWYER Say how, and in what manner.   175
DOG I'll tell thee. When thou wishest ill,
  Corn, man, or beast would spoil or kill,
  Turn thy back against the sun
  And mumble this short orison:
  'If thou to death or shame pursue 'em,   180
  Sanctibicetur nomen tuum'.°

ELIZABETH SAWYER 'If thou to death or shame pursue 'em,
　　Sanctibecetur nomen tuum'.
DOG Perfect. Farewell. Our first-made promises
　　We'll put in execution against Banks.　　　　　　　　　　185
　　　　Exit
ELIZABETH SAWYER *Contaminetur*° *nomen tuum*. I'm an expert
　　scholar.
　　Speak Latin, or I know not well what language,
　　As well as the best of 'em. But who comes here?
　　　　Enter Cuddy Banks
　　The son of my worst foe. 'To death pursue 'em　　　　　　190
　　Et sanctabecetur nomen tuum'.
CUDDY BANKS What's that she mumbles? The devil's *pater noster*?
　　Would it were else! Mother Sawyer, good morrow.
ELIZABETH SAWYER Ill morrow to thee, and all the world that flout a
　　poor old woman.　　　　　　　　　　　　　　　　　　　195
　　'To death pursue 'em,
　　And *sanctabecetur nomen tuum*'.
CUDDY BANKS Nay, good Gammer Sawyer, whate'er it please my
　　father to call you, I know you are—
ELIZABETH SAWYER A witch.　　　　　　　　　　　　　　200
CUDDY BANKS A witch? Would you were else i'faith!
ELIZABETH SAWYER Your father knows I am by this.
CUDDY BANKS I would he did.
ELIZABETH SAWYER And so in time may you.
CUDDY BANKS I would I might else. But, witch or no witch, you are a　　205
　　motherly woman, and though my father be a kind of God-bless-us,°
　　as they say, I have an earnest suit to you. And if you'll be so kind to
　　ka me one good turn, I'll be so courteous as to kob you° another.
ELIZABETH SAWYER What's that? To spurn, beat me and call me witch,
　　as your kind father doth?　　　　　　　　　　　　　　210
CUDDY BANKS My father? I am ashamed to own him. If he has hurt
　　the head of thy credit there's money to buy thee a plaster [*offers her
　　money*], and a small courtesy I would require at thy hands.
ELIZABETH SAWYER You seem a good young man, [*aside*] and I must
　　dissemble, the better to accomplish my revenge. [*To Cuddy*] But　　215
　　for this silver, what wouldst have me do? Bewitch thee?
CUDDY BANKS No, by no means, I am bewitched already. I would
　　have thee so good as to unwitch me, or witch another with me for
　　company.
ELIZABETH SAWYER I understand thee not. Be plain, my son.　　　220

CUDDY BANKS As a pike-staff, mother. You know Kate Carter?

ELIZABETH SAWYER The wealthy yeoman's daughter. What of her?

CUDDY BANKS That same party has bewitched me.

ELIZABETH SAWYER Bewitched thee?

CUDDY BANKS Bewitched me, *hisce auribus*.° I saw a little devil fly   225
out of her eye like a bird-bolt, which sticks at this hour up to the
feathers in my heart. Now my request is to send one of thy what-
d'ye-call-'ems, either to pluck that out, or stick another as fast in
hers. Do, and here's my hand, I am thine for three lives.

ELIZABETH SAWYER [*aside*] We shall have sport. [*Aloud*] Thou art   230
in love with her?

CUDDY BANKS Up to the very hilts, mother.

ELIZABETH SAWYER And thou'dst have me make her love thee too?

CUDDY BANKS [*aside*] I think she'll prove a witch in earnest. [*Aloud*]
Yes, I could find in my heart to strike her three quarters deep in   235
love with me too.

ELIZABETH SAWYER But dost thou think that I can do't, and I alone?

CUDDY BANKS Truly, Mother Witch, I do verily believe so and,
when I see it done, I shall be half persuaded so too.

ELIZABETH SAWYER It's enough. What art can do, be sure of. Turn to   240
the west, and whatsoe'er thou hearest or seest, stand silent and be
not afraid.

She stamps. Enter the Dog; he fawns and leaps upon her

CUDDY BANKS Afraid, Mother Witch? Turn my face to the west? I
said I should always have a back-friend of her, and now it's out. An
her little devil should be hungry, come sneaking behind me like   245
a cowardly catchpole and clap his talons on my haunches! 'Tis
woundy cold sure. I dudder and shake like an aspen-leaf° every
joint of me.

ELIZABETH SAWYER 'To scandal and disgrace pursue 'em
Et sanctabicetur nomen tuum'.°   250
How now, my son, how is't?

Exit Dog

CUDDY BANKS Scarce in a clean life, Mother Witch. But did your
goblin and you spout Latin together?

ELIZABETH SAWYER A kind of charm I work by. Didst thou hear me?

CUDDY BANKS I heard I know not the devil what mumble in a scurvy   255
base tone, like a drum that had taken cold in the head the last
muster. Very comfortable° words. What were they? And who taught
them you?

ELIZABETH SAWYER A great learned man.

CUDDY BANKS Learned man! Learned devil it was as soon! But what,   260
what comfortable news about the party?

ELIZABETH SAWYER Who? Kate Carter? I'll tell thee. Thou know'st the
stile at the west end of thy father's pease-field. Be there tomorrow
night after sunset and the first live thing thou seest be sure to
follow, and that shall bring thee to thy love.   265

CUDDY BANKS In the pease-field? Has she a mind to codlings already?°
The first living thing I meet, you say, shall bring me to her?

ELIZABETH SAWYER To a sight of her, I mean. She will seem
wantonly coy and flee thee, but follow her close and boldly. Do but
embrace her in thy arms once and she is thine own.   270

CUDDY BANKS At the stile at the west end of my father's pease-land,
the first live thing I see, 'follow and embrace her and she shall be
thine'. Nay, an I come to embracing once, she shall be mine. I'll go
near to make at eaglet else.°
Exit

ELIZABETH SAWYER A ball well bandied! Now the set's half won.   275
The father's wrong I'll wreak upon the son.
Exit

2.2

Enter Old Carter, Warbeck, and Somerton

OLD CARTER How now, gentlemen? Cloudy? I know, Master
Warbeck, you are in a fog° about my daughter's marriage.

WARBECK And can you blame me, sir?

OLD CARTER Nor you me justly. Wedding and hanging are tied up
both in a proverb,° and destiny is the juggler° that unties the knot.   5
My hope is you are reserved to a richer fortune than my poor
daughter.

WARBECK However, your promise—

OLD CARTER Is a kind of debt, I confess it.

WARBECK Which honest men should pay.   10

OLD CARTER Yet some gentlemen break in that point now and then,
by your leave, sir.

SOMERTON I confess thou hast had a little wrong in the wench, but
patience is the only salve to cure it. Since Thorney has won the
wench, he has most reason to wear° her.   15

WARBECK Love in this kind admits no reason to wear her.

OLD CARTER Then love's a fool, and what wise man will take exception?

SOMERTON Come, frolic, Ned. Were every man master of his own fortune, fate might pick straws and destiny go a-wool-gathering.   20

WARBECK You hold yours in a string,° though. 'Tis well, but if there be any equity, look thou to meet the like usage ere long.

SOMERTON In my love to her sister Katherine? Indeed, they are a pair of arrows drawn out of one quiver and should fly at an even length. If she do run after her sister—   25

WARBECK Look for the same mercy at my hands as I have received at thine.

SOMERTON She'll keep a surer compass. I have too strong a confidence to mistrust her.

WARBECK And that confidence is a wind that has blown many a   30
married man ashore at Cuckold's Haven,° I can tell you. I wish yours more prosperous though.

OLD CARTER Whate'er you wish, I'll master° my promise to him.

WARBECK Yes, as you did to me.

OLD CARTER No more of that, if you love me. But for the more   35
assurance, the next offered occasion shall consummate the marriage, and that once sealed—

Enter Frank Thorney and Susan

SOMERTON Leave the manage of the rest to my care. But see, the bride-groom and bride come, the new pair of Sheffield knives fitted both to one sheath.°   40

WARBECK The sheath might have been better fitted if somebody had their due. But—

SOMERTON No harsh language, if thou lovest me. Frank Thorney has done—

WARBECK No more than I, or thou, or any man, things so standing,   45
would have attempted.

SOMERTON Good morrow, master bridegroom.

WARBECK Come, give thee joy. Mayst thou live long and happy in thy fair choice.

FRANK THORNEY I thank ye, gentlemen. Kind Master Warbeck, I   50
find you loving.

WARBECK Thorney, that creature [*aside*] much good do thee with her,
[*aloud*] Virtue and beauty hold fair mixture in her.
She's rich, no doubt, in both. Yet were she fairer
Thou art right worthy of her. Love her, Thorney;   55
'Tis nobleness in thee, in her but duty.

The match is fair and equal, the success
I leave to censure. Farewell, mistress bride:
Till now elected, thy old scorn deride.
            Exit

SOMERTON Good Master Thorney.   60
            [*Exit*]

OLD CARTER Nay, you shall not part till you see the barrels run a-tilt,°
gentlemen.
            Exit

SUSAN Why change you your face, sweetheart?

FRANK THORNEY Who? I? For nothing.

SUSAN Dear, say not so. A spirit of your constancy cannot endure   65
this change for nothing. I have observed strange variations in you.

FRANK THORNEY In me?

SUSAN In you, sir. Awake you seem to dream, and in your sleep you
utter sudden and distracted accents, like one at enmity with peace.
Dear loving husband, if I may dare to challenge any interest in   70
you, give me the reason fully. You may trust my breast as safely as
your own.

FRANK THORNEY With what? You half amaze me. Prithee—

SUSAN Come, you shall not, indeed, you shall not shut me from
partaking the least dislike that grieves you. I am all yours.   75

FRANK THORNEY And I all thine.

SUSAN You are not, if you keep the least grief from me. But I find the
cause: it grew from me.

FRANK THORNEY From you?

SUSAN From some distaste in me or my behaviour. You are not kind   80
in the concealment. 'Las, sir, I am young, silly,° and plain; more,
strange to those contents a wife should offer. Say but in what I fail,
I'll study satisfaction.

FRANK THORNEY Come, in nothing.

SUSAN I know I do. Knew I as well in what, you should not long be   85
sullen. Prithee, love, if I have been immodest or too bold, speak't in
a frown; if peevishly too nice, show't in a smile. Thy liking is the
glass by which I'll habit my behaviour.

FRANK THORNEY Wherefore dost weep now?

SUSAN You, sweet, have the power to make me passionate as an April 90
day; now smile, then weep; now pale, then crimson red. You are
the powerful moon of my blood's sea, to make it ebb or flow into
my face as your looks change.

FRANK THORNEY Change thy conceit, I prithee.
    Thou art all perfection. Diana herself   95
    Swells in thy thoughts and moderates thy beauty.
    Within thy left eye amorous Cupid sits
    Feathering love-shafts, whose golden heads he dipped
    In thy chaste breast. In the other lies
    Blushing Adonis scarfed in modesties.°   100
    And still as wanton Cupid blows love-fires,
    Adonis quenches out unchaste desires.
    And from these two I briefly do imply
    A perfect emblem of thy modesty.
    Then, prithee, dear, maintain no more dispute,   105
    For where thou speakst, it's fit all tongues be mute.
SUSAN Come, come, those golden strings of flattery
    Shall not tie up my speech, sir. I must know
    The ground of your disturbance.
FRANK THORNEY   Then look here,
    For here, here is the fen in which this Hydra°   110
    Of discontent grows rank.
SUSAN   Heaven shield it! Where?
FRANK THORNEY In mine own bosom, here the cause has root.
    The poisoned leeches twist about my heart,
    And will, I hope, confound me.
SUSAN   You speak riddles.
FRANK THORNEY Take 't plainly then. 'Twas told me by a woman,   115
    Known and approved in palmistry,
    I should have two wives.
SUSAN Two wives? Sir, I take it exceeding likely. But let not conceit
    hurt you. You are afraid to bury me?°
FRANK THORNEY No, no, my Winifred.   120
SUSAN How say you? Winifred? You forget me.
FRANK THORNEY No, I forget myself, Susan.
SUSAN In what?
FRANK THORNEY Talking of wives I pretend Winifred,°
    A maid that at my mother's waited on me   125
    Before thyself.
SUSAN   I hope, sir, she may live
    To take my place. But why should all this move you?
FRANK THORNEY [aside] The poor girl, she has 't before thee,°
    And that's the fiend torments me.

SUSAN   Yet why should this
   Raise mutiny within you? Such presages   130
   Prove often false; or say it should be true?
FRANK THORNEY That I should have another wife?
SUSAN   Yes, many;
   If they be good, the better.
FRANK THORNEY   Never any equal
   To thee in goodness.
SUSAN   Sir, I could wish I were
   Much better for you. Yet if I knew your fate   135
   Ordained you for another, I could wish,
   So well I love you and your hopeful pleasure,
   Me in my grave, and my poor virtues added
   To my successor.
FRANK THORNEY Prithee, prithee, talk not
   Of death or graves. Thou art so rare a goodness   140
   As death would rather put itself to death
   Than murder thee. But we, as all things else,
   Are mutable and changing.
SUSAN   Yet you still move
   In your first sphere of discontent. Sweet, chase
   Those clouds of sorrow, and shine clearly on me.   145
FRANK THORNEY At my return I will.
SUSAN Return? Ah me! Will you then leave me?
FRANK THORNEY For a time I must. But how? As birds their young,
   or loving bees their hives, to fetch home richer dainties.
SUSAN Leave me? Now has my fear met its effect. You shall not;   150
   cost it° my life, you shall not.
FRANK THORNEY Why? Your reason?
SUSAN Like to the lapwing° have you all this while with your false
   love deluded me, pretending counterfeit senses for your discontent,
   And now at last it is by chance stole from you.   155
FRANK THORNEY What! What by chance?
SUSAN Your pre-appointed meeting of single combat with young
   Warbeck.
FRANK THORNEY Ha!
SUSAN Even so! Dissemble not, 'tis too apparent. Then in his look I 160
   read it. Deny it not, I see't apparent. Cost it my undoing, and unto
   that my life, I will not leave you.
FRANK THORNEY Not until when?
SUSAN   Till he and you be friends.
   Was this your cunning, and then flam me off

With an old witch, two wives and Winifred? 165
You're not so kind indeed as I imagined.

FRANK THORNEY And you more fond by far than I expected.
It is a virtue that attends thy kind.
But of our business within; and by this kiss
I'll anger thee no more, 'troth, chuck, I will not. 170
    [*Kisses her*]

SUSAN You shall have no just cause.

FRANK THORNEY   Dear Sue, I shall not.
    Exeunt

3.1

Enter Cuddy Banks and Morris-dancers

FIRST DANCER Nay, Cuddy, prithee do not leave us now. If we part all this night, we shall not meet before day.

SECOND DANCER I prithee, Banks, let's keep together now.

CUDDY BANKS If you were wise, a word would serve; but as you are, I must be forced to tell you again: I have a little private business, an hour's work; it may prove but a half-hour's, as luck may serve, and then I take horse along with you. Have we e'er a witch in the morris?

FIRST DANCER No, no; no woman's part but Maid Marian and the hobby-horse.°

CUDDY BANKS I'll have a witch. I love a witch.

FIRST DANCER Faith, witches themselves are so common nowadays that the counterfeit will not be regarded. They say we have three or four in Edmonton, besides Mother Sawyer.

SECOND DANCER I would she would dance her part with us.

THIRD DANCER So would not I, for, if she comes, the devil and all comes along with her.

CUDDY BANKS Well, I'll have a witch. I have loved a witch ever since I played at cherry-pit.° Leave me and get my horse dressed. Give him oats, but water him not till I come. Whither do we foot it first?

SECOND DANCER To Sir Arthur Clarington's first, then whither thou wilt.

CUDDY BANKS Well, I am content. But we must first up to Carter's, the rich yeoman. I must be seen on hobby-horse there.

FIRST DANCER O, I smell him now. I'll lay my ears Banks is in love and that's the reason he would walk melancholy by himself.

CUDDY BANKS Ha! Who was that said I was in love?

FIRST DANCER Not I.

SECOND DANCER Not I.

CUDDY BANKS Go to, no more of that. When I understand what you speak, I know what you say. Believe that.

FIRST DANCER Well 'twas I, I'll not deny it. I meant no hurt in't. I have seen you walk up to Carter's of Cheshunt. Banks, were not you there last Shrovetide?°

CUDDY BANKS Yes, I was ten days together there the last Shrovetide.

SECOND DANCER How could that be when there are but seven days in the week?

CUDDY BANKS Prithee peace! I reckon *stila nova* as a traveller.° Thou understandest as a freshwater° farmer that never sawest a week

beyond sea. Ask any soldier that ever received his pay but in the
Low Countries, and he'll tell thee there are eight days in the week°   40
there hard by. How dost thou think they rise in High Germany,
Italy and those remoter places?

THIRD DANCER Ay, but simply there are but seven days in the week
yet.

CUDDY BANKS No, simply as thou understandest. Prithee, look but in   45
the lover's almanac. When he has been but three days absent, 'O',
says he, 'I have not seen my love these seven years.' There's a long
cut.° When he comes to her again and embraces her, 'O', says he,
'now methinks I am in heaven', and that's a pretty step. He that can
get up to heaven in ten days need not repent his journey. You may   50
ride a hundred days in a caroche, and be further off than when you
set forth. But I pray you, good morris-mates, now leave me. I will
be with you by midnight.

FIRST DANCER Well, since he will be alone, we'll back again and
trouble him no more.   55

DANCERS But remember, Banks.

CUDDY BANKS The hobby-horse shall be remembered. But hark you,
get Poldavis° the barber's boy for the witch, because he can show
his art better than another.
       Exeunt [Dancers]
Well, now to my walk. I am near the place where I should meet I   60
know not what. Say I meet a thief, I must follow him, if to the
gallows. Say I meet a horse, or hare, or hound, still I must follow.
Some slow-paced beast, I hope; yet love is full of lightness in the
heaviest lovers.°
       [Enter the Dog]
Ha! My guide is come. A water-dog. I am thy first man, sculler.°   65
I go with thee. Ply no other but myself. Away with the boat
Land me but at Katherine's Dock,° my sweet Katherine's Dock,
and I'll be a fare to thee.
       [The Dog starts to move]
That way? Nay, which way thou wilt, thou know'st the way better
than I. *[Aside]* Fine gentle cur it is, and well brought up, I warrant   70
him. *[To the Dog]* We go a-ducking, spaniel; thou shalt fetch me the
ducks,° pretty kind rascal.
       Enter a Spirit in the shape of Katherine,
       vizarded; she takes the vizard off

SPIRIT *[aside]* Thus throw I off mine own essential horror,
       And take the shape of a sweet lovely maid
       Whom this fool dotes on. We can meet his folly,   75

But from his virtues must be runaways.
We'll sport with him, but when we reckoning call,
We know where to receive. Th' witch pays for all.
    The Dog barks
CUDDY BANKS Ay? Is that the watchword? She's come. Well, if ever
we be married, it shall be at Barking Church° in memory of thee.   80
Now come behind, kind cur.
            And have I met thee, sweet Kate?
            I will teach thee to walk so late.°
O, see, we meet in metre. What? Dost thou trip from me? O
that I were upon my hobby-horse, I would mount after thee   85
so nimble. 'Stay, nymph, stay, nymph,' singed Apollo.°
            Tarry and kiss me, sweet nymph, stay.
            Tarry and kiss me, sweet.
            We will to Cheshunt Street,
            And then to the house stands in the highway.   90
Nay, by your leave, I must embrace you.
    [*Exeunt Spirit and Cuddy Banks*]
[*Within*] O, help, help! I am drowned, I am drowned!
DOG Ha, ha, ha, ha!
    Enter [Cuddy Banks] wet
CUDDY BANKS This was an ill night to go a-wooing in; I find it now
in Pond's almanac.° Thinking to land at Katherine's Dock, I was   95
almost at Gravesend.° I'll never go to a wench in the dog-days
again. Yet 'tis cool enough. Had you never a paw in this dog- trick?
A mange take that black hide of yours! I'll throw you in at
Limehouse° in some tanner's pit or other.
DOG Ha, ha, ha, ha!   100
CUDDY BANKS How now! Who's that laughs at me? Hist to him.
    The Dog barks
Peace, peace! Thou didst but thy kind neither.° 'Twas my own
fault.
DOG Take heed how thou trustest the devil another time.
CUDDY BANKS How now! Who's that speaks? I hope you have not your   105
reading° tongue about you?
DOG Yes, I can speak.
CUDDY BANKS The devil you can! You have read Aesop's fables,
then. I have played one of your parts then, the dog that catched at
the shadow in the water.° Pray you, let me catechize you a little.   110
What might one call your name, dog?

DOG My dame calls me Tom.

CUDDY BANKS 'Tis well, and she may call me ass, so there's an whole
one betwixt us, Tom-ass. She said I should follow you, indeed.
Well, Tom, give me thy fist: we are friends. You shall be mine ingle.   115
I love you, but I pray you let's have no more of these ducking devices.

DOG Not if you love me. Dogs love where they are beloved. Cherish
me, and I'll do anything for thee.

CUDDY BANKS Well, you shall have jowls° and livers. I have butchers
to my friends that shall bestow 'em, and I will keep crusts and bones   120
for you, if you'll be a kind dog, Tom.

DOG Anything. I'll help thee to thy love.

CUDDY BANKS Wilt thou? That promise shall cost me a brown loaf,
though I steal it out of my father's cupboard. You'll eat stolen
goods, Tom, will you not?   125

DOG O, best of all. The sweetest bits, those.

CUDDY BANKS You shall not starve, ningle Tom, believe that. If you
love fish, I'll help you to maids and soles.° I'm acquainted with a
fishmonger.

DOG Maids and soles? O, sweet bits! Banqueting stuff, those.   130

CUDDY BANKS One thing I would request you, ningle, as you have
played the knavish cur with me a little, that you would mingle
amongst our morris-dancers in the morning. You can dance?

DOG Yes, yes, anything. I'll be there, but unseen to any but thyself.
Get thee gone before. Fear not my presence. I have work tonight.   135
I serve more masters, more dames, than one.°

CUDDY BANKS He can serve mammon and the devil too.°

DOG It shall concern thee and thy love's purchase.
There's a gallant rival loves the maid,
And likely is to have her. Mark what a mischief,   140
Before the morris ends, shall light on him.

CUDDY BANKS O, sweet ningle, thy neuf once again. Friends must
part for a time. Farewell, with this remembrance, shalt have bread
too when we meet again. If ever there were an honest devil, 'twill be
the Devil of Edmonton,° I see. Farewell, Tom. I prithee dog me as   145
soon as thou canst.

    Exit Cuddy Banks

DOG I'll not miss thee, and be merry with thee.
Those that are joys denied must take delight
In sins and mischiefs; 'tis the devil's right.

    Exit the Dog

3.2

Enter Frank Thorney, Winifred dressed as a boy, [weeping]

FRANK THORNEY Prithee no more. Those tears give nourishment
  To weeds and briars in me, which shortly will
  O'ergrow and top my head. My shame will sit
  And cover all that can be seen of me.
WINIFRED I have not shown this cheek in company;°   5
  Pardon me now. Thus singled with yourself,
  It calls a thousand sorrows round about;°
  Some going before and some on either side,
  But infinite behind; all chained together.
  Your second adulterous marriage leads,   10
  That's the sad eclipse: the effects must follow°
  As plagues of shame, spite, scorn and obloquy.
FRANK THORNEY Why? Hast thou not left one hour's patience
  To add to all the rest? One hour bears us
  Beyond the reach of all these enemies.   15
  Are we not now set forward in the flight,
  Provided with the dowry of my sin
  To keep us in some other nation?
  While we together are, we are at home
  In any place.
WINIFRED   'Tis foul ill-gotten coin,   20
  Far worse than usury or extortion.
FRANK THORNEY Let my father then make the restitution,
  Who forced me take the bribe. It is his gift
  And patrimony to me; so I receive it.
  He would not bless, nor look a father on me,°   25
  Until I satisfied his angry will.
  When I was sold, I sold myself again
  (Some knaves have done't in lands, and I in body)
  For money, and I have the hire. But, sweet, no more.
  'Tis hazard of discovery, our discourse,°   30
  And then prevention takes off all our hopes,
  For, only but to take her leave of me,
  My wife is coming.
WINIFRED   Who coming? Your wife!
FRANK THORNEY No, no, thou art here. The woman—I knew
  Not how to call her now, but after this day   35

She shall be quite forgot and have no name
In my remembrance. See, see, she's come.
    Enter Susan
Go lead the horses to the hill's top, there I'll meet thee.°
SUSAN Nay, with your favour, let him stay a little.
  I would part with him too, because he is°   40
  Your sole companion, and I'll begin with him,
  Reserving you the last.
FRANK THORNEY   Ay, with all my heart.
SUSAN You may hear, if it please you, sir.
FRANK THORNEY   No, 'tis not fit.
  Some rudiments, I conceive, they must be,
  To overlook my slippery footings. And so—°   45
SUSAN No, indeed, sir.
FRANK THORNEY   Tush, I know it must be so
  And 'tis necessary. On, but be brief.
    [*He walks away from Susan and Winifred*]
WINIFRED What charge soe'er you lay upon me, mistress,
  I shall support it faithfully, being honest,°
  To my best strength.   50
SUSAN Believe't shall be no other. I know you were
  Commended to my husband by a noble knight.
    [*Winifred bursts into tears*]
WINIFRED O, gods! O, mine eyes!
SUSAN   How now? What ail'st thou, lad?
WINIFRED Something hit mine eye, it makes it water still,
  Even as you said 'commended to my husband'.   55
  Some dor I think it was. I was, forsooth,
  Commended to him by Sir Arthur Clarington.
SUSAN Whose servant once my Thorney was himself.
  That title, methinks, should make you almost fellows,
  Or at least much more than a servant,   60
  And I am sure he will respect you so.
  Your love to him, then, needs no spur from me,
  And what for my sake you will ever do,
  'Tis fit it should be bought with something more
  Than fair entreats. Look! Here's a jewel for thee,   65
  A pretty wanton label for thine ear,°
  And I would have it hang there, still to whisper
  These words to thee, 'Thou hast my jewel with thee'.°
  It is but earnest of a larger bounty

When thou returnest with praises of thy service,   70
Which I am confident thou wilt deserve.
Why, thou art many now besides thyself.
Thou mayst be servant, friend, and wife to him.
A good wife is them all. A friend can play
The wife and servant's part, and shift enough,   75
No less the servant can the friend and wife.
'Tis all but sweet society, good counsel,
Interchanged loves, yes, and counsel-keeping.°

FRANK THORNEY Not done yet?

SUSAN Even now, sir.   80

WINIFRED Mistress, believe my vow. Your severe eye,
Were it present to command, your bounteous hand,
Were it then by to buy or bribe my service,
Shall not make me more dear or near unto him,
Than I shall voluntary. I'll be all your charge,   85
Servant, friend, wife to him.

SUSAN   Wilt thou?
Now blessings go with thee for't! Courtesies
Shall meet thee coming home.

WINIFRED   Pray you, say plainly,
Mistress, are you jealous of him? If you be,
I'll look to him that way too.

SUSAN   Sayst thou so?   90
I would thou hadst a woman's bosom now.
We have weak thoughts within us. Alas,
There's nothing so strong in us as suspicion.
But I dare not, nay, I will not think
So hardly of my Thorney.

WINIFRED   Believe it, mistress,   95
I'll be no pander to him, and if I find
Any loose lubric scapes in him, I'll watch him,
And at my return protest I'll show you all.
He shall hardly offend without my knowledge.

SUSAN Thine own diligence is that I press,   100
And not the curious eye over his faults.
Farewell. If I should never see thee more,
Take it forever.

FRANK THORNEY Prithee take that along with thee,
        Gives [Winifred] his sword
And haste thee to the hill's top. I'll be there instantly.

SUSAN No haste, I prithee, slowly as thou canst.   105
　　　Exit Winifred
　　Pray let him obey me now.
　　'Tis happily his last service to me.°
　　My power is e'en a-going out of sight.
FRANK THORNEY Why would you delay? We have no other
　　Business now but to part.   110
SUSAN And will not that, sweetheart, ask a long time?
　　Methinks it is the hardest piece of work
　　That e'er I took in hand.
FRANK THORNEY　　　　　Fie, fie! Why, look,
　　I'll make it plain and easy to you. Farewell.
　　　Kisses her
SUSAN Ah, 'las! I am not half perfect in it yet.°   115
　　I must have it read over a hundred times.
　　Pray you take some pains, I confess my dullness.
FRANK THORNEY [*aside*] What a thorn this rose grows on! Parting
　　were sweet,
　　But what a trouble 'twill be to obtain it!
　　[*Aloud*] Come.
　　　Kisses her
　　　　　　Again and again. Farewell. Yet wilt return?   120
　　All questions of my journey, my stay, employment
　　And revisitation, fully I have answered all.
　　There's nothing now behind, but nothing.°
SUSAN And that nothing is more hard than anything,
　　Than all the everythings. This request—
FRANK THORNEY　　　　　　　　What is it?   125
SUSAN That I may bring you through one pasture more
　　Up to yon knot of trees. Amongst those shadows
　　I'll vanish from you, they shall teach me how.
FRANK THORNEY Why, 'tis granted. Come, walk then.
SUSAN　　　　　　　　　　　　　Nay, not
　　too fast.
　　They say slow things have best perfection;   130
　　The gentle shower wets to fertility,
　　The churlish storm may mischief with his bounty;
　　The baser beasts take strength, even from the womb,
　　But the lord lion's whelp is feeble long.
　　　Exeunt

3.3

Enter the Dog

DOG Now for an early mischief and a sudden.
    The mind's about it now. One touch from me
    Soon sets the body forward.°
        Enter Frank Thorney and Susan
FRANK THORNEY Your request is out. Yet will you leave me?
SUSAN What? So churlishly? You'll make me stay for ever,   5
    Rather than part with such a sound from you.°
FRANK THORNEY Why, you almost anger me. Pray you, be gone.
    You have no company, and 'tis very early;
    Some hurt may betide you homewards.
SUSAN   Tush! I fear none.°
    To leave you is the greatest hurt I can suffer.   10
    Besides, I expect your father and mine own
    To meet me back, or overtake me with you.
    They began to stir when I came after you;
    I know they'll not be long.
FRANK THORNEY [*aside*] So, I shall have more trouble.   15
        The Dog rubs him
    Thank you for that. Then I'll ease all at once. 'Tis done now, what
    I ne'er thought on. [*Aloud*] You shall not go back.
SUSAN Why, shall I go along with thee? Sweet music!
FRANK THORNEY No, to a better place.
SUSAN   Any place, I.
    I'm there at home where thou pleasest to have me.   20
FRANK THORNEY At home? I'll leave you in your last lodging.
    I must kill you.
SUSAN   O, fine! You'd fright me from you.
FRANK THORNEY You see I had no purpose, I'm unarmed. 'Tis this
    minute's decree, and it must be. Look, this will serve your turn.
        [*He draws a knife*]
SUSAN I'll not turn from it if you be earnest, sir. Yet you may tell me   25
    wherefore you'll kill me.
FRANK THORNEY Because you are a whore.
SUSAN There's one deep wound already: a whore?
    'Twas ever further from me than the thought
    Of this black hour. A whore?
FRANK THORNEY   Yes, I'll prove it,   30
    And you shall confess it. You are my whore.

No wife of mine. The word admits no second.
I was before wedded to another, have her still.
I do not lay the sin unto your charge,
'Tis all mine own. Your marriage was my theft,   35
For I espoused your dowry, and I have it.
I did not purpose to have added murder;
The devil did not prompt me. Till this minute°
You might have safe returned; now you cannot.
You have dogged your own death.
   He stabs her

SUSAN   And I deserve it.°   40
I'm glad my fate was so intelligent.°
'Twas some good spirit's motion. Die? O, 'twas time!
How many years might I have slept in sin?
Sin of my most hatred too, adultery!°

FRANK THORNEY Nay, sure, 'twas likely that the most was past,   45
For I meant never to return to you
After this parting.

SUSAN   Why, then I thank you more.
You have done lovingly, leaving yourself,
That you would thus bestow me on another.
Thou art my husband, Death, and I embrace thee   50
With all the love I have. Forget the stain
Of my unwitting sin, and then I come
A crystal virgin to thee. My soul's purity
Shall with bold wings ascend the doors of mercy,
For innocence is ever her companion.   55

FRANK THORNEY Not yet mortal? I would not linger you,°
Or leave you a tongue to blab.
   [*He stabs her again*]

SUSAN Now heaven reward you ne'er the worse for me.
I did not think that Death had been so sweet,
Nor I so apt to love him. I could ne'er die better   60
Had I stayed forty years for preparation,°
For I'm in charity with all the world.°
Let me for once be thine example, heaven.
Do to this man as I him free forgive,
And may he better die and better live.   65
   She dies

FRANK THORNEY 'Tis done, and I am in! Once past our height,
We scorn the deep'st abyss. This follows now,

To heal her wounds by dressing of the weapon.
Arms, thighs, hands, any place, we must not fail
   He wounds himself
Light scratches, giving such deep ones. The best I can   70
To bind myself to this tree. Now's the storm,°
Which, if blown o'er, many fair days may follow.
   The Dog ties him
So, so, I'm fast. I did not think I could
Have done so well behind me. How prosperous
And effectual mischief sometimes is! Help! Help!   75
Murder, murder, murder!
   [*Exit the Dog.*] *Enter Old Carter and Old Thorney*

OLD CARTER Ha! Whom tolls the bell for?

FRANK THORNEY O! O!°

OLD THORNEY Ah me! The cause appears too soon; my child, my son!

OLD CARTER Susan, girl, child! Not speak to thy father? Ha!   80

FRANK THORNEY O lend me some assistance to o'ertake° this hapless
woman.

OLD THORNEY Let's o'ertake the murderers. Speak whilst thou canst,
anon may be too late. I fear thou hast death's mark upon thee too.

FRANK THORNEY I know them both, yet such an oath is passed   85
As pulls damnation up if it be broke.
I dare not name 'em. Think what forced men do.

OLD THORNEY Keep oath with murderers! That were a conscience to
hold the devil in.

FRANK THORNEY Nay, sir, I can describe 'em;   90
Shall show them as familiar as their names.
The taller of the two at this time wears
His satin doublet white but crimson lined,
Hose of black satin, cloak of scarlet—

OLD THORNEY Warbeck, Warbeck, Warbeck! Do you list to this, sir?   95

OLD CARTER Yes, yes, I listen you. Here's nothing to be heard.

FRANK THORNEY Th'other's cloak branched velvet, black, velvet-
lined his suit.

OLD THORNEY I have 'em already; Somerton, Somerton!
Binal revenge all this. [*To Old Carter*] Come, sir, the first work   100
Is to pursue the murderers, when we have removed
These mangled bodies hence.

OLD CARTER Sir, take that carcass there, and give me this.°
I'll not own her now, she's none of mine.
Bob me off with a dumb show? No, I'll have life.°   105

This is my son too, and while there's life in him,
'Tis half mine. Take you half that silence for't.
When I speak I look to be spoken to.
Forgetful slut!

OLD THORNEY   Alas, what grief may do now!
Look, sir, I'll take this load of sorrow with me.   110
     [*He picks up Susan's body*]

OLD CARTER   Ay, do, and I'll have this. How do you, sir?

FRANK THORNEY   O, very ill, sir.

OLD CARTER   Yes, I think so, but 'tis well you can speak yet.
There's no music but in sound, sound it must be.
I have not wept these twenty years before,   115
And that I guess was ere that girl was born;
Yet now methinks, if I but knew the way,
My heart's so full, I could weep night and day.
     Exeunt

3.4

     Enter Sir Arthur Clarington, Warbeck, and Somerton

SIR ARTHUR   Come, gentlemen, we must all help to grace
The nimble-footed youth of Edmonton,
That are so kind to call us up today
With a high morris.

WARBECK   I could wish it for the best it were the worst now.   5
Absurdity's in my opinion ever the best dancer in a morris.

SOMERTON   I could rather sleep than see 'em.

SIR ARTHUR   Not well, sir?

SOMERTON   Faith, not ever thus leaden, yet I know no cause for't.

WARBECK   Now am I beyond mine own condition highly disposed to   10
mirth.

SIR ARTHUR   Well, you may have yet a morris to help both;
To strike you in a dump, and make him merry.
     *Enter Sawgut the fiddler and the Morris-dancers, all but Cuddy
     Banks*

SAWGUT   Come, will you set yourselves in morris-'ray?° The fore-bell,
second-bell, tenor and great-bell; Maid Marian for the same bell.   15
But where's the weathercock° now? The hobby-horse?

FIRST DANCER   Is not Banks come yet? What a spite 'tis!

SIR ARTHUR When set you forward, gentlemen?

SECOND DANCER We stay but for the hobby-horse, sir. All our footmen
are ready.   20

SOMERTON 'Tis marvel your horse should be behind your foot.°

SECOND DANCER Yes, sir, he goes further about. We can come in at the
wicket, but the broad gate must be opened for him.°

    Enter Cuddy Banks dressed as a Hobby-Horse, and the Dog

SIR ARTHUR O, we stayed for you, sir.

CUDDY BANKS Only my horse wanted a shoe, sir, but we shall make   25
you amends ere we part.

SIR ARTHUR Ay, well said. Make 'em drink ere they begin.

    Enter servants with beer

CUDDY BANKS A bowl, I prithee, and a little for my horse; he'll mount
the better. Nay, give me. I must drink to him, he'll not pledge° else.
[*Drinks*] Here, Hobby.   30

    Holds him the bowl°

I pray you. No? Not drink? You see, gentlemen, we can but
bring our horse to the water; he may choose whether he'll drink
or no.

SOMERTON A good moral made plain by history.

SECOND DANCER Strike up, Father° Sawgut, strike up.   35

SAWGUT E'en when you will, children. Now in the name of the best
foot forward—

    [*Sawgut starts to play his fiddle, but there is no sound*]

How now! Not a word in thy guts?° I think, children, my instrument
has caught cold° on the sudden.

CUDDY BANKS [*aside*] My ningle's knavery; Black Tom's doing.   40

DANCERS° Why, what mean you, Father Sawgut?

CUDDY BANKS Why, what would you have him do? You hear his
fiddle is speechless.

SAWGUT I'll lay mine ear to my instrument that my poor fiddle is
bewitched. I played 'The Flowers in May'° e'en now as sweet as a   45
violet. Now 'twill not go against the hair.° You see, I can make
no more music than a beetle of a cow-turd.

CUDDY BANKS Let me see, Father Sawgut.

    [*He takes the fiddle from Sawgut*]

Say once you had a brave hobby-horse that you were beholding to.
I'll play and dance too. [*Aside to the Dog*] Ningle, away with it. 50

DANCERS [*to Cuddy Banks*] Ay, marry, sir.

    [*Cuddy Banks gives the fiddle to the Dog.*] *The Dog plays the*

morris; [the dancers perform their morris;] which ended, enter a
Constable and officers

CONSTABLE Away with jollity! 'Tis too sad an hour.
Sir Arthur Clarington, your own assistance,
In the King's name, I charge, for apprehension
Of these two murderers, Warbeck and Somerton.   55

SIR ARTHUR Ha! Flat° murderers?

SOMERTON Ha, ha, ha! This has awakened my melancholy.

WARBECK And struck my mirth down flat. Murderers?

CONSTABLE The accusation is flat against you, gentlemen.
Sir, you may be satisfied with this.   60

[He shows his warrant]

I hope you'll quietly obey my power.
'Twill make your cause the fairer.

SOMERTON *and* WARBECK O, with all our hearts, sir.

CUDDY BANKS *[aside]* There's my rival taken up for hangman's meat.
Tom told me he was about a piece of villainy. *[To the dancers]*   65
Mates and morris-men, you see here's no longer piping, no longer
dancing. This news of murder has slain the morris. You that go the
footway, fare ye well. I am for a gallop.

[He gives the fiddle back to Sawgut]

[Aside to the Dog] Come, Ningle.

Exeunt Cuddy Banks and the Dog

SAWGUT (*strikes° his fiddle*) Ay? Nay, an my fiddle be come to himself   70
again, I care not. I think the devil has been abroad amongst us today.
I'll keep thee out of thy fit now, if I can.

Exeunt [Sawgut and the Morris-dancers]

SIR ARTHUR These things are full of horror, full of pity.
But if this time be constant to the proof,
The guilt of both these gentlemen I dare take   75
Upon mine own danger. Yet, howsoever, sir,
Your power must be obeyed.

WARBECK O, most willingly, sir.
'Tis a most sweet affliction! I could not meet
A joy in the best shape with better will.   80
Come, fear not, sir. Nor judge, nor evidence
Can bind him o'er who's freed by conscience.

SOMERTON Mine stands so upright to the middle zone
It takes no shadow to 't, it goes alone.°

Exeunt

4.1

Enter Old Banks and two or three Countrymen

OLD BANKS My horse this morning runs most piteously of the glanders,° whose nose yesternight was as clean as any man's here now coming from the barber's. And this, I'll take my death upon 't, is long of this jadish witch, Mother Sawyer.

FIRST COUNTRYMAN I took° my wife and a servingman in our town of Edmonton threshing in my barn together such corn as country wenches carry to market.° And examining my polecat° why she did so, she swore in her conscience she was bewitched, and what witch have we about us but Mother Sawyer?

SECOND COUNTRYMAN Rid the town of her, else our wives will do nothing else but dance about our country maypoles.

THIRD COUNTRYMAN Our cattle fall, our wives fall, our daughters fall and maidservants fall; and we ourselves shall not be able to stand if this beast be suffered to graze amongst us.

Enter W. Hamluc, with thatch and a link

HAMLUC Burn the witch, the witch, the witch, the witch!

OLD BANKS *and* COUNTRYMEN What hast got there?

HAMLUC A handful of thatch plucked off a hovel of hers; and they say when 'tis burning, if she be a witch, she'll come running in.

OLD BANKS Fire it, fire it! I'll stand between thee and home° for any danger.

[*Hamluc ignites the thatch with the link.*] *As that burns, enter Elizabeth Sawyer*

ELIZABETH SAWYER Diseases, plagues, the curse of an old woman follow and fall upon you!

ALL Are you come, you old trot?

OLD BANKS You hot whore, must we fetch you with fire in your tail?°

FIRST COUNTRYMAN This thatch is as good as a jury to prove she is a witch.

ALL Out, witch! Beat her, kick her, set fire on her!

ELIZABETH SAWYER Shall I be murdered by a bed of serpents? Help, help!

Enter Sir Arthur Clarington and a Justice

ALL Hang her, beat her, kill her!

JUSTICE How now? Forebear this violence!

ELIZABETH SAWYER A crew of villains, a knot of bloody hangmen set to torment me, I know not why!

JUSTICE Alas, neighbour Banks, are you a ringleader in mischief?
　　Fie, to abuse an aged woman!   35
OLD BANKS Woman? A she-hellcat, a witch! To prove her one, we no
　　sooner set fire on the thatch of her house, but in she came running
　　as if the devil had sent her in a barrel of gunpowder; which trick as
　　surely proves her a witch as the pox in a snuffling nose° is a sign a
　　man is a whore-master.   40
JUSTICE Come, come. Firing her thatch? Ridiculous! Take heed, sirs,
　　what you do. Unless your proofs come better armed, instead of
　　turning her into a witch, you'll prove yourselves stark fools.
OLD BANKS *and* COUNTRYMEN Fools?
JUSTICE Arrant fools.   45
OLD BANKS Pray, Master Justice What-do-you-call-'em, hear me but
　　in one thing. This grumbling devil owes me, I know, no good will
　　ever since I fell out with her.
ELIZABETH SAWYER And breakedst my back with beating me.
OLD BANKS I'll break it worse.   50
ELIZABETH SAWYER Wilt thou?
JUSTICE You must not threaten her; 'tis against law. Go on.
OLD BANKS So, sir, ever since, having a dun cow tied up in my
　　backside,° let me go thither or but cast mine eye at her, and, if I
　　should be hanged, I cannot choose, though it be ten times in an hour, 55
　　but run to the cow and taking up her tail kiss (saving your worship's
　　reverence) my cow behind, that the whole town of Edmonton has
　　been ready to bepiss themselves with laughing me to scorn.
JUSTICE And this is long of her?
OLD BANKS Who the devil else? For is any man such an ass to be such   60
　　a baby if he were not bewitched?
SIR ARTHUR Nay, if she be a witch, and the harms she does end in
　　such sports, she may 'scape burning.°
JUSTICE Go, go; pray vex her not. She is a subject, and you must not
　　be judges of the law to strike her as you please.   65
OLD BANKS *and* COUNTRYMEN No, no, we'll find cudgel enough to
　　strike her.
OLD BANKS Ay, no lips to kiss but my cow's ——!°
　　　　　Exeunt [*Old Banks, Hamluc, and the Countrymen*]
ELIZABETH SAWYER Rots and foul maladies eat up thee and thine!
JUSTICE Here's none now, Mother Sawyer, but this gentleman,   70
　　myself, and you. Let us to some mild questions; have you mild
　　answers? Tell us honestly and with a free confession (we'll do our
　　best to wean you from it): are you a witch or no?

ELIZABETH SAWYER I am none!

JUSTICE Be not so furious.   75

ELIZABETH SAWYER I am none. None but base curs so bark at me. I
    am none. Or would I were! If every poor old woman be trod on thus
    by slaves, reviled, kicked, beaten, as I am daily, she, to be revenged,
    had need turn witch.

SIR ARTHUR And you to be revenged have sold your soul to th' devil.   80

ELIZABETH SAWYER Keep thine own° from him.

JUSTICE You are too saucy and too bitter.

ELIZABETH SAWYER Saucy? By what commission can he send my
    soul on the devil's errand more than I can his? Is he a landlord of
    my soul to thrust it, when he list, out of door?   85

JUSTICE Know whom you speak to.°

ELIZABETH SAWYER A man; perhaps no man. Men in gay clothes,
    whose backs are laden with titles and honours, are within far more
    crooked than I am, and if I be a witch, more witch-like.

SIR ARTHUR You're a base hell-hound. And now, sir, let me tell you,   90
    far and near she's bruited for a woman that maintains a spirit that
    sucks her.°

ELIZABETH SAWYER I defy thee.

SIR ARTHUR Go, go. I can, if need be, bring a hundred voices, e'en here
    in Edmonton, that shall loud proclaim thee for a secret and   95
    pernicious witch.

ELIZABETH SAWYER Ha, ha!

JUSTICE Do you laugh? Why laugh you?

ELIZABETH SAWYER At my name, the brave name this knight gives
    me—witch!   100

JUSTICE Is the name of witch so pleasing to thine ear?

SIR ARTHUR Pray, sir, give way, and let her tongue gallop on.

ELIZABETH SAWYER A witch? Who is not?
    Hold not that universal name in scorn then.
    What are your painted things in princes' courts,   105
    Upon whose eyelids lust sits, blowing fires
    To burn men's souls in sensual hot desires,
    Upon whose naked paps a lecher's thought°
    Acts sin in fouler shapes than can be wrought?

JUSTICE But those work not as you do.

ELIZABETH SAWYER   No, but far worse.   110
    These by enchantments can whole lordships change
    To trunks of rich attire, turn ploughs and teams
    To Flanders mares and coaches, and huge trains
    Of servitors to a French butterfly.°

Have you not city-witches who can turn   115
  Their husbands' wares, whole standing shops of wares,
  To sumptuous tables, gardens of stol'n sin;
  In one year wasting what scarce twenty win?
  Are not these witches?
JUSTICE   Yes, yes; but the law
  Casts not an eye on these.
ELIZABETH SAWYER   Why then on me   120
  Or any lean old beldam? Reverence once
  Had wont to wait on age. Now an old woman
  Ill-favoured grown with years, if she be poor
  Must be called bawd or witch. Such so abused
  Are the coarse witches, t'other are the fine,   125
  Spun for the devil's own wearing.
SIR ARTHUR   And so is thine.
ELIZABETH SAWYER She on whose tongue a whirlwind sits to blow
  A man out of himself, from his soft pillow
  To lean his head on rocks and fighting waves,
  Is not that scold a witch? The man of law   130
  Whose honeyed hopes the credulous client draws,
  As bees by tinkling basins, to swarm to him
  From his own hive to work the wax in his;
  He is no witch, not he!
SIR ARTHUR   But these men-witches
  Are not in trading with hell's merchandise   135
  Like such as you are, that for a word, a look,
  Denial of a coal of fire, kill men,
  Children and cattle.
ELIZABETH SAWYER   Tell them, sir, that do so.
  Am I accused for such an one?
SIR ARTHUR   Yes, 'twill be sworn
ELIZABETH SAWYER Dare any swear I ever tempted maiden,   140
  With golden hooks flung at her chastity,
  To come and lose her honour, and, being lost,
  To pay not a denier for't? Some slaves have done it.
  Men-witches can, without the fangs of law
  Drawing once one drop of blood, put counterfeit pieces   145
  Away for true gold.
SIR ARTHUR   By one thing she speaks°
  I know now she's a witch, and dare no longer
  Hold conference with the fury.
JUSTICE   Let's then away.

Old woman, mend thy life, get home and pray.
  Exeunt [Sir Arthur Clarington and Justice]
ELIZABETH SAWYER For his confusion.
  Enter the Dog

         My dear Tom-boy, welcome! 150
I am torn in pieces by a pack of curs
Clapped all upon me, and for want of thee.
Comfort me; thou shalt have the teat anon.
DOG Bow-wow! I'll have it now.
ELIZABETH SAWYER   I am dried up
With cursing and with madness, and have yet 155
No blood to moisten these sweet lips of thine.
Stand on thy hind-legs up. Kiss me, my Tommy,
And rub away some wrinkles on my brow
By making my old ribs to shrug for joy
Of thy fine tricks. What hast thou done? Let's tickle. 160
  [She embraces the Dog]
Hast thou struck the horse lame as I bid thee?
DOG Yes, and nipped the sucking child.
ELIZABETH SAWYER   Ho, ho, my dainty,
My little pearl! No lady loves her hound,
Monkey or parakeet, as I do thee.
DOG The maid had been churning butter nine hours, but it shall not 165
 come.
ELIZABETH SAWYER Let 'em eat cheese and choke.
DOG   I had rare sport
Amongst the clowns i'th' morris.
ELIZABETH SAWYER   I could dance
Out of my skin to hear thee. But, my curl-pate,
That jade, that foul-tongued whore, Nan Ratcliffe, 170
Who, for a little soap licked by my sow,
Struck and almost had lamed it; did not I charge thee
To pinch that quean to th' heart?
DOG Bow-wow-wow! Look here else.
  Enter Anne Ratcliffe mad
ANNE RATCLIFFE See, see, see! The Man i'th' Moon has built a new 175
 windmill, and what running there's from all quarters of the city
 to learn the art of grinding.
ELIZABETH SAWYER Ho, ho, ho! I thank thee, my sweet mongrel.
ANNE RATCLIFFE Hey-day! A pox of the devil's false hopper! All the
 golden meal runs into the rich knaves' purses, and the poor have 180

nothing but bran. Hey derry down! Are not you Mother
Sawyer?

ELIZABETH SAWYER No, I am a lawyer.

ANNE RATCLIFFE Art thou! I prithee let me scratch thy face, for thy
pen has flayed off a great many men's skins. You'll have brave   185
doings in the vacation, for knaves and fools are at variance in
every village. I'll sue Mother Sawyer, and her own sow shall give in
evidence against her.

ELIZABETH SAWYER [*to the Dog*] Touch her.
 [*The Dog rubs against Anne Ratcliffe*]

ANNE RATCLIFFE O, my ribs are made of a paned hose,° and they break.   190
There's a Lancashire hornpipe° in my throat. Hark, how it
tickles it, with doodle, doodle, doodle, doodle! Welcome, sergeants!
Welcome, devil! Hands, hands, hold hands and dance around,
around, around.
 Enter Old Banks, his son Cuddy Banks the Clown, Old
 Ratcliffe, and Country Fellows

OLD RATCLIFFE She's here. Alas, my poor wife is here!   195

OLD BANKS Catch her fast, and have her into some close chamber,°
do, for she's as many wives are, stark mad.

CUDDY BANKS The witch, Mother Sawyer! The witch, the devil!

OLD RATCLIFFE O, my dear wife! Help, sirs!
 [*Old Ratclffe and the Country Fellows*] *carry Anne off*

OLD BANKS You see your work, Mother Bombie.°   200

ELIZABETH SAWYER My work? Should she and all you here run mad,
is the work mine?

CUDDY BANKS No, on my conscience, she would not hurt a devil of
two years old.
 Enter Old Ratcliffe and the [*Country Fellows*]
How now? What's become of her?   205

OLD RATCLIFFE Nothing. She's become nothing but the miserable
trunk of a wretched woman. We were in her hands as reeds in a
mighty tempest. Spite of our strengths away she brake, and nothing
in her mouth being heard but 'the devil, the witch, the witch, the
devil', she beat out her own brains, and so died.   210

CUDDY BANKS It's any man's case, be he never so wise, to die when
his brains go a-wool-gathering.

OLD BANKS Masters, be ruled by me, let's all to a justice. Hag, thou
hast done this, and thou shalt answer it.

ELIZABETH SAWYER Banks, I defy thee.   215

OLD BANKS Get a warrant first to examine her, then ship her

to Newgate. Here's enough, if all her other villainies were
pardoned, to burn her for a witch. You have a spirit, they say,
comes to you in the likeness of a dog; we shall see your cur at one
time or other. If we do, unless it be the devil himself, he shall go   220
howling to the jail in one chain, and thou in another.

ELIZABETH SAWYER Be hanged thou in a third, and do thy worst!

CUDDY BANKS How, father! You send the poor dumb thing howling
to th' jail? He that makes him howl makes me roar.

OLD BANKS Why, foolish boy, dost thou know him?   225

CUDDY BANKS No matter if I do or not. He's bailable, I am sure, by
law. But if the dog's word will not be taken, mine shall.

OLD BANKS Thou bail for a dog?

CUDDY BANKS Yes, or a bitch either, being my friend. I'll lie by the
heels myself before Puppison° shall; his dog-days° are not come yet,   230
I hope.

OLD BANKS What manner of dog is it? Didst ever see him?

CUDDY BANKS See him? Yes, and given him a bone to gnaw twenty
times. The dog is no court foisting° hound that fills his belly full by
base wagging his tail. Neither is it a citizen's water-spaniel, enticing   235
his master to go a-ducking twice or thrice a week whilst his wife
makes ducks and drakes° at home. This is no Paris Garden° bandog
neither, that keeps a bow-wow-wowing to have butchers bring their
curs thither, and when all comes to all they run away like sheep.
Neither is this the Black Dog of Newgate.°   240

OLD BANKS No, goodman son-fool, but the dog of hell-gate.

CUDDY BANKS I say, goodman father-fool, it's a lie.

ALL He's bewitched.

CUDDY BANKS A gross lie as big as myself. The devil in St Dunstan's
will as soon drink with this poor cur as with any Temple Bar°   245
laundress that washes and wrings lawyers.

DOG Bow-wow-wow-wow!

ALL O, the dog's here,° the dog's here!

OLD BANKS It was the voice of a dog.

CUDDY BANKS The voice of a dog? If that voice were a dog's, what   250
voice had my mother? So am I a dog; bow-wow-wow! It was I that
barked so, father, to make coxcombs of these clowns.

OLD BANKS However, we'll be coxcombed no longer; away, therefore
to th' justice for a warrant, and then, Gammer Gurton,° have at
your needle of witchcraft!   255

ELIZABETH SAWYER And prick thine own eyes out. Go, peevish fools!
        Exeunt [Old Banks, Old Ratcliffe and Countrymen]

CUDDY BANKS Ningle, you had like to have spoiled all with your
bowings. I was glad to put 'em off with one of my dog-tricks on a
sudden. I am bewitched, little cost-me-nought, to love thee—a pox,
that morris makes me spit in thy mouth.° I dare not stay. Farewell,   260
Ningle, you whoreson dog's nose. Farewell, witch.

    Exit

DOG Bow-wow-wow-wow.

ELIZABETH SAWYER Mind him not, he's not worth thy worrying.
Run at a fairer game, that foul-mouthed knight, scurvy Sir Arthur.
Fly at him, my Tommy, and pluck out's throat.   265

DOG No, there's a dog already biting's conscience.

ELIZABETH SAWYER That's a sure bloodhound.° Come, let's home
and play.
Our black work ended, we'll make holiday.

    Exeunt

4.2

    Enter Katherine: a bed thrust forth,° on it Frank Thorney
    in a slumber

KATHERINE Brother, brother! So sound asleep? That's well.

FRANK THORNEY No, not I, sister. He that's wounded here,°
As I am—All my other hurts are bitings
Of a poor flea, but he that here once bleeds
Is maimed incurably.

KATHERINE   My good sweet brother,   5
For now my sister must grow up in you,°
Though her loss strikes you through, and that I feel
The blow as deep, I pray thee be not cruel
To kill me too by seeing you cast away
In your own helpless sorrow. Good love, sit up,   10
And if you can give physic to yourself,
I shall be well.

FRANK THORNEY I'll do my best.

KATHERINE   I thank you.
What do you look about for?

FRANK THORNEY   Nothing, nothing;
But I was thinking, sister.

KATHERINE   Dear heart, what?

FRANK THORNEY Who but a fool would thus be bound to a bed   15
    Having this room to walk in?
KATHERINE   Why do you talk so?
    Would you were fast asleep.
FRANK THORNEY   No, no, I'm not idle;°
    But here's my meaning: being robbed as I am,
    Why should my soul, which married was to hers,
    Live in divorce, and not fly after her?   20
    Why should not I walk hand in hand with death
    To find my love out?
KATHERINE   That were well, indeed,
    Your time being come. When death is sent to call you,
    No doubt you shall meet her.
FRANK THORNEY   Why should not I go
    Without calling?
KATHERINE   Yes, brother, so you might,   25
    Were there no place to go to when you're gone,
    But only this.
FRANK THORNEY
                    Troth, sister, thou sayst true,°
    For when a man has been a hundred years
    Hard travelling o'er the tottering bridge of age,
    He's not the thousand part upon his way.   30
    All life is but a wandering to find home.
    When we are gone, we are there. Happy were man
    Could here his voyage end. He should not then
    Answer how well or ill he steered his soul
    By heaven's or hell's compass; how he put in,   35
    Losing bless'd goodness' shore at such a sin;
    Nor how life's dear provision he has spent;
    Nor how far he in's navigation went
    Beyond commission. This were a fine reign;
    To do ill and not hear of it again.   40
    Yet then were man more wretched than a beast,
    For, sister, our dead pay is sure the best.°
KATHERINE 'Tis so, the best or worst, and I wish heaven
    To pay, and so I know it will, that traitor,
    That devil Somerton (who stood in mine eye   45
    Once as an angel) home to his deservings.
    What villain but himself, once loving me,

With Warbeck's soul would pawn his own to hell
To be revenged on my poor sister?
FRANK THORNEY   Slaves!
A pair of merciless slaves! Speak no more of them.   50
KATHERINE I think this talking hurts you.
FRANK THORNEY   Does me no good, I'm sure.
I pay for't everywhere.
KATHERINE   I have done then.
Eat, if you cannot sleep. You have these two days
Not tasted any food. Jane, is it ready?
FRANK THORNEY What's ready? What's ready?   55
          [*Enter Jane, a maidservant, with chicken*]
KATHERINE I have made ready a roasted chicken for you.
Sweet, wilt thou eat?
FRANK THORNEY   A pretty stomach on a sudden; yes—
There's one in the house can play upon a lute.
[*To Jane*] Good girl, let's hear him too.
KATHERINE   You shall, dear brother.
          [*Exit Jane*]
Would I were a musician, you should hear   60
How I would feast your ear.
          A lute plays [*within*]
Stay, mend your pillow and raise you higher.
FRANK THORNEY I am up too high, am I not, sister, now?
KATHERINE No, no, 'tis well. Fall to,° fall to.—A knife. Here's
never a knife. Brother, I'll look out yours.   65
          [*She picks up his coat and begins looking in the pockets.*]
          Enter the Dog, shrugging as it were for joy, and dances
FRANK THORNEY Sister, O, sister, I am ill upon a sudden and can eat
nothing.
KATHERINE In very deed you shall. The want of food makes you so faint.
          [*She finds his knife, still bloody, in his coat pocket*]
Ha! Here's none° in your pocket. I'll go fetch a knife.
FRANK THORNEY Will you? 'Tis well, all's well.   70
          *She's gone, he searches first one, then the other pocket. Knife
          found. Dog runs off. He lies on one side. The Spirit of Susan
          his second wife comes to the bedside. He stares at it, and turning
          to the other side, it's there too.° In the meantime, Winifred, as
          a page, comes in, stands at his bed's feet sadly. He, frighted, sits
          upright. The Spirit vanishes.*

FRANK THORNEY What art thou?

WINIFRED A lost creature.

FRANK THORNEY So am I too.—Win? Ah, my she-page!

WINIFRED For your sake I put on
    A shape that's false, yet do I wear a heart   75
    True to you as your own.

FRANK THORNEY   Would mine and thine
    Were fellows in one house. Kneel by me here.
    On this side now! How dar'st thou come to mock me
    On both sides of my bed?

WINIFRED   When?

FRANK THORNEY   But just now;
    Outface me, stare upon me with strange postures,   80
    Turn my soul wild by a face in which were drawn
    A thousand ghosts leapt newly from their graves
    To pluck me into a winding-sheet.

WINIFRED   Believe it,
    I came no nearer to you than yon place
    At your bed's feet, and of the house had leave,   85
    Calling myself your horse-boy, in to come
    And visit my sick master.

FRANK THORNEY   Then 'twas my fancy.
    Some windmill in my brains for want of sleep.°

WINIFRED Would I would never sleep so you could rest.
    But you have plucked a thunder on your head,   90
    Whose noise cannot cease suddenly. Why should you
    Dance at the wedding of a second wife,
    When scarce the music which you heard at mine
    Had ta'en a farewell of you? O this was ill!
    And they who thus can give both hands away   95
    In th' end shall want their best limbs.

FRANK THORNEY   Winifred,
    The chamber-door fast?

WINIFRED   Yes.

FRANK THORNEY   Sit thee then down,
    And when thou'st heard me speak, melt into tears.
    Yet I, to save those eyes of thine from weeping,
    Being to write a story of us two,   100
    Instead of ink, dipped my sad pen in blood,
    When of thee I took leave, I went abroad
    Only for pillage, as a freebooter,

What gold soe'er I got to make it thine.
To please a father I have heaven displeased.   105
Striving to cast two wedding rings in one,
Through my bad workmanship I now have none;
I have lost her and thee.
WINIFRED   I know she's dead,
  But you have me still.
FRANK THORNEY   Nay, her this hand
  Murdered, and so I lose thee too.
WINIFRED   O, me!   110
FRANK THORNEY Be quiet, for thou my evidence art,
  Jury and judge. Sit quiet and I'll tell all.
          As they whisper, enter at one end of the stage Old Carter and
          Katherine, the Dog at the other, pawing softly at Frank Thorney
KATHERINE I have run madding up and down to find you,
  Being laden with the heaviest news that ever
  Poor daughter carried.
OLD CARTER   Why? Is the boy dead?   115
KATHERINE Dead, sir! O, father, we are cozened. You are told
  The murderer sings in prison, and he laughs here.
  This villain killed my sister. See else, see,
  A bloody knife in's pocket.
OLD CARTER   Bless me, patience!
FRANK THORNEY The knife,° the knife, the knife!   120
KATHERINE What knife?
          Exit the Dog
FRANK THORNEY To cut my chicken up, my chicken.
  Be you my carver, father.
OLD CARTER   That I will.
KATHERINE [*aside*] How the devil steels our brows after doing ill!
FRANK THORNEY My stomach and my sight are taken from me. All 125
  is not well within me.
OLD CARTER I believe thee, boy; I that have seen so many moons clap
  their horns on other men's foreheads° to strike them sick, yet mine
  to scape and be well. I that never cast away a fee upon urinals,° but
  am as sound as an honest man's conscience when he's dying,   130
  I should cry out as thou dost, 'All is not well within me', felt I but
  the bag of thy imposthumes.° Ah, poor villain! Ah, my wounded
  rascal! All my grief is, I have now small hope of thee.
FRANK THORNEY Do the surgeons say my wounds are dangerous then?
OLD CARTER Yes, yes and there's no way with thee but one.   135

FRANK THORNEY Would he were here to open them.

OLD CARTER I'll go to fetch him. I'll make a holiday° to see thee as I wish.

    Exit to fetch officers

FRANK THORNEY A wondrous kind old man.

WINIFRED [*aside*] Your sin's the blacker so to abuse his goodness.
    [*Aloud*] Master, how do you?   140

FRANK THORNEY Pretty well now, boy. I have such odd qualms come
    'cross my stomach. I'll fall to. Boy, cut me.°

WINIFRED [*aside*] You have cut me, I'm sure. [*Aloud*] A leg or wing,
    sir?

FRANK THORNEY No, no, no; a wing. [*Aside*] Would I had wings but   145
    to soar up yon tower.° But here's a clog° that hinders me.

    Enter Old Carter with Susan's body in a coffin°

What's that?

OLD CARTER That? What? O, now I see her; 'tis a young wench, my
    daughter, sirrah, sick to the death, and hearing thee to be an
    excellent rascal for letting blood,° she looks out at a casement and   150
    cries, 'Help, help! Stay that man! Him I must have, or none'.

FRANK THORNEY For pity's sake, remove her. See, she stares
    With one broad open eye still in my face.

OLD CARTER Thou puttest both hers out, like a villain as thou art. Yet
    see, she is willing to lend thee one again to find out the murderer,   155
    and that's thyself.

FRANK THORNEY Old man, thou liest!

OLD CARTER So shalt thou: i'th' jail. Run for officers!

KATHERINE O, thou merciless slave!
    She was, though yet above ground, in her grave   160
    To me; but thou hast torn it up again.
    Mine eyes too much drowned, now must feel more rain.

OLD CARTER Fetch officers.

    Exit Katherine

FRANK THORNEY For whom?

OLD CARTER For thee, sirrah, sirrah! Some knives have foolish posies°   165
    upon them, but thine has a villainous one. Look! O, it is enamelled
    with the heart-blood of thy hated wife, my beloved daughter. What
    sayst thou to this evidence? Is't not sharp? Does 't not strike home?°
    Thou canst not answer honestly and without a trembling heart to
    this one point, this terrible bloody point.   170

WINIFRED I beseech you, sir, strike him no more; you see he's dead
    already.

OLD CARTER O, sir, you held his horses. You are as arrant a rogue as
    he. Up,° go you too.

FRANK THORNEY As you are a man, throw not upon that woman your   175
   loads of tyranny, for she's innocent.

OLD CARTER How! How! A woman? Is't grown to a fashion for women
    in all countries to wear the breeches?

WINIFRED I am not as my disguise speaks me, sir, his page,
    But his first, only wife, his lawful wife.   180

OLD CARTER How! How! More fire i'th' bedstraw?

WINIFRED The wrongs which singly fell upon your daughter,
    On me are multiplied. She lost a life,
    But I a husband and myself must lose
    If you call him to a bar for what he has done.   185

OLD CARTER He has done it then?

WINIFRED   Yes, 'tis confessed to me.

FRANK THORNEY Dost thou betray me?

WINIFRED O, pardon me, dear heart! I am mad to lose thee,
    And know not what I speak; but if thou didst,
    I must arraign this father for two sins,°   190
    Adultery and murder.

      Enter Katherine

KATHERINE   Sir, they are come.

OLD CARTER Arraign me for what thou wilt, all Middlesex knows me
    better for an honest man than the middle of a market-place
    knows thee for an honest woman. Rise, sirrah, and don your
    tacklings;° rig yourself for the gallows, or I'll carry thee thither on   195
    my back. Your trull shall to the jail go with you. There be as fine
    Newgate birds as she that can draw him in. Pox on's wounds!

FRANK THORNEY I have served thee, and my wages now are paid;
    Yet my worst punishment shall, I hope, be stayed.°

      Exeunt

5.1

Enter Elizabeth Sawyer alone

ELIZABETH SAWYER Still wronged by every slave, and not a dog
    Bark in his dame's defence? I am called witch,
    Yet am myself bewitched from doing harm.°
    Have I given up myself to thy black lust
    Thus to be scorned? Not see me in three days!   5
    I'm lost without my Tomalin. Prithee come.
    Revenge to me is sweeter far than life;
    Thou art my raven on whose coal-black wings
    Revenge comes flying to me. O my best love!
    I am on fire, even in the midst of ice,   10
    Raking my blood up till my shrunk knees feel
    Thy curled head leaning on them. Come then, my darling.
    If in the air thou hover'st, fall upon me
    In some dark cloud; and as I oft have seen
    Dragons and serpents in the elements,   15
    Appear thou now so to me. Art thou i' th' sea?
    Muster up all the monsters from the deep,
    And be the ugliest of them. So that my bulch
    Show but his swart cheek to me, let earth cleave
    And break from hell, I care not! Could I run   20
    Like a swift powder-mine beneath the world,°
    Up would I blow it all to find out thee,
    Though I lay ruined in it. Not yet come!
    I must then fall to my old prayer,
    Sanctibiceter nomen tuum.   25
    Not yet come! Worrying of wolves, biting of mad dogs, the
    manges and the—

    Enter the Dog. [It is now white]

DOG How now! Whom art thou cursing?

ELIZABETH SAWYER Thee! Ha! No, 'tis my black cur I am cursing for
    not attending on me.   30

DOG I am that cur.

ELIZABETH SAWYER Thou liest. Hence, come not nigh me.

DOG Bow-wow!

ELIZABETH SAWYER Why dost thou thus appear to me in white,
    As if thou wert the ghost of my dear love?   35

DOG I am dogged, list not to tell thee. Yet, to torment thee, my
  whiteness puts thee in mind of thy winding sheet.
ELIZABETH SAWYER Am I near death?
DOG Yes, if the dog of hell be near thee. When the devil comes to thee
  as a lamb,° have at thy throat!   40
ELIZABETH SAWYER Off, cur!
DOG He has the back of a sheep, but the belly of an otter; devours by sea
  and land.° Why am I in white? Didst thou not pray to me?
ELIZABETH SAWYER Yes, thou dissembling hell-hound!
  Why now in white more than at other times?   45
DOG Be blasted with the news! Whiteness is day's foot-boy, a
  forerunner to light which shows thy old rivelled face: villains are
  stripped naked;° the witch must be beaten out of her cockpit.
ELIZABETH SAWYER Must she? She shall not! Thou art a lying spirit.
  Why to mine eyes art thou a flag of truce?   50
  I am at peace with none: 'tis the black colour,
  Or none, which I fight under. I do not like
  Thy puritan paleness. Glowing furnaces°
  Are far more hot than they which flame outright.
  If thou my old dog art, go and bite such as I shall set thee on.   55
DOG I will not.
ELIZABETH SAWYER I'll sell my self to twenty thousand fiends
  To have thee torn in pieces then.
DOG Thou canst not. Thou art so ripe to fall into hell, that no more of
  my kennel will so much as bark at him that hangs thee.   60
ELIZABETH SAWYER I shall run mad.
DOG Do so. Thy time is come to curse, and rave, and die. The glass of
  thy sins is full, and it must run out at gallows.
ELIZABETH SAWYER It cannot, ugly cur. I'll confess nothing,
  And not confessing, who dare come and swear   65
  I have bewitched them? I'll not confess one mouthful.
DOG Choose, and be hanged or burned.
ELIZABETH SAWYER Spite of the devil and thee, I'll muzzle up my
  tongue from telling tales.
DOG Spite of thee and the devil, thou'lt be condemned.   70
ELIZABETH SAWYER Yes, when?
DOG And ere the executioner catch thee full in's claws, thou'lt
  confess all.
ELIZABETH SAWYER Out, dog!

DOG   Out, witch! Thy trial is at hand.
   Our prey being had, the devil does laughing stand.   75
          The Dog stands aloof. Enter Old Banks, Ratcliffe and Countrymen
OLD BANKS She's here. Attach her. Witch, you must go with us.
ELIZABETH SAWYER Whither? To hell?
OLD BANKS No, no, no, old crone. Your *mittimus* shall be made
   thither, but your own jailers shall receive you. Away with her!
          [*They seize her*]
ELIZABETH SAWYER My Tommy! My sweet Tom-boy! O thou dog!   80
   Dost thou now fly to thy kennel and forsake me? Plagues and
   consumptions—
          Exeunt [*all but the Dog*]
DOG Ha, ha, ha, ha!
   Let not the world witches or devils condemn:
   They follow us, and then we follow them.°   85
          Enter Cuddy Banks to the Dog
CUDDY BANKS I would fain meet with mine ingle once more. He has
   had a claw amongst 'em. My rival, that loved my wench, is like to
   be hanged like an innocent. A kind cur where he takes, but where
   he takes not, a dogged rascal. I know the villain loves me.
          The Dog barks
   No! Art thou there? That's Tom's voice, but 'tis not he. This is a dog   90
   of another hair, this. Bark and not speak to me? Not Tom then.
   There's as much difference betwixt Tom and this as betwixt
   white and black.
DOG Hast thou forgot me?
          [*The Dog barks*]
CUDDY BANKS That's Tom again. Prithee, ningle, speak. Is thy name   95
   Tom?
DOG Whilst I served my old Dame Sawyer 'twas. I'm gone from
   her now.
CUDDY BANKS Gone? Away with the witch then, too! She'll never
   thrive if thou leavest her. She knows no more how to kill a cow, or   100
   a horse, or a sow without thee, than she does to kill a goose.
DOG No, she has done killing now, but must be killed for what she has
   done. She's shortly to be hanged.
CUDDY BANKS Is she? In my conscience, if she be, 'tis thou hast brought
   her to the gallows, Tom.   105
DOG Right; I served her to that purpose. 'Twas part of my wages.
CUDDY BANKS This was no honest servant's part, by your leave,
   Tom. This remember, I pray you, between you and I, I entertained
   you ever as a dog, not as a devil.

DOG True, and so I used thee doggedly, not devilishly. I have deluded 110
  thee for sport to laugh at. The wench thou seekst after thou never
  spakest with, but a spirit in her form, habit and likeness. Ha, ha!

CUDDY BANKS I do not then wonder at the change of your garments,
  if you can enter into shapes of women too.

DOG Any shape to blind such silly eyes as thine, but chiefly those coarse 115
  creatures, dog or cat, hare, ferret, frog, toad.

CUDDY BANKS Louse or flea?

DOG Any poor vermin.

CUDDY BANKS It seems you devils have poor thin souls that you can
  bestow yourselves in such small bodies. But pray you, Tom, one 120
question at parting—I think I shall never see you more—where do
  you borrow those bodies that are none of your own? The garment-
  shape you may hire at broker's.

DOG Why wouldst thou know that, fool? It avails thee not.

CUDDY BANKS Only for my mind's sake, Tom, and to tell some of my 125
  friends.

DOG I'll thus much tell thee. Thou never art so distant
  From an evil spirit but that thy oaths,
  Curses, and blasphemies pull him to thine elbow.
  Thou never tell'st a lie but that a devil 130
  Is within hearing it; thy evil purposes
  Are ever haunted. But when they come to act,
  As thy tongue slandering, bearing false witness,
  Thy hand stabbing, stealing, cozening, cheating,
  He's then within thee. Thou play'st, he bets upon thy part.° 135
  Although you lose, yet he will gain by thee.

CUDDY BANKS Ay? Then he comes in the shape of a rook.°

DOG The old cadaver of some self-strangled wretch
  We sometimes borrow, and appear human.
  The carcass of some disease-slain strumpet 140
  We varnish fresh, and wear as her first beauty.
  Didst never hear? If not, it has been done.
  A hot luxurious lecher in his twines,
  When he has thought to clip his dalliance,
  There has provided been for his embrace 145
  A fine hot flaming devil in her place.

CUDDY BANKS Yes, I am partly a witness to this, but I never could
  embrace her. I thank thee for that, Tom. Well again I thank thee,
  Tom, for all this counsel; without a fee too. There's few
  lawyers of thy mind° now. Certainly, Tom, I begin to pity thee. 150

DOG Pity me? For what?

CUDDY BANKS Were it not possible for thee to become an honest dog yet? 'Tis a base life you lead, Tom, to serve witches, to kill innocent children, to kill harmless cattle, to 'stroy corn and fruit, etcetera.° 'Twere better yet to be a butcher and kill for yourself. 155

DOG Why? These are all my delights, my pleasures, fool.

CUDDY BANKS Or, Tom, if you could give your mind to ducking,° I know you can swim, fetch and carry. Some shop-keeper in London would take great delight in you and be a tender master over you. Or if you have a mind to the game either at bull or bear,° I think I 160 could prefer you to Moll Cutpurse.°

DOG Ha, ha! I should kill all the game, bulls, bears, dogs, and all, not a cub to be left.

CUDDY BANKS You could do, Tom, but you must play fair; you should be staved off° else. Or, if your stomach did better like to 165 serve in some nobleman's, knight's, or gentleman's kitchen, if you could brook the wheel° and turn the spit—your labour could not be much—when they have roast meat, that's but once or twice in the week at most; here you might lick your own toes° very well. Or if you could translate yourself into a lady's arming puppy, there you 170 might lick sweet lips and do many pretty offices. But to creep under an old witch's coats° and suck like a great puppy! Fie upon't! I have heard beastly things of you, Tom.

DOG Ha, ha! The worse thou heardst of me the better 'tis.
Shall I serve thee, fool, at the self-same rate? 175

CUDDY BANKS No, I'll see thee hanged, thou shalt be damned first! I know thy qualities too well. I'll give no suck to such whelps, therefore henceforth I defy thee. Out and avaunt!

DOG Nor will I serve for such a silly soul.
I am for greatness now, corrupted greatness. 180
There I'll shug in, and get a noble countenance,°
Serve some Briarean footcloth-strider°
That has a hundred hands to catch at bribes,
But not a finger's nail of charity.
Such, like the dragon's tail, shall pull down hundreds° 185
To drop and sink with him. I'll stretch myself
And draw this bulk small as a silver wire,
Enter at the least pore tobacco fume
Can make a breach for. Hence, silly fool,
I scorn to prey on such an atom soul.° 190

CUDDY BANKS Come out, come out, you cur! I will beat thee out of the bounds of Edmonton, and tomorrow we go in procession,° and after thou shalt never come in again. If thou goest to

London I'll make thee go about by Tyburn, stealing in by Thieving
Lane.° If thou canst rub thy shoulder against a lawyer's gown   195
as thou passest by Westminster Hall, do; if not, to the stairs°
amongst the bandogs, take water, and the devil go with thee.

Exeunt Cuddy Banks and the Dog, who barks

5.2

*Enter the Justice, Sir Arthur Clarington, Warbeck, [Somerton],
Old Carter, and Katherine*

JUSTICE Sir Arthur, though the bench hath mildly censured your
errors, yet you have indeed been the instrument that wrought all
their misfortunes. I would wish you paid down your fine speedily
and willingly.

SIR ARTHUR I'll need no urging to it.   5

OLD CARTER If you should 'twere a shame to you, for, if I should
speak my conscience, you are worthier to be hanged of the two, all
things considered; and now make what you can of it. But I am glad
these gentlemen are freed.

WARBECK We knew our innocence.   10

SOMERTON And therefore feared it not.

KATHERINE But I am glad that I have you safe.

Noise within

JUSTICE How now! What noise is that?

OLD CARTER Young Frank is going the wrong way. Alas, poor youth!
Now I begin to pity him.   15

[Exeunt]

5.3

*Enter Frank Thorney and [Officers with] halberds. [They pass
over the stage and exeunt.] Enter as to see the execution Old Carter, Old
Thorney, Katherine, and Winifred weeping*

OLD THORNEY Here let our sorrows wait him. To press nearer
The place of his sad death, some apprehensions
May tempt our grief too much, at height already.°
Daughter, be comforted.

WINIFRED   Comfort and I
    Are too far separated to be joined   5
    But in eternity. I share too much
    Of him that's going thither.
OLD CARTER   Poor woman,
    'Twas not thy fault. I grieve to see thee weep
    For him that hath my pity too.
WINIFRED My fault was lust, my punishment was shame.   10
    Yet I am happy that my soul is free
    Both from consent, foreknowledge, and intent
    Of any murder but of mine own honour.
    Restored again by a fair satisfaction,
    And since not to be wounded.   15
OLD THORNEY Daughter, grieve not for what necessity forceth; rather
    resolve to conquer it with patience. Alas, she faints!
WINIFRED My griefs are strong upon me. My weakness scarce can bear
    them.
VOICES [*within*] Away with her! Hang her! Witch!   20
        Enter Elizabeth Sawyer to execution, Officers with halberds,
        and Country people
OLD CARTER The witch, that instrument of mischief! Did not she
    witch the devil into my son-in-law when he killed my poor
    daughter? Do you hear, Mother Sawyer?
ELIZABETH SAWYER What would you have? Cannot a poor old woman
    have your leave to die without vexation?   25
OLD CARTER Did you not bewitch Frank to kill his wife? He could never
    have done't without the devil.
ELIZABETH SAWYER Who doubts it? But is every devil mine?
    Would I had one now whom I might command
    To tear you all in pieces.   30
    Tom would have done't before he left me.
OLD CARTER Thou didst bewitch Anne Ratcliffe to kill herself.
ELIZABETH SAWYER Churl, thou liest, I never did her hurt. Would
    you were all as near your ends as I am, that gave evidence against
    me for it.   35
FIRST COUNTRYMAN I'll be sworn, Master Carter, she bewitched
    Gammer Washbowl's sow to cast her pigs a day before she would have
    farrowed,° yet they were sent up to London, and sold for as good
    Westminster dog-pigs at Bartholomew Fair° as ever great-bellied ale-
    wife longed for.   40
ELIZABETH SAWYER These dogs will mad me. I was well resolved
    To die in my repentance. Though 'tis true

I would live longer if I might, yet since
I cannot, pray torment me not, my conscience
Is settled as it shall be. All take heed   45
How they believe the devil; at last he'll cheat you.

OLD CARTER Thou'dst best confess all truly.

ELIZABETH SAWYER   Yet again?
Have I scarce breath enough to say my prayers,
And would you force me to spend that in bawling?
Bear witness. I repent all former evil;   50
There is no damned conjuror like the devil.

ALL Away with her! Away!

> [*Exeunt Elizabeth Sawyer with Officers.*] *Enter Frank Thorney
> to execution, Officers, Justice, Sir Arthur Clarington, Warbeck
> and Somerton*

OLD THORNEY Here's the sad object which I yet must meet
With hope of comfort, if a repentant end
Make him more happy than misfortune would   55
Suffer him here to be.

FRANK THORNEY   Good sirs, turn from me.
You will revive affliction almost killed
With my continual sorrow.

OLD THORNEY   O Frank, Frank!
Would I had sunk in mine own wants, or died°
But one bare minute ere thy fault was acted.   60

FRANK THORNEY To look upon your sorrows executes me
Before my execution.

WINIFRED   Let me pray you, sir—

FRANK THORNEY Thou much wronged woman, I must sigh for thee
As he that's only loath to leave the world
For that he leaves thee in it unprovided,   65
Unfriended; and for me to beg a pity
From any man to thee when I am gone
Is more than I can hope; nor, to say truth,
Have I deserved it. But there is a payment
Belongs to goodness from the great exchequer   70
Above; it will not fail thee, Winifred.
Be that thy comfort.

OLD THORNEY   Let it be thine, too,
Untimely lost young man.

FRANK THORNEY   He is not lost
Who bears his peace within him. Had I spun
My web of life out at full length, and dreamed   75

Away my many years in lusts, in surfeits,
Murders of reputations, gallant sins
Commended or approved; then, though I had
Died easily, as great and rich men do,
Upon my own bed, not compelled by justice,   80
You might have mourned for me indeed: my miseries
Had been as everlasting, as remediless.
But now the law hath not arraigned, condemned
With greater rigour my unhappy fact
Than I myself have every little sin   85
My memory can reckon from my childhood.
A court hath been kept here where I am found
Guilty. The difference is, my impartial judge
Is much more gracious than my faults
Are monstrous to be named; yet they are monstrous.   90
OLD THORNEY Here's comfort in this penitence.
WINIFRED   It speaks
How truly you are reconciled, and quickens
My dying comfort that was near expiring
With my last breath. Now this repentance makes thee
As white as innocence, and my first sin with thee,   95
Since which I knew none like it, by my sorrow
Is clearly cancelled. Might our souls together
Climb to the height of their eternity,
And there enjoy what earth denied us, happiness.
But since I must survive and be the monument   100
Of thy loved memory, I will preserve it
With a religious care, and pay thy ashes
A widow's duty, calling that end best
Which, though it stain the name, makes the soul blest.
FRANK THORNEY Give me thy hand, poor woman. Do not weep.   105
Farewell. Thou dost forgive me?
WINIFRED   'Tis my part
To use that language.
FRANK THORNEY   O, that my example
Might teach the world hereafter what a curse
Hangs on their heads who rather choose to marry
A goodly portion than a dower of virtues!   110
Are you there, gentlemen? There is not one
Amongst you whom I have not wronged. [*To Old Carter*] You most:

I robbed you of a daughter, but she is
In heaven, and I must suffer for it willingly.

OLD CARTER Ay, ay, she's in heaven, and I am glad to see thee so 115
well prepared to follow her. I forgive thee with all my heart. If thou
hadst not had ill counsel thou wouldst not have done as thou didst;
the more shame for them.°

SOMERTON Spare your excuse to me, I do conceive
What you would speak. I would you could as easily 120
Make satisfaction to the law as to my wrongs.
I am sorry for you.

WARBECK   And so am I,
And heartily forgive you.

KATHERINE   I will pray for you
For her sake, who I am sure did love you dearly.

SIR ARTHUR Let us part friendly too. I am ashamed 125
Of my part in thy wrongs.

FRANK THORNEY   You are all merciful,
And send me to my grave in peace. Sir Arthur,
Heavens send you a new heart. [*To Old Thorney*] Lastly to you, sir;
And though I have deserved not to be called
Your son, yet give me leave upon my knees 130
To beg a blessing. [*Kneels*]

OLD THORNEY Take it. Let me wet thy cheeks with the last
Tears my griefs have left me. O Frank, Frank, Frank!

FRANK THORNEY Let me beseech you, gentlemen,
To comfort my old father. Keep him with ye; 135
Love this distressèd widow, and as often
As you remember what a graceless man
I was, remember likewise that these are
Both free, both worthy of a better fate
Than such a son or husband as I have been. 140
All help me with your prayers. [*To the Officers*] On, on, 'tis just
That law should purge the guilt of blood and lust.
    Exit Frank [*with the Officers*]

OLD CARTER Go thy ways. I did not think to have shed one tear for
thee, but thou hast made me water my plants spite of my heart.
Master Thorney, cheer up, man. Whilst I can stand by you, you 145
shall not want help to keep you from falling. We have lost our
children, both on's the wrong way, but we cannot help it. Better or
worse, 'tis now as 'tis.

OLD THORNEY I thank you, sir. You are more kind than I have cause to
    hope or look for.   150
OLD CARTER Master Somerton, is Kate yours or no?
SOMERTON We are agreed.
KATHERINE And but my faith is passed,° I should fear to be married.
    Husbands are so cruelly unkind. Excuse me that I am thus troubled.
SOMERTON Thou shalt have no cause.   155
JUSTICE Take comfort, Mistress Winifred. Sir Arthur,
    For his abuse to you and to your husband,
    Is by the bench enjoined to pay you down
    A thousand marks.
SIR ARTHUR   Which I will soon discharge.°
WINIFRED Sir, 'tis too great a sum to be employed   160
    Upon my funeral.
OLD CARTER Come, come. If luck had served, Sir Arthur, and every
    man had his due, somebody might have tottered ere this without
    paying fines, like it as you list. Come to me, Winifred; shalt be
    welcome. Make much of her, Kate, I charge you. I do not think   165
    but she's a good wench and hath had wrong as well as we. So let's
    every man home to Edmonton with heavy hearts, yet as merry
    as we can, though not as we would.
JUSTICE Join, friends, in sorrow, make of all the best.
    Harms past may be lamented, not redressed.   170
        Exeunt [all but Winifred]

Epilogue

WINIFRED I am a widow still, and must not sort
    A second choice without a good report,
    Which though some widows find, and few deserve,
    Yet I dare not presume, but will not swerve
    From modest hopes. All noble tongues are free;   5
    The gentle may speak one kind word for me.
        Exit

ADDITIONAL PASSAGES

The following passages, printed in Q (1658), did not form part of the play as it was originally staged in 1621.

1. Argument

The whole argument is this distich:

> Forced marriage murder, murder blood requires.
> Reproach revenge, revenge hell's help desires.

2. Prologue

The town of Edmonton hath lent the stage
A devil and a witch, both in an age.°
To make comparisons it were uncivil
Between so even a pair, a witch and devil.
But as the year doth with his plenty bring   5
As well a latter as a former spring,
So has this witch enjoyed the first, and reason
Presumes she may partake the other season.°
In acts deserving name, the proverb says,
Once good, and ever; why not so in plays?   10
Why not in this? Since, gentlemen, we flatter
No expectation, here is mirth and matter.

THE ENGLISH TRAVELLER

THOMAS HEYWOOD

THE PERSONS OF THE PLAY

PROLOGUE

YOUNG GERALDINE, an unmarried gentleman, Old Geraldine's son;
   a traveller
DALAVILL, a gentleman, Geraldine's friend
ROGER, the clown, Wincott's servant, the clown
WINCOTT, an old married man
WINCOTT'S WIFE, a young woman
PRUDENTILLA, Mrs Wincott's unmarried sister
OLD GERALDINE, a widower, Young Geraldine's father
A GENTLEMAN, Dalavill's companion
BESS, Mrs Wincott's chambermaid
A DRAWER at a Barnet tavern

YOUNG LIONEL, Old Lionel's only son
REIGNALD, the steward of Old Lionel's city house
ROBIN, a servant in Old Lionel's country house
BLANDA, a whore
SCAPHA, an old bawd
RIOTER, a spendthrift
TWO GALLANTS, Rioter's companions
TWO PROSTITUTES, Lionel's guests
OLD LIONEL, a merchant, Young Lionel's father
WATERMEN
TWO SERVANTS of Old Lionel
A USURER
THE USURER'S MAN
MASTER RICOTT, an old merchant; Old Lionel's next-door
   neighbour
THE PREVIOUS OWNER of Old Lionel's house

The English Traveller

Prologue

[Enter the Prologue]

PROLOGUE A strange play you are like to have, for know,
We use no drum, nor trumpet, nor dumb show
No combat, marriage, not so much today
As song, dance, masque, to bombast out a play.°
Yet these all good, and still in frequent use   5
With our best poets. Nor is this excuse
Made by our author as if want of skill
Caused this defect: it's rather his self-will.°
Will you the reason know? There have so many
Been in that kind, that he desires not any   10
At this time in his scene: no help, no strain,
Or flash that's borrowed from another's brain.
Nor speaks he this, that he would have you fear it,
He only tries if once bare lines will bear it.
Yet may't afford, so please you silent sit,   15
Some mirth, some matter, and perhaps some wit.

[Exit the Prologue]

1.1

Enter Young Geraldine and Master Dalavill

DALAVILL O friend,
That I to mine own notion had joined
But your experience. I have the theoric,
But you the practic.

YOUNG GERALDINE   I, perhaps, have seen
What you have only read of.

DALAVILL   There's your happiness.   5
A scholar in his study knows the stars,
Their motion and their influence, which are fixed
And which are wandering; can decipher seas°
And give each several land his proper bounds;
But set him to the compass, he's to seek,°   10
When a plain pilot can direct his course
From hence unto both th' Indies, can bring back°
His ship and charge with profits quintuple.
I have read Jerusalem, and studied Rome,
Can tell in what degree each city stands,   15
Describe the distance of this place from that—
All this the scale in every map can teach—
Nay, for a need could punctually recite
The monuments in either, but what I have
By relation only, knowledge by travel,   20
Which still makes up a complete gentleman,
Proves eminent in you.

YOUNG GERALDINE   I must confess
I have seen Jerusalem and Rome, have brought
Mark from the one, from th' other testimony,°
Know Spain and France, and from their airs have sucked   25
A breath of every language. But no more
Of this discourse, since we draw near the place
Of them we go to visit.

Enter Roger the Clown

ROGER Noble Master Geraldine, worshipful Master Dalavill.

DALAVILL I see thou still remember'st us.   30

ROGER Remember you? I have had so many memorandums from the
multiplicities of your bounties that not to remember you were to
forget myself. You are both most ingeniously and nobly welcome.

YOUNG GERALDINE And why ingeniously and nobly?

ROGER Because had I given your welcomes other attributes than I have   35
the one being a soldier and the other seeming a scholar, I should
have lied in the first and showed myself a kind of blockhead in the last.

YOUNG GERALDINE I see your wit is nimble as your tongue.
But how doth all at home?

ROGER Small doings° at home, sir, in regard that the age of my master   40
corresponds not with the youth of my mistress, and you know cold
January and lusty May° seldom meet in conjunction.

DALAVILL I do not think but this fellow in time may for his wit and
understanding make almanacs!

ROGER Not so, sir; you being more judicious than I, I'll give you   45
the pre-eminence in that, because I see by proof you have such
judgement in times and seasons.

DALAVILL And why in times and seasons?

ROGER Because you have so seasonably made choice to come so just
at dinner-time. You are welcome, gentlemen. I'll go tell my master   50
of your coming.

    Exit Roger

DALAVILL A pleasant knave.

YOUNG GERALDINE   This fellow, I perceive,
Is well acquainted with his master's mind.
O, 'tis a good old man.

DALAVILL   And she a lady,
For beauty and for virtue unparalleled,
Nor can you name that thing to grace a woman   55
She has not in a full perfection.
Though in their years might seem disparity,
And therefore at the first a match unfit,
Imagine but his age and government,°
Withal her modesty and chaste respect,   60
Betwixt them there's so sweet a sympathy
As crowns a noble marriage.

YOUNG GERALDINE   'Tis acknowledged.
But to the worthy gentleman himself
I am so bound in many courtesies
That not the least, by all th' expression   65
My labour or my industry can show,
I will know how to cancel.

DALAVILL   O, you are modest.

YOUNG GERALDINE He studies to engross me to himself
And is so wedded to my company   70

He makes me stranger to my father's house
Although so near a neighbour.

DALAVILL   This approves you°
To be most nobly propertied, that from one
So exquisite in judgement can attract
So affectionate an eye.

YOUNG GERALDINE   Your character   75
I must bestow on his unmerited love
As one that know I have it, and yet ignorant
Which way I should deserve it. Here both come.°

        Enter Old Master Wincott, his Wife, and Prudentilla, her sister

WINCOTT Gentlemen, welcome. But what need I use
A word so common, unto such to whom   80
My house was never private? I expect
You should not look for such a needless phrase,
Especially you, Master Geraldine.
Your father is my neighbour, and I know you
Ever from the cradle. Then I loved your infancy   85
And since, your riper growth bettered by travel.
My wife and you in youth were playfellows
And nor now be strangers; as I take it,
Not above two years different in your age.

WIFE So much he hath outstripped me.

WINCOTT   I would have you   90
Think this your home, free as your father's house,
And to command it as the master on't,
Call boldly here, and entertain your friends
As in your own possessions. When I see't
I'll say you love me truly, not till then.   95
O what a happiness your father hath,
Far above me, one to inherit after him
Where I, heaven knows, am childless.

YOUNG GERALDINE   That defect
Heaven hath supplied in this your virtuous wife,°
Both fair and full of all accomplishments.   100
My father is a widower, and herein
Your happiness transcends him.

WIFE   O Master Geraldine,
Flattery in men's an adjunct of their sex.
This country breeds it, and for that, so far
You needed not to have travelled.

YOUNG GERALDINE   Truth's a word   105
  That should in every language relish well,
  Nor have I that exceeded.
WIFE   Sir, my husband
  Hath took much pleasure in your strange discourse
  About Jerusalem and the Holy Land,
  How the new city differs from the old,   110
  What ruins of the Temple yet remain
  And whether Sion and those hills about
  With their adjacent towns and villages
  Keep that proportioned distance as we read;
  And then in Rome, of that great pyramis°   115
  Reared in the front, on four lions mounted;
  How many of those idol temples stand,
  First dedicated to their heathen gods,
  Which ruined, which to better use repaired;
  Of their Pantheon and their Capitol,°   120
  What structures are demolished, what remain.
WINCOTT And what more pleasure to an old man's ear,
  That never drew save his own country's air,
  Than hear such things related? I do exceed him
  In years, I must confess, yet he much older   125
  Than I in his experience.
PRUDENTILLA   Master Geraldine,
  May I be bold to ask you but one question
  That which I'd be resolved in?
YOUNG GERALDINE   Anything
  That lies within my knowledge.
WINCOTT   Put him to't.
  Do, sister, you shall find him (make no doubt)   130
  Most pregnant in his answer.
PRUDENTILLA   In your travels
  Through France, through Savoy, and through Italy,
  Spain and the Empire, Greece and Palestine,°
  Which breeds the choicest beauties?
YOUNG GERALDINE   In troth, lady,
  I never cast on any in those parts   135
  A curious eye of censure, since my travel°
  Was only aimed at language, and to know.°
  These passed me but as common objects did,
  Seen, but not much regarded.

PRUDENTILLA   O, you strive
  To express a most unheard-of modesty
  And seldom found in any traveller,
  Especially of our country, thereby seeking
  To make yourself peculiar.
YOUNG GERALDINE   I should be loath°
  Profess in outward show to be one man
  And prove myself another.
PRUDENTILLA   One thing more:
  Were you to marry, you that know these climes,
  Their states and their conditions, out of which
  Of all these countries would you choose your wife?
YOUNG GERALDINE I'll answer you in brief. As I observe,
  Each several clime, for object, fare, or use
  Affords within itself for all of these
  What is most pleasing to the man there born.
  Spain, that yields scant of food, affords the nation
  A parsimonious stomach, where our appetites
  Are not content but with the large excess
  Of a full table. Where the pleasingest fruits
  Are found most frequent, there they best content.
  Where plenty flows, it asks abundant feasts,
  For so hath provident Nature dealt with all.
  So in the choice of women. The Greek wantons,
  Compelled beneath the Turkish slavery,°
  Vassal themselves to all men, and such best
  Please the voluptuous that delight in change.°
  The French is of one humour, Spain another,
  The hot Italian, he's a strain from both,°
  All pleased with their own nations. Even the Moor:
  He thinks the blackest the most beautiful.
  And, lady, since you so far tax my choice,
  I'll thus resolve you: being an Englishman,
  'Mongst all these nations I have seen or tried,
  To please me best, here would I choose my bride.
PRUDENTILLA And happy were that lady, in my thoughts,
  Whom you would deign that grace to.
WIFE   How now, sister?
  This is a fashion that's but late come up
  For maids to court their husbands.

140

145

150

155

160

165

170

WINCOTT   I would, wife,   175
  It were no worse, upon condition
  They had my helping hand and purse to boot,
  With both in ample measure. O this gentleman
  I love, nay almost dote on.
WIFE   You've my leave
  To give it full expression.
WINCOTT   In these arms then.   180
     [Wincott embraces Young Geraldine]
  O, had my youth been blessed with such a son
  To have made my estate to my name hereditary,
  I should have gone contented to my grave
  As to my bed, to death as to my sleep.
  But heaven hath will in all things. Once more welcome,   185
  [To Dalavill] And you, sir, for your friend's sake.
DALAVILL   Would I had in me
  That which he hath, to have claimed it for mine own.
  However, I much thank you.
     Enter Roger the Clown
WINCOTT Now sir, the news with you?
ROGER Dancing news, sir, for the meat stands piping hot upon the   190
  dresser, the kitchen's in a heat, and the cook hath so bestirred
  himself that he's in a sweat, the jack° plays music, and the spits turn
  round to't.
WINCOTT This fellow's my best clock. He still strikes true to dinner.
ROGER And to supper, too, sir. I know not how the day goes with you,   195
  but my stomach hath struck twelve, I can assure you that.
WINCOTT You take us unprovided, gentlemen,
  Yet something you shall find, and we would rather
  Give you the entertain of household guests
  Than compliment of strangers. I pray, enter.   200
     Exeunt all but Roger the Clown
ROGER I'll stand to't, that in good hospitality there can be nothing found
  that's ill. He that's a good housekeeper keeps a good table; a good
  table is never without good stools; good stools seldom without good
  guests; good guests never without good cheer; good cheer cannot
  be, without good stomachs; good stomachs, without good digestion.   205
  Good digestion keeps men in good health, and therefore, *[to the*
  audience] all good people that bear good minds, as you love goodness,
  be sure to keep good meat and drink in your houses, and so you

shall be called good men, and nothing can come on't but good, I
warrant you.   210
    Exit

1.2

    Enter two servingmen, Reignald and Robin

REIGNALD Away, you Corydon.°

ROBIN Shall I be beat out of my master's house thus?

REIGNALD Thy master? We are lords amongst ourselves
  And here we live and reign. Two years already
  Are past of our great empire, and we now   5
  Write *anno tertio.*

ROBIN   But the old man lives°
  That shortly will depose you.

REIGNALD   I' th' meantime
  I, as the mighty lord and seneschal
  Of this great house and castle, banish thee
  The very smell o'the kitchen. Be it death   10
  To appear before the dresser.

ROBIN   And why so?

REIGNALD Because thou stink'st of garlic. Is that breath
  Agreeing with our palace, where each room°
  Smells with musk, civet and rich ambergris,
  Aloes, cassia, aromatic gums,   15
  Perfumes and powders? One whose very garments
  Scent of the folds and stables? O, fie, fie,
  What a base and nasty rogue 'tis!

ROBIN   Yet your fellow.

REIGNALD Then let us put a carthorse in rich trappings
  And bring him to the tiltyard.

ROBIN   Prank it, do:°   20
  Waste, riot and consume; misspend your hours
  In drunken surfeits; lose your days in sleep
  And burn the nights in revels; drink and drab;
  Keep Christmas all year long, and blot lean Lent°
  Out of the calendar; all that mass of wealth   25
  Got by my master's sweat and thrifty care
  Havoc in prodigal uses; make all fly,°

Pour't down your oily throats, or send it smoking
Out at the tops of chimneys. At his departure,
Was it the old man's charge to have his windows   30
Glister all night with stars, his modest house
Turned to a common stews, his beds to pallets
Of lusts and prostitutions, his buttery hatch
Now made more common than a tavern's bar,
His stools, that welcomed none but civil guests,   35
Now only free for panders, whores and bawds,
Strumpets and such?
REIGNALD   I suffer thee too long.
What is to me thy country, or to thee
The pleasure of our city? Thou hast cows,
Cattle and beeves to feed, *oves* and *boves*.°   40
These that I keep and in this pasture graze
Are dainty damosellas, bonny girls.
If thou be'st born to hedge, ditch, thresh and plough
And I to revel, banquet and carouse,
Thou, peasant, to the spade and pickaxe, I   45
The baton and stiletto, think it only°
Thy ill, my good. Our several lots are cast
And both must be contented.
ROBIN   But when both
Our services are questioned—
REIGNALD   Look thou to one.
My answer is provided.
                    Enter Young Lionel
ROBIN   Farewell, musk-cat.°   50
        Exit Robin
REIGNALD Adieu, good cheese and onions. Stuff thy guts°
With speck and barley-pudding for digestion,
Drink whig and sour milk, whilst I rinse my throat
With Bordeaux and canary.
YOUNG LIONEL   What was he?
REIGNALD   A spy, sir.
One of their hinds o' th' country, that came prying   55
To see what dainty fare our kitchen yields,
What guests we harbour and what rule we keep,
And threats to tell the old man when he comes.
I think I sent him packing.
YOUNG LIONEL   It was well done.

REIGNALD A whoreson jackanapes, a base baboon,
  To insinuate in our secrets.
YOUNG LIONEL   Let such keep°
  The country, where their charge is.
REIGNALD   So I said, sir.
YOUNG LIONEL And visit us when we command them thence,
  Not search into our counsels.
REIGNALD   'Twere not fit.
YOUNG LIONEL Who in my father's absence should command   65
  Save I, his only son?
REIGNALD   It is but justice.
YOUNG LIONEL For am not I now lord?
REIGNALD   Dominus factotum.
  And am not I your steward?
YOUNG LIONEL   Well remembered.°
  This night I have a purpose to be merry,
  Jovial and frolic. How doth our cash hold out?   70
REIGNALD The bag's still heavy.
YOUNG LIONEL   Then my heart's still light.
REIGNALD I can assure you, yet 'tis pretty deep,
  Though scarce a mile to the bottom.
YOUNG LIONEL   Let me have
  To supper, let me see, a duck—
REIGNALD   Sweet rogue!
YOUNG LIONEL A capon—
REIGNALD   Geld the rascal!
YOUNG LIONEL   Then a turkey—   75
REIGNALD Now spit him for an infidel!
YOUNG LIONEL   Green plover, snipe,
  Partridge, lark, cock and pheasant.
REIGNALD   Ne'er a widgeon°
YOUNG LIONEL Yes, wait thyself at table.
REIGNALD   Where I hope
  Yourself will not be absent.
YOUNG LIONEL   Nor my friends.
REIGNALD We'll have them then in plenty.
YOUNG LIONEL   Caviare,   80
  Sturgeon, anchovies, pickle-oysters. Yes,
  And a potato pie. Besides all these
  What thou think'st rare and costly.
REIGNALD   Sir, I know
  What's to be done, the stock that must be spent°

    Is in my hands, and what I have to do
    I will do suddenly.   85
YOUNG LIONEL   No butcher's meat;°
    Of that beware in any case.
REIGNALD   I still remember
    Your father was no grazier. If he were,
    This were a way to eat up all his fields,
    Hedges and all.
YOUNG LIONEL You will be gone, sir?   90
REIGNALD Yes, and you are i'the way going.
       Exit
YOUNG LIONEL To what may young men best compare themselves?
    Better to what, than to a house new built,
    The fabric strong, the chambers well contrived,
    Polished within, without well beautified,   95
    When all that gaze upon the edifice
    Do not alone commend the workman's craft
    But either make it their fair precedent
    By which to build another, or at least
    Wish there to inhabit? Being set to sale,   100
    In comes a slothful tenant, with a family
    As lazy and debauched. Rough tempests rise,
    Untile the roof, which, by their idleness
    Left unrepaired, the stormy showers beat in,
    Rot the main posts and rafters, spoil the rooms,   105
    Deface the ceilings, and in little space
    Bring it to utter ruin; yet the fault
    Not in the architect that first reared it
    But him that should repair it. So it fares   110
    With us young men: we are those houses made,
    Our parents raise these structures, the foundation
    Laid in our infancy; and as we grow
    In years, they strive to build us by degrees
    Storey on storey higher. Up at height
    They cover us with counsel, to defend us   115
    From storms without; they polish us within
    With learnings, knowledge, arts, and disciplines.
    All that is naught and vicious they sweep from us
    Like dust and cobwebs, and our rooms concealed
    Hang with the costliest hangings: 'bout the walls   120
    Emblems and beauteous symbols pictured round.
    But when that lazy tenant, Love, steps in

And in his train brings Sloth and Negligence,   125
Lust, Disobedience and Profuse Excess,
The thrift with which our fathers tiled our roofs
Submits to every storm and winter's blast,
And, yielding place to every riotous sin,
Gives way without, to ruin what's within.
Such is the state I stand in.   130
    Enter Blanda, a whore, and Scapha, a bawd. [They do not see
    Young Lionel]

BLANDA And how doth this tire become me?

SCAPHA Rather ask, how your sweet carriage and court behaviour
doth best grace you. For lovers regard not so much the outward
habit as that which the garment covers.

YOUNG LIONEL [*aside*] O here's that hail, shower, tempest, storm and gust 135
That shattered hath this building, let in lust,
Intemperance, appetite to vice; withal,
Neglect of every goodness. Thus I see
How I am sinking in mine own disease
Yet can I not abide it.   140

BLANDA And how this gown? I prithee, view me well
And speak with thy best judgement.

SCAPHA What do you talk of gowns and ornaments
That have a beauty precious in itself
And becomes anything?   145

YOUNG LIONEL [*aside*] Let me not live, but she speaks naught but truth,
And I'll for that reward her.

BLANDA All's one to me, become they me or not,°
Or be I fair or foul in others' eyes,°
So I appear so to my Lionel.   150
He is the glass in whom I judge my face,
By whom in order I will dress these curls
And place these jewels, only to please him.
Why dost smile?

SCAPHA To hear a woman that thinks herself so wise speak so foolishly; 155
that knows well, and does ill.

BLANDA Teach me wherein I err.

SCAPHA I'll tell thee, daughter: in that thou knowest thyself to be
beloved of so many, and settlest thy affection only upon one. Doth
the mill grind only when the wind sits in one corner? Or ships only 160
sail when it's in this or that quarter? Is he a cunning fencer that lies
but at one guard, or he a skilful musician that plays but on one string?
Is there but one way to the wood, and but one bucket that belongs

to the well? To affect one and despise all other becomes the precise°
matron, not the prostitute; the loyal wife, not the loose wanton. Such   165
have I been as you are now, and should learn to sail with all winds,
defend all blows, make music with all strings, know all the ways to
the wood, and, like a good travelling hackney, learn to drink of all
waters.

YOUNG LIONEL [*aside*] May I miscarry in my Blanda's love   170
     If I that old damnation do not send
     To hell before her time.

BLANDA I would not have you, mother, teach me aught
     That tends to injure him.

SCAPHA Well, look to't when 'tis too late, and then repent at leisure, as   175
     I have done. Thou seest here's nothing but prodigality and pride,
     wantoning and wasting, rioting and revelling, spoiling and spending,
     gluttony and gormandising. All goes to havoc. And can this hold out?
     When he hath nothing left to help himself, how can he harbour thee?
     Look at length to drink from a dry bottle and feed from an empty   180
     knapsack. Look to't, 'twill come to that.

YOUNG LIONEL [*aside*] My parsimony shall begin in thee
     And instantly; for from this hour, I vow
     That thou no more shalt drink upon my cost
     Nor taste the smallest fragment from my board.   185
     I'll see thee starve i'the street first.

SCAPHA Live to one man? A jest! Thou may'st as well tie thyself to
     one gown; and what fool but will change with the fashion? Yes, do,
     confine thyself to one garment and use no variety, and see how soon
     it will rot and turn to rags.   190

YOUNG LIONEL [*to Scapha*] Those rags be thy reward! [*To Blanda*]
          O, my sweet Blanda,
     Only for thee I wish my father dead
     And ne'er to rouse us from our sweet delight.
     But for this hag, this beldam, she whose back
     Hath made her items in my mercer's books,°   195
     Whose ravenous guts I have stuffed with delicates,
     Nay, even to surfeit, and whose frozen blood
     I have warmed with *aqua-vitae*: be this day
     My last of bounty to a wretch ingrate,
     But unto thee a new indenture sealed   200
     Of an affection fixed and permanent.
     I'll love thee still, be't but to give the lie
     To this old cankered worm.

BLANDA   Nay, be not angry.

213

YOUNG LIONEL With thee my soul shall ever be at peace,
  But with this love-seducer, still at war.   205
      Enter Rioter and two Gallants
SCAPHA Hear me but speak.
YOUNG LIONEL Ope but thy lips again, it makes a way
  To have thy tongue plucked out.
RIOTER   What, all in tempest?
YOUNG LIONEL Yes, and the storm raised by that witch's spells.
  O, 'tis a damned enchantress!
RIOTER   What's the business?   210
BLANDA Only some few words, slipped her unawares.
  For my sake, make her peace.
RIOTER   You charge me deeply.
  Come, friend, will you be moved at women's words,
  A man of your known judgement?
YOUNG LIONEL   Had you but heard
  The damned erroneous doctrine that she taught,   215
  You would have judged her to the stake.
BLANDA   But sweetheart,°
  She now recants those errors. Once more number her
  Amongst your household servants.
RIOTER   Shall she beg,
  And be denied aught from you?
BLANDA   Come, this kiss
  Shall end all former quarrels.
RIOTER   'Tis not possible   220
  Those lips should move in vain, that two ways plead,
  Both in their speech and silence.
YOUNG LIONEL   You have prevailed,
  But upon this condition, no way else:
  I'll censure her as she hath sentenced thee,
  But with some small inversion.
RIOTER   Speak, how's that?   225
BLANDA Not too severe, I prithee. See, poor wretch,
  She at the bar stands quaking.
YOUNG LIONEL [*to Scapha*]   Now, hold up—°
RIOTER How, man, how?°
YOUNG LIONEL Her hand, I mean. And now I'll sentence thee
  According to thy counsel given to her: 230
  Sail by one wind, thou shalt; to one tune sing;
  Lie at one guard; and play but on one string.

Henceforth I will confine thee to one garment
And that shall be a cast one, like thyself,°
Just past all wearing, and thou, past all use,
And not to be renewed till 't be as ragged   235
As thou art rotten.

BLANDA   Nay, sweet!

YOUNG LIONEL   That for her habit.

SCAPHA A cold suit I have on 't.

YOUNG LIONEL   To prevent surfeit,
Thy diet shall be to one dish confined
And that, too, rifled with as unclean hands   240
As e'er were laid on thee.

SCAPHA What he scants me in victuals, would he but allow me in drink.

YOUNG LIONEL That shall be the refuse of the flagons, jacks,
And snuffs, such as the nastiest breaths shall leave.
Of wine and of strong water never hope   245
Henceforth to smell.

SCAPHA   O me, I faint already!

YOUNG LIONEL If I sink in my state, of all the rest
Be thou excused. What thou proposed to her,
Beldam, is now against thyself decreed:
Drink from dry springs, from empty knapsacks feed.   250

SCAPHA No burnt wine, nor hot-waters!

            She swoons

YOUNG LIONEL   Take her hence.

BLANDA Indeed you are too cruel.

YOUNG LIONEL   Yes, to her,
Only of purpose to be kind to thee.
Are any of my guests come?

RIOTER   Fear not, sir,
You will have a full table.

YOUNG LIONEL   What, and music?

RIOTER Best consort in the city for six parts.   255

YOUNG LIONEL We shall have songs, then!

            Rioter whispers [to Young Lionel]

RIOTER By th' ear.

YOUNG LIONEL And wenches?

RIOTER Yes, by th' eye.   260

BLANDA Ha, what was that you said?

RIOTER We shall have such to bear you company
As will no doubt content you.

YOUNG LIONEL   Enter then.
    In youth there is a fate that sways us still
    To know what's good, and yet pursue what's ill.   265
        Exeunt

2.1

Enter Old Master Wincott and his Wife

WINCOTT And what's this Dalavill?

WIFE   My apprehension
Can give him no more true expression
Than that he first appears: a gentleman
And well conditioned.

WINCOTT   That for outward show.
But what in him have you observèd else   5
To make him better known?

WIFE   I have not eyes
To search into the inward thoughts of men
Nor ever was I studied in that art
To judge of men's affection by the face.
But that which makes me best opinioned of him   10
Is that he's companion and the friend
Beloved of him whom you so much commend,
The noble Master Geraldine.

WINCOTT   Thou hast spoke
That which not only crowns his true desert
But now instates him in my better thoughts,   15
Making his worth unquestioned.

WIFE   He pretends
Love to my sister Pru. I have observed him
Single her out to private conference.

WINCOTT But I could rather for her own sake wish
Young Geraldine would fix his thoughts that way   20
And she towards him. In such affinity,
Trust me, I would not use a sparing hand.

WIFE But love in these kinds should not be compelled,
Forced, nor persuaded. When it freely springs
And of itself takes voluntary root   25
It grows, it spreads, it ripens and brings forth
Such an usurious crop of timely fruit°
As crowns a plenteous autumn.

WINCOTT   Such a harvest
I should not be th' ungladdest man to see,
Of all thy sister's friends.

[*Enter Roger the Clown*]

Now, whence come you?   30

ROGER Who, I, sir? From a lodging of largesse, a house of hospitality,
and a palace of plenty; where there's feeding like horses, and drinking
like fishes; where for pints we're served in pottles, and instead of
pottle-pots, in pails; instead of silver tankards we drink out of water
tankards;° claret runs as freely as the cocks,° and canary, like the   35
conduits of a coronation day.° Where there's nothing but feeding
and frolicking, carving and kissing, drinking and dancing, music
and madding, fiddling and feasting.

WINCOTT And where, I pray thee, are all these revels kept?

ROGER They may be rather called wreaks than revels. As I came along   40
by the door, I was called up amongst them, he-gallants and she-
gallants. I no sooner looked out, but saw them out with their knives,
slashing of shoulders, mangling of legs and lancing of loins, till
there was scarce a whole limb left amongst them.

WINCOTT A fearful massacre.   45

ROGER One was hacking to cut off a neck. This was mangling a breast,
his knife slipped from the shoulder, and only cut off a wing. One
was picking the brains out of a head, another was knuckle-deep in
a belly. One was groping for a liver, another searching for the
kidneys. I saw one pluck the soul° from the body (goose that she   50
was to suffer't), another pricked into the breast with his own bill—
woodcock to endure it.

WIFE How fell they out at first?

ROGER I know not that, but it seems one had a stomach° and another
had a stomach. But there was such biting and tearing with their   55
teeths that I am sure I saw some of their poor carcasses pay for't.

WINCOTT Did they not send for surgeons?

ROGER Alas, no; surgeons' help was too late. There was no stitching up
of those wounds where limb was plucked from limb, nor any salve
for those scars which all the plaster of Paris cannot cure.   60

WINCOTT Where grew the quarrel first?

ROGER It seems it was first broached in the kitchen, certain creatures
being brought in thither by some of the house. The cook, being a
choleric fellow, did so touse them and toss them, so pluck them
and pull them, till he left them as naked as my nail, pinioned some   65
of them like felons,° cut the spurs from others off their heels.° Then
down went his spits; some of them he ran in at the throat and out at
the backside. About went his basting-ladle, where he did so besauce
them that many a shrewd turn° they had amongst them.

WIFE But in all this, how did the women scape?   70

ROGER They fared best, and did the least hurt that I saw, but for
quietness' sake were forced to swallow what is not yet digested.°
Yet everyone had their share, and she that had least, I am sure by
this time hath her belly full.

WINCOTT And where was all this havoc kept?   75

ROGER Marry, sir, at your next neighbour's, young Master Lionel,
where there is nothing but drinking out of dry-fats and healthing°
in half-tubs. His guests are fed by the belly,° and beggars served
at his gate° in baskets. He's the adamant of this age, the daffodil°
of these days, the prince of prodigality, and the very Caesar of all   80
young citizens.

WINCOTT Belike then 'twas a massacre of meat, not as I apprehended?

ROGER Your gravity hath guessed aright. The chiefest that fell in this
battle were wild fowl and tame fowl. Pheasants were wounded instead
of alferes, and capons for captains; anchovies stood for ensigns, and   85
caviar for corporals. Dishes were assaulted instead of ditches,° and
rabbits were cut to pieces upon the ravelins. Some lost their legs, whilst
other of their wings were forced to fly.° The pioneer undermined
nothing but pie-crust, and—

WINCOTT Enough, enough; your wit hath played too long   90
Upon our patience. Wife, it grieves me much
Both for the young and old man; the one greys
His head with care, endures the parching heat
And biting cold, the terrors of the lands
And fears at sea in travel, only to gain   95
Some competent estate to leave his son.
Whiles all that merchandise through gulfs, cross-tides,
Pirates, and storms he brings so far, th'other
Here shipwrecks in the harbour.

WIFE   'Tis the care
Of fathers, and the weakness incident   100
To young that wants experience.°

        Enter Young Geraldine, Dalavill and Prudentilla,
        laughing

ROGER I was at the beginning of the battle, but here comes some that
it seems were at the rifling of the dead carcasses, for by their mirth
they have had part of the spoil.

WINCOTT You are pleasant, gentlemen. What, I entreat,   105
Might be the subject of your pleasant sport?
It promiseth some pleasure.

PRUDENTILLA   If their recreation
  Be, as I make no question, on truth grounded,
  'Twill beget sudden laughter.
WIFE   What's the project?
DALAVILL Who shall relate it?
WINCOTT   Master Geraldine,   110
  If there be anything can please my ear
  With pleasant sounds, your tongue must be the instrument
  On which the string must strike.
DALAVILL   Be't his, then.
PRUDENTILLA Nay, hear it, 'tis a good one.
WIFE   We entreat you,
  Possess us o' th' novel.
WINCOTT   Speak, good sir.°   115
YOUNG GERALDINE I shall, then, with a kind of barbarism
  Shadow a jest that asks a smoother tongue,
  For in my poor discourse, I do protest,
  'Twill but lose his lustre.
WIFE   You are modest.
WINCOTT However, speak, I pray; for my sake do't.   120
ROGER [aside] This is like a hasty pudding, longer in eating than it
  was in making.
YOUNG GERALDINE Then thus it was: this gentleman and I
  Passed but just now by your next neighbour's house,
  Where, as they say, dwells one young Lionel.   125
ROGER Where I was tonight at supper.
WINCOTT An unthrift youth, his father now at sea.
YOUNG GERALDINE Why, that's the very subject upon which
  It seems this jest is grounded. There this night
  Was a great feast.
ROGER   Why, so I told you, sir.   130
WINCOTT Be thou still dumb. 'Tis he that I would hear.
YOUNG GERALDINE In the height of their carousing, all their brains
  Warmed with the heat of wine, discourse was offered
  Of ships, and storms at sea; when suddenly,
  Out of his giddy wildness, one conceives   135
  The room wherein they quaffed to be a pinnace,
  Moving and floating, and the confused noise
  To be the murmuring winds, gusts, mariners;
  That their unsteadfast footing did proceed
  From rocking of the vessel. This conceived,   140

Each one begins to apprehend the danger
And to look out for safety. 'Fly', saith one,
'Up to the main-top, and discover.' He°
Climbs by the bed-post to the tester, there
Reports a turbulent sea and tempest towards,°   145
And wills them, if they'll save their ship and lives,
To cast their lading overboard. At this
All fall to work, and hoist into the street,
As to the sea, what next come to their hand:
Stools, tables, trestles, trenchers, bedsteads, cups,   150
Pots, plate, and glasses. Here a fellow whistles;
They take him for the boatswain. One lies struggling
Upon the floor, as if he swum for life.
A third takes the bass viol for the cock-boat,
Sits in the belly on't, labours and rows,   155
His oar the stick with which the fiddler played.
A fourth bestrides his fellows, thinking to scape
As did Arion on the dolphin's back,°
Still fumbling on a gittern.

ROGER   Excellent sport.

WINCOTT But what was the conclusion?

YOUNG GERALDINE   The rude multitude,   160
Watching without, and gaping for the spoil
Cast from the windows, went by th' ears about it.
The constable is called to atone the broil,°
Which done, and hearing such a noise within,
Of imminent shipwreck, enters the house and finds them   165
In this confusion. They adore his staff
And think it Neptune's trident, and that he
Comes with his Tritons (so they called his watch)
To calm the tempest and appease the waves;
And at this point we left them.   170

ROGER Come what will, I'll steal out of doors and see the end of it,
that's certain.

    Exit Roger

WINCOTT Thanks, Master Geraldine, for this discourse.
In troth, it hath much pleased me, but the night
Begins to grow fast on us. For your parts   175
You are all young, and you may sit up late.
My eyes begin to summon me to sleep,
And nothing's more offensive unto age

Than to watch long and late.

YOUNG GERALDINE   Now good rest with you.
     [*Exit Wincott*]

DALAVILL What says fair Prudentilla? Maids and widows   180
     And we young bachelors, such as indeed
     Are forced to lie in solitary beds
     And sleep without disturbance, we methinks
     Should desire later hours, when married wives,
     That in their amorous arms hug their delights,   185
     To often wakings subject, their more haste
     May better be excused.

PRUDENTILLA   How can you,
     That are, as you confess, a single man,
     Enter so far into these mystical secrets
     Of marriage, which as yet you never proved?   190

DALAVILL There's, lady, an instinct innate in man
     Which prompts us to the apprehensions
     Of th' uses we were born to, such we are
     Aptest to learn, ambitious most to know,
     Of which our chief is marriage.

PRUDENTILLA   What you men   195
     Most meditate, we women seldom dream of.

DALAVILL When dream maids most?

PRUDENTILLA When think you?

DALAVILL When you lie upon your backs. Come, come, your ear.
     Exeunt Dalavill and Prudentilla

YOUNG GERALDINE We now are left alone.   200

WIFE Why, say we be; who should be jealous of us?
     This is not first of many hundred nights
     That we two have been private; from the first
     Of our acquaintance, when our tongues but clipped
     Our mother's-tongue and could not speak it plain,   205
     We knew each other. As in stature, so
     Increased our sweet society. Since your travel°
     And my late marriage, through my husband's love
     Midnight hath been as mid-day, and my bedchamber
     As free to you as your own father's house,   210
     And you as welcome to't.

YOUNG GERALDINE   I must confess
     It is in you your noble courtesy,
     In him a more than common confidence,
     And in this age can scarce find precedent.

WIFE Most true; it is withal an argument   215
    That both our virtues are so deep impressed
    In his good thoughts, he knows we cannot err.
YOUNG GERALDINE A villain were he to deceive such trust,°
    Or (were there one) a much worse character.
WIFE And she no less, whom either beauty, youth,   220
    Time, place or opportunity could tempt
    To injure such a husband.
YOUNG GERALDINE   You deserve,
    Even for his sake, to be forever young,
    And he for yours, to have his youth renewed,
    So mutual is your true conjugal love.   225
    Yet had the Fates so pleased—
WIFE   I know your meaning.
    It was once voiced that we two should have matched.
    The world so thought, and many tongues so spake.
    But heaven hath now disposed us otherways,
    And being as it is (a thing in me   230
    Which, I protest, was never wished nor sought)
    Now done, I not repent it.
YOUNG GERALDINE   In those times,
    Of all the treasures of my hopes and love
    You were th' exchequer, they were stored in you;
    And had not my unfortunate travel crossed them,   235
    They had been here reserved still.
WIFE   Troth, they had;
    I should have been your trusty treasurer.
YOUNG GERALDINE However, let us love still, I entreat:
    That neighbourhood and breeding will allow.
    So much the laws divine and human both   240
    'Twixt brother and a sister will approve;
    Heaven then forbid that they should limit us
    Wish well to one another.
WIFE   If they should not,
    We might proclaim they were not charitable,
    Which were a deadly sin but to conceive.   245
YOUNG GERALDINE Will you resolve me one thing?
WIFE   As to one
    That in my bosom hath a second place
    Next my dear husband.
YOUNG GERALDINE   That's the thing I crave,
    And only that: to have a place next him.

WIFE Presume on that already. But perhaps   250
  You mean to stretch it further?
YOUNG GERALDINE   Only thus far:
  Your husband's old, to whom my soul doth wish
  A Nestor's age, so much he merits from me.
  Yet if (as proof and Nature daily teach
  Men cannot always live, especially   255
  Such as are old and crazed) he be called hence,°
  Fairly, in full maturity of time,
  And we two be reserved to after life,°
  Will you confer your widowhood on me?
WIFE You ask the thing I was about to beg.   260
  Your tongue hath spake mine own thoughts.
YOUNG GERALDINE   Vow to that.
WIFE As I hope mercy.
YOUNG GERALDINE   'Tis enough; that word
  Alone instates me happy. Now, so please you,
  We will divide, you to your private chamber,
  I to find out my friend.
WIFE   Nay, Master Geraldine   265
  One ceremony rests yet unperformed.
  My vow is past, your oath must next proceed,
  And as you covet to be sure of me
  Of you I would be certain.
YOUNG GERALDINE   Make ye doubt?
WIFE No doubt. But love's still jealous, and in that   270
  To be excused. You, then, shall swear by heaven,
  And as in all your future acts you hope
  To thrive and prosper, as the day may yield
  Comfort, or the night rest, as you would keep
  Entire the honour of your father's house   275
  And free your name from scandal and reproach,
  By all the goodness that you hope to enjoy
  Or ill to shun—
YOUNG GERALDINE You charge me deeply, lady.
WIFE Till that day come, you shall reserve yourself
  A single man, converse nor company   280
  With any woman, contract nor combine
  With maid or widow; which expected hour,
  As I do wish not haste, so when it happens

It shall not come unwelcome. You hear all.
Vow this.   285
YOUNG GERALDINE By all that you have said, I swear,
  And by this kiss confirm.
WIFE   You're now my brother,
  But then, my second husband.
      Exeunt

2.2

*Enter Young Lionel, Rioter, Blanda, Scapha, two gallants and
two wenches, as newly waked from sleep*
YOUNG LIONEL We had a stormy night on't.
BLANDA   The wine still works,
  And with the little rest they have took tonight
  They are scarce come to themselves.
YOUNG LIONEL   Now 'tis a calm,
  Thanks to those gentle sea-gods that have brought us
  To this safe harbour. Can you tell their names?   5
SCAPHA He with the painted staff I heard you call Neptune.
YOUNG LIONEL The dreadful god of seas,
  Upon whose back ne'er stuck March fleas.
FIRST GALLANT One with the bill keeps Neptune's porpoises,
  So Ovid says in's *Metamorphoses*.°   10
SECOND GALLANT A third the learned poets write on,
  And as they say, his name is Triton.
YOUNG LIONEL These are the marine gods to whom my father
  In his long voyage prays, too. Cannot they,
  That brought us to our haven, bury him   15
  In their abyss? For if he safe arrive,
  I, with these sailors, sirens and what not,
  Am sure here to be shipwrecked.
FIRST WENCH [*to Rioter*]   Stand up stiff.°
RIOTER But that the ship so totters; I shall fall.
FIRST WENCH If thou fall, I'll fall with thee.
RIOTER   Now I sink,   20
  And, as I dive and drown, thus by degrees
  I'll pluck thee to the bottom.°
      They fall. Enter Reignald

YOUNG LIONEL Amain for England! See, see,
   The Spaniard now strikes sail.
REIGNALD   So must you all.°
FIRST GALLANT Whence is your ship? From the Bermudas?   25
REIGNALD Worse, I think: from Hell.
   We are lost, split, shipwrecked, and undone;
   This place is a mere quicksands.
SECOND GALLANT   So we feared.
REIGNALD Where's my young master?
YOUNG LIONEL   Here man. Speak: the news?
REIGNALD The news is, I, and you—   30
YOUNG LIONEL What?
REIGNALD She, and all these—
BLANDA I?
REIGNALD We, and all ours, are in one turbulent sea
   Of fear, despair, disaster and mischance   35
   Swallowed. Your father, sir—
YOUNG LIONEL   Why, what of him?
REIGNALD He is—O, I want breath—
YOUNG LIONEL   Where?
REIGNALD Landed, and at hand.
YOUNG LIONEL Upon what coast? Who saw him?
REIGNALD   I, these eyes.
YOUNG LIONEL O heaven, what shall I do, then?
REIGNALD   Ask ye me   40
   What shall become of you that have not yet
   Had time of study to dispose myself?
   I say again, I was upon the quay,
   I saw him land and this way bend his course.
     [*Sees Rioter on the ground*]
   What drunkard's this, that can outsleep a storm   45
   Which threatens all our ruins? Wake him.
BLANDA Ho, Rioter, awake!
RIOTER   Yes, I am 'wake.
   How dry hath this salt water made me. Boy,
   Give me th' other glass.
YOUNG LIONEL   Arise, I say.
   My father's come from sea.
RIOTER   If he be come,   50
   Bid him be gone again.
REIGNALD   Can you trifle

At such a time, when your inventions, brains,
Wits, plots, devices, stratagems and all
Should be at one in action? Each of you
That love your safeties, lend your helping hands,   55
Women and all, to take this drunkard hence
And to bestow him elsewhere.
BLANDA   Lift, for heaven's sake!
          [*Young Lionel, Blanda, Scapha, the Gallants, and the Wenches*]
          carry Rioter in.
REIGNALD But what am I the nearer? Were all these
Conveyed to sundry places, and unseen,
The stain of our disorders still remain,   60
Of which the house will witness, and the old man
Must find when he enters; and for these
I am here left to answer.
          Enter [*Young Lionel, Blanda, and Scapha*]
                              What, is he gone?
YOUNG LIONEL But whither? But into the self-same house
That harbours him, my father's, where we all   65
Attend from him surprisal.
REIGNALD   I will make
That prison of your fears your sanctuary.
Go, get you in together.
YOUNG LIONEL   To this house?
REIGNALD Your father's, with your sweetheart, these and all.
Nay, no more words, but do't.
BLANDA   That were   70
To betray us to his fury.
REIGNALD   I have't here
To bail you hence at pleasure. And in th' interim
I'll make this supposed jail to you as safe
From th' injured old man's just incensèd spleen
As were you now together i' th' Low Countries,   75
Virginia, or i' th' Indies.
BLANDA   Present fear
Bids us to yield unto the faint belief
Of the least hopèd safety.
REIGNALD   Will you in?
YOUNG LIONEL, BLANDA *and* SCAPHA
By thee we will be counselled.
          [*Exeunt Blanda and Scapha*]

REIGNALD   Shut them fast.

YOUNG LIONEL And thou and I to leave them?

REIGNALD   No such thing,   80
  For you shall bear your sweetheart company,
  And help to cheer the rest.

YOUNG LIONEL   And so thou
  Meanest to escape alone?

REIGNALD   Rather, without
  I'll stand a champion for you all within.
  Will you be swayed? One thing in any case   85
  I must advise: the gates bolted and locked,
  See that 'mongst you no living voice be heard,
  No, not so much as a dog to howl
  Or cat to mew. All silence: that I charge,
  As if this were a mere forsaken house   90
  And none did there inhabit.

YOUNG LIONEL   Nothing else?

REIGNALD And though the old man thunder at the gates
  As if he meant to ruin what he had reared,
  None, on their lives, to answer.

YOUNG LIONEL   'Tis my charge.
  Remains there nothing else?

REIGNALD   Only the key,   95
  For I must play the jailer for your durance,
  To be the Mercury in your release.°

YOUNG LIONEL Me and my hope I in this key deliver
  To thy safe trust.
        [*He gives Reignald the key*]

REIGNALD   When you are fast, you are safe.
        [*Young Lionel goes in; Reignald locks the door behind him*]
  And with this turn 'tis done. What fools are these,   100
  To trust their ruined fortunes to his hands
  That hath betrayed his own, and make themselves
  Prisoner to one deserves to lie for all,°
  As being cause of all! And yet something prompts me,
  I'll stand it at all dangers, and to recompense   105
  The many wrongs unto the young man done,
  Now if I can doubly delude the old—
  My brain, about it, then. All's hushed within;
  The noise that shall be, I must make without,
  And he, that part for gain and part for wit   110

So far hath travelled, strive to fool at home.
Which to effect, art must with knavery join
And smooth dissembling meet with impudence.
I'll do my best, and howsoe'er it prove
My praise or shame, 'tis but a servant's love.   115
    [*Reignald withdraws.*] *Enter Old Lionel like a civil merchant,*
    with Watermen and Two Servants with burdens and caskets
OLD LIONEL [*to a Servant*] Discharge these honest sailors that have
    brought
Our chests ashore, and pray them have a care
Those merchandise be safe we left aboard.
As heaven hath blessed us with a fortunate voyage,
In which we bring home riches with our healths,   120
So let not us prove niggards in our store.
See them paid well and to their full content.
FIRST SERVANT I shall, sir.
OLD LIONEL   Then return.
    [*Exit First Servant and Watermen*]
                      These special things
And of most value we'll not trust aboard.
Methinks they are not safe till they see home   125
And there repose where we will rest ourselves
And bid farewell to travel; for I vow
After this hour no more to trust the seas
Nor throw me to such danger.
REIGNALD [*aside*]   I could wish
You had took your leave o' th' land, too.   130
OLD LIONEL And now it much rejoiceth me to think
What a most sudden welcome I shall bring
Both to my friends and private family.
    [*Enter First Servant*]
REIGNALD [*aside*] O, but how much more welcome had he been
That had brought certain tidings of thy death.   135
OLD LIONEL But soft, what's this? My own gates shut upon me
And bar their master entrance? Who's within there?
    Knocks aloud°
How, no man speak? Are all asleep, or dead,
That no soul stirs to open?
    [*Reignald comes forward*]
REIGNALD What madman's that who, weary of his life,   140
Dares once lay hand on these accursèd gates?

OLD LIONEL Who's that? My servant Reignald.
REIGNALD   My old master,
  Most glad I am to see you. Are you well, sir?
OLD LIONEL Thou seest I am.
REIGNALD   But are you sure you are?
  Feel you no change about you? Pray you, stand off.   145
OLD LIONEL What strange and unexpected greeting's this
  That thus a man may knock at his own gates,
  Beat with his hands and feet and call thus loud,
  And no man give him entrance?
REIGNALD   Said you, sir,
  Did your hand touch that hammer?
OLD LIONEL   Why, whose else°   150
REIGNALD But are you sure you touched it?
OLD LIONEL   How else, I prithee,
  Could I have made this noise?
REIGNALD   You touched it, then?
OLD LIONEL I tell thee yet, I did.
REIGNALD   O, for the love I bear you—
  O, me most miserable! You, for your own sake,
  Of all alive most wretched! Did you touch it?   155
OLD LIONEL Why, say I did?
REIGNALD   You have then a sin committed
  No sacrifice can expiate to the dead.
  But yet I hope you did not.
OLD LIONEL   'Tis past hope,
  The deed is done, and I repent it not.
REIGNALD You and all yours will do 't. In this one rashness   160
  You have undone us all. Pray be not desperate,
  But first thank heaven that you have escaped thus well.
  Come from the gate.
      [*Old Lionel moves away*]
          Yet further.
      [*Old Lionel moves a little further away*]
          Further yet,
  And tempt your fate no more. Command your servants
  Give off and come no nearer. They are ignorant   165
  And do not know the danger, therefore pity
  That they should perish in 't. 'Tis full seven months
  Since any of your house durst once set foot
  Over that threshold.

OLD LIONEL   Prithee, speak the cause.

REIGNALD First look about: beware that no man hear.   170
  Command these to remove.

OLD LIONEL   Begone.
    Exeunt Servants

                              Now speak.

REIGNALD O, sir, this house is grown prodigious,
  Fatal, disastrous unto you and yours.

OLD LIONEL What fatal? What disastrous?

REIGNALD Some host that hath been owner of this house   175
  In it his guest hath slain, and we suspect
  'Twas he of whom you bought it.

OLD LIONEL   How came this
  Discovered to you first?

REIGNALD   I'll tell you, sir.
  But further from the gate. Your son one night
  Supped late abroad, I within. O, that night   180
  I never shall forget. Being safe got home,
  I saw him in his chamber laid to rest,
  And after went to mine, and being drowsy,
  Forgot by chance to put the candle out.
  Being dead asleep, your son affrighted calls   185
  So loud that I soon wakened, brought in light
  And found him almost drowned in fearful sweat.
  Amazed to see 't, I did demand the cause,
  Who told me that this murdered ghost appeared,
  His body gashed and all o'erstruck with wounds,   190
  And spake to him as follows.

OLD LIONEL   O, proceed,
  'Tis that I long to hear.

REIGNALD   'I am', quoth he,
  'A transmarine by birth, who came well stored
  With gold and jewels to this fatal house,
  Where seeking safety I encountered death.   195
  The covetous merchant, landlord of this rent,
  To whom I gave my life and wealth in charge,
  Freely to enjoy the one robbed me of both.
  Here was my body buried, here my ghost
  Must ever walk, till that have Christian rite;   200
  Till when, my habitation must be here.
  Then fly, young man, remove thy family

And seek some safer dwelling. For my death
This mansion is accursed: 'tis my possession,
Bought at the dear rate of my life and blood.   205
None enter here, that aims at his own good:'
And with this charge he vanished.

OLD LIONEL   O my fear,
Whither wilt thou transport me?

REIGNALD   I entreat,
Keep further from the gate, and fly.

OLD LIONEL   Fly whither?
Why dost not thou fly too?

REIGNALD   What need I fear?   210
The ghost and I am friends.

OLD LIONEL   But Reignald—

REIGNALD [*speaks towards the door*]   Tush,
I nothing have deserved, nor aught transgressed;
I came not near the gate.

OLD LIONEL   To whom was that
Thou spakest?

REIGNALD   Was't you, sir, namèd me?
Now as I live, I thought the dead man called   215
To enquire for him that thundered at the gate
Which he so dearly paid for. Are you mad,
To stand a foreseen danger?

OLD LIONEL   What shall I do?

REIGNALD Cover your head and fly, lest looking back
You spy your own confusion.   220

OLD LIONEL Why dost not thou fly, too?

REIGNALD   I tell you, sir,
The ghost and I am friends.

OLD LIONEL   Why didst thou quake, then?

REIGNALD In fear lest some mischance may fall on you
That have the dead offended. For my part,
The ghost and I am friends. Why fly you not,   225
Since here you are not safe?

OLD LIONEL   Some blest powers guard me

REIGNALD Nay sir, I'll not forsake you. [*Aside*] I have got the start,
But ere the goal 'twill ask both brain and art.
        Exeunt

3.1

Enter Old Master Geraldine, Young Geraldine,
Master Wincott and his Wife, Dalavill and
Prudentilla

WINCOTT We are bound to you, kind Master Geraldine,
    For this great entertainment. Troth, your cost
    Hath much exceeded common neighbourhood.
    You have feasted us like princes.
OLD GERALDINE   This, and more
    Many degrees, can never countervail   5
    The oft and frequent welcomes given my son.
    You have took him from me quite, and have, I think,
    Adopted him into your family,
    He stays with me so seldom.
WINCOTT   And in this
    By trusting him to me, of whom yourself   10
    May have both use and pleasure, you're as kind
    As moneyed men, that might make benefit
    Of what they are possessed, yet to their friends°
    In need will lend it gratis.
WIFE   And like such
    As are indebted more than they can pay   15
    We more and more confess ourselves engaged
    To you for your forbearance.
PRUDENTILLA   Yet you see,
    Like debtors such as would not break their day°
    The treasure late received we tender back,
    The which the longer you can spare, you still   20
    The more shall bind us to you.
OLD GERALDINE   Most kind ladies,
    Worthy you are to borrow, that return
    The principal with such large use of thanks.°
DALAVILL [*aside*] What strange felicity these rich men take
    To talk of borrowing, lending, and of use,   25
    The usurer's language right.
WINCOTT   You've, Master Geraldine,
    Fair walks and gardens; I have praisèd them
    Both to my wife and sister.

OLD GERALDINE   You would see them?
  There's no pleasure that the house can yield
  That can be debarred from you. Prithee, son,   30
  Be thou the usher to those mounts and prospects
  May one day call thee master.
YOUNG GERALDINE   Sir, I shall.
  Please you to walk?
PRUDENTILLA   What, Master Dalavill,
  Will you not bear us company?
DALAVILL   'Tis not fit
  That we should leave our noble host alone.   35
  Be you my friend's charge, and this old man mine.
PRUDENTILLA Well, be't then at your pleasure.
    Exeunt all but Dalavill and Old Geraldine
DALAVILL [*aside*] You to your prospects, but there's project here
  That's of another nature. [*To Old Geraldine*] Worthy sir,
  I cannot but approve your happiness   40
  To be the father of so brave a son,
  So every way accomplished and made up,
  In which my voice is least. For I, alas,
  Bear but a mean part in the common choir,
  When with much louder accents of his praise   45
  So all the world reports him.
OLD GERALDINE   Thank my stars:
  They have lent me one who, as he always was
  And is my present joy, if their aspect
  Be no ways to our goods malevolent,
  May be my future comfort.   50
DALAVILL Yet must I hold him happy above others,
  As one that solely to himself enjoys
  What many others aim at but in vain.
OLD GERALDINE How mean you that?
DALAVILL   So beautiful a mistress.
OLD GERALDINE A mistress, said you?
DALAVILL   Yes, sir, or a friend,°   55
  Whether you please to style her.
OLD GERALDINE   Mistress? Friend?°
  Pray, be more open-languaged.
DALAVILL   And indeed
  Who can blame him to absent himself from home
  And make his father's house but as a grange,
  For a beauty so attractive? Or blame her,   60

Hugging so weak an old man in her arms,
To make a new choice of an equal youth
Being in him so perfect? Yet in troth
I think they both are honest.

OLD GERALDINE   You, have, sir,
Possessed me with such strange fancies.

DALAVILL   For my part   65
How can I love the person of your son
And not his reputation? His repair
So often to the house is voiced by all
And frequent in the mouths of the whole country.
Some equally addicted, praise his happiness,   70
But others, more censorious and austere,
Blame and reprove a course so dissolute.
Each one in general pity the good man
As one unfriendly dealt with; yet in my conscience
I think them truly honest.

OLD GERALDINE   'Tis suspicious.
                                                     75
DALAVILL True, sir, at best; but what when scandalous tongues
Will make the worst, and what good in itself
Sully and stain by fabulous misreport?
For, let men live as chary as they can,
Their lives are often questioned; then no wonder   80
If such as give occasion of suspicion
Be subject to this scandal. What I speak
Is as a noble friend unto your son,
And therefore, as I glory in his fame
I suffer in his wrong. For, as I live,
                                                     85
I think they both are honest.

OLD GERALDINE   Howsoever,
I wish them so.

DALAVILL   Some course might be devised
To stop this clamour ere it grow too rank,
Lest that which yet but inconvenience seems
May turn to greater mischief. This I speak   90
In zeal to both: in sovereign care of him
As of a friend, and tender of her honour
As one to whom I hope to be allied
By marriage with her sister.

OLD GERALDINE   I much thank you,
For you have clearly given me light of that
                                                     95
Till now I never dreamt on.

DALAVILL   'Tis my love,
  And therefore, I entreat you, make not me
  To be the first reporter.
OLD GERALDINE   You have done
  The office of a noble gentleman,
  And shall not be so injured.
> *Enter again, as from walking, Wincott, his Wife, Young Geraldine,*
> *and Prudentilla.* [*The Wife and Prudentilla are wearing flowers*]

WINCOTT   See, Master Geraldine,   100
  How bold we are; especially these ladies
  Play little better than the thieves with you,
  For they have robbed your garden.
WIFE   You might, sir,
  Better have termed it sauciness than theft.
  You see we blush not what we took in private   105
  To wear in public view.
PRUDENTILLA   Besides, these cannot
  Be missed out of so many; in full fields
  The gleanings are allowed.
OLD GERALDINE   These and the rest
  Are, ladies, at your service.
WINCOTT   Now to horse.
  But one thing ere we part I must entreat,   110
  In which my wife will be joint suitor with me,
  My sister, too.
OLD GERALDINE In what, I pray?
WINCOTT   That he
  Which brought us hither may but bring us home:
  Your much respected son.
OLD GERALDINE [*aside*]   How men are borne
  To woo their own disasters.
WIFE   But to see us   115
  From whence he brought us, sir, that's all.
OLD GERALDINE [*aside*] This second motion makes it palpable
  To note. A woman's cunning: make her husband°
  Bawd to her own lascivious appetite
  And to solicit his own shame.
PRUDENTILLA   Nay, sir,   120
  When all of us join in so small a suit
  It were some injury to be denied.

OLD GERALDINE [*aside*] And work her sister, too! What will not woman
    To accomplish her own ends? But this disease
    I'll seek to physic ere it grow too far.   125
    [*Aloud*] I am most sorry to be urged, sweet friends
    In what at this time I can no ways grant.
    Most, that these ladies should be aught denied
    To whom I owe all service; but occasions
    Of weighty and important consequence   130
    Such as concern the best of my estate
    Call him aside. Excuse us both this once;
    Presume, this business is no sooner over
    But he's at his own freedom.

WINCOTT   'Twere no manners
    In us to urge it further. We will leave you,   135
    With promise, sir, that he shall in my will
    Not be the last remembered.

OLD GERALDINE   We are bound to you.
    [*To Young Geraldine*] See them to horse, and instantly return;
    We have employments for you.

YOUNG GERALDINE   Sir, I shall.

DALAVILL [*to Old Geraldine*] Remember your last promise.

OLD GERALDINE   Not to do't   140
    I should forget myself.

        [*Exeunt Wincott and his Wife, Dalavill, Prudentilla and*
        Young Geraldine]
                 If I find him false
    To such a friend, be sure he forfeits me.
    In which to be more punctually resolved
    I have a project how to sift his soul
    How 'tis inclined, whether to yonder place,°   145
    The clear bright palace, or black dungeon.
        Enter Young Geraldine
                      See,
    They are onward on the way, and he returned.

YOUNG GERALDINE I now attend your pleasure.

OLD GERALDINE You are grown perfect man, and now you float
    Like to a well-built vessel 'tween two currents,   150
    Virtue and vice. Take this, you steer to harbour,
    Take that, to eminent shipwreck.

YOUNG GERALDINE   Pray, your meaning?°

OLD GERALDINE What fathers' cares are, you shall never know
    Till you yourself have children. Now my study
    Is how to make you such that you in them   155
    May have a feeling of my love to you.
YOUNG GERALDINE Pray, sir, expound yourself, for I protest
    Of all the languages I yet have learned
    This is to me most foreign.
OLD GERALDINE   Then I shall:
    I have lived to see you in your prime of youth   160
    And height of fortune, so you will but take
    Occasion by the forehead. To be brief°
    And cut off all superfluous circumstance,
    All the ambition that I aim at now
    Is but to see you married.
YOUNG GERALDINE   Married, sir?   165
OLD GERALDINE And to that purpose, I have found out one
    Whose youth and beauty may not only please
    A curious eye, but her immediate means°
    Able to strengthen a state competent°
    Or raise a ruined fortune.
YOUNG GERALDINE   Of all which   170
    I have, believe me, neither need nor use,
    My competence best pleasing as it is
    And this my singularity of life
    Most to my mind contenting.
OLD GERALDINE [*aside*] I suspect, but yet must prove him further. 175
    [*Aloud*] Say to my care I add a father's charge,
    And couple with my counsel my command?
    To that how can you answer?
YOUNG GERALDINE   That I hope
    My duty and obedience still unblamed
    Did never merit such austerity,   180
    And from a father never yet displeased.
OLD GERALDINE Nay then, to come more near unto the point,
    Either you must resolve for present marriage
    Or forfeit all your interest in my love.
YOUNG GERALDINE Unsay that language, I entreat you, sir,   185
    And do not so oppress me. Or if needs
    Your heavy imposition stand in force.
    Resolve me by your counsel: with more safety

May I infringe a sacred vow to heaven
Or to oppose me to your strict command,
Since one of these I must?   190

OLD GERALDINE [*aside*]   Now, Dalavill,
I find thy words too true.

YOUNG GERALDINE   For marry, sir,
I neither may nor can.

OLD GERALDINE   Yet whore you may,
And that's no breach of any vow to heaven;
Pollute the nuptial bed with mechal sin,   195
Asperse the honour of a noble friend,
Forfeit thy reputation here below
And th' interest that thy soul might claim above
In yon bless'd city; these you may, and can,
With untouched conscience. O, that I should live   200
To see the hopes that I have stored so long
Thus in a moment ruined, and the staff
On which my old decrepit age should lean
Before my face thus broken, on which trusting,
I thus abortively, before my time,   205
Fall headlong to my grave.
          Falls on the earth

YOUNG GERALDINE   It yet stands strong,
Both to support you unto future life
And fairer comfort.

OLD GERALDINE   Never, never, son;
For till thou canst acquit thyself of scandal
And me of my suspicion, here, even here,
Where I have measured out my length of earth   210
I shall expire my last.

YOUNG GERALDINE   Both these I can.
Then rise, sir, I entreat you; and that innocency
Which, poisoned by the breath of calumny
Cast you thus low, shall, these few stains wiped off,   215
With better thoughts erect you.
          [*He helps Old Geraldine up*]

OLD GERALDINE   Well, say on.

YOUNG GERALDINE
There's but one fire from which this smoke may grow,
Namely the unmatched yoke of youth and age;°

In which, if ever I occasion was
Of the smallest breach, the greatest implacable mischief   220
Adultery can threaten fall on me;
Of you may I be disavowed a son,
And unto heaven a servant. For that lady,
As she is beauty's mirror, so I hold her°
For chastity's examples. From her tongue   225
Never came language that arrived my ear
That even censorious Cato, lived he now,°
Could misinterpret. Never from her lips
Came unchaste kiss, or from her constant eye
Look savouring of the least immodesty.   230
Further—

OLD GERALDINE Enough. One only thing remains,
  Which on thy part performed assures firm credit
  To these thy protestations.
YOUNG GERALDINE   Name it then.
OLD GERALDINE Take hence th' occasion of this common fame
  Which hath already spread itself so far   235
  To her dishonour and thy prejudice.
  From this day forward to forbear the house,
  This do, upon my blessing.
YOUNG GERALDINE   As I hope it,
  I will not fail your charge.
OLD GERALDINE   I am satisfied.
    Exeunt

3.2

Enter at one door an Usurer and his man, at the other
Old Lionel with his servant, in the midst Reignald

REIGNALD [*aside*] To which hand shall I turn me? Here's my master
  Hath been to inquire of him that sold the house
  Touching the murder. Here's an usuring rascal
  Of whom we have borrowed money to supply
  Our prodigal expenses, broke our day,   5
  And owe him still the principal and use.
  Were I to meet them single, I have brain
  To oppose both and to come off unscarred.
  But if they do assault me, and at once,

Not Hercules himself could stand that odds,   10
Therefore I must encounter them by turns;
And to my master first. [*To Old Lionel*] O, sir, well met.
OLD LIONEL What, Reignald? I but now met with the man
  Of whom I bought yon house.
REIGNALD   What, did you, sir?
  But did you speak of aught concerning that
  Which I last told you?   15
OLD LIONEL   Yes, I told him all.
REIGNALD [*aside*] Then am I cast. [*Aloud*] But I pray tell me, sir,°
  Did he confess the murder?
OLD LIONEL   No such thing;
  Most stiffly he denies it.
REIGNALD   Impudent wretch;
  Then serve him with a warrant. Let the officer
  Bring him before a justice. You shall hear   20
  What I can say against him. 'Sfoot, deny 't!
  But I pray, sir, excuse me; yonder's one
  With whom I have some business. Stay you here,
  And but determine what's best course to take,
  And note how I will follow't.   25
OLD LIONEL   Be brief, then.
REIGNALD [*aside*] Now if I can as well put off my use-man,
  This day I shall be master of the field.
USURER That should be Lionel's man.
MAN   The same, I know him.
USURER After so many frivolous delays
  There's now some hope. He that was wont to shun us   30
  And to absent himself, accosts us freely
  And with a pleasant countenance. Well met, Reignald;
  What, 's this money ready?
REIGNALD   Never could you
  Have come in better time.
USURER   Where's your master,
  Young Lionel? It something troubles me   35
  That he should break his day.
REIGNALD   A word in private.
USURER Tush, private me no privates. In a word,
  Speak, are my moneys ready?
REIGNALD   Not so loud.
USURER I will be louder yet. Give me my moneys;
  Come, tender me my moneys.   40

REIGNALD We know you have a throat wide as your conscience,
    You need not use it now. Come, get you home.
USURER Home?
REIGNALD Yes, home, I say. Return by three o'clock,   45
    And I will see all cancelled.°
USURER 'Tis now past two, and I can stay till three;°
    I'll make that now my business. Otherwise
    With these loud clamours I will haunt thee still:
    Give me my use, give me my principal.   50
REIGNALD [aside] This bur will still cleave to me. What, no means°
    To shake him off? I ne'er was caught till now.
    [Aloud] Come, come, you're troublesome.
USURER   Prevent that trouble,
    And without trifling pay me down my cash.
    I will be fooled no longer.
REIGNALD   So, so, so.   55
USURER I have been still put off from time to time
    And day to day. These are but cheating tricks,
    And this is the last minute I'll forbear
    Thee or thy master. Once again I say
    Give me my use, give me my principal.   60
REIGNALD [aside] Pox o' this use, that hath undone so many,
    And now will confound me.
OLD LIONEL   Hast thou heard this?
SERVANT Yes, sir, and to my grief.
OLD LIONEL   Come hither, Reignald.
REIGNALD Here, sir. [Aside] Nay, now I am gone.
OLD LIONEL   What use is this,
    What principal he talks of, in which language   65
    He names my son, and thus upbraideth thee?
    What is't you owe this man?
REIGNALD   A trifle, sir.
    Pray stop his mouth and pay't him.
OLD LIONEL   I, pay? What?
REIGNALD If I say pay't him, pay't him.
OLD LIONEL   What's the sum?
REIGNALD A toy: the main about five hundred pounds,°   70
    And the use fifty.
OLD LIONEL   Call you that a toy?
    To what use was it borrowed? At my departure

I left my son sufficient in his charge,
With surplus, to defray a large expense
Without this need of borrowing.

REIGNALD   'Tis confessed.   75
Yet stop his clamorous mouth, and only say
That you will pay't tomorrow.

OLD LIONEL   I, pass my word?

REIGNALD Sir, if I bid you, do't. Nay, no more words,
But say you'll pay't tomorrow.

OLD LIONEL   Jest indeed.
But tell me how these moneys were bestowed.   80

REIGNALD Safe, sir, I warrant you.

OLD LIONEL   The sum still safe?
Why do you not then tender it yourselves?

REIGNALD Your ear, sir. This sum joined to the rest, your son
Hath purchased land and houses.

OLD LIONEL   Land, dost thou say?

REIGNALD A goodly house and gardens.

OLD LIONEL   Now joy on him,   85
That, whilst his father merchandised abroad,
Had care to add to his estate at home.
But Reignald, wherefore houses?

REIGNALD   Now, Lord, sir,
How dull you are. This house possessed with spirits,
And there no longer stay, would you have had   90
Him, us, and all your other family
To live and lie i' th' streets? It had not, sir,
Been for your reputation.

OLD LIONEL   Blessing on him
That he is grown so thrifty.

USURER   'Tis struck three;
My money's not yet tendered.

REIGNALD   Pox upon him.   95
See him discharged, I pray, sir.

OLD LIONEL   Call upon me
Tomorrow, friend, as early as thou wilt;
I'll see thy debt defrayed.

USURER   It is enough,
I have a true man's word.

              Exeunt Usurer and his man

OLD LIONEL   Now tell me, Reignald,
  For thou hast made me proud of my son's thrift,   100
  Where, in what country, doth this fair house stand?°
REIGNALD [*aside*] Never in all my time so much to seek;°
  I know not what to answer.
OLD LIONEL   Wherefore studiest thou?
  Use men to purchase lands at a dear rate
  And know not where they lie?
REIGNALD   'Tis not for that,   105
  I only had forgot his name that sold them.
  'Twas—let me see, see—
OLD LIONEL   Call thyself to mind.
REIGNALD [*aside*] Nonplussed or never, now. Where art thou, brain?
  [*Aloud*] O, sir, where was my memory? 'Tis this house
  That next adjoins to yours.
OLD LIONEL   My neighbour Ricott's?   110
REIGNALD The same, the same, sir. We had pennyworths in't,
  And, I can tell you, have been offered well
  Since, to forsake our bargain.
OLD LIONEL   As I live,
  I much commend your choice.
REIGNALD   Nay, 'tis well seated,
  Roughcast without, but bravely lined within.   115
  You have met with few such bargains.
OLD LIONEL   Prithee knock
  And call the master or the servant on't
  To let me take free view on't.
REIGNALD [*aside*] Puzzle again on puzzle. [*Aloud*] One word, sir.
  The house is full of women. No man knows   120
  How on the instant they may be employed.
  The rooms may lie unhandsome, and maids stand
  Much on their cleanliness and housewifery.
  To take them unprovided were disgrace:
  'Twere fit they had some warning. Now, do you   125
  Fetch but a warrant from the justice, sir—
  You understand me?
OLD LIONEL   Yes I do.
REIGNALD   To attach
  Him of suspected murder; I'll see't served.
  (Did he deny't?) And in the interim I

Will give them notice you are now arrived   130
And long to see your purchase.
OLD LIONEL   Counselled well.
And meet some half-hour hence.
REIGNALD [*aside*]   This plunge well past
All things fall even, to crown my brain at last.
          Exeunt

3.3

          Enter Dalavill and a Gentleman
GENTLEMAN Where shall we dine today?
DALAVILL   At th' ordinary.
I see, sir, you are but a stranger here.
This Barnet is a place of great resort,
And commonly upon the market days
Here all the country gentlemen appoint
A friendly meeting; some about affairs   5
Of consequence and profit, bargain, sale,
And to confer with chapmen; some for pleasure,
To match their horses, wager in their dogs
Or try their hawks; some to no other end   10
But only meet good company, discourse,
Dine, drink and spend their money.
GENTLEMAN   That's the market
We have to make this day.
DALAVILL   'Tis a commodity
That will be easily vended.
          Enter Old Geraldine and Young Geraldine
                          What, my worthy friend,
You are happily encountered. O, you're grown strange   15
To one that much respects you. Troth, the house
Hath all this time seemed naked without you.
The good old man doth never sit to meat
But next his giving thanks he speaks of you;
There's scarce a bit that he at table tastes
That can digest without a 'Geraldine',   20
You are in his mouth so frequent, he and she

Both wondering what distaste from one or either
So suddenly should alienate a guest
To them so dearly welcome.

OLD GERALDINE   Master Dalavill,   25
Thus much let me for him apology:
Divers designs have thronged upon us late
My weakness was not able to support
Without his help. He hath been much abroad
At London, or elsewhere. Besides, 'tis term°   30
And lawyers must be followed; seldom at home,
And scarcely then at leisure.

DALAVILL   I am satisfied,
And I would they were so, too. [*Aside to Old Geraldine*]
    But I hope, sir,
In this restraint you have not used my name?

OLD GERALDINE [*aside to Dalavill*] Not as I live.

DALAVILL [*aside to Old Geraldine*]   You're noble. Who
    [*Aloud*] had thought.   35
To have met with such good company. You're, it seems,
But new alighted. Father and son, ere part,
I vow we'll drink a cup of sack together;
Physicians say it doth prepare the appetite
And stomach against dinner.

OLD GERALDINE   We old men   40
Are apt to take these courtesies.

DALAVILL   What say you, friend?

YOUNG GERALDINE I'll but inquire for one at the next inn
And instantly return.

DALAVILL   'Tis enough.

Exeunt [Dalavill, the Gentleman, and Old Geraldine.]
Enter Bess meeting with Young Geraldine

YOUNG GERALDINE Bess, how dost thou, girl?

BESS Faith, we may do how we list for you, you are grown so great a   45
stranger. We are more beholding to Master Dalavill; he's a constant
guest, and howsoe'er to some (that shall be nameless) his presence
may be graceful, yet to others—I could say somewhat.

YOUNG GERALDINE He's a noble fellow, and my choice friend.

BESS Come, come, he is what he is, and that the end will prove.   50

YOUNG GERALDINE And how's all at home?
    Nay, we'll not part without a glass of wine,

And meet so seldom. Boy!
   Enter Drawer
DRAWER Anon, anon, sir.
YOUNG GERALDINE A pint of claret, quickly.
   Exit Drawer

          Nay, sit down. 55
The news, the news, I pray thee. I am sure
I have been much inquired of thy old master,
And thy young mistress, too.
BESS   Ever your name
Is in my master's mouth, and sometimes, too,
In hers, when she hath nothing else to think of. 60
Well, well, I could say somewhat.
   Enter Drawer
DRAWER Here's your wine, sir.
YOUNG GERALDINE Fill, boy.
   [*The Drawer pours out their wine.*] *Exit Drawer*
        Here, Bess; this glass to both their healths.
Why dost weep, my wench?
BESS Nay, nothing, sir. 65
YOUNG GERALDINE Come, I must know.
BESS   In troth, I love you, sir,
And ever wished you well. You are a gentleman
Whom always I respected; know the passages
And private whisperings of the secret love
Betwixt you and my mistress, I dare swear 70
On your part well intended, but—
YOUNG GERALDINE   But what?
BESS You bear the name of landlord, but another
Enjoys the rent; you dote upon the shadow,
But another he bears away the substance.
YOUNG GERALDINE Be more plain. 75
BESS You hope to enjoy a virtuous widowhood,
But Dalavill, whom you esteem your friend,
He keeps the wife in common.
YOUNG GERALDINE   You're to blame,°
And, Bess, you make me angry. He's my friend,
And she my second self. In all their meetings° 80
I never saw so much as cast of eye
Once entertained betwixt them.
BESS   That's their cunning.

YOUNG GERALDINE For her, I have been with her at all hours,
    Both late and early; in her bedchamber,
    And often singly ushered her abroad.   85
    Now, would she have been any man's alive,
    She had been mine. You wrong a worthy friend
    And a chaste mistress. You're not a good girl.
       [*He gives Bess money*]
    Drink that; speak better of her. I could chide you,°
    But I'll forbear. What you have rashly spoke   90
    Shall ever here be buried.
BESS   I am sorry
    My freeness should offend you, but yet know
    I am her chambermaid.
YOUNG GERALDINE   Play now the market maid,
    And prithee, 'bout thy business.
BESS   Well, I shall—
    That man should be so fooled!
      Exit
YOUNG GERALDINE   She a prostitute?   95
    Nay, and to him? My troth-plight and my friend?
    As possible it is that heaven and earth
    Should be in love together, meet and kiss,
    And so cut off all distance. What strange frenzy
    Came in this wench's brain, so to surmise?   100
    Were she so base, his nobleness is such
    He would not entertain it, for my sake;
    Or he so bent, his hot and lust-burnt appetite
    Would be soon quenched at the mere contemplation
    Of her most pious and religious life.   105
    The girl was much to blame. Perhaps her mistress
    Hath stirred her anger by some word or blow
    Which she would thus revenge, not apprehending
    At what a high price honour's to be rated;
    Or else someone that envies her rare virtue   110
    Might hire her thus to brand it; or who knows
    But the young wench may fix a thought on me
    And to divert me from her mistress' love
    May raise this false aspersion? Howsoever,
    My thoughts on these two columns fixèd are: 115
    She's good as fresh, and purely chaste as fair.
      Enter Roger the Clown with a letter [*and a pot of liquor*]

ROGER O sir, you are the needle, and if the whole county of Middlesex
    had been turned to mere bottle of hay, I had been enjoined to
    have found you out, or never more returned back to my old master.
    There's a letter, sir.   120
    [*Hands Young Geraldine the letter*]
YOUNG GERALDINE I know the hand that superscribed it well.
    Stay but till I peruse it, and from me
    Thou shalt return an answer.
    [*Reads the letter*]
ROGER I shall, sir. [*Aside*] This is market-day, and here acquaintance
    commonly meet. And whom have I encountered? My gossip Pint-   125
    pot, and brimful; nay, I mean to drink with you before I part. And
    how doth all your worshipful kindred: your sister Quart, your *pater*
    Pottle (who was ever a gentleman's fellow) and your old grandsire
    Gallon? They cannot choose but be all in health, since so many
    healths have been drunk out of them. I could wish them all here,   130
    and in no worse state than I see you are in at this present. Howsoever,
    gossip, since I have met you hand to hand, I'll make bold to drink
    to you—nay, either you must pledge me, or get one to do 't for you.
    Do you open your mouth° towards me? Well, I know what you would
    say: 'Here, Roger, to your master and mistress and all our good   135
    friends at home.' Gramercy, gossip; if I should not pledge thee,
    I were worthy to be turned out to grass and stand no more at livery.
    And now in requital of this courtesy I'll begin one health to you
    and all your society in the cellar: to Peter Pipe, Harry Hogshead,
    Bartholomew Butt and little Master Randal Runlet, to Timothy   140
    Taster and all your other great and small friends.
YOUNG GERALDINE He writes me here
    That at my discontinuance he's much grieved,
    Desiring me, as I have ever tendered
    Or him or his, to give him satisfaction   145
    Touching my discontent, and that in person
    By any private meeting.
ROGER Ay, sir, 'tis very true; the letter speaks no more than he
    wished me to tell you by word of mouth.
YOUNG GERALDINE Thou art, then, of his counsel?°   150
ROGER His privy, an 't please you.
YOUNG GERALDINE [*aside*] Though ne'er so strict hath been my
    father's charge,
    A little I'll dispense with 't, for his love.
    [*To Roger*] Commend me to thy master; tell him from me

On Monday night (then will my leisure serve)   155
I will by heaven's assistance visit him.

ROGER On Monday, sir? That's, as I remember, just the day before
Tuesday.

YOUNG GERALDINE But 'twill be midnight first, at which late hour
Please him to let the garden door stand ope;   160
At that I'll enter, but conditionally
That neither wife, friend, servant, no third soul
Save him and thee to whom he trusts this message,
Know of my coming in or passing out.
When, tell him, I will fully satisfy him   165
Concerning my forced absence.

ROGER I am something oblivious;° your message would be the trulier
delivered if it were set down in black and white.

YOUNG GERALDINE I'll call for pen and ink, and instantly dispatch it.
Exeunt

4.1

Enter Reignald

REIGNALD Now impudence but steel my face this once,
　　Although I ne'er blush after. Here's the house.
　　　　[He knocks at the door]
　　Ho, who's within? What, no man to defend
　　These innocent gates from knocking?
　　　　Enter Master Ricott

RICOTT　　　　　　　　　　　Who's without there?

REIGNALD One, sir, that ever wished your worship's health,　　　5
　　And those few hours I can find time to pray in
　　I still remember it.

RICOTT　　　　　　Gramercy, Reignald,
　　I love all those that wish it. You are the men
　　Lead merry lives, feast, revel and carouse:
　　You feel no tedious hours, time plays with you;　　　10
　　This is your golden age.

REIGNALD　　　　　　　　It was. But now, sir,
　　That gold is turned to worse than alchemy:°
　　It will not stand the test. Those days are past,
　　And now our nights come on.

RICOTT Tell me, Reignald, is he returned from sea?　　　15

REIGNALD Yes, to our grief, already; but we fear
　　Hereafter it may prove to all our costs.

RICOTT Suspects thy master anything?

REIGNALD　　　　　　　　　　Not yet, sir.
　　Now, my request is that your worship, being
　　So near a neighbour, therefore most disturbed,　　　20
　　Would not be first to peach us.

RICOTT　　　　　　　　　Take my word;
　　With other neighbours make what peace you can,
　　I'll not be your accuser.

REIGNALD　　　　　　Worshipful sir,
　　I shall be still your beadsman. Now, the business
　　That I was sent about: the old man my master,　　　25
　　Claiming some interest in acquaintance past,
　　Desires (might it be no way troublesome)
　　To take free view of all your house within.

RICOTT View of my house? Why, 'tis not set to sale,
    Nor bill upon the door. Look well upon 't.   30
    View of my house?
REIGNALD   Nay, be not angry, sir;
    He no way doth disable your estate;°
    As far to buy, as you are loath to sell.°
    Some alterations in his own he'd make,
    And, hearing yours by workmen much commended,   35
    He would make that his precedent.
RICOTT   What fancies
    Should at this age possess him, knowing the cost,
    That he should dream of building?
REIGNALD   'Tis supposed
    He hath late found a wife out for his son.
    Now, sir, to have him near him, and that nearness,   40
    Too, without trouble (though beneath one roof,
    Yet parted in two families), he would build
    And make what's pitched a perfect quadrangle°
    Proportioned just with yours, were you so pleased°
    To make it his example.
RICOTT   Willingly.   45
    I will but order some few things within
    And then attend his coming.
        Exit
REIGNALD   Most kind coxcomb.
    Great Alexander and Agathocles,°
    Caesar, and others, have been famed, they say,°
    And magnified for high facinorous deeds;   50
    Why claim not I an equal place with them,
    Or rather, a precedent? These commanded
    Their subjects and their servants; I, my master
    And every way his equals, where I please
    Lead by the nose along. They placed their burdens   55
    On horses, mules, and camels; I, old men
    Of strength and wit load with my knavery
    Till both their backs and brains ache. Yet, poor animals,
    They ne'er complain of weight.
        Enter Old Lionel [with a warrant]
                   O, are you come, sir?
OLD LIONEL I made what haste I could.   60
REIGNALD And brought the warrant?

OLD LIONEL See, here I have't.

REIGNALD 'Tis well done; but speak, runs it both without bail and
  mainprize?°

OLD LIONEL Nay, it carries both form and power.   65

REIGNALD Then I shall warrant him. I have been yonder, sir.

OLD LIONEL And what says he?

REIGNALD   Like one that offers you
  Free ingress, view, and regress, at your pleasure,
  As to his worthy landlord.

OLD LIONEL   Was that all?

REIGNALD He spake to me, that I would speak to you,   70
  To speak unto your son; and then again
  To speak to him, that he would speak to you,
  You would release his bargain.

OLD LIONEL   By no means.
  Men must advise before they part with land,
  Not after to repent it. 'Tis most just
  That such as hazard and disburse their stocks   75
  Should take all gains and profits that accrue
      Enter Master Ricott again, walking before
      the gate
  As well in sale of houses as in barter
  And traffic of all other merchandise.

REIGNALD See, in acknowledgement of a tenant's duty   80
  He attends you at the gate. Salute him, sir.

OLD LIONEL My worthy friend.

RICOTT Now as I live, all my best thoughts and wishes
  Impart with yours, in your so safe return.
  Your servant tells me you have great desire   85
  To take survey of this my house within.

OLD LIONEL Be 't, sir, no trouble to you.

RICOTT   None. Enter boldly,
  With as much freedom as it were your own.
      [*Old Lionel and Reignald speak aside*]

OLD LIONEL As it were mine? Why, Reignald, is it not?

REIGNALD Lord, sir, that in extremity of grief   90
  You'll add unto vexation. See you not
  How sad he's on the sudden?

OLD LIONEL   I observe it.

REIGNALD To part with that which he hath kept so long,
  Especially his inheritance. Now, as you love°

Goodness and honesty, torment him not   95
With the least word of purchase.

OLD LIONEL   Counselled well;
Thou teachest me humanity.

RICOTT   Will you enter?
Or shall I call a servant to conduct you
Through every room and chamber?

OLD LIONEL   By no means;
I fear we are too much troublesome of ourselves.   100

REIGNALD See, what a goodly gate!

OLD LIONEL   It likes me well.

REIGNALD What brave carved posts! Who knows but here
In time, sir, you may keep your shrievalty,
And I be one o' th' sergeants.

OLD LIONEL   They are well carved.°

RICOTT And cost me a good price, sir. Take your pleasure.   105
I have business in the town.

                    Exit

REIGNALD   Poor man, I pity him.
H' 'ath not the heart to stay and see you come,
As 'twere, to take possession. Look that way, sir,
What goodly fair bay windows!

OLD LIONEL   Wondrous stately.°

REIGNALD And what a gallery, how costly ceiled,   110
What painting round about!

OLD LIONEL   Every fresh object
To good adds betterness.

REIGNALD   Terraced above,
And how below supported! Do they please you?

OLD LIONEL All things beyond opinion. Trust me, Reignald,
I'll not forgo the bargain for more gain   115
Than half the price it cost me.

REIGNALD   If you would,
I should not suffer you; was not the money
Due to the usurer took upon good ground
That proved well built on? We were no fools
That knew not what we did.

OLD LIONEL   It shall be satisfied.   120

REIGNALD Please you to trust me with 't, I'll see 't discharged.

OLD LIONEL He hath my promise, and I'll do 't myself.
Never could son have better pleased a father

254

Than in this purchase. Hie thee instantly
Unto my house i' th' country: give him notice   125
Of my arrive, and bid him with all speed
Post hither.

REIGNALD   Ere I see the warrant served?

OLD LIONEL It shall be thy first business; for my soul
Is not at peace till face to face I approve
His husbandry, and much commend his thrift.   130
Nay, without pause, begone.

REIGNALD [*aside*]   But a short journey,
For he's not far that I am sent to seek.
I have got the start: the best part of the race
Is run already. What remains is small,
And, tire now, I should but forfeit all.   135

OLD LIONEL Make haste, I do entreat thee.

      Exeunt

4.2

    Enter Roger the Clown

ROGER This is the garden gate, and here am I set to stand sentinel and
to attend the coming of young Master Geraldine. Master Dalavill's
gone to his chamber, my mistress to hers. 'Tis now about midnight,
a banquet prepared, bottles of wine in readiness, all the whole
household at their rest; and no creature by this honestly stirring,°   5
saving I and my old master; he in a by-chamber prepared of purpose
for their private meeting; and I here to play the watchman against
my will.

    Enter Young Geraldine

Qui va la?° Stand. Who goes there?

YOUNG GERALDINE A friend.   10

ROGER The word?°

YOUNG GERALDINE Honest Roger!

ROGER That's the word, indeed; you have leave to pass freely without
calling my corporal.°

YOUNG GERALDINE How go the affairs within?   15

ROGER According to promise: the business is composed and the
servants disposed; my young mistress reposed, my old master,
according as you proposed, attends you, if you be exposed to give

him meeting, nothing in the way being interposed to transpose you
to the least danger; and this I dare be deposed,° if you will not take   20
my word, as I am honest Roger.

YOUNG GERALDINE Thy word shall be my warrant, but secured
Most in thy master's promise; on which building,
By this known way I enter.

ROGER Nay, by your leave, I that was late but a plain sentinel will now   25
be your captain conductor. Follow me.
        Exeunt

4.3

*A table and stools are set out, with lights, a banquet, and wine.
Enter Master Wincott*

WINCOTT I wonder whence this strangeness should proceed,
Or wherein I, or any of my house,
Should be th' occasion of the least distaste.
Now, as I wish him well, it troubles me.
But now the time grows on, from his own mouth   5
To be resolved, and I hope satisfied.
        Enter Roger the Clown and Young Geraldine
Sir, as I live, of all my friends, to me
Most wishedly you are welcome. Take that chair,
I this. Nay, I entreat, no compliment.
[*To Roger*] Attend: fill wine.   10

ROGER Till the mouths of the bottles yawn directly upon the floor,
and the bottoms turn their tails up to the ceiling, Whilst there's
any blood in their bellies, I'll not leave them.
        [*Roger serves wine. Wincott drinks to Young Geraldine*]

WINCOTT I first salute you thus.

YOUNG GERALDINE   It could not come
From one whom I more honour. Sir, I thank you.   15

ROGER Nay, since my master begun it, I'll see 't go round to all three.

WINCOTT Now give us leave.°

ROGER Talk you by yourselves, whilst I find something to say to this.
I have a tale to tell him shall make his stony heart relent.
        Exit

YOUNG GERALDINE Now first, sir, your attention I entreat;   20
Next, your belief that what I speak is just,
Maugre all contradiction.

WINCOTT   Both are granted.
YOUNG GERALDINE Then I proceed, with due acknowledgement
    Of all your more than many courtesies:
    You've been my second father, and your wife   25
    My noble and chaste mistress; all your servants
    At my command, and this your bounteous table
    As free and common as my father's house.
    Neither 'gainst any or the least of these
    Can I commence just quarrel.
WINCOTT   What might then be   30
    The cause of this constraint, in thus absenting
    Yourself from such as love you?
YOUNG GERALDINE   Out of many,
    I will propose some few: the care I have
    Of your (as yet unblemishèd) renown;
    The untouched honour of your virtuous wife;   35
    And (which I value least, yet dearly, too)
    My own fair reputation.
WINCOTT   How can these
    In any way be questioned?
YOUNG GERALDINE   O, dear sir,
    Bad tongues have been too busy with us all;
    Of which I never yet had time to think,
    But with sad thoughts and griefs unspeakable.   40
    It hath been whispered by some wicked ones,
    But loudly thundered in my father's ears
    By some that have maligned our happiness
    (Heaven, if it can brook slander, pardon them)
    That this my customary coming hither   45
    Hath been to base and sordid purposes:
    To wrong your bed, injure her chastity,
    And be mine own undoer. Which, how false—
WINCOTT As heaven is true, I know't.
YOUNG GERALDINE   Now, this calumny   50
    Arriving first unto my father's ears,
    His easy nature was induced to think
    That these things might perhaps be possible.
    I answered him as I would do to heaven,
    And cleared myself in his suspicious thoughts
    As truly as the high all-knowing Judge   55
    Shall of these stains acquit me, which are merely
    Aspersions and untruths. The good old man,

Possessed with my sincerity, and yet careful
Of your renown, her honour, and my fame,   60
To stop the worst that scandal could inflict
And to prevent false rumours, charges me,
The cause removed, to take away the effect,
Which only could be to forbear your house,
And this upon his blessing. You hear all.   65

WINCOTT And I of all acquit you. This your absence,
With which my love most cavilled, orators
In your behalf. Had such things passed betwixt you,
Not threats nor chidings could have driven you hence:
It pleads in your behalf, and speaks in hers,   70
And arms me with a double confidence
Both of your friendship and her loyalty.
I am happy in you both, and only doubtful
Which of you two doth most impart my love.
You shall not hence tonight.

YOUNG GERALDINE   Pray pardon, sir.   75

WINCOTT You are in your lodging.

YOUNG GERALDINE   But my father's charge.

WINCOTT My conjuration shall dispense with that.
You may be up as early as you please,
But hence tonight you shall not.

YOUNG GERALDINE   You are powerful.

WINCOTT This night, of purpose, I have parted beds,   80
Feigning myself not well, to give you meeting,
Nor can be aught suspected by my wife,
I have kept all so private. Now 'tis late;
I'll steal up to my rest. But howsoever,
Let's not be strange in our writing: that way, daily   85
We may confer without the least suspect
In spite of all such base calumnious tongues.
So now, goodnight, sweet friend.

YOUNG GERALDINE   May he that made you
So just and good still guard you.

     Exit Wincott

                              Not to bed;
So I perhaps might oversleep myself   90
And then my tardy waking might betray me
To the more early household. Thus as I am
I'll rest me on this pallet.°

     [*Lies down*]

But in vain;°
I find no sleep can fasten on mine eyes,
There are in this disturbèd brain of mine   95
So many mutinous fancies. This to me
Will be a tedious night. How shall I spend it?
No book that I can spy? No company?
A little let me recollect myself.
O, what more wished company can I find,   100
Suiting the apt occasion, time and place,
Than the sweet contemplation of her beauty
And the fruition, too, time may produce
Of what is yet lent out? 'Tis a sweet lady,°
And every way accomplished. Hath mere accident   105
Brought me thus near, and I not visit her?
Should it arrive her ear, perhaps might breed
Our lasting separation; for 'twixt lovers
No quarrel's to unkindness. Sweet opportunity
Offers prevention, and invites me to 't;   110
The house is known to me, the stairs and rooms,
The way unto her chamber frequently
Trodden by me at midnight and all hours.
How joyful to her would a meeting be,
So strange and unexpected; shadowed, too,   115
Beneath the veil of night. I am resolved
To give her visitation in that place
Where we have passed deep vows: her bedchamber.
My fiery love this darkness makes seem bright,
And this the path that leads to my delight.   120
        He goes in at one door and comes out at another
And this the gate unto't. I'll listen first
Before too rudely I disturb her rest
And gentle breathing. Ha! She's sure awake,
For in the bed two whisper, and their voices
Appear to me unequal: one a woman's,   125
And hers. Th' other should be no maid's tongue,
It bears too big a tone. And hark, they laugh.
Damnation! But list further: tother sounds—
Like—'tis the same false perjured traitor, Dalavill,
To friend and goodness. Unchaste, impious woman,   130
False to all faith and true conjugal love.
There's met a serpent and a crocodile,
A Sinon and a Circe. O, to what°

May I compare you? But my sword—
I'll act a noble execution   135
On two unmatched for sordid villainy.
I left it in my chamber, and thanks, heaven,
That I did so: it hath prevented me
From playing a base hangman. Sin securely,°
Whilst I, although for many, yet less, faults   140
Strive hourly to repent me. I once loved her,
And was to him entired. Although I pardon,
Heaven will find time to punish. I'll not stretch
My just revenge so far as once by blabbing
To make your brazen impudence to blush.   145
Damn on—revenge too great—and, to suppress°
Your souls yet lower, without hope to rise,
Heap Ossa upon Pelion. You have made me°
To hate my very country, because here bred
Near two such monsters. First I'll leave this house   150
And then my father's; next I'll take my leave
Both of this clime and nation, travel till
Age snow upon this head. My passions now
Are unexpressable. I'll end them thus:
Ill man, bad woman; your unheard-of treachery   155
This unjust censure on a just man give,
To seek out place where no two such can live.
        Exit

4.4

Enter Dalavill in a nightgown, Wincott's Wife in a night-tire,
as coming from bed

DALAVILL A happy morning now betide you, lady,
    To equal the content of a sweet night.
WIFE It hath been to my wish and your desire,
    And this your coming, by pretended love
    Unto my sister Pru, cuts off suspicion   5
    Of any such converse 'twixt you and me.
DALAVILL It hath been wisely carried.
WIFE   One thing troubles me.
DALAVILL What's that, my dearest?

WIFE   Why your friend Geraldine
    Should on the sudden thus absent himself.
    Has he had, think you, no intelligence   10
    Of these our private meetings?
DALAVILL   No, on my soul,
    For therein hath my brain exceeded yours:
    I, studying to engross you to myself,
    Of his continued absence have been cause;
    Yet he of your affection no way jealous,   15
    Or of my friendship. How the plot was cast
    You at our better leisure shall partake.
    The air grows cold: have care unto your health.
    Suspicious eyes are o'er us, that yet sleep,
    But with the dawn will open. Sweet, retire you   20
    To your warm sheets, I now to fill my own
    That have this night been empty.
WIFE   You advise well.
    O, might this kiss dwell ever on thy lips
    In my remembrance.
DALAVILL   Doubt it not, I pray,
    Whilst day frights night, and night pursues the day.   25
    Good morrow.
        Exeunt

4.5

*Enter Reignald, Young Lionel, Blanda, Scapha, Rioter,
and two gallants, Reignald with a key in his hand*

REIGNALD Now is the jail-delivery. Through this back gate
    Shift for yourselves: I here unprison all.
YOUNG LIONEL But tell me, how shall we dispose ourselves?
    We are as far to seek now as at the first.
    What is it to reprieve us for few hours   5
    And now to suffer? Better had it been
    At first to have stood the trial, so by this
    We might have passed our penance.
BLANDA Sweet Reignald.
YOUNG LIONEL Honest rogue.   10
RIOTER If now thou failest us, then we are lost for ever.

REIGNALD This same 'sweet Reignald', and this 'honest rogue',
    Hath been the burgess under whose protection
    You all this while have lived free from arrests;
    But now the sessions of my power's broke up   15
    And you exposed to actions, warrants, writs,
    For all the hellish rabble are broke loose
    Of sergeants, sheriffs and bailiffs.
ALL   Guard us, heaven!
REIGNALD I tell you as it is. Nay, I myself
    That have been your protector, now as subject   20
    To every varlet's pestle, for you know
    How I am engaged with you—[*He starts*] At whose suit, sir?
ALL Why didst thou start?
        All start
REIGNALD I was afraid some catchpole stood behind me
    To clap me on the shoulder.
RIOTER   No such thing,   25
    Yet I protest thy fear did fright us all.
REIGNALD I knew your guilty consciences.
YOUNG LIONEL   No brain left?
BLANDA No crotchet for my sake?
REIGNALD   One kiss then, sweet.
    Thus shall my crotchets and your kisses meet.
        [*Blanda and Reignald kiss*]
YOUNG LIONEL Nay, tell us what to trust to.
REIGNALD   Lodge yourselves   30
    In the next tavern. There's the cash that's left.
        [*Reignald gives Young Lionel money*]
    Go, health it freely for my good success,
    Nay, drown it all; let not a tester 'scape
    To be consumed in rot-gut. I have begun,
    And I will stand the period.
YOUNG LIONEL   Bravely spoke.   35
REIGNALD Or perish in the conflict.
RIOTER   Worthy Reignald.
REIGNALD Well, if he now come off well, fox you all;
    Go, call for wine; for singly of myself
    I will oppose all danger. But I charge you,
    When I shall faint or find myself distressed   40
    If I like brave Orlando wind my horn,°
    Make haste unto my rescue.

YOUNG LIONEL   And die in't.

REIGNALD Well hast thou spoke, my noble Charlemagne
    With these thy peers about thee.

YOUNG LIONEL   May good speed
    Attend thee still.

REIGNALD   The end still crowns the deed.   45

    Exeunt

4.6

Enter Old Lionel and the first Owner of the house

OWNER Sir, sir, your threats nor warrants can fright me.
    My honesty and innocency's known
    Always to have been unblemished. Would you could
    As well approve your own integrity
    As I shall doubtless acquit myself   5
    Of this surmisèd murder.

OLD LIONEL   Rather surrender
    The price I paid, and take into thy hands
    This haunted mansion, or I'll prosecute
    My wrongs, even to the utmost of the law,
    Which is no less than death.

OWNER   I'll answer all,   10
    Old Lionel, both to thy shame and scorn.
    This for thy menaces!

    [*The Owner gestures.*] *Enter Roger the Clown*

ROGER [*aside*] This is the house, but where's the noise that was wont
    to be in't? I am sent hither to deliver a note to two young gentlemen
    that here keep revel-rout; I remember it since the last massacre of   15
    meat that was made in 't; but it seems that the great storm that
    was raised then is chased now. I have other notes to deliver, one to
    Master Ricott, and—I shall think on them all in order. My old master
    makes a great feast for the parting of young Master Geraldine, who
    is presently upon his departure for travel, and the better to grace it, 20
    hath invited many of his neighbours and friends, where will be old
    Master Geraldine, his son, and I cannot tell how many. But this is
    strange, the gates shut up at this time o' day; belike they are all
    drunk and laid to sleep. If they be, I'll wake them, with a murrain!

    Roger knocks at the door

OLD LIONEL What desperate fellow's this, that, ignorant   25
    Of his own danger, thunders at these gates?

ROGER Ho, Reignald! Riotous Reignald! Revelling Reignald!

OLD LIONEL What madness doth possess thee, honest friend,
    To touch the hammer's handle?

ROGER What madness doth possess thee, honest friend,   30
    To ask me such a question?

OLD LIONEL [to the owner] Nay, stir not you.

OWNER Not I; the game begins.

OLD LIONEL How dost thou? Art thou well?

ROGER Yes, very well, I thank you. How do you, sir?   35

OLD LIONEL No alteration? What change about thee?

ROGER Not so much change about me at this time as to change you a
    shilling into two testers.

OLD LIONEL Yet I advise thee, fellow, for thy good,
    Stand further from the gate.   40

ROGER And I advise thee, friend, for thine own good, stand not betwixt
    me and the gate, but give me leave to deliver my errand. Ho, Reignald,
    you mad rascal!

OLD LIONEL In vain thou thunder'st at these silent doors
    Where no man dwells to answer, saving ghosts,   45
    Furies and sprites.

ROGER Ghosts! Indeed, there has been much walking in and about the
    house after midnight.

OLD LIONEL Strange noise oft heard?

ROGER Yes, terrible noise, that none of the neighbours could take any   50
    rest for it. I have heard it myself.

OLD LIONEL You hear this? Here's more witness.

OWNER Very well, sir.

OLD LIONEL Which you shall dearly answer. Whooping?

ROGER And hallooing.   55

OLD LIONEL And shouting?

ROGER And crying out, till the whole house rung again.

OLD LIONEL Which thou hast heard?

ROGER Oftener than I have toes and fingers.

OLD LIONEL Thou wilt be deposed of this?   60

ROGER I'll be sworn to 't, and that's as good.

OLD LIONEL Very good still. [To the Owner] Yet you are innocent!
    [To Roger] Shall I entreat thee, friend, to avouch as much
    Hereby, to the next justice?

ROGER I'll take my soldier's oath on 't.   65

OLD LIONEL A soldier's oath, what's that?

ROGER My corporal oath. And you know, sir, a corporal is an office
  belonging to a soldier.

OLD LIONEL [*to the Owner*] Yet you are clear? Murder will come to light.

OWNER So will your gullery, too.   70

     Enter Robin, the old serving-man

ROBIN [*aside*] They say my old master's come home. I'll see if he will
  turn me out of doors as the young man has done. I have laid rods
  in piss° for somebody, scape Reignald as he can; and with more
  freedom than I durst late, I boldly now dare knock.

     Robin knocks

OLD LIONEL More madmen yet. I think, since my last voyage,   75
  Half of the world's turned frantic. [*To Robin*] What dost mean?
  Or long'st thou to be blasted?

ROBIN O sir, you are welcome home; 'twas time to come
  Ere all was gone to havoc.

OLD LIONEL   My old servant?
  Before I shall demand of further business,   80
  Resolve me why thou thunder'st at these doors
  Where thou know'st none inhabits?

ROBIN   Are they gone, sir?
  'Twas well yet they have left the house behind,
  For all the furniture, to a bare bench,
  I am sure is spent and wasted.

OLD LIONEL   Where's my son,   85
  That Reignald, posting for him with such speed,
  Brings him not from the country?

ROBIN   Country, sir?
  'Tis a thing they know not. Here they feast,
  Dice, drink and drab. The company they keep,
  Cheaters and roaring lads, and these attended°   90
  By bawds and queans. Your son hath got a strumpet
  On whom he spends all that your sparing left,
  And here they keep court, to whose damned abuses
  Reignald gives all encouragement.

OLD LIONEL   But stay, stay;
  No living soul hath for these six months' space   95
  Here entered, but the house stood desolate.

ROBIN Last week I am sure, so late, and th' other day,
  Such revels were here kept.

OLD LIONEL   And by my son?

ROBIN Yes, and his servant Reignald.

OLD LIONEL   And this house
  At all not haunted?

ROBIN   Save, sir, with such sprites.   100

OWNER This murder will come out.
    Enter Master Ricott

OLD LIONEL But see, in happy time comes my neighbour
  Of whom he bought this mansion. He, I am sure,
  More amply can resolve me. I pray, sir,
  What sums of moneys have you late received   105
  Of my young son?

RICOTT   Of him? None, I assure you.

OLD LIONEL What of my servant Reignald?

RICOTT   But devise
  What to call less than nothing, and that sum
  I will confess received.

OLD LIONEL   Pray sir, be serious.
  I do confess myself indebted to you   110
  A hundred pound.

RICOTT You may do well to pay 't then, for here's witness
  Sufficient of your words.

OLD LIONEL   I speak no more
  Than what I purpose; just so much I owe you,
  And ere I sleep will tender.

RICOTT   I shall be   115
  As ready to receive it, and as willing
  As you can be to pay't.

OLD LIONEL   But provided
  You will confess seven hundred pounds received
  Beforehand of my son.

RICOTT   But by your favour,
  Why should I yield seven hundred received   120
  Of them I never dealt with? Why? For what?
  What reason? What condition? Where or when
  Should such a sum be paid me?

OLD LIONEL Why? For this bargain. And for what? This house.
  Reason? Because you sold it. The conditions? Such   125
  As were agreed between you. Where and when?
  That only hath escaped me.

RICOTT   Madness, all.

OLD LIONEL Was I not brought to take free view thereof
  As of mine own possession?

RICOTT   I confess
　　Your servant told me you had found out a wife   130
　　Fit for your son, and that you meant to build,
　　Desired to take a friendly view of mine
　　To make it your example. But for selling,
　　I tell you, sir, my wants be not so great
　　To change my house to coin.

OLD LIONEL   Spare, sir, your anger   135
　　And turn it into pity. Neighbours and friends,
　　I am quite lost. Was never man so fooled,
　　And by a wicked servant. Shame and blushing
　　Will not permit to tell the manner how,
　　Lest I be made ridiculous to all.   140
　　My fears are, to inherit what's yet left,
　　He hath made my son away.

ROBIN   That's my fear, too.

OLD LIONEL Friends, as you would commiserate a man
　　Deprived at once both of his wealth and son,
　　And in his age, by one I ever tendered   145
　　More like a son than servant, by imagining
　　My case were yours, have feeling of my griefs
　　And help to apprehend him. Furnish me
　　With cords and fetters; I will lay him safe
　　In prison within prison.   150

RICOTT We'll assist you.

ROBIN And I.

ROGER And all. [*Aside*] But not to do the least hurt to my old friend
　　Reignald.

OLD LIONEL His legs will be as nimble as his brain,   155
　　And 'twill be difficult to seize the slave,
　　Yet your endeavours, pray. Peace, here he comes.
　　　　Enter Reignald with a horn in his pocket. They withdraw
　　　　behind the arras

REIGNALD My heart misgives, for 'tis not possible
　　But that in all these windings and indents
　　I shall be found at last. I'll take that course   160
　　That men both troubled and affrighted do:
　　Heap doubt on doubt, and as combustions rise
　　Try if from many I can make my peace
　　And work mine own atonement.

OLD LIONEL   Stand you close,
　　Be not yet seen, but at your best advantage   165

Hand him and bind him fast, whilst I dissemble
As if I yet knew nothing.
    [*He comes forward*]

REIGNALD [*aside*]   I suspect,
And find there's trouble in my master's looks;
Therefore I must not trust myself too far
Within his fingers.

OLD LIONEL   Reignald?

REIGNALD   Worshipful sir.   170

OLD LIONEL What says my son i'the country?

REIGNALD   That tomorrow
Early i'the morning he'll attend your pleasure
And do as all such duteous children ought:
Demand your blessing, sir.

OLD LIONEL   Well; 'tis well.

REIGNALD [*aside*] I do not like his countenance.   175

OLD LIONEL But Reignald, I suspect the honesty
And the good meaning of my neighbour here,
Old Master Ricott. Meeting him but now,
And having some discourse about the house,
He makes all strange, and tells me in plain terms   180
He knows of no such matter—

REIGNALD   Tell me that, sir?

OLD LIONEL I tell thee as it is—nor that such moneys,
Took up at use, were ever tendered him
On any such conditions.

REIGNALD   I cannot blame
Your worship to be pleasant, knowing at what   185
An under-rate we bought it; but you ever
Were a most merry gentleman.

OLD LIONEL [*aside*]   Impudent slave!
[*Aloud*] But Reignald, he not only doth deny it
But offers to depose himself and servants
No such thing ever was.

REIGNALD   Now, heaven to see   190
To what this world's grown to. I will make him—

OLD LIONEL Nay more, this man will not confess the murder.

REIGNALD Which both shall dearly answer; you have warrant
For him already. But for the other sir,
If he deny it, he had better—

OLD LIONEL [*softly*]   Appear gentlemen,   195

'Tis a fit time to take him.

REIGNALD [aside]   I discover
  The ambush that's laid for me.

OLD LIONEL Come nearer, Reignald.

REIGNALD   First, sir, resolve me
  One thing: amongst other merchandise
  Bought in your absence by your son and me   200
  We engrossed a great commodity of combs;
  And how many sorts, think you?

OLD LIONEL   You might buy
  Some of the bones of fishes, some of beasts,
  Box combs, and ivory combs.

REIGNALD   But besides these,
  We have for horses, sir, mane-combs and curry-combs.   205
  Now, sir, for men, we have head-combs, beard-combs, ay, and
  coxcombs, too. Take view of them at your pleasure, whilst for
  my part I thus bestow myself.

       They all appear with cords and shackles, whilst he gets up°

ROGER Well said, Reignald! Nobly put off, Reignald! Look to thyself,
  Reignald!   210

OLD LIONEL Why dost thou climb thus?

REIGNALD   Only to practise
  The nimbleness of my arms and legs
  Ere they prove your cords and fetters.

OLD LIONEL   Why to that place?

REIGNALD Why? Because, sir, 'tis your own house. It hath been my
  harbour long, and now it must be my sanctuary; dispute now, and   215
  I'll answer.

OWNER Villain, what devilish meaning hadst thou in't
  To challenge me of murder?

REIGNALD O sir, the man you killed is alive at this present to justify it:
  'I am', quoth he, 'A transmarine by birth'—   220

RICOTT Why challenge me
  Receipt of moneys, and to give abroad
  That I had sold my house?

REIGNALD   Why? Because, sir,
  Could I have purchased houses at that rate
  I had meant to have bought all London.   225

ROGER Yes, and Middlesex, too, and I would have been thy half,
  Reignald.

OLD LIONEL   Yours are great,

My wrongs insufferable: as, first, to fright me
From mine own dwelling till they had consumed
The whole remainder of the little left;   230
Besides, out of my late stock got at sea
Discharge the clamorous usurer; make me accuse
This man of murder; be at charge of warrants;
And challenging this my worthy neighbour of
Forswearing sums he never yet received;   235
Fool me to think my son that had spent all
Had by his thrift bought land; ay, and him too
To open all the secrets of his house
To me, a stranger. O, thou insolent villain,
What to all these canst answer?

REIGNALD   Guilty, guilty.   240

OLD LIONEL But to my son's death, what, thou slave?

REIGNALD   Not guilty.

OLD LIONEL Produce him, then. I' th' meantime, and—
    Honest friends, get ladders.

REIGNALD Yes, and come down in your own ropes.°

OWNER I'll fetch a piece and shoot him.   245

REIGNALD So the warrant in my master's pocket will serve for my
    murder, and ever after shall my ghost haunt this house.

ROGER And I will say like Reignald, 'This ghost and I am friends.'

OLD LIONEL Bring faggots; I'll set fire upon the house
    Rather than this endure.   250

REIGNALD To burn houses is felony, and I'll not out
    Till I be fired out. But since I am besieged thus,
    I'll summon supplies unto my rescue.
        He winds a horn. Enter Young Lionel, Rioter, two gallants,
        Blanda, and others

YOUNG LIONEL Before you chide, first hear me. Next, your blessing
    That on my knees I beg. I have but done   255
    Like misspent youth, which, after wit dear bought,
    Turns his eyes inward, sorry and ashamed.
    These things in which I have offended most
    Had I not proved, I should have thought them still
    Essential things, delights perdurable,   260
    Which now I find mere shadows, toys and dreams,
    Now hated more than erst I doted on.
    Best natures are soonest wrought on; such was mine.
    As I the offences, so the offenders throw
    Here at your feet, to punish as you please.   265

[*He kneels*]
You have but paid so much as I have wasted
To purchase to yourself a thrifty son
Which I from henceforth vow.

OLD LIONEL   See what fathers are,
That can three years' offences, foul ones too,
Thus in a minute pardon, and thy faults   270
Upon myself chastise in these my tears.
Ere this submission I had cast thee off.
Rise in my new adoption. But for these—

ROGER The one you have nothing to do withal; here's his ticket for his
discharge. [*Hands out invitations*] Another for you, sir, to summon   275
you to my master's feast; for you, and you, where I charge you all
to appear, upon his displeasure and your own apperils.

YOUNG LIONEL This is my friend; the other one I loved.
Only because they have been dear to him
That now will strive to be more dear to you   280
Vouchsafe their pardon.

OLD LIONEL   All dear to me, indeed,
For I have paid for 't soundly; yet for thy sake
I am atoned with all. Only that wanton:
Her and her company abandon quite.
So doing, we are friends.   285

YOUNG LIONEL A just condition, and willingly subscribed to.

OLD LIONEL But for that villain, I am now devising
What shame, what punishment remarkable
To inflict on him.

REIGNALD   Why, master, have I laboured,
Plotted, contrived, and all this while for you,   290
And will you leave me to the whip and stocks,
Not mediate my peace?

OLD LIONEL   Sirrah, come down.

REIGNALD Not till my pardon's sealed; I'll rather stand here
Like a statue in the forefront of your house
For ever, like the picture of Dame Fortune   295
Before the Fortune playhouse.

YOUNG LIONEL   If I have here°
But any friend amongst you, join with me
In this petition.

ROGER Good sir, for my sake. I resolved you truly concerning
whooping, the noise, the walking, and the sprites, and for a need   300
can show you a ticket for him, too.

271

OWNER I impute my wrongs rather to knavish cunning
    Than least pretended malice.
RICOTT   What he did
    Was but for his young master; I allow it
    Rather as sports of wit than injuries;   305
    No other, pray, esteem them.
OLD LIONEL   Even as freely
    As you forgot my quarrels made with you,
    Raised from the errors first begot by him,
    I here remit all free. I now am calm,
    But had I seized upon him in my spleen—   310
REIGNALD I knew that; therefore this was my invention,
    For policy's the art still of prevention.
ROGER Come down, then, Reignald, first on your hands and feet, and
    then on your knees to your master.
       [Exit Reignald from above]
    Now gentlemen, what do you say to your inviting to my master's feast?   315
RICOTT We will attend him.
OLD LIONEL Nor do I love to break good company,
    For Master Wincott is my worthy friend
    And old acquaintance.
       Enter Reignald
              O thou crafty wag-string,
    And couldst thou thus delude me? But we are friends.   320
    Nor, gentlemen, let not what's hereto passed
    In your least thoughts disable my estate:
    This my last voyage hath made all things good,
    With surplus, too; be that your comfort, son.
    Well, Reignald—but no more.
REIGNALD   I was the fox,   325
    But I from henceforth will no more the cox-
    Comb put upon your pate.
OLD LIONEL   Let's walk, gentlemen.
       Exeunt

5.1

Enter Old Geraldine and Young Geraldine

OLD GERALDINE Son, let me tell you, you are ill advised
  And doubly to be blamed, by undertaking
  Unnecessary travel, grounding no reason
  For such a rash and giddy enterprise.
  What profit aim you at you have not reaped?   5
  What novelty affords the Christian world
  Of which your view hath not participated
  In a full measure? Can you either better
  Your language or experience? Your self-will
  Hath only purpose to deprive a father   10
  Of a loved son, and many noble friends
  Of your much wished acquaintance.
YOUNG GERALDINE   O, dear sir,
  Do not, I entreat you, now repent you
  Of your free grant, which with such care and study
  I have so long, so often, laboured for.   15
OLD GERALDINE Say that may be dispensed with, show me reason
  Why you desire to steal out of your country
  Like some malefactor that had forfeited
  His life and freedom. Here's a worthy gentleman
  Hath for your sake invited many guests   20
  To his great charge, only to take of you
  A parting leave. You send him word you cannot,
  After, you may not come. Had not my urgence,
  Almost compulsion, driven you to his house,
  Th' unkindness might have forfeited your love   25
  And rased you from his will, in which he hath given you
  A fair and large estate; yet you of all this strangeness
  Show no sufficient ground.
YOUNG GERALDINE   Then understand,
  The ground thereof took his first birth from you.
  'Twas you first charged me to forbear the house,   30
  And that upon your blessing. Let it not then
  Offend you, sir, if I so great a charge
  Have strived to keep so strictly.

OLD GERALDINE   Me perhaps
  You may appease, and with small difficulty
  Because a father; but how satisfy   35
  Their dear, and, on your part, unmerited, love?
  But this your last obedience may salve all.
  We now grow near the house.
YOUNG GERALDINE [aside]   Whose doors to me
  Appear as horrid as the gates of hell.
  Where shall I borrow patience, or from whence,   40
  To give a meeting to this viperous brood°
  Of friend and mistress?
      Enter Wincott, his Wife, Ricott, the two Lionels, the Owner,
      Dalavill, Prudentilla, Reignald, and Rioter
WINCOTT You've entertained me with a strange discourse
  Of your man's knavish wit, but I rejoice
  That in your safe return all ends so well.   45
  Most welcome to you, and you, and indeed all,
  To whom I am bound that at so short a warning
  Thus friendly you will deign to visit me.
OLD LIONEL It seem my absence hath begot some sport,
  Thank my kind servant here.
REIGNALD   Not so much worth, sir.   50
OLD LIONEL But though their riots tripped at my estate
  They have not quite o'erthrown it.
WINCOTT   But see, gentlemen,
  These whom we most expected come at length.
  This I proclaim the master of the feast,
  In which, to express the bounty of my love,   55
  I'll show myself no niggard.
YOUNG GERALDINE   Your choice favours:
  I still taste in abundance.
WIFE Methinks it would not misbecome me, sir,
  To chide your absence, that have made yourself
  To us so long a stranger.
      He turns away sad, as not being minded
YOUNG GERALDINE [to Old Lionel] Pardon me, sir,   60
  That have not yet, since your return from sea,
  Voted the least fit opportunity
  To entertain you with a kind salute.
OLD LIONEL Most kindly, sir, I thank you.
DALAVILL   Methinks, friend,

You should expect green rushes to be strewed   65
After such discontinuance.

YOUNG GERALDINE   Mistress Pru,
I have not seen you long, but greet you thus:
May you be lady of a better husband
Than I expect a wife.

WINCOTT   I like that greeting.
Nay, enter, gentlemen. Dinner perhaps   70
Is not yet ready, but the time we stay
We'll find some fresh discourse to spend away.
          Exeunt. Dalavill remains

DALAVILL Not speak to me, nor once vouchsafe an answer,
But slight me with a poor and base neglect?
No, nor so much as cast an eye on her,   75
Or least regard, though in a seeming show
She courted a reply? 'Twixt him and her,
Nay, him and me, this was not wont to be.
If she have brain to apprehend as much
As I have done, she'll quickly find it out.   80
          Enter Young Geraldine and Wife
Now, as I live, as our affections meet,
So our conceits, and she hath singled him
To some such purpose. I'll retire myself,
Not interrupt their conference.
          Exit

WIFE   You are sad, sir.

YOUNG GERALDINE I know no cause.

WIFE   Then can I show you some: 85
Who could be otherways, to leave a father
So careful, and each way so provident?
To leave so many and such worthy friends?
To abandon your own country? These are some,
Nor do I think you can be much the merrier   90
For my sake.

YOUNG GERALDINE
          Now your tongue speaks oracles,
For all the rest are nothing; 'tis for you,
Only for you, I cannot.

WIFE   So I thought.
Why, then, have you been all this while so strange?
Why will you travel, suing a divorce   95

Betwixt us of a love inseparable?
For here shall I be left as desolate
Unto a frozen, almost widowed bed,
Warmed only in that future stored in you,
For who can in your absence comfort me?   100

YOUNG GERALDINE [*aside*] Shall my oppressed sufferance yet
    break forth
Into impatience, or endure her more?

WIFE But since by no persuasion, no entreats,
    Your settled obstinacy can be swayed,
    Though you seem desperate of your own dear life,   105
    Have care of mine, for it exists in you.
    O sir, should you miscarry I were lost,
    Lost and forsaken. Then, by our past vows
    And by this hand once given me, by these tears
    Which are but springs begetting greater floods,   110
    I do beseech thee, my dear Geraldine,
    Look to thy safety and preserve thy health;
    Have care into what company you fall;
    Travel not late, and cross no dangerous seas;
    For till heavens bless me in thy safe return   115
    How will this poor heart suffer!

YOUNG GERALDINE [*aside*]   I had thought
    Long since the Sirens had been all destroyed;°
    But one of them I find survives in her;
    She almost makes me question what I know,
    An heretic unto my own belief.   120
    O, thou mankind's seducer.

WIFE   What, no answer?

YOUNG GERALDINE Yes, thou hast spoke to me in showers;
    I will reply in thunder: thou adulteress,
    That hast more poison in thee than the serpent
    Who was the first that did corrupt thy sex,   125
    The devil.

WIFE   To whom speaks the man?

YOUNG GERALDINE   To thee,
    Falsest of all that ever man termed fair.
    Hath impudence so steeled thy smooth soft skin
    It cannot blush? Or sin so obdured thy heart
    It doth not quake and tremble? Search thy conscience;   130
    There thou shalt find a thousand clamorous tongues
    To speak as loud as mine doth.

WIFE   Save from yours,
    I hear no noise at all.
YOUNG GERALDINE   I'll play the doctor
    To open thy deaf ears: Monday the ninth
    Of the last month; canst thou remember that?   135
    That night; more black in thy abhorred sin
    Than in the gloomy darkness. That the time.
WIFE Monday?
YOUNG GERALDINE Wouldst thou the place know? Thy polluted
    chamber,
    So often witness of my sinless vows.   140
    Wouldst thou the person? One not worthy name,
    Yet to torment thy guilty soul the more
    I'll tell him thee: that monster Dalavill.
    Wouldst thou your bawd know? Midnight, that the hour.
    The very words thou spake? 'Now what would Geraldine   145
    Say if he saw us here?' To which was answered,
    'Tush, he's a coxcomb, fit to be so fooled.'
    No blush? What, no faint fever on thee yet?
    How hath thy black sins changed thee! Thou Medusa.°
    Those hairs that late appeared like golden wires   150
    Now crawl with snakes and adders. Thou art ugly.
WIFE And yet my glass till now ne'er told me so.
    Who gave you this intelligence?
YOUNG GERALDINE   Only He°
    That, pitying such an innocency as mine
    Should by two such delinquents be betrayed,   155
    He brought me to that place by miracle
    And made me an ear-witness of all this.
WIFE I am undone.
YOUNG GERALDINE But think what thou hast lost
    To forfeit me. Ay, notwithstanding these
    (So fixed was my love and unalterable)   160
    I kept this from thy husband, nay, all ears,
    With thy transgressions smothering mine own wrongs
    In hope of thy repentance.
WIFE   Which begins
    Thus low upon my knees.
YOUNG GERALDINE   Tush, bow to heaven,
    Which thou hast most offended. I, alas,   165
    Save in such scarce unheard-of treachery,
    Most sinful like thyself. Wherein, O wherein,

Hath my unspotted and unbounded love deserved
The least of these? Sworn to be made a stale
For term of life, and all this for my goodness?   170
Die, and die soon; acquit me of my oath,
But prithee, die repentant. Farewell ever;
'Tis thou, and only thou, hast banished me
Both from my friends and country.

WIFE   O, I am lost.
      She sinks down. Enter Dalavill meeting Young Geraldine
      going out

DALAVILL Why, how now, what's the business?   175

YOUNG GERALDINE Go take her up whom thou hast oft thrown down,
  Villain.
      Exit

DALAVILL [*aside*] That was no language from a friend,
  It had too harsh an accent. But how's this,
  My mistress thus low cast upon the earth,
  Gravelling and breathless? Mistress, lady, sweet—   180

WIFE O tell me if thy name be Geraldine;
  Thy very looks will kill me!

DALAVILL   View me well,
  I am no such man; see, I am Dalavill.

WIFE Th' art then a devil, that presents before me
  My horrid sins, persuades me to despair,   185
  When he, like a good angel sent from heaven,
  Besought me of repentance. Swell, sick heart,
  Even till thou burst the ribs that bound thee in.
  So, there's one string cracked. Flow, and flow high,
  Even till thy blood distil out of mine eyes   190
  To witness my great sorrow.

DALAVILL   Faint again!
  [*Calls*] Some help within there! No attendant near?
  Thus to expire! In this I am more wretched
  Than all the sweet fruition of her love
  Before could make me happy.
      Enter Wincott, Old Geraldine, Young Geraldine, the two Lionels,
      Ricott, the Owner, Prudentilla, Reignald, and Roger the Clown

WINCOTT   What was he   195
  Clamoured so loud, to mingle with our mirth
  This terror and affright?

DALAVILL　　　　　　　　See, sir, your wife
　　In these my arms expiring.
WINCOTT　　　　　　　　　　How?
PRUDENTILLA　　　　　　　　　My sister!
WINCOTT Support her, and by all means possible
　　Provide for her dear safety.
OLD GERALDINE　　　　　　　See, she recovers.　　　　　　　200
WINCOTT Woman, look up.
WIFE　　　　　　　　　　O sir, your pardon.
　　Convey me to my chamber; I am sick,
　　Sick even to death. [*To Dalavill*] Away, thou sycophant,
　　Out of my sight! I have, besides thyself,
　　Too many sins about me.
ROGER　　　　　　　　　　My sweet mistress!　　　　　　　205
　　　　　[*Prudentilla and Roger take the Wife away*]
DALAVILL　The storm's coming, I must provide for harbour.
　　　　　Exit Dalavill
OLD LIONEL　What strange and sudden alteration's this?
　　How quickly is this clear day overcast.
　　But such and so uncertain are all things
　　That dwell beneath the moon.
YOUNG LIONEL　　　　　　　A woman's qualm,°　　　　210
　　Frailties that are inherent to her sex,
　　Soon sick, and soon recovered.
WINCOTT　　　　　　　　　If she misfare°
　　I am a man more wretched in her loss
　　Than had I forfeited life and estate,
　　She was so good a creature.
OLD GERALDINE　　　　　　I the like　　　　　　　215
　　Suffered when I my wife brought unto her grave.
　　So you, when you were first a widower;
　　Come, arm yourself with patience.
RICOTT　　　　　　　　　　These are casualties
　　That are not new, but common.
REIGNALD [*aside*]　　　　　Burying of wives—
　　As stale as shifting shirts—or for some servants　　　220
　　To flout and gull their masters.
OWNER　　　　　　　　　Best to send
　　　And see how her fit holds her.
　　　　　Enter Prudentilla and Clown [*with a letter*]

PRUDENTILLA   Sir, my sister
  In these few lines commends her last to you,
  For she is now no more. What's therein writ
  Save heaven and you, none knows. This she desired   225
  You would take view of, and with these words expired.
WINCOTT Dead?
YOUNG GERALDINE [*aside*] She hath made me then a free release
  Of all the debts I owed her.
          [*Wincott reads the letter*]
WINCOTT [*aside*] 'My fear is, beyond pardon Dalavill
  Hath played the villain, but for Geraldine,   230
  He hath been each way noble. Love him still.
  My peace already I have made with heaven;
  O, be not you at war with me; my honour
  Is in your hands, to punish or preserve.
  I am now confessed, and only Geraldine   235
  Hath wrought on me this unexpected good.
  The ink I write with, I wish had been my blood
  To witness my repentance.' Dalavill!
  Where's he? Go, seek him out.
ROGER   I shall, I shall, sir.
          Exit Roger the Clown
WINCOTT [*aside*] The wills of dead folk should be still obeyed;   240
  However false to me, I'll not reveal 't.
  Where heaven forgives, I pardon. [*Aloud*] Gentlemen,
  I know you all commiserate my loss;
  I little thought this feast should have been turned
  Into a funeral.
          Enter Clown
                    What's the news of him?   245
ROGER He went presently to the stable, put the saddle upon his horse,
  put his foot into the stirrup, clapped his spurs into his sides, and
  away he's galloped as if he were to ride a race for a wager.
WINCOTT All our ill lucks go with him. Farewell he,
  [*To Young Geraldine*] But all my best of wishes wait on you   250
  As my chief friend. This meeting that was made
  Only to take of you a parting leave
  Shall now be made a marriage of our love
  Which none save only death shall separate.
YOUNG GERALDINE It calls me from all travel, and from henceforth   255
  With my country I am friends.
WINCOTT   The lands that I have left

You lend me for the short space of my life;
As soon as heaven calls me, they call you lord.
First feast, and after mourn. We'll, like some gallants
That bury thrifty fathers, think't no sin   260
To wear blacks without, but other thoughts within.
    Exeunt

DEDICATION AND
ADDRESS TO THE READER

When the play was published in 1633, Heywood added a dedication
and an address to the reader, reprinted here.

The Epistle Dedicatory

To the Right Worshipful Sir Henry Appleton,° Knight, Baronet, &c.

Noble Sir,
For many reasons I am induced to present this poem to your favourable
acceptance; and not the least of them, that alternate love and those fre
quent courtesies, which interchangeably passed betwixt yourself and   5
the good old gentleman mine uncle (Master Edmund Heywood) whom
you pleased to grace by the title of Father. I must confess, I had altogether slept (my weakliness and bashfulness discouraging me) had
they not been wakened and animated by that worthy gentleman, your
friend and my countryman, Sir William Elwes,° whom (for his unmer-   10
ited love many ways extended towards me) I much honour. Neither,
sir, need you to think it any undervaluing of your worth to undertake
the patronage of a poem in this nature, since the like hath been done
by Roman Laelius,° Scipio,° Maecenas,° and many other mighty princes
and captains, nay, even by Augustus Caesar° himself, concerning whom   15
Ovid is thus read (*Trist.* 2):

> *Inspice ludorum sumptus, Auguste, tuorum:*
> *empta tibi magno talia multa leges.*
> *Haec tu spectasti spectandaque saepe dedisti*
> *(maiestas adeo comis ubique tua est).*°   20

So highly were they respected in the most flourishing estate of the
Roman Empire; and if they have been vilified of late by any separistical
humourist, as in the now questioned *Histriomastix,*° I hope by the
next term (*Minerva assistente*)° to give such satisfaction° to the world,
by vindicating many particulars in that work maliciously exploded and   25
condemned, as that no gentleman of quality and judgement but shall
therein receive a reasonable satisfaction. I am loath by tediousness to
grow troublesome, therefore conclude with a grateful remembrance of
my service, intermixed with myriads of zealous wishes for your health

of body and peace of mind, with superabundance of earth's blessings,   30
and Heaven's graces, ever remaining,

Your most observant,
Thomas Heywood.

To the Reader

If, reader, thou hast of this play been an auditor, there is less apology
to be used by entreating thy patience. This tragicomedy (being one
reserved amongst two hundred and twenty in which I have had either
an entire hand or at the least a main finger) coming accidentally to the
press, and I have intelligence thereof, thought it not fit that it should   5
pass *filius populi*,° a bastard without a father to acknowledge it. True it
is that my plays are not exposed unto the world in volumes to bear the
title of *Works*, as others'°. One reason is that many of them, by shifting and change of companies, have been negligently lost; others of
them are still retained in the hands of some actors, who think it against   10
their peculiar profit to have them come in print; and a third, that it
never was any great ambition in me to be in this kind voluminously
read. All that I have further to say at this time is only this: censure, I
entreat, as favourably as it is exposed to thy view freely. Ever

studious of thy pleasure and profit,   15
Thomas Heywood

APPENDIX 1

THE UNKNOWN AUTHOR OF
ARDEN OF FAVERSHAM

When *Arden of Faversham* was first published in 1592, its title-page gave no indication of its authorship. This was not in the least unusual: Thomas Kyd's *The Spanish Tragedy*, Christopher Marlowe's *Tamburlaine*, and Shakespeare's *Henry VI* were likewise effectively anonymous works when they debuted in print in the first half of the 1590s. The difference is that these plays were later securely ascribed to named dramatists and, for Marlowe and Shakespeare at least, assimilated into larger authorial canons, whereas *Arden* remains an orphan. Four centuries on, we shall never know for sure who wrote it, but we can infer several things about the author.

He is far more likely to have been a man than a woman: the only known female dramatists of the sixteenth century wrote literary tragedies in the classical tradition, not plays like *Arden* in the milieu of the developing commercial theatre. He had received a broader-than-usual classical education: in the opening scene he comfortably appropriates a passage from one of the erotic poems of Ovid, which were not on any Elizabethan grammar-school syllabus. And he knew north Kent intimately: the marshy ground where it tends to get misty and unwary men risk falling into bogs, the places where roads fork and fellow-travellers with different destinations must leave one another, the fact that Faversham, a few miles inland, nevertheless has ready access to the sea; throughout, the action has an unostentatious geographical precision which is usually only found in plays set in London. Beyond that, we are in ignorance, and must be content to say that *Arden* was the work of an otherwise unknown dramatist.

Yet there is a powerful temptation to father the play on someone we already know. Optimistic people have seized on a misprinted ascription to Shakespeare in Edward Archer's play catalogue of 1656 and given it far more weight than it deserves. Archer's unreliability emerges forcefully when you consider that he also names Shakespeare as the author of, among others, *The Spanish Tragedy*, Henry Chettle's *Hoffman*, Thomas Middleton's *A Trick to Catch the Old One*, and John Fletcher's *The Chances*, the last of which was written some years after Shakespeare died. (Archer is, moreover, responsible for centuries of confusion arising from his misattribution of Middleton's *The Revenger's Tragedy* to Cyril Tourneur.) However, there was one commercial playwright working at the time who fits the *Arden* author's profile with uncanny exactitude. Christopher Marlowe was born in Canterbury and educated at Cambridge, and not only translated Ovid's *Amores* into English but also puts into the mouth of the doomed Doctor Faustus the Latin original of the very line that Arden adapts to describe his once happy sex life with Alice. If the style of *Arden* is unlike the lush, early Marlovian verse of the *Tamburlaine* plays (1587) and *Doctor Faustus* (1588), so too is Marlowe's own mature, 'greyer' writing in *Edward II* (1592) and *The Massacre at Paris* (1593).

An ascription to Marlowe would make perfect circumstantial sense, but it will not do. The internal evidence of the play tells us one other thing about the *Arden* author: that he was not a theatre professional. He was certainly familiar with the new wave of tragedy which developed in the late 1580s, driven by the innovations of Marlowe and Kyd. He had seen and appreciated *The Spanish Tragedy*, which was still unpublished when *Arden* first saw print, for he imitates one of its more memorable lines (4.88). He knew the theatre, but he did not really know how it worked: as a practical stage-writer he was immensely inexperienced, even naïve. There is a minor blunder in his plot management concerning Greene's letter which Bradshaw carries back to Faversham (see note to 8.157), and the play intermittently shows a striking disregard for the techniques and limitations of the theatre. In particular, no playwright with a jot of backstage experience would have written a woman's part like Alice Arden. At around 600 lines, it is the most substantial role in the play, almost twice the combined length of the two next largest (Arden and Mosby), and well beyond what Elizabethan acting companies usually expected of their boy apprentices. (In the early 1590s, a principal female character, such as Queen Margaret in the *Henry VI* plays, typically spoke 200–300 lines per play, compared with 600–800 lines for a leading man.) It is as if the dramatist is so caught up with telling his powerful story that he forgets it will also have to be realized on stage.

The original stage directions are very distinctively worded, using the formula 'here enters' and often stating that 'then' such-and-such an event happens. It is possible to infer that, in his mind's eye, the author imagined the action from the audience's point of view: he is aware of the doors set in the back wall of the stage, and twice mentions them (at the heads of Scenes 7 and 12), but he never thinks beyond them into the backstage area. At one point he does not see the theatre at all: '*Then Shakebag falls into a ditch*' (12.18 SD). Elizabethan stages were not ordinarily equipped with ditches: he is evidently thinking in terms of the real location, a Kentish marsh. To simulate the incident in the theatre, the actor would need to drop through a trapdoor, then climb out again. While out of sight under the stage, he has to become 'bewrayed' (50)— covered in filth. In theory, there were two ways of achieving this. The simpler option, involving a stage hand and a bucket of mud, would leave the company with an unwelcome and tedious cleaning operation after each and every performance: no matter how down-at-heel the murderers may look, Shakebag cannot start off with a costume already muddy from the play's previous outing. But clothing was expensive, and frequent heavy cleaning would have shortened its useful life. The sensible alternative would have been a quick change into a duplicate costume already covered in mud, if only that were possible in the time available. But between Shakebag's falling into the trap and being helped out, there are only three short speeches between Black Will and the Ferryman, taking perhaps fifteen or twenty seconds' playing time: the actor scarcely has the chance to catch his breath, let alone fiddle with the manifold fastenings of Elizabethan clothes. The author, of course, has never thought it through in terms of practical staging.

It is useful to contrast the handling of a similar issue in *The Witch of Edmonton*, the work of two very experienced theatre men (Dekker and Rowley) and a promising newcomer (Ford). When Cuddy Banks falls into the pond, Rowley, who wrote as well as played Cuddy, sends himself off the stage so that the mishap can be imagined rather than having to be seen. He then quickly re-enters 'wet' (3.1.93 SD), presumably after an off-stage splash as he drenched himself. The incident is cannily placed just before Cuddy is due for a costume change, so he will not need to stay in the wet clothes after the scene is over: when we next see him, in 3.4, he is dressed in his hobby-horse outfit for the morris dance. No mud has been involved, only water, so the costume will dry off of its own accord and will not need to be cleaned. Rowley has skilfully anticipated and circumvented all the staging problems which the *Arden* dramatist failed even to see.

Both plays include points when the action needs momentarily to be suspended so that a necessary event can take place. In *The Witch of Edmonton*, it is the unremarkable but narratively important moment in 1.2 when Old Thorney reads Sir Arthur Clarington's letter averring untruthfully that Frank has not married Winifred, and so is free to marry Susan Carter. Dekker deftly covers the interval of silent reading by giving Frank an aside about how fate seems inexorably to be leading him the wrong way (189–91). In *Arden*, however, words fail and things simply come to a standstill. It happens twice, at moments of significantly greater tension, in the opening scene when Arden begins to eat the poisoned broth, and in the murder scene when the killers bundle his dead body away for outdoor disposal, leaving Alice alone on stage with nothing to say or do. Of course, there are opportunities there for skilful theatre practitioners: in the 1970 Royal Shakespeare Company production, Dorothy Tutin made much of the way Alice ran out of both words and stratagems once the murder was done, and in the earlier scene it is possible to create an intense, uncomfortable focus on Arden as the other characters watch him start what two of them hope will be his last meal on earth. But equally it is a tyro author who unwittingly puts such difficulties in his actors' way.

All of this makes it possible to say with confidence that *Arden of Faversham*, though not inherently a bad play, was certainly not written by a mid-career Marlowe, nor by a Shakespeare making his first tentative move across from acting into script-writing, nor by Kyd, nor Greene, nor Peele, nor any other experienced commercial playwright, nor an enterprising actor. All these people would have known and understood the theatre practices which *Arden* flouts. Of course, even established authors are not immune from error, but the *Arden* playwright makes rather more than his fair share. The play's strengths and weaknesses suggest instead the work of an enthusiastic amateur—or, in modern terms, a fan. If by some miracle we ever found out his name, it would probably not mean very much to us, because he seems to have written nothing else that survives. For once we must do without our habitual fondness for placing literary works into larger groups defined by their common authorship: with *Arden of Faversham*, the play itself really is the thing.

APPENDIX 2

THE DATE OF *THE ENGLISH TRAVELLER*

Historians of English drama have customarily dated the writing of *The English Traveller* around 1626–7, in the belief that Heywood's source for the main plot was 'A Modern History of an Adulteress'; the story appears in his *Gunaikeion*, a collection of narratives about women published in 1624. Two passing references also seem to point to a date in the second half of the 1620s. But all this 'evidence' disintegrates under closer scrutiny.

The two apparently topical allusions both occur in relation to Young Lionel's drunken revelry in the second act. First, Roger the clown says that canary wine runs 'like the conduits of a coronation day' (2.1.35–6), referring to the traditional civic festivities when London's public drinking fountains were charged with wine instead of the usual water. King Charles I was crowned on 2 February 1626; but a serious outbreak of plague made it an atypical event which passed without the usual municipal celebrations (though these were, notoriously, not cancelled before the city had incurred expenses amounting to £4,300 by way of preparation). But Young Lionel is prodigal, not parsimonious, in the supply of liquor: the coronation reference must be read 'straight', without the sardonic irony it would necessarily have had if written in or soon after 1626.

In the next scene, when Young Lionel develops an extended nautical metaphor, he issues a warning to his English ship making its way home: 'The Spaniard now strikes sail' (2.2.24). The allusion is to a Spanish man-of-war preparing to attack, and this would seem to fix the writing of the play after war with Spain was declared in 1625. But in fact, anti-Spanish sentiments were rife in the summer of 1624, and were pointedly not being restrained by the Revels Office, the government censor of commercial stage plays: early in August, Spain and its agents were lampooned in Thomas Middleton's *A Game at Chess*, and a key incident in the comedy *A Wedding* by John Webster and William Rowley, licensed for performance at the end of July, is a sea battle between an English vessel and a hostile flotilla of Spanish warships—the very type of event which provides Young Lionel with his metaphor. Anglo-Spanish friction was well advanced before the formal declaration of war the following year, so all the reference tells us for sure is that *The English Traveller* was not written before late 1623, when England was still pursuing a pro-Spanish foreign policy and attempting to negotiate a Spanish marriage for the heir to the throne.

This leaves us with the supposed source in *Gunaikeion*. Heywood compiled the book in considerable haste (it took him just seventeen weeks, he said), and he used whatever material came conveniently to hand, including the plots of several plays, such as *The Honest Man's Fortune* (1613) by Nathan Field and John Fletcher, and his own *The Captives*, which he completed in the late summer of 1624 (it was licensed on 3 September). Another was the main plot of *The English Traveller*. The reason scholars used to think the *Gunaikeion* version came first is that Heywood calls the tale 'a modern History lately happening, and in mine own knowledge' (sig. S1^r): in other words, he represents it as a true story, forcing the inference that the play was a later reworking. In fact, however, *The English Traveller*'s last editor, Paul Merchant, demonstrated with a close verbal analysis that the *Gunaikeion* story derived from the play rather than vice versa: it had happened 'lately' in that it was performed in London, presumably at the Cockpit theatre by Heywood's usual company, Lady Elizabeth's Men.[1]

In turn, the play drew the narrative from Heywood's own tragedy of twenty years before, *A Woman Killed with Kindness*. The two main plots correspond closely, with the added complication that Mrs Wincott is both a present and future wife to two different men: in proposing this arrangement, Young Geraldine accepts the same celibacy that Frankford imposes on himself in banishing but not killing the adulterous Anne; he is betrayed by a friend, Dalavill, as Frankford is by Wendoll, and there are closely parallel night scenes (Scene 13 and 4.3) in which the two men discover the guilty couples asleep in bed together. 'A Modern History of an Adulteress' is not the true story it claims to be; on the contrary, it is doubly fictitious, a tale whose immediate source was itself a reworking of another fiction.

All this enables us to date *The English Traveller* with some precision, after the shift in government policy towards Spain, but before the seventeen-week period, probably at the end of 1624, that Heywood spent churning out *Gunaikeion*. In all likelihood the play was written in the late spring or early summer of that year: dramatists would have become more cautious in their Spanish references after August, when *A Game at Chess* caused a diplomatic scandal and the issue of a warrant for Middleton's arrest. In terms of Heywood's career, that places *The English Traveller* between *Fortune by Land and Sea* (*c*.1623), another play about the complications arising from marriage and the transmission of property, and *The Captives*, which draws its main plot, as *The English Traveller* does its sub-plot, from a Latin comedy by Plautus.

---

[1] Thomas Heywood, *Three Marriage Plays*, ed. Paul Merchant, Revels Plays Companion Library (Manchester, 1996), 14.

EXPLANATORY NOTES

Arden of Faversham

THE PERSONS OF THE PLAY

Lord Cheyne: Sir Thomas Cheyne (1485?–1558), an important court figure; historically he was not a lord. The name is pronounced 'Chainey'.

1.2 *Duke of Somerset*: Edward Seymour (*c.*1506–1552), Lord Protector of England 1547–9.

4 *his majesty*: the reference to a male sovereign economically establishes for the play's first audiences, ruled by Elizabeth I for more than three decades, that the action is not contemporary: it takes place during the reign of Edward VI (1547–53).

2–5 *My . . . Faversham*: after the dissolution of the monasteries in the mid-sixteenth century, ecclesiastical lands were confiscated by the crown and distributed to court favourites or for money.

11 *nothing . . . torments*: nothing other than that which torments.

12 *And . . . eyes*: this phrase is governed by 'shows me nothing but' in the previous line.

13 *for*: instead of.

17 *the ring*: at this time it was usual for a wedding ring to be worn only by the bride.

25 *at the first*: in social origin.

30 *his silken gown*: the pronoun refers to Lord Clifford, not Mosby: the gown is his livery (distinctive colours worn by a nobleman's servants).

32 *Lord Clifford*: Henry Clifford, 2nd Earl of Cumberland (died 1570), a Catholic nobleman.

43 *channels*: the blood is imagined flowing freely from open wounds.

47 *race*: penetrate.

48 *jealous*: frequently pronounced with three syllables (compare Q spelling *jelious*).

51 *term*: one of the four law terms, when the courts were in session. Many of the country gentry would take up temporary residence in London during term-time. The terms were of unequal length (Michaelmas Term, October–November, was the longest), but all four put together lasted little more than three months: Arden will not be long away from home.

52 *will not*: do not wish to.

53 *outrageous*: excessive; here, excessively lascivious.

54 *abhors from*: is at variance with.

59 *rise*: risen (pronounced *riz*).

60 *Ovid*: a Roman erotic poet (43 BC–AD 17), banished by the Emperor Augustus and popular in Renaissance England. The rest of Arden's sentence plays on Ovid's *Amores* 1.13, in which he rebukes the early arrival of the dawn to interrupt his love-making, and calls on the horses of the night to run slowly.

64 *Ocean*: in classical mythology, the Atlantic Ocean, from which the goddess of dawn rises, and where she spends every night with her lover.

67 *like*: likely, probable.

74 *credit*: credibility.

81 *presently*: immediately.

85 *come again*: return.

88 *fetch*: fetches. Verbs in this play frequently disobey modern rules of grammatical concord.

89 *the quay*: Faversham is situated on a creek which leads down to the coast; thus Arden can go to the quay and be back in time for breakfast later in the scene.

99 *he*: Arden.

102 *title*: right of possession.

104 S.D. *the Flower-de-Luce*: an inn in Abbey Street, Faversham.

111 *in any case*: whatever the circumstances.

113 *take no knowledge*: show no awareness.

116 *Hercules*: hero in classical mythology, who went mad and killed his own children.

117 *of force*: exceptionally strong.

128 *but along*: only outside; Mosby more habitually comes indoors at her house.

135 *marrow-prying*: deeply inquisitive, as if prying with X-ray eyes into the very marrow of her bones.

152 *a dagger . . . heart*: a lover's token signifying the pains of an unrequited passion. This could be a trinket like the dice Alice has just sent to Mosby, or a painted emblem; Michael seems to take it literally (compare 159–60).

153 *stolen*: plagiarized.

a painted cloth: hung over the walls of sixteenth-century rooms; they were often decorated with narrative pictures and verses.

156 *both write and read*: reading and writing were distinct skills in the period; not everyone who could read (as Michael can) could also write.

158–60 *such . . . head*: the letter will taunt Clarke, the painter, and so make him ridiculous in Susan's eyes; thus she will no longer value his love-token, and reject him.

165 *took*: caught, arrested.

166–7 *Susan . . . shrieve*: it was popularly believed that a virgin could save a condemned man from hanging by taking him for her husband.

167 *of . . . shrieve*: from the sheriff (the officer supervising the execution).

173 *Boughton*: a village near Faversham.

181 *'Tis . . . fear*: the scene takes place in the early morning, so nobody is about yet to witness their meeting.

191 *closet*: private chamber.

201 *countenance*: be appropriate to, 'suit'.

202–3 *Being . . . gentleman*: refers to Alice herself, not Mosby.

204 *may'st*: might.

209 *strange*: stand-offish.

213 *So . . . song*: mermaids were thought to lure sailors who listened to their songs to steer a course onto rocks.

221 *our children*: these may only be *potential* children, not yet begotten, although in the source, Holinshed's *Chronicles*, the Ardens have a daughter.

225 *We'll . . . there*: prevent him from going (by killing him before his departure).

229 *oil*: the oil paints Clarke uses. It takes a skilful ('cunning') man to mix ('temper') this concoction because oil was widely thought to be the antithesis of poison.

231 *beams*: Renaissance optical theories depended on the notion of invisible beams connecting the eye with the object seen; authorities disagreed which of the two produced these beams, but here they are credulously imagined as the channel through which the poison will transmit itself into the body.

233 *counterfeit*: portrait.

242 *that*: something that.

256 *Muse*: inspiration; from the nine Muses, goddesses of the arts in classical mythology.

260 *but*: unless.

use her well: treat her kindly.

271 *venture life*: gamble with life (because murder was punishable by death).

274 *control*: restraint, check.

295 *Sir Anthony Aucher*: member of a minor gentry family of Otterden, Kent (died 1558). A former supporter of Thomas Cromwell, he was knighted by Edward VI on Shrove Tuesday 1547 and became Master of the King's Jewels.

307 *pocket up*: put up with, tolerate.

311 *The . . . artificers*: by a statute of 1363, then still in force, wearing of swords was restricted to the ranks of gentlemen and above. Arden is calling attention to Mosby's lowly status as a mere craftsman ('artificer'), and proceeds to confiscate his illicit sword.

312 *warrant that*: have authority (from the statute) for what.

312–13 *bodkin . . . pressing-iron*: the implements of Mosby's former trade as a botcher.

315 *goodman*: a mode of address implying lower rank.

327 *elected saints*: the phrase is ambiguous: it can be taken to refer to saints in the usual sense, chosen ('elected') by God, who played an important role in Catholic devotional practice; Protestants, however, used the phrase to refer to the whole community of blessed souls in heaven. Mosby is perhaps exploiting the ambiguity to obscure his doctrinal allegiances.

340 *I'll be friends*: Arden may give Mosby back his sword at about this point.

341 *base terms*: insulting words.

359 *light . . . weigh*: trivial . . . judge.

361 *Master Mosby*: Arden pointedly retracts the more demeaning term 'goodman' which he used at line 315.

362 *for company*: to be sociable.

373 *convinced*: proven guilty, convicted.

375 *hang*: only metaphorically; hanging was not the penalty for adultery, or for a wife's murder of her husband (see note on 18.31).

378 *doubts*: dubious accusations.

395 *again*: back.

395 S.D. *Enter Michael*: Michael does not speak in this part of the scene. He was sent to prepare the horses at line 363, but is back on stage by line 416, when he is included in the exit direction. His entrance could be placed anywhere in the passage (he could, for example, clean up the broth spilt on the stage by Alice at line 367), but if he enters now it silently conveys the information that the horses are ready, and so prompts Franklin's next line.

407 *tide*: hour of the day.

422 *he's . . . he*: Arden.

425 *gross and populous*: crude and obvious; but perhaps alternatively implying cheap and nasty, fit for the vulgar rather than a 'designer' poison.

439 *proved*: as if by academic reasoning; in the universities students were taught to 'prove' propositions by syllogistic logic.

461 *Generally intitled*: granted legal possession (of the lands) without regard for prior claims.

465 *in state*: by right of legal ownership.

468 *Chancery*: the court of the Lord Chancellor, the highest in the land.

470 *touched*: affected (could mean either wronged or upset).

472–3 *only . . . portion*: all Greene has left from his inheritance is the land ('living') which Arden has now acquired.

481 *so*: so much.

490 *what you brought*: her dowry.

496 *content*: be enough for.

498 *at home*: i.e. in Faversham.

522 *wager*: bribe.

522–3 *ten pound . . . twenty*: when the play was written, the best-paid skilled workers rarely received wages in excess of £10 per annum.

539 *them*: the news.

540 *tempered*: made pliable, persuaded.

545 *books*: favour.

547 *make a gree*: come to terms.

560 *interest*: rights to a share in the land.

562 *choler*: one of the four humours of Renaissance medical theory. The balance of the humours in a person's bloodstream was thought to determine his psychological state; an excess of choler would make him irascible (and, therefore, prone to commit murder).

580 *make . . . open*: reveal.

582 *Forewarned, forearmed*: proverbial (Tilley H.54).

596 *lays . . . life*: paints a vivid, accurate image.

601 *It . . . grant*: as head of the family, Mosby has the right of veto over his sister's choice of husband.

617 *toucheth*: has to do with.

622 *draw . . . out*: put the finishing touches to.

629 *offend . . . sight*: i.e. make him ill through his eyes.

632 *softly as*: as comfortably as if it were.

2.8 *Boulogne*: French seaport, garrisoned by the English, 1544–50. Many of the soldiers there were recruited in Kent, often from the criminal classes.

12 *a crown*: a gold coin worth five shillings (25p).

29–30 *share crowns with*: i.e. rob.

36 *Sir Anthony Cooke*: 1504–76; formerly the King's tutor, an important Protestant statesman.

48 *Long hair*: a conventional mark of criminality; there are other hirsute villains in Marlowe's *The Jew of Malta* and Anthony Munday's *Sir Thomas More*. The reference could have an ironic undertone if Black Will and Shakebag are also long-haired (see note on 4.73).

53 *The . . . show*: the doublet was so ragged that more of the lining was visible than the outside.

54 *seam rent*: split at the seams.

59 *trolled the bowl*: passed round the drink (literally, cup).

59–60 *the tapster's . . . Lion*: the head of the tapster at the Lion inn.

64 *thy plate*: i.e. the plate Bradshaw has been talking about (which does not belong to him).

68 *forth*: henceforward (or, possibly, out of prison).

70–1 *the Isle of Sheppey*: Sir Thomas Cheyne lived at Shurland Castle on Sheppey (an island in the Thames Estuary). Bradshaw's errand has some urgency: the law term is about to start, so Fitten's trial and likely execution are imminent.

82 *profound*: able to conceal (the murder plot) deeply.

92 *platform*: plot, scheme.

93–4 *stab . . . wall*: this was considered a cowardly way to kill one's opponent, because he was unable to defend himself.

96 *Aldersgate Street*: an up-market residential area in the north-west of the City of London, where many noblemen lived.

103 *occupation*: recognized trade.

104 *warden . . . company*: the head of the imagined professional guild of murderers.

3.5 *the turtle . . . alone*: in English folklore turtle-doves were thought to mate only once, for life, and were therefore a traditional emblem of constancy in love.

6 *Paul's*: St Paul's Cathedral, widely used as a concourse for secular business; in the churchyard, where this scene takes place, there were many stationers' stalls. Walking up and down the Cathedral nave was also a way of touting for employment; Michael may mean to suggest that, though he already has a master, without Susan he shares the distress of these hungry, unemployed men.

11 *a plaster of pitch*: used to seal horses' wounds.

3-13 *My duty . . . end*: Michael's letter is written in the 'euphuistic' prose style popularized by John Lyly's romance *Euphues* (1578), characterized by elegantly balanced syntax and abundant analogies with classical mythology and natural history.

30 *rouse . . . house*: i.e. sack her.

38 *speed him*: see him on his way, i.e. kill him.

39 *this coward*: Greene's modestly self-mocking term for himself: he always absents himself from the scene whenever Black Will and Shakebag are about to attempt the murder. In this instance he plans to wait for them at the Nag's Head, a tavern on the corner of Friday Street, a few hundred yards from the Cathedral.

43 *Blackfriars*: residential district in the south-eastern corner of the City, formerly ecclesiastical land; as such it still retained freedom from local authority jurisdiction, and wanted criminals could still claim rights of sanctuary there. Because it abutted the river, it offered an easy escape route.

48 *old filching*: shoplifting.

press: crowd.

48 S.D. *lets . . . window*: the prentice's stall has a counter window with a shutter which can be propped over it like an awning. In the theatre, the stall could be represented by a booth on stage, or a frontage set up in one of the doors at the rear of the stage.

49 S.D. *other tradesmen . . . brawl*: Q leaves the stage action here unclear, but it is later established (line 74) that a brawl has taken place. Presumably Black Will and Shakebag draw their swords to retaliate after the accident and provoke the prentice to defend himself. The involvement of other tradesmen is indicated by the prentice's use of the plural in his next line, 'We'll tame you', and by Black Will's threat to take revenge by pulling down their shop signs (line 59); they too may be apprentices, who were notorious for riotous behaviour.

58 *Counter*: there were two London prisons of this name. The one nearer to St Paul's was in Bread Street at the time of the action (but moved to Wood Street in 1555).

75 *forbearance . . . acquittance*: you don't get even by putting up with things; proverbial (Tilley F.584).

87 *a lap of crowns*: the lap of her dress filled with coins.

99 *panting*: beating its last after being eviscerated.

111 *earth . . . blood*: a latent irony cuts against Greene: it was popularly believed that the earth would refuse to absorb blood spilled by murder.

122 *eighteen-pence ordinary*: fixed-price eatery.

125 *There . . . it*: it is mere bad luck.

135 *have I*: even if I had.

149 *underhand*: both (*a*) clandestine and (*b*) already under way.

155 *a member*: a (metaphorical) limb; an accomplice in the plot rather than its principal agent.

173 *against*: in readiness for when.

175 *inner court*: entrance hall.

181 *go wrong with*: be the worse for.

198 *deal currently*: promptly do what was agreed.

4.5 *couch*: cause to germinate and grow.

  6 *'join*: enjoin.

 13 *Hydra's . . . decay*: in classical mythology, the Hydra was a water-serpent which grew two new heads for every one that was cut off; commonly used a metaphor for anything undesirable, fast-breeding, and hard to control. (The closest modern equivalent might be a cancer.)

 24 *these two*: i.e. Alice's reformation or death.

     fall: come to pass, happen.

 29 *room*: place.

 32 *Here, here*: Arden may mean either his heart (implying a deeply felt grief) or his forehead (implying the shame of being a cuckold, thought to grow horns there); the actor's choice will reflect whether Arden is understood as a betrayed, loving husband or a man more concerned with his social honour.

 55 *bare*: past tense of *bear*.

 73 *bolstered hair*: the precise meaning is unclear. To bolster something can be either to prop it up or to pad it out, so Michael could be imagining either (*a*) a bristly 'punk' hairstyle bolstered with grease or egg-white, or (*b*) long hair so luxuriant that it resembles a well-stuffed pillow.

 76 *Insulting*: arrogantly triumphing.

 88 *What . . . rest?*: the line echoes Hieronimo's words on overhearing his son's murder in Thomas Kyd's *The Spanish Tragedy* (1587): 'What outcries pluck me from my naked bed?' (2.4.63)

 92 *to*: against.

103 *not half contenteth*: seriously dissatisfies.

5.1 S.D. *Here . . . Shakebag*: The placing of this stage direction, after the first line of Shakebag's speech, follows Q. The intention may be to suggest that the audience should hear Shakebag approaching before he can be seen, thus adding to the suspense.

  5 *such as we*: i.e. robbers and murderers.

6–8 *The lazy . . . complete*: the night hours seem long until the murder is done. Shakebag wraps up the thought in a conceit of the minutes dawdling, so that each hour contains more than the correct amount of time due to it (audit = reckoning).

19 *bugs and fears*: imaginary terrors.

20 *their fancy's work*: by working upon the murderers' fancies (= imaginations).

24 *slipped*: passed over, deferred.

37 *Knock . . . sword*: it is left ambiguous whether Shakebag follows Black Will's advice and knocks fruitlessly, or cannily assesses the situation and decides not to draw attention to themselves by creating a disturbance.

6.1 *Billingsgate*: the easternmost wharf in the City of London, where Arden and Franklin plan to take a boat across the Thames and pick up the Old Kent Road in Southwark. They avoid crossing from a nearer wharf, because it would mean passing through the disreputable Bankside area south of the river. They need to catch the tide, because at other times the boat could only be reached by an unpleasant walk across mud-flats.

4 *flood*: flood-tide.

7 *toil*: a snare of nets set up ('pitched') by huntsmen.

15 *late*: previously.

38 *note*: take any notice of.

40 *use*: practice.

   mockery: futile waste of time.

7.12 *bethink himself*: remember.

23 *As true . . . true*: as true as the fact that I'm telling it to you.

25 *the Salutation*: a tavern in Billingsgate.

26–7 *you shall . . . master*: by neglecting his errand, Michael will delay Franklin and Arden by half a day until the next high tide; this will give the murderers a chance to get to Rainham Down first, where they will lie in wait to ambush Arden.

29 *except of*: do without.

8.17 *starry*: the word may suggest how high Mosby imagines himself to be nesting. Alternatively, Q's *stary* might be an otherwise unrecorded adjective from *stare* (= starling): a fifteenth-century collective noun for a flock of starlings was *murmuration*, which is appropriate to the gentleness of the breeze.

37 *Yet*: still. Mosby's imagination carries him ahead to the time when all his other accomplices will have been permanently silenced.

37–8 *Yet . . . one*: in English law, a wife was not usually considered competent to give evidence against her husband; Mosby can therefore silence Alice by marrying her.

39 *what for that*: what if, despite that.

73 *honest wife*: chaste wife.

78 *Woe worth*: may ill befall.

84 *stated me*: placed me in a particular (high) rank, i.e. promoted.

91 *for changing*: in exchange for.

92 *wrapped*: entangled, compromised.

93 *that . . . thine!*: you haven't mentioned that!

97 *showed . . . dove*: persuaded him that Alice was a good, beautiful ('fair') woman when she was really a bad, plain one.

98 *viewed thee not*: didn't see you properly.

122 *hold . . . sect*: follow no other religion.

126 *sighted as the eagle*: the eagle had proverbially sharp vision (Tilley E.6).

127 *heard . . . hare*: the hare was proverbially timorous (Tilley H.147) because at this time it was the principal animal hunted with dogs; the animal's good hearing was probably inferred from its long ears.

133 *A . . . still*: when you stir up mud in a fountain, the water does not stay muddy indefinitely.

135–9 *I am . . . gentles are*: all this is an offended, derisive paraphrase of what Alice has said to him.

150 *with . . . seal up*: this moment is open to two distinct realizations on stage: either Alice and Mosby kiss and break off when Mosby sees Bradshaw, suggesting that Bradshaw may have seen them; or Mosby sees Bradshaw first and prevents the kiss before it happens.

157 *We . . . London*: the letter creates a significant discontinuity in the plot: Bradshaw was given it in Scene 2, before Greene had arrived in London or even hired Black Will and Shakebag.

166 *I to*: I will go to.

9.4 *whether*: the word was often pronounced as a monosyllable in the period.

5 *here's a coil!*: what a fuss!

6 *took in hand*: prepared.

9 *flashing of the fire*: when the gun ('dag') discharges.

26 *for*: because of.

29 *Aesop's talk*: Aesop was a legendary Greek writer (sixth century BC) of moral fables, many of them about animals. The particular story Greene goes on to tell was proverbial (Tilley D. 545) and does not come from Aesop.

32 *striving . . . manhood*: fighting about who is more macho.

36 S.D. *kneels . . . heaven*: presumably Black Will silently invokes the heavens to avenge the insult if he should fail to do it himself.

37 *fittest standings*: best positions for ambush (literally, to shoot game).

38 *Lime . . . bird*: small birds were caught by smearing birdlime, a viscous, sticky substance, onto twigs.

40 *Make towards*: come back.

41 *coucheth*: lies down.

be off: fires, goes off.

55 *overtake*: catch up with.

61 *onwards . . . tale*: Arden and Franklin are on the pilgrim's road from London to Canterbury. It is surely a literary joke that they pass the time by listening to Franklin's tale (the word is used three times, as if for emphasis). In Chaucer's *Canterbury Tales*, 'The Franklin's Tale' concerns a virtuous wife who unwittingly finds herself honour-bound to commit adultery; this Franklin tells of a more impudent adulteress who is caught in the act and gets away with it by a witty answer. The play includes too little of the tale to ascribe a specific source, though a number of Renaissance short stories deal with similar situations (e.g. Boccaccio, *Decameron* 6.7 and Bandello, *Novelle* 4.19).

69 *brook*: agree.

85 *hemmed . . . seem*: went 'hem' as if to clear her throat.

92 *tell it out*: finish telling it.

94 *Stand to it*: prepare to fire.

121 *your beadsman*: this was a conventional way of saying 'your humble servant', but Will also plays on the more technical sense of someone paid to say prayers for his employer's soul.

125–7 *If . . . truss*: if you are accused of even a very trivial offence, and come to trial, you are sure to be hanged (literally, trussed up for the hangman).

128 *four mile together*: the distance from Rainham to Sittingbourne, where Lord Cheyne will take the road for Sheppey while Arden and Franklin continue on to Faversham.

131 *chops me in*: intervenes; 'me' is the grammatical inflection known as the ethical dative, common in the sixteenth century but now obsolete, which is used to imply indirect involvement in an action.

132 *his*: Arden's.

133 *I . . . throat*: Cheyne's largesse is trivial in comparison with the fee for the murder (the equivalent of 120 crowns).

144 *'Preserved'. . . him*: at the heart of the retort is a contrast between the heavenly and earthly lords as agents of Arden's escape, with Black Will atheistically attributing to chance what Greene piously saw as providence. Some previous editors have proposed that the Q reading (as printed here) makes no sense, and that Will originally said something like 'The Lord of Heaven – a fig!', only to be censored into incoherence; they have emended accordingly, transforming Q's rough hexameter line into an irruption of prose. But perhaps we should not require full rational coherence and lightning wit of an exasperated and not altogether competent murderer

who has just been baulked of his quarry; instead, Will seizes on Greene's most irritating word, 'preserved', and caps it with an expletive.

145 *Shurland*: see note on 2.70–1.

146 *by the way*: *en route* to Shurland.

154 *plot the news*: lay a new plot; possibly a misprint for 'plot anew'.

10.1 *the Hours*: in classical mythology, the daughters of Jupiter who guarded the entrance to heaven and presided over the changes of the seasons.

3–4 *Sol . . . car*: in classical mythology, the sun-god Sol drove a chariot across the heavens each day.

6 *pretend*: intend.

45 *broom close*: field of furze.

46 *long home*: final resting-place.

59–60 *carry . . . over*: have your eye on.

11.1 S.D. *the Ferryman*: Arden and Franklin need to be ferried across the water to Sheppey. After Michael's remarks in the previous scene (10.47), the character also acts as an ironic allusion to Charon, the ferryman in classical mythology who carried the souls of the dead to the underworld. A number of minor characters in 1590s tragedy have similar ominous, partly symbolic associations with death, such as the mower in Marlowe's *Edward II* (1592) or the skeletal apothecary in Shakespeare's *Romeo and Juliet* (1595), who both intervene at key moments which precipitate the protagonist's downfall. In contrast, the effect here is one of misdirection.

4 *what . . . here*: the mainland area opposite Sheppey is marshy and so prone to morning fog.

5 *mystical*: thick, hard to see through.

17 *governed by the moon*: the moon was proverbially changeable (Tilley M.1111). The ferryman may mean, more particularly, that his wife's menstrual cycle makes her moody and emotionally capricious.

27 *the man in the moon*: here the moon suggests the ferryman's wife's vagina.

29 *bramble-bush*: a traditional attribute of the man in the moon.

32 *bold yeomanry*: amusing talk typical of the yeoman class.

12.8 *pot-finger*: an unidentified sexual activity, presumably involving either finger or penis; the 'pot' is obviously a vagina.

18 S.D. *a ditch*: this would be represented by one of the stage trapdoors. Shakebag must be temporarily out of vision so that his clothes can be muddied. (See Appendix 1 for a discussion of the staging difficulties here.)

23 *well enough served*: i.e. unwise.

32 *get his way*: take himself off.

33 *Hock Monday*: Easter Monday, when local people customarily detained passers-by to collect money for parish purposes.

56 *Let . . . state*: let me deal with this: it is my job to do so.

66 *your tenement*: the Flower-de-Luce where Mosby is staying.

68 *Hornsby*: an offensive nickname alluding to a cuckold's horns (see note on 4.32) and playing on the name of Alice's intended next husband, Mosby (probably pronounced 'Morsby').

13.1 *to little end*: pointless.

85 S.D. *They fight*: the action here is described in detail by Black Will at 14.50–9.

128 *cried him mercy*: apologized to him.

147 *Work . . . debates*: cause discordant arguments.

14.4 *hanged . . . door*: murderers were sometimes hanged at the scene of the crime rather than the normal place of execution, to signify the connection between crime and punishment.

6–7 *taking the wall*: the preferred walking position in sixteenth-century city streets was alongside the wall, because the drainage gutter or 'kennel' ran down the middle, making that part of the street not only wet but filthy; 'taking the wall' was considered offensive and sometimes provoked street-fights.

7 *silver noses*: prosthetic false noses (to replace those cut off by Black Will).

8 *cracked . . . blades*: either (*a*) broken other men's sword blades, or (*b*) injured brave opponents.

14 *Thames Street*: parallel to the north bank of the river; the street was thronged with carts carrying wares.

16 *tallies*: financial accounts were kept by cutting notches in wooden rods called 'tallies'.

20–1 *All . . . hand*: i.e. each alehouse keeper offered Black Will a drink.

23 *lattice*: alehouses were recognized not only by their signs but also by their painted window lattices.

29 *he*: Arden.

38 *the fair*: the historical Thomas Ardern was murdered on the night of 14 February 1551 after attending the annual fair held in Faversham on that day.

39 *steal from*: slip away from.

43 *bid*: invite.

74 *favour*: a token of affection given by a woman to her lover and worn prominently by him; refers here to the bandage around his arm. Given the precariousness in adversity of Mosby's relationship with Alice, the line could also be played with sardonic undercurrent of the word's usual meaning, implying 'This is what your favour has done for me.'

112–13 *Place . . . stool*: seating signified status, with a backless stool considered lowlier than a chair. Mosby, as a guest in the house, will have the seat of honour usually occupied by Arden himself.

133 *adventure on*: dare to attack.

135 *this door*: the staging of the scene requires three doors: one represents the counting-house, which is locked after the hired killers hide there; another is the street door through which characters enter the house; and the third leads to the rest of the house, from whence the servants fetch the various domestic artefacts used in the scene.

138 *Tisiphone*: in classical mythology, one of the snake-haired Furies who pursued evil-doers. Ironically Alice imagines Tisiphone's torments driving her on to commit the murder rather than punishing her afterwards.

141 *spheres*: in Renaissance cosmology, the stars were fixed on concentric, rotating crystal spheres.

143–7 *chaste Diana . . . Endymion*: in classical mythology, Diana was the goddess of the moon and chastity; Endymion was a beautiful youth who fell in love with the moon.

146 *silly*: trivial.

151 *tables*: a backgammon set, not furniture.

162 *or*: before.

170 *given . . . supper*: i.e. driven away my appetite.

213 *pledge*: drink after another person, from the same cup, as a mark of friendship.

223 *creep . . . legs*: at this point, Michael is standing, as instructed, in front of the counting-house door, masking it from Arden.

228 *take . . . up*: engage with.

229 *the pressing-iron . . . of*: in the opening scene, 1.313.

237 *Southwark*: a disreputable suburb of London south of the Thames.

249 *The . . . out*: the Elizabethans believed that providence operated to reveal murderers by such miraculous means as indelible bloodstains (compare note on 3.111).

267 *What . . . weep?*: what has made you cry?

318 *bring . . . doors*: accompany them to their front doors.

323 *I counsel!*: who am I to give advice?

330 *weep that will*: let those who want to weep, do so.

336 *the watch*: a night patrol with powers of arrest, comprising, or paid for by, the householders of the parish.

346 S.D. *Alice . . . stage*: unusually, no lines are supplied to cover the break in the action at this point; presumably Alice frets silently.

395 *slipshoe*: a light, indoor shoe or slipper; Arden was obviously not out in the snow when he was killed.

15.1 *kept*: this could mean either (*a*) habitually visited, (*b*) supported as a mistress, or (*c*) pimped.

9 *sanctuary*: wanted criminals could claim freedom from arrest in certain ecclesiastical buildings and land. Shakebag is in Southwark, and may intend to cross the river to seek sanctuary at Blackfriars (see note on 3.43).

16.0 S.D. *discovered*: revealed, by pulling aside the traverse curtains across a recess (known as the 'discovery space') in the rear stage wall.

4–6 *The more . . . falls*: it was widely believed that a murdered corpse's wounds would bleed again in the presence of the killer. The phenomenon was considered providential and was sometimes admitted in evidence in murder trials.

17.2 *hues and cries*: spontaneous collective pursuit of a suspected criminal by members of the public, immediately after a crime was discovered.

6 *Flushing*: a Dutch seaport, outside English jurisdiction at the time of the action (though, ironically, not when the play was written).

8 *full . . . adventures*: recklessly at full speed.

11 *Gads Hill*: notorious haunt of highway robbers on the road from London to Rochester.

18.24 *given consent to*: been an accessory in.

29 *Smithfield*: one of the regular places of execution in London.

31 *burnt*: wives who murdered their husbands (and servants who murdered their employers) were guilty of the aggravated offence of petty treason, punishable by burning at the stake rather than hanging.

37 *with*: at the same time as.

EPILOGUE

7 *Ospringe*: about a mile south of Faversham.

14 *naked*: unadorned.

15 *filèd points*: elaborate literary artifices.

A Woman Killed with Kindness

PROLOGUE

2 *these preparations*: this may refer to the sounding of trumpets at the playhouse before the start of the performance, or perhaps to the dressing of the stage, which was hung with black for some tragedies.

3 *state*: splendour.

5 *afford . . . twig*: wish this twig were.

7 *drone*: mistakenly considered lazy and unproductive, in contrast with the honey bee.

10 *our bat's . . . sight*: bats were proverbially blind and eagles proverbially clear-sighted (Tilley O.92, E.6).

13 *give the foil*: defeat or (in wrestling) throw down.

13–14 *But . . . spoil*: the prologue appeals to the audience's gentility (and gentleness) to make allowance for the play's admitted faults, and refrain from over-zealous criticism.

14 *spoil*: despoil.

1.2 *'The . . . Sheets'*: a popular tune and ballad, but also referring to wedding-night sex.

4 *the dance . . . dance*: the dance of death, mentioned in the ballad 'The Shaking of the Sheets'.

6 *Music, ho!*: the music does not actually begin until Sir Francis commands, 'Sound', at line 9. If there has been no obvious response to this first order, then there may be a note of irritation in the second; alternatively, we may see the musicians obediently enter the stage to play, or hear them tuning up off stage.

16 *qualified*: endowed.

25 *yours*: i.e. your heart.

28 *approve*: demonstrate to be true (in choosing her for his wife).

32 *they*: Anne's accomplishments.

47 *against*: in anticipation of the time when.

48 *takes . . . down*: dominates, establishes supremacy over.

53 *to . . . entailed*: an entail was a legal device which predetermined the future ownership of property, irrespective of the wishes of the immediate heir. Here, old Acton did not 'bequeath' his personal quirks to both his children equally, but only to the one who inherited the land.

62 *unseasoned frieze*: coarse woollen cloth with a nap, used in winter coats and therefore unseasonable ('unseasoned') in the summer.

84 *bride-laces*: ribbons, often of gold or silk lace, used to tie up the nosegays of rosemary traditionally worn at weddings.

86 *on the hoigh*: excited.

87 *They . . . mill-horses*: horses driving a mill walk round in circles, like the movement of the locals' country dances.

88–9 *not . . . cutting*: the rustics' dances are not unduly elaborate or flashy: there are no nimble pirouettes (turning 'on the toe'), and none of the steps (capers) involve high kicks ('cutting'). Compare Samuel Rowlands's satirical portrait of a dancer in *Look to it, for I'll Stab Ye* (1604): 'You nimble skipjack, turning on the toe | . . . You that do leap about and caper so, | Esteeming our old country dances stale . . .' (sig. E3ᵛ).

95 *chevy chase*: Chevy Chase in Northumberland was the scene of a celebrated Anglo-Scottish border battle of 1388; but references in Scenes 6 and 11 establish that the play is set in Yorkshire. There is a parish near Wakefield called Chevet, and woodland north of Leeds called the Chevin, either of which may have been intended. Alternatively, the phrase may be simply a periphrasis for hunting: 'chevy' is recorded in the *Oxford English Dictionary* as a hunting cry, though no examples are known before the late eighteenth century. Or perhaps the anomaly might just be a sign that, at this early stage in the writing, Heywood had not yet decided on a Yorkshire setting. (The play was printed from an authorial draft manuscript incorporating a number of superseded first thoughts; see the Note on the Text.)

107–8 *clap . . . bargain*: shake hands or it isn't a deal.

2.6 *dancing . . . foot it*: he can dance in a rudimentary way rather than elaborately (confirming the condescension of Sir Francis in 1.87–9).

6–7 *I am . . . Milk-pail*: in the previous line, Nick was to dance with Joan Miniver, and Sisly Milk-pail was assigned to Jack Slime; presumably unspoken stage business indicates that this arrangement is not to the liking of one of the parties, most probably Jack or Joan, so that Nick ends up with Sisly.

9 *serving courtiers*: the point of the apparent oxymoron is that courtiers, who belonged to the highest rank and were understood to be sophisticated in their tastes, were also the household servants of the monarch.

15–16 *comparisons are odious*: proverbial (Tilley C.576).

31 *deserved a cushion*: worked hard enough to have earned a cushy life.

32 *the cushion dance*: a country dance in which the dancers pair off by laying a cushion in front of their chosen partner, then dance in a ring.

42 *come cleanly off*: be performed well, with bawdy double entendre about taking off the wenches' underwear (smocks).

43 *put . . . musicians*: let the musicians decide for themselves.

29–44 *Rogero . . . Round*: the seven titles in this passage refer to popular dance tunes, most of which are reprinted in William Chappell, *Old English Popular Music* (London, 1893), vol. i; 'Sellenger's Round', the tune which is actually played, appears on pp. 256–7.

49 S.D. *speaks . . . fashion*: the servants talk to one another as they dance, ad libbing the lines; most of the dialogue reflects their lowly station; Nicholas, however, attempts a more dignified ('stately') style of speech, but does it badly ('scurvily').

3.0 S.D. *Enter . . . Falconers*: the action may be enhanced by the inclusion of two hawks, one brought on now by Sir Francis's falconer and the other later by Sir Charles's; but live birds would pose obvious difficulties of control, even if hooded, when violence breaks out at line 40, while stuffed ones would become unconvincing at the same point. In any event, it is notable that the text is written to obviate the need to show Sir Charles's hawk in flight: he has just released it the moment before he enters, and his falconer is later told to go and fetch it rather than call it back.

Malby: the character plays no further part in the scene, not even taking sides in the quarrel; it is possible that his inclusion in this stage direction is an error, or Heywood's superseded first thought.

1–3 *Aloft . . . earth*: both hunting bird and prey are flying up from the ground ('at the souse') when the hawk makes the kill; the dead bird then falls to the ground, followed by the hawk.

7–9 *Now . . . bells*: the hawk has landed with its prey, and has started to pluck its feathers ('plume her'). Sir Charles orders the falconer not to call the bird back ('rebeck her not') but to go and fetch it, making a chirruping noise to reassure it ('chirk her'), and then taking hold of its harness ('gets'), leg straps ('jesses'), and attached bells (worn on the hawk's legs to enable the falconer to trace it).

11–13 *My hawk . . . ferre*: Sir Francis's hawk has made an easier kill than Sir Charles's: the prey was on the ground ('at the querre'), whereas Sir Charles's attacked its quarry while flying upwards ('at the mount'). Sir Francis's bird also made the mistake of failing to make the kill on the far side of the river ('at the ferre') when it had the opportunity. Presumably they are hunting waterfowl.

14–19 *our . . . hawk*: Sir Francis's hawk was the first to draw feathers from the prey ('plumed the fowl') and chased it back ('renewed') from the river on two occasions. (Wendoll may refer to the bird eventually killed by Sir Charles's hawk, implying that its kill was helped by its rival.) Moreover, the bird's flight is hampered by what Wendoll judges to be sub-standard bells. It was recommended that hawks' bells should be of even weight but pitched a semitone apart. Ironically Milan, famous for fine metalwork such as needles and cutlery, was usually thought to supply the best silver bells for hawking.

19 *'Tis lost*: referring to Sir Francis's wager.

22 *petty singles . . . long singles*: the hawk's short and long claws.

24–6 *The terrials . . . away*: the hawk not only tore out ('discomfited') some of the prey's feathers, but drew blood, as could be seen on its 'terrials' (an unidentified hawking term); however, the prey bird escaped ('brake away') on this occasion.

27 *rifler*: a hawk that seizes feathers without drawing blood; Sir Francis is suggesting that Sir Charles's hawk made a luckier, less efficient kill. He may also mean to imply that his own bird first wounded the prey which Sir Charles's hawk finished off (compare note on lines 14–19); the word 'rifler' could also imply 'thief'.

27 S.D. *Enter . . . Falconer*: the falconer left the stage at line 10 and has returned by the time the fight breaks out at line 40, but there is no clear indication of precisely when he does so. An entrance at this point, when Sir Charles's hawk is under discussion, would be pointedly relevant, especially if he has the bird with him (compare note on the scene's opening SD).

36 *strike home*: i.e. 'kill you'.

37 *long home*: permanent home, i.e. the grave.

40 S.D. *fight*: at least some of the combatants fight with sword and dagger: Sir Francis has told his followers to draw (39), and Sir Charles later surrenders his 'weapons' to the Sheriff (103).

others . . . wounded: one character who is not wounded is Sir Francis (as mentioned at 4.53–4).

58 *fear*: fearful event.

63–4 *at the heart . . . at the heart*: Susan means 'mortally', but her brother takes the phrase to mean spiritually.

70 *great*: powerful.

71 *danger*: penalty.

82 *So*: so long as.

84 *rank*: profusely.

109 S.D. *with the bodies*: the Sheriff's officers came to fight Sir Charles's living friends, but their real theatrical function is to remove his dead enemies.

4.0 S.D. *in a study*: wrapped up in his thoughts.

4–6 *A king's . . . gentleman*: though no longer a member of the court elite, Frankford remains prosperous.

9 *been . . . proficient*: made profitable use.

26–7 *his . . . observation*: observing his behaviour has given me great pleasure.

29 *seen*: skilled, accomplished.

32 *house*: family.

33 *a second place*: i.e. second to Anne.

47 *banding sides*: taking sides, forming hostile parties.

48 *Where*: whereupon.

53 *brother*: brother-in-law.

57–8 *Had . . . it*: you would have preferred to bring better news if you could.

59 *find . . . friends*: i.e. his associates will prove harsh to him.

70 *table*: meals (compare the modern 'board').

75 *last remembrance*: most recent courtesy.

85 *earns*: grieves.

88 *lie*: reside (but, with proleptic irony, the word could also mean 'have sex').

92 *him*: Wendoll.

99 *no boot*: useless.

   deny: refuse.

99–100 *given . . . coat*: servants' livery uniforms were provided by their master.

100–1 *brush . . . wand*: a master was entitled to beat his servants; a holly stick was a usual implement for this purpose.

104–6 *though . . . yet*: the play is being performed in the afternoon (the usual time in this period), but in the action it is only late morning, dinner being a midday meal.

5.3 *try*: experience, undergo.

 10 *fees*: prisoners had to pay the jailer for their own imprisonment.

 22 *owe*: possess.

 26 *want*: need.

 33 *for fail*: just in case three should prove too little.

 35 *hold law*: litigate.

 46 *house of pleasure*: summerhouse.

 49 *lies*: is situated.

6.15 *balls*: eyeballs.

 32 *alliance*: blood-tie.

 35 *Of*: from being.

 47 *name*: reputation (which would be damaged if he became a cuckold).

114 *tried*: experienced.

125 *table*: record.

165 *the nick*: the exact moment, the nick of time.

168 *pocket up*: have to tolerate.

172–3 *stand To*: abide by (hence, fulfil).

181 *a . . .*: this edn. (Q a &c.). The missing word is, obviously, *whore*. Though this could be an offensive term, its omission was probably not an act of censorship either by Heywood or Q's printer, William Jaggard: their other work indicates that neither man had any particular sensitivity to the word. However, such coyness seems entirely characteristic of Nicholas, with his tendency to speak in verse and his earlier attempts to ape the gentility of his betters' discourse (see 2.49 SD and note).

7.2 *To . . . unsold*: to keep unsold this poor house remaining to us.

6 *old Sir Charles*: this could refer either to their father or to the present Sir Charles's former self.

8 S.D. *Sergeant*: officer with powers of arrest.

14 *lordship*: aristocratic estate; it seems this is not the first time that Shafton has profited from the financial misfortunes of the upper classes.

16 *successively*: continuously down the generations.

19 *He . . . began*: the first Mountford who could call himself a gentleman.

30 *brought . . . execution*: procured a court order for repayment of the loan.

35 *trouble*: misfortune.

57 *changed . . . away*: utterly transformed my customary way of life.

58 *Arrest him*: a sergeant would arrest a man by clapping him on the shoulder or striking him with his mace of office.

Actions: lawsuits.

60–1 *I'll . . . question*: Shafton threatens to initiate a prosecution for crimes which Sir Charles allegedly committed before his reformation.

71 *irons*: this may either be a humiliating metonymy for the arrested man, treating him as nothing more than the prison chains which will bind him, or else an order to the Sergeant to shackle him.

78–9 *cry . . . sake*: impoverished prisoners could beg for food at a barred prison window ('the grate') onto the street.

98 *what cheer*: 'how are you feeling?'

107 *whether*: which.

8.0 S.D. *voider*: a receptacle into which crumbs and other table refuse are scraped (using the wooden knife).

carpet: an embroidered rug to cover the table.

2–3 *spread . . . hall*: now that the masters have eaten, it is time for the servants' supper.

7 *daily*: i.e. resident.

20 *Fall*: happen, befall.

23 *stayed*: waited for.

29 *husband*: thrifty person.

42 *make . . . good*: prove his claim to love Frankford better than Anne.

46 *comparisons*: insinuations.

63 *Dives*: a wealthy man who goes to hell in a biblical parable (Luke 16: 19–31); Jesus preached that it was supremely difficult for a rich man to go to heaven (Matthew 19: 24).

86 *discourse . . . circumstance*: 'give you the details'.

88 *strangers*: visitors to the house, guests.

100 *Judas*: the disciple who betrayed Jesus; hence a byword for a traitor.

115 *pair*: pack.

116 *counters*: used for keeping score in card games.

119 *say . . . goose*: proverbial (Tilley B.481) for a trifling act of daring.

121 *take my part*: be my partner.

123 *sit out*: cannot join in the game.

125 *match*: (*a*) agreement; (*b*) partnership (not just at cards).

128 *take . . . up*: play against them (and, by implication, win).

131 *playing false*: cheating (at cards, and in other ways).

133 *forfeit . . . set*: lose the game.

134 *It . . . you*: this sentence, like some of Frankford's other pointed remarks, could be spoken aside; but in a sequence so permeated with double meanings, it could as easily be spoken aloud as part of his pretence of amiable competitiveness.

136 *noddy*: (*a*) a card game similar to cribbage; (*b*) fool, dupe.

138 *double-ruff*: (*a*) a card game similar to whist; (*b*) sexual passion.

139 *together*: (*a*) teamed up at cards; (*b*) having sex.

140 *double hand*: (*a*) double-ruff; (*b*) duplicity.

143 *knave . . . doors*: the full name of this card game is 'beat the knave out of doors', which is, taken literally, Nicholas's advice on how to deal with Wendoll: eject him forcibly from the house.

144 *loadum*: a card game in which the loser wins (as Wendoll has 'won' Anne even though he is not her husband).

145 *saint*: more properly *cent*, a card game similar to piquet; the original spelling is retained here to preserve Frankford's pun in the next line.

148 *new-cut*: (*a*) a card game; (*b*) implying virginity ('new cunt'), which was not always differentiated from married chastity: the chaste wife was said to give her husband 'each night a maidenhead' (Robert Herrick, 'A Country Life', 42).

soonest hitter: the first to score (at cards and in bed).

150 *draw out*: pick the losing cards.

154 *post and pair*: a card game played with three cards; in the following lines, Wendoll makes this emblematic of the triangular relationship, casting himself and Anne as the pair.

156 *kiss the post*: be shut out (proverbial, Tilley P.494).

157 *Whoever . . . cost*: there is something ominously threatening about the way this line turns Wendoll's jesting couplet into a triplet; it may well be spoken aside.

158 *make honours*: cut for the highest cards ('honours'), usually king, queen, and knave (or jack).

160 *except*: exclude.

161 *Lift*: cut the cards.

165 *grossest pair*: (*a*) most coarsely textured (perhaps dirtiest?) pack of cards; (*b*) most egregious couple of adulterers.

167 *lost . . . dealing*: i.e. lost count.

179 *Booty . . . play*: to play booty is to cheat, often with an accomplice, with a view to taking all a fellow player's money.

187 *to deal*: (*a*) deal the cards; (*b*) seduce Anne.

189 *see your chamber*: retire to bed.

203 *My self*: Anne.

212 *set*: predetermined.

213 *securely play*: have illicit sex without fear of discovery.

9.10 *the . . . sake*: for the sake of the family's good name.

12–13 *He . . . laid*: he is not allowed to move about the prison but is kept locked up in the worst dungeon ('the hole').

15 *it . . . to*: you have the power to.

19 *took . . . of*: been laid in; the old man's body is conceived as a measuring rod the same length as the grave.

37 *Charity . . . heaven*: in classical mythology, the goddess of justice left the earth at the end of the golden age; here Susan reapplies the idea to her brother's circumstances.

51 *you*—: this edn. (Q you &c.). It is unclear whether Malby whispers the rest of his line or Susan interrupts, cutting it off. (Later, at 14.20, the Q printer uses '&c.' to signify interruption.) The ambiguity is important to the way we conceive the characters of Susan and Sir Francis: an indecent proposal is either made by Malby (on Acton's behalf, in the whispered part of the line) or mistakenly inferred by Susan.

68 *lies in execution*: is imprisoned. 'Execution' refers to the carrying-out of a court order, not necessarily a death sentence.

70 *appeal is sued*: prosecution is in progress. An appeal was a legal process initiated by the plaintiff, and for serious crimes had largely been superseded by indictment; this suggests that the prosecution partly originates in Acton's personal malice.

10.0 S.D. *feet*: Q1 reads '*face*', which might possibly mean that, as a prisoner, Sir Charles has had his beard shaved off, and possibly also his hair.

1 *Of . . . miserable*: an elaborate vocative apostrophizing himself.

12 *left*: ceased.

66 *chased*: hunted.

69 *A . . . alliance*: any bond of kinship.

71 *Drudges too much*: egregiously base men.

75 *remember*: remind.

102 *with . . . balance*: objectively weigh up.

111–12: *from . . . deeds*: strangers are less prone than friends to do ('execute') kindnesses.

11.1 *play the touch*: act as a touchstone, which tested whether an object was truly made of gold. The status of Anne and Wendoll as 'angels' (2) is being tested in numismatic as well as in celestial and moral terms. (An angel was also a gold coin.)

23–5 *you . . . Charles*: Frankford might have enough influence with Sir Francis to persuade him to be more lenient with Sir Charles.

42 *alacrity*: brisk cheerfulness.

46 *attends*: waits for.

49 *March beer*: a strong beer, named after the month in which it is brewed.

50 *Trojan*: a good, sociable fellow.

61 *Content ye*: I assure you (with apologetic overtones).

67 *Appointed*: armed.

86 *Dissembling . . . heart*: the lips which do not match ('suit not with') the heart within may belong either to Frankford himself or to Anne; Anne's heart can be called his because she is his wife (see note on 13.184).

91 *abroad so publicly*: i.e. in the main dining room of the house.

97 *spared from*: excused attendance at.

104 *pale offenders*: i.e. those who approach their misdeeds without full-blooded relish and vigour.

109 *puritan*: conscientiously scrupulous person; moral prude.

111 *plead custom*: claim that the act has been legitimated by regular practice ('custom').

114 *Once . . . sin*: sin is not like wading through a river: once you start, there is no difference between being up to your ankles or up to your head.

12.0 S.D. *other Servingmen*: the scene presumes a minimum of four unnamed servingmen (two of whom may be Jack Slime and Roger Brickbat from Scene 2): at least two enter here, and at least another two after line 13. Frankford's is evidently a well-to-do household.

5 *Mum*: discreet silence.

When . . . play: Tilley C.175.

7 *I . . . rat*: Jenkin caps Sisly's proverb with another (Tilley R.31).

8 *answer*: justify.

19 *for this night*: it is usually Nicholas's responsibility to lock up.

25 *as snug . . . pease-straw*: proverbial (Tilley P.296); pease-straw was from the pea plant, and was used for animal bedding and fodder.

13.0 S.D. *dark lantern*: a sealed lantern with a shutter enabling a beam of light to be shown or hidden at will; this allowed a person to move about at night without attracting attention.

8 *outward gate*: the front door of the house.

9 *withdrawing chamber*: private room adjacent to the hall.

11 *Fountain and spring*: original source.

17 *Now . . . gate*: without representational scenery to tie the action down, location was often fluid on the early seventeenth-century stage: characters might shift from place to place within a scene, without actually moving (e.g. the way the action of Scene 17 unobtrusively migrates inside Anne's bedchamber). This sequence is unusual because it calls attention to the doors and thresholds which must be unlocked and crossed as Frankford and Nicholas enter the house. It is not impossible that this was simply mimed, but one way of staging it in an Elizabethan theatre might be to use the two doors on either side of the discovery space in the back wall of the stage. Thus Frankford and Nicholas would exit through one door as they enter the house at line 18 or 20, then immediately return, probably through the same door. (Alternatively, they could quickly cross the backstage area to enter through the door on the opposite side of the stage; but this would entail a brief interruption of the action.) They would then cross the stage to the other door, representing the entrance to the bedroom, arriving there at line 23.

18 *Cripplegate*: one of the city gates of London, which presumably opened with a notorious creak.

20 *reach me*: hand over.

the rest: the other doors which must be unlocked.

22 *surprised*: overcome.

33 *circumstance*: ado, palaver.

35–7 *An . . . there*: if Nicholas were in Frankford's position, he would have dealt with his wife and her lover with greater immediacy.

43–6 *But . . . judgement*: it was believed that people who died suddenly would be damned for the sins they had been unable to repent; to kill someone unexpectedly, especially during or soon after the commission of some sin, was therefore considered especially horrible. In Frankford's eyes it would also be improperly wasteful of God's mercy, since the Christian doctrine of atonement held that Jesus bought humanity the opportunity to repent at the cost of his own crucifixion.

47 *met*: i.e. ended at the same moment; but the word also carries a nasty suggestion of the two bodies skewered together on the sword.

53 *glass*: hourglass.

63 *cast . . . moon*: conjecture wildly (proverbial, Tilley M.1114); literally, try to throw something up higher than the orbit of the moon, which was the farthest edge of space in traditional cosmology.

66 S.D. *night-gown*: dressing gown.

   smock: an undergarment, worn in bed.

76 *Judas-like . . . tree*: Judas (see note on 8.100) hanged himself (Matthew 27: 5); the tree was traditionally thought to be an elder.

79–80 *I . . . husband*: I am as far from the happy state of being able to call you husband as Lucifer (in Christian mythology, the first fallen angel) is from heaven.

96–7 *for . . . souls*: i.e. for Jesus' sake.

109 *calling*: station in life. Sumptuary laws prescribed the opulence of dress permitted to each rank in the social hierarchy, but these were often flouted, and were repealed soon after the play was written.

114 S.D. *two infant children*: it is left open whether these are represented as babes-in-arms or toddlers. Babies are easier, since they may be simulated by props, but would have less sentimental impact than a pair of very young child actors. The age of the children will also bear on the audience's sense of the overall duration of the Frankfords' marriage.

124 *stained . . . bastardy*: Frankford is not suggesting that the children actually were fathered by Wendoll, only that their mother's adultery means that their legitimacy will forever be doubted.

135 *strappadoed*: the strappado was a torture in which the victim's hands were tied behind his back; he was then repeatedly hoisted up by the wrists and let down with a jerk. Later in the seventeenth century the verb is recorded as meaning simply to beat with a strap.

147 *shirt*: nightshirt.

156 *Good . . . Cranwell*: the subtext is probably 'don't try to intervene'.

159 *nothing . . . mistress*: none of your possessions.

162 *hangings*: decorative painted or embroidered cloths hung against the wall (instead of modern wallpaper).

166 *by*: nearby.

168 *limit*: permit.

172 *book of life*: in Christian mythology, a book in which an angel recorded the names of all who were destined to go to heaven.

184 *cut . . . one*: Frankford plays on the biblical statement that husband and wife are one flesh (Matthew 19: 5), conceiving his heart and Anne's to be a single organ divided into two by her actions.

315

14.1 *tricked me*: dressed me up

3 *estate*: worldly circumstances.

5 *kern*: Irish foot-soldier; strongly pejorative, as the Irish were fighting a guerrilla war against the English settlers at the time the play was written.

8 *staring*: wild-eyed.

14 *beam*: a large alien object stuck in the eye; literally a plank of wood (alluding to Jesus' metaphor of the mote and the beam, Matthew 7: 3−5).

35 *challenge*: claim; accept the offer.

kindred . . . apart: discount the duties of kinship.

48 *jewel*: a common metaphor for virginity.

59 *Sue*: this edn (Q1 Jane; Q2 sister).

85 *shall*: that shall.

87 *grant*: agreement (to be offered to Acton).

88 *soothe . . . suit*: satisfy those to whom I am obliged (and who therefore have the right to take legal action, a suit).

110 *I . . . earnest*: the line may either be spoken aside or to Malby.

113 *interest*: share of ownership. As the patriarchal head of his family, Sir Charles has the right to bestow his sister in marriage on whom he pleases (though the bride also had to consent).

123 *engaged*: under obligation of gratitude.

131 *Do . . . her*: in raping Susan, Acton will do all the things Sir Charles has just said.

rely: depend upon.

136 *engage*: stake, risk.

15.14 *run . . . division*: played a rapid melodic passage.

16.7 *by*: about.

8 *manners*: incorporating the homophone, 'manors'; in performance, both senses are equally present. (Q1 has 'mannor . . . maners', which most editors modernize as 'manor . . . manors'; but it is clear that Heywood wrote two different words rather than singular and plural of the same one.)

18 *time*: harmony.

22 *he . . . that*: implying that Frankford is heart-broken; his heart has therefore depreciated in value, and so could be given ('afforded') to Anne.

37 *lay it to*: set it against, compare it with.

46 *turtles*: turtle-doves. See note on *Arden* 3.5

48 *several*: separate.

50 *Orpheus*: in classical mythology, a poet and musician whose melody was so beautiful that even inanimate objects were moved to dance to it.

Some Renaissance mythographers rationalized the story as referring to the civilizing influence of the arts upon the common people ('hinds', literally servants or farm labourers).

66 *what's . . . do?*: 'what's going on here?' Nicholas is surprised that tears have suddenly welled up in his eyes.

70 *break . . . wheel*: the lute will be taken off stage to be smashed: the prop is valuable, and a new one cannot be provided for every performance. The text does not specify which of Anne's attendants is given the job, but Jenkin and the carters remain on stage until later; the Coachman seems a more fitting candidate than Sisly.

115 *unseasoned*: unseasonable, ill-timed.

119–20 *and be hanged*: may you be hanged; in modern terms, 'Get knotted'.

120 *kept this coil*: caused this trouble.

124 *Cain*: in Judaeo-Christian mythology, the first murderer, whose punishment was to become a perpetual fugitive (Genesis 4).

129 *travel*: (*a*) usual modern sense; (*b*) hard work, travail.

130 *Gotten . . . tongues*: become fluent in the respective countries' languages.

131 *in . . . abate*: subside after coming to a head, and then be forgotten.

132 *divine*: foresee.

17.1 *these troubles*: the misfortunes of his sister, Anne.

4 *atoned*: reconciled (literally, made one).

4–6 *I would . . . ours*: i.e. he wishes that Anne's situation will have a happy outcome, like theirs.

9 *demeans*: expresses.

13–14 *She . . . well*: i.e. Sir Francis rejects the possibility that Anne had any prior inclination (a disposition 'of herself') to adultery.

35 *the good hour*: the moment of her death (which is 'good' because it is the moment when her soul will enter heaven).

37 S.D. *in her bed*: the bed would either be 'discovered' (see note on *Arden* 16.0 SD) or pushed onto the stage through the discovery space.

54 *Master Frankford*: Q1 (Q2 reads 'brother Acton'). Though Frankford has not yet arrived, the reading makes sense as expressing the momentary confusion or delirium of a woman who is seriously ill and preoccupied with the question of whether her husband will visit her.

64 *brawls*: loud rebukes.

68 *cross*: the primary meaning is 'misfortune', but there may also be a latent allusion to the cross made on the forehead at baptism, implying that worldly affliction is the lot of every Christian (compare line 71).

71 *to*: to undergo.

77 *spotted*: corrupt, impure.

88 *usurped upon*: assumed power over.

93 *my . . . death*: Jesus asked God to forgive those who crucified him (Luke 23: 34).

99–102 *all . . . stay*: in Anne's death, Acton will not truly lose a sibling, because Frankford will replace her: Acton will regard him as if he were a brother by blood ('the nearest way') rather than just by marriage.

104 *scarlet*: the colour of judges' robes of office.

120 *Once . . . wife*: i.e. she who is now once more thy wife.

EPILOGUE

3 *like a cherry*: probably refers to the round, ruddy cheeks of a beaming man; the redness of the cherry was proverbial (Tilley C.277).

4 *neat*: unadulterated and undiluted.

6 *runs . . . lee*: has been drawn from the bottom of the barrel, and so is mixed with the sediment (lee) that accumulates there.

8 *flat*: lacking in taste.

13 *allude*: obliquely compare.

The Witch of Edmonton

THE PERSONS OF THE PLAY

Hamluc: it is possible that this is not the character's name but that of the actor who played the role in the mid-1630s. However, there is no other record of such an actor.

1.1 S.D.: *with child*: visibly pregnant.

3 *in their cups*: drunkenly.

12–15 *the longest . . . thrift*: by temporarily living apart from his wife, Frank will be able to save more money for their future together.

19 *occasions*: causes.

38 *Waltham Abbey*: in Hertfordshire, about five miles from Edmonton.

53 *'less*: unless.

88 *forfeit shame*: lose her sense of shame.

106 *continual friend*: Sir Arthur promises to be Frank's 'friend for life' if he accepts the offer.

123 *occasions*: needs, obligations (here, in a specifically financial sense).

126–7 *Then . . . woman*: some other editions mark this as an aside, indicating that there is more to Sir Arthur's solicitude than meets the eye; but it may as easily be played as a bluff remark about 'making an honest woman of her'.

132 *bring*: escort.

143 *Lowly*: humbly.

152 *Am I a talker?*: i.e. 'Surely you know that you can count on my silence.'
Draw: draft, prepare in writing.

156 *cuckoo*: cuckold.

170−2 *It . . . practice*: Winifred's marriage is taken, wrongly, to be a convenience to cover her pregnancy; this shows her to be a skilled deceiver who will easily be able to fool her husband next time she and Sir Arthur have sex ('practice').

182 *For trial*: as a test (of virtue or constancy).

199 *upon a rock*: i.e. on the firmest possible foundation; the metaphor derives from a biblical parable (Matthew 7: 24−5).

202 *either*: one another.

209 *as much . . . lies*: with all your might.

212 *Get . . . nunnery*: echoes a famous line from *Hamlet* (3.1.123), playing on the fact that Winifred is going to live near an abbey.

216 *honesty*: chastity.

218 *want*: need.

224−5 *Thorney . . . fortune*: Sir Arthur had expected to have to pay Thorney to take the pregnant Winifred off his hands, but turns out to have given him a desirable commodity, an honest woman and loving wife; so instead of owing him money, Sir Arthur is now his creditor, while Frank is like the proverbial fool (Tilley F.536) who falls on his feet.

1.2.6 *proved one*: shown to match up.

12 *the proverb*: Tilley M.502.

15 *tarriers*: hindrances; but, since 'terriers' was also spelt 'tarriers' in the seventeenth century, this may also be the start of the play's run of canine imagery. Terriers were known as implacable hunting dogs which worried their prey and would not easily let go after biting.

16 *present*: immediate.

25 *black bags*: worn to conceal or protect a woman's face. Compare Thomas Jordan, 'A Paradox on his Mistress' (1646), ll. 31−2: 'Thou need'st no scarfs, no black bags here prevail; | Thy face is both thy beauty and thy veil.'

31−2 *Barber-Surgeons' Hall*: the headquarters of the Barber-Surgeons' Company in Monkswell Street, London. Public dissections took place there, and afterwards the skeletons were displayed outside.

38 *a loose gown*: a waistless, floor-length dress fitted only at the shoulders; starting to go out of fashion in the 1620s, but sometimes worn to conceal pregnancy.

48 *Yea and nay*: in the Sermon on the Mount, Jesus prohibits swearing: 'let your communication be, Yea, yea; Nay, nay' (Matthew 5: 37).

76 *roaring lads*: riotous delinquents, more commonly called roaring boys.

80–1 *by five . . . stone-weight*: in imperial weights, fourteen pounds make a stone (approximately 6½ kilograms metric).

85 *such another——*: the long rule in Q may indicate that Carter tails off, or that the printer has censored an expletive; compare 4.1.68.

89 *jointure*: money settled on a woman by her husband as part of their marriage contract.

90 *I think by sea*: Susan disparages the value of Warbeck's offer: wealth is at greater risk tied up in merchant shipping than in land.

115–16 *Master Thorney . . . Somerton*: Carter pointedly does not name Warbeck.

124 *clew*: ball of thread; in classical mythology, used by Theseus to find his way through the labyrinth on Crete.

152 *Heaven . . . it*: a non-committal answer ('God willing'), hence his father's response.

203 *plain Dunstable*: Dunstable was proverbially associated with simple plain-speaking (Tilley D.646).

208 *challenge*: claim.

210 *at a burden*: in one pregnancy.

217 *go scrape*: since there is now no job for them here, the unemployed fiddlers can go and scrape both their bowstrings and their living elsewhere.

217–18 *dance at night*: metaphorically, when they consummate the marriage. Heywood uses the same joke in *Woman*, 1.2.

2.1.9 *ignorant of myself*: the phrase applies to Mother Sawyer, not her accusers: she has learned witchcraft from them, having previously known nothing of it.

36 S.D. *Morris Dancers*: Q calls only for '*three or four more*' (and assigns dialogue to four).

39 *Crooked Lane*: a street in London; the Black Bell inn was on the corner.

41 *Trebles*: punning on the highest range of musical sound, above the mean (middle) and bass (lowest).

45 *Rowland*: the second dancer is named after a popular comic playlet of the 1580s, known as a 'jig' (although the modern implication of dance is irrelevant). Jigs commonly had bawdy plots, and were sometimes performed after plays.

47 *hunting counter*: following a quarry's scent or trail in the wrong direction.

48 *Enfield Chase*: a royal deer park in Middlesex.

48–9 *for . . . serve*: it will not take much effort to cast the morris dance.

55 *hobby-horse*: a lightweight horse costume worn by a single morris dancer, fastened over the shoulders; the horse's head and hindquarters projected from the dancer's midriff. Hobby-horses were known for their disruptive sexual antics during the morris.

64 *forget the hobby-horse*: playing on 'The hobby-horse is forgot', the refrain of a well-known and often quoted ballad (of which no full text survives).

82 *Let . . . back*: the joke is that, if the hobby-horse were a real one, it would need a strong back to carry Cuddy, who is fat. The part was originally played by the play's co-author, William Rowley, who often wrote parts for himself which made joking references to his own rotundity.

87–8 *curse . . . out*: this implies that Elizabeth Sawyer is one-eyed.

89 *Ungirt*: wearing no girdle (belt); the proverb is Tilley U.10.

98 *ground*: cause.

132 *deed of gift*: a written legal instrument transferring ownership by gift.

135–6 *If . . . pieces*: devils were thought to compel acquiescence by the threat of bodily pain. The action here draws on Christopher Marlowe's *Doctor Faustus* (1588), 5.1, in which Mephistopheles forces Faustus to sign a deed of gift in his own blood, under threat of being torn piecemeal.

173–4 *make . . . but me*: a perversion of the First Commandment: 'Thou shalt have no other gods before me' (Exodus 20: 3).

176–81 *I'll . . . tuum*: the Dog begins to speak in rhyming trochaic tetrameter, conventionally an indication of a supernatural figure in Elizabethan and Jacobean drama.

181 *Sanctibicetur . . . tuum*: a variant of the Latin for the second line of the Lord's Prayer, 'Hallowed be thy name' (Matthew 6: 9; it should be *sanctificetur*); the Dog, being a devil, gets it wrong, and Mother Sawyer progressively compounds the error when she repeats it in lines 183 and 186.

186 *Contaminetur*: corrupted be (Latin).

206 *a kind of God-bless-us*: a man of religious convictions.

208 *ka me . . . kob you*: proverbial (Tilley K.1), meaning 'you scratch my back and I'll scratch yours'. 'Ka' is pronounced 'kay', like the letter of the alphabet.

225 *hisce auribus*: with these ears (Latin).

247 *aspen-leaf*: the leaves of the asp (a tree of the poplar family) are especially prone to tremble.

250 *Et . . . tuum*: Cuddy's next line (252–3) implies that the Dog should say the Latin along with Mother Sawyer; but Cuddy is later surprised to learn that the Dog can speak (3.1.107–8).

257 *comfortable*: comforting.

266 *codlings*: (*a*) peascods (given as a love-token); (*b*) testicles.

273–4 *I'll . . . else*: if he fails to embrace her, he will remain in need of Mother Sawyer's guidance (like a young eagle, still being trained by its parents).

2.2.1–2 *Cloudy . . . in a fog*: melancholy.

5 *a proverb*: 'Wedding and hanging go by destiny' (Tilley W.232).

5 *juggler*: conjuror.

15 *wear*: possess.

21 *hold . . . string*: have your destiny under your own control.

30–1 *that . . . Haven*: men who trust their wives too much are more likely to be cuckolded. Cuckold's Haven was an area of the south bank of the Thames, downstream from central London, which got its name from the legend that King John granted the land to a man whose wife he had seduced.

33 *master*: keep.

39–40 *new pair . . . sheath*: a pair of knives, commonly given as a wedding gift, is here used as a periphrasis for the married couple themselves. Sheffield was, and remains, a centre of cutlery production in England.

61 *run a-tilt*: some country wedding festivities included jousts ('tilts'), as parodied in Ben Jonson's 1633 royal entertainment at Welbeck; barrels sometimes served as targets for the horsemen's lances.

81 *silly*: innocent.

100 *Adonis*: in classical mythology, a chaste young hunter, who rejected the sexual advances of Venus, goddess of love.

110 *Hydra*: see note on *Arden* 4.13.

119 *bury me*: i.e. outlive her.

124 *pretend*: excuse myself with reference to. Frank claims that Winifred waited on him as if she were his wife, in order to conceal the fact that she really is.

128 *has 't*: has Susan's place as his wife.

151 *cost it*: even if it should cost.

153 *lapwing*: the bird was known for decoying intruders away from its nest.

3.1.8–9 *the hobby-horse*: Cuddy himself plays the hobby-horse: the suggestion that it is a woman's part is probably a laddish jibe.

18 *cherry-pit*: a children's game in which cherrystones are thrown into a small hole.

33 *Shrovetide*: the Sunday, Monday, and Tuesday before Lent, a period of festivity before Lenten abstinence. In 1621, this was 11–13 February.

37 *reckon . . . traveller*: since 1582, continental Europe had used the Gregorian calendar, whereas until 1752 England retained the Julian calendar, which

was ten days behind. Travel overseas consequently entailed reckoning dates '*stila nova*' (new style). Cuddy's joke is that, by conflating the two calendars, Shrovetide can be made to last ten days.

38 *freshwater*: unskilled, inexperienced.

40 *eight . . . week*: because soldiers were paid both unpunctually and poorly: seven days' pay for eight days' work, and late to boot.

47–9 *There's . . . cut*: it is unclear whether this sentence is part of the text Cuddy is quoting or his own comment on it. The primary meaning of 'a long cut' is an extended period of unhappiness, but it also contains bawdy innuendo ('a deep vagina').

58 *Poldavis*: Poldavis was coarse sacking material; the word was often used as a name for a lowly tradesman.

62–4 *a horse . . . heaviest lovers*: fat Cuddy will have a hard time keeping up with a swift-moving quarry.

65 *sculler*: a waterman. In London, watermen would ferry paying passengers along and across the Thames, like a modern taxi service.

67 *Katherine's Dock*: a London landing-place immediately east of the Tower, with a bawdy secondary meaning ('Kate's bottom').

72 *ducks*: playing on 'duck' as a term of endearment; Cuddy intends an amorous expedition rather than a sporting one.

80 *Barking Church*: a London church in Great Tower Street (with an obvious canine pun).

83 *I . . . late*: it was held that to be out of doors late at night was to risk assault by night-walking criminals. Cuddy's remark carries an undertone of sexual threat to Kate.

86 *'Stay . . . Apollo*: the classical god Apollo sings this as he pursues the nymph Daphne in a popular contemporary ballad.

95 *Pond's almanac*: a popular almanac by Edward Pond, published annually from 1601.

96 *Gravesend*: a Kentish port thirty miles downriver from the City of London. The primary point of the geographical reference is to facilitate a pun (falling in the pond has almost killed him), but it also suggests how far Cuddy's wooing has drifted off course.

99 *Limehouse*: an east London district where leather was tanned.

102 *Thou . . . neither*: i.e. the dog was only behaving as dogs do ('kind' here means species).

106 *reading*: reprimanding.

108–10 *Aesop's fables . . . water*: in the *Fables* of Aesop (see note on *Arden* 9.29), a dog carrying a piece of meat sees itself in the water and attacks the reflection in the hope of getting a second meal.

119 *jowls*: fish heads.

128 *maids and soles*: species of edible fish. The Dog, of course, is more interested in corrupting maidens and stealing souls.

136 *I serve . . . than one*: alluding to the biblical precept that no man can serve two masters (Luke 16: 13).

137 *mammon and the devil*: in the Bible, one cannot serve both God and Mammon (Matthew 6: 24).

145 *the Devil of Edmonton*: *The Merry Devil of Edmonton* (1602) was a popular farce about a benevolent, tricksy conjuror who helps a pair of young lovers to marriage.

3.2.5 *shown . . . company*: wept in public.

6–7 *Thus . . . about*: now that she is alone with Frank, all her sorrows, hitherto unwept, overwhelm her.

11 *eclipse*: thought to be a portent of disastrous public events; Winifred applies the idea to her personal situation.

25 *look . . . me*: treat me as a father should treat his son.

30 *'Tis . . . discourse*: talking at this length entails the risk of our being caught together.

38 *Go . . . thee*: until now Frank has spoken to Winifred in verse, but now drops into prose as he pretends, for Susan's ears, to be addressing his horse-boy.

40 *part with*: say goodbye to.

44–5 *Some . . . footings*: he supposes that Susan intends to ask 'the horse-boy' to keep an eye on him in her absence and report any marital misdemeanours.

49 *being honest*: provided the task is an honest one.

66 *label*: (here) pendent earring.

68 *jewel*: Frank. A jewel was often used as a metaphor for female virginity, but the implication here is of male post-marital fidelity.

78 *counsel-keeping*: keeping his secrets.

107 *happily*: in all likelihood.

115 *perfect*: thoroughly instructed (as of a lesson wholly learnt and internalized).

123 *behind*: left to tell.

3.3.2–3 *The mind's . . . forward*: Frank is already premeditating an evil deed; it will only take a small intervention by the Dog for him to turn these thoughts into action.

6 *part . . . sound*: leave with his brusque words ringing in her ears.

9 *homewards*: on your way home.

38 *The devil . . . me*: Frank is unaware of the Dog's influence on him.

40 *dogged*: pursued, punning on the Dog's agency in the murder.

41 *intelligent*: intelligible.

44 *Sin . . . hatred*: the sin I hate most of all.

56 *linger*: cruelly force her to die slowly (literally, detain).

61 *stayed*: waited.

62 *in . . . world*: have no enemies.

71 *this tree*: early seventeenth-century theatres often had two pillars supporting a canopy over the stage; they were often used to stand in for trees.

78 *O! O!*: a groan.

81 *o'ertake*: catch up with; he is asking them to finish him off so that he can be dead with Susan.

103 *that carcass there*: Susan's body.

105 *dumb show*: mime, often used in drama to compress action or comment allegorically upon it; as Carter's disdainful metaphor suggests, they were often considered a low, crude device.

3.4.14 *morris-'ray*: morris-dancing costumes.

14–16 *The fore-bell . . . weathercock*: Sawgut imagines the morris dancers, who are wearing bells, in terms of a church tower with a peal of bells inside and a weathercock on top.

19 *horse . . . foot*: in battle, the cavalry would charge ahead of the foot soldiers.

22–3 *We . . . for him*: Cuddy is slow because he is fat; metaphorically, he must wait for the big gate to be opened for him, whereas his slimmer colleagues can slip in through the wicket gate ahead of him.

29 *pledge*: see note on *Arden* 14.213.

30 S.D. *Holds him the bowl*: holds the cup of beer in front of the hobby-horse's mouth.

35 *Father*: a familiar mode of address to any old man, not suggesting a blood relationship.

38 *guts*: the strings of the fiddle (made of catgut).

39 *caught cold*: lost its voice.

41, 51 S.P. *DANCERS*: this edn.; Q reads '*Omn.*'

45 *'The Flowers in May'*: a dance tune.

46 *hair*: bowstring.

56 *Flat*: downright.

70 S.D. *strikes*: plays a note on.

83–4 *Mine . . . alone*: anything which stands perfectly vertical at the equator ('the middle zone') casts no shadow.

4.1.2 *glanders*: a contagious disease in horses, with symptoms including a runny nose.

5 *took*: caught, unexpectedly discovered.

6–7 *threshing . . . market*: having sex.

7 *polecat*: loose woman, whore.

19 *stand . . . home*: protect you.

24 *with . . . tail*: there is a bawdy secondary meaning, in which the woman's 'tail' is her vagina and the 'fire' signifies sexual excitement.

39 *a snuffling nose*: a nose partly eaten away by syphilis.

54 *backside*: back yard.

63 *burning*: perhaps refers to the reprisals which the countrymen were about to take earlier in the scene; in England, the legal penalty for witchcraft was hanging, not burning (but compare line 218 below).

68 *cow's* ——: the long rule (standing for the word 'arse') may indicate either censorship by Q's printer or polite self-abbreviation by Banks.

81 *thine own*: i.e. his own soul.

86 *Know . . . to*: 'Keep a civil tongue in your head.'

92–3 *a spirit that sucks her*: witches were thought to suckle their familiar spirits with blood from a third nipple—'the teat' which Mother Sawyer later offers the Dog (153). This nipple was not necessarily in the usual place: Cuddy Banks later bawdily suggests that Mother Sawyer's is somewhere below her waist (5.1.172); witnesses in the trial of the historical Elizabeth Sawyer claimed to have seen it just above her anus.

108 *naked paps*: some fashionable young women at the Jacobean court wore dresses which left their breasts bare.

111–14 *These . . . butterfly*: the passage refers to the contemporary aristocratic practice of selling landed estates to finance a lifestyle of conspicuous consumption: by sacrificing his agricultural land, a lord would be able to buy himself up-to-the-minute transport and chic clothing (which might be flimsy, like a butterfly, and of foreign cut); his former servants would become unemployed.

146 *one thing*: Sir Arthur guiltily supposes that Mother Sawyer's attack on the seduction of maidens by upper-class men (143–6) refers specifically to his liaison with Winifred; and, in order to know about that, he assumes, she must be a witch.

190 *paned hose*: breeches made in sections ('panes'), which were liable to split at the seams.

191 *Lancashire hornpipe*: a musical pipe with a horn bell at the bottom end.

196 *close chamber*: confinement in a dark room was a seventeenth-century treatment for madness.

200 *Mother Bombie*: an old fortune-teller in a comedy of the same name by John Lyly (*c*.1590); often used as a nickname for a witch.

230 *Puppison*: an affectionate diminutive of 'puppy'.

dog-days: literally, the hottest time of the year, in July and August. If 2.1 takes place around midsummer (24 June; see 2.1.57), and 5.3 during or after Bartholomew Fair (24 August–2 September; see 5.3.39), then this scene may indeed be set during the dog-days; but the primary sense, of course, is the canine joke.

234 *foisting*: (*a*) deceitfully flattering, like a courtier; (*b*) farting, like a dog.

237 *makes . . . drakes*: (*a*) behaves improvidently; (*b*) commits adultery.

237 *Paris Garden*: the London home of bear-baiting, on the south bank of the Thames; the sport involved using dogs to attack and kill a tethered bear.

240 *Black Dog of Newgate*: a spectral hound said to appear in the streets around Newgate prison at the time of executions. Sceptics alternatively defined the phrase as either (*a*) the dark mood of the conscience-stricken prisoners, or (*b*) a large black stone in the condemned cell.

244–5 *St Dunstan's . . . Temple Bar*: Temple Bar in Fleet Street was the westward limit of the City of London local authority's jurisdiction. Next to it was the Devil tavern, whose sign depicted St Dunstan taking the devil by the nose with fire-tongs. (Both were in the parish of St Dunstan's.) The district was the city's legal centre, with barristers living in all-male collegiate societies, the Inns of Court, serviced by the local laundresses and others.

248 *the dog's here*: the Dog has been there all the time, invisible to them all; they only become aware of his presence when he barks.

254 *Gammer Gurton*: an old woman who loses her needle in William Stephenson's academic comedy, *Gammer Gurton's Needle* (*c*.1553), which was later staged commercially.

260 *spit . . . mouth*: a way of showing affection to a dog.

267 *bloodhound*: often used as a synonym for 'murderer'.

4.2.0 S.D. *a bed thrust forth*: the bed would be pushed onto the stage through the large central aperture in the back wall.

2 *here*: the heart.

6 *my sister . . . you*: the assumption is that the dead continue to exist in those who live on and remember them.

17 *idle*: raving in delirium.

26–7 *no place . . . only this*: if only the material world existed, and there were no afterlife, there would be no reason not to commit suicide (whereas, for those who believe in heaven and hell, suicide could lead to damnation).

42 *dead pay*: here, the reward of the true believer after death. This is the best kind of dead pay in that the term's more usual meaning was money appropriated by a corrupt military officer and accounted for as wages paid to soldiers who were actually dead.

64 *Fall to*: 'tuck in', start eating.

69 *Here's none*: Katherine has found the murder weapon, but makes an excuse to allow her to go and fetch her father.

70 S.D. *it's there too*: in the Jacobean theatre, the effect would probably have been achieved using two trapdoors, one on each side of the bed: as Frank begins to turn, the ghost would descend into one trap, and emerge through the other as Frank completes the movement. This might have involved two actors in identical costumes, to simplify the timing and obviate the need for swift transit in the under-stage area. The second trap would then have been used to facilitate the ghost's disappearance moments later.

88 *windmill:* bizarre, fanciful notion.

120 *The knife*: Frank thinks Katherine has returned with the cutlery she went to fetch.

127–8 *moons . . . foreheads*: the crescent moon was said to have horns, as were cuckolds.

129 *urinals*: doctors (whose professional equipment included a urinal for examining patients' water).

132 *bag . . . imposthumes*: a cyst inside the body, containing noxious fluid.

137 *make a holiday*: take time away from everyday pursuits, 'go out of my way'; but also implying celebration.

142 *cut me*: carve the chicken for me.

146 *tower*: heaven.

clog: literally, a heavy block of wood tied to a man's leg to impede his movement and prevent him escaping. Here Winifred is the clog, a metonymy for Frank's bigamy, which will debar him from heaven.

S.D. *coffin*: at least one servant will also be required to carry the coffin, or two if Old Carter does not share in the job himself.

150 *letting blood*: if she were ill, Susan might need bloodletting, a surgical procedure used in the seventeenth century to drain infected blood out of the body. Frank, as a murderer, is good at drawing blood in a different sense, but Old Carter expects that now she will bleed again: it was believed that a corpse's wounds would do so in the presence of its murderer.

165 *posies*: engraved verses.

168 *strike home*: hit the intended target; the evidence is figuratively like the knife itself.

174 *Up*: either Winifred is still sitting on the bed or she has knelt to beg Carter for mercy.

190 *this father*: Frank, the father of her unborn child; Old Carter mistakes it as a reference to himself (line 192).

194 *don . . . tacklings*: get dressed; Frank is still in bed. 'Tacklings' literally means a ship's rigging.

199 *worst punishment*: damnation.

5.1.3 *bewitched*: supernaturally prevented.

21 *powder-mine*: in siege warfare, an excavation beneath a city's defensive walls; a gunpowder explosion inside the mine was used to make the walls collapse.

40 *lamb*: lambs are white, as the Dog is now, but the image is also suggestively topsy-turvy: dogs usually tear out lambs' throats, but here the 'lamb' is to savage the witch; and the lamb, as a conventional image of Christ, is an unexpected metaphorical guise for a hell-hound.

42–3 *He . . . land*: the different body parts make the devil amphibious: he can get you anywhere. The otter itself, thought to be neither fish nor flesh, continues the suggestion of transgressive topsy-turvydom.

48 *stripped naked*: exposed for what they are by the coming of light.

53 *puritan*: pure.

84–5 *Let . . . them*: a declaration of mutual irresponsibility: devils are not to blame for enticing witches because it is the witch who initiates the contract; but witches are not to blame for their own damnation because it is effected by devils.

135 *play'st*: gamble.

137 *rook*: (*a*) black, crow-like bird; (*b*) card-sharper.

149–50 *There's . . . mind*: most lawyers charge exorbitant fees for giving advice.

155 *etcetera*: this edn. (Q & c.). This is probably not an invitation to improvise, since the sense carries on uninterrupted into the next sentence. Perhaps Cuddy becomes momentarily and uncharacteristically Latinate to mark his own elevation above the baseness of the Dog's life.

157 *ducking*: hunting ducks, a sport in which dogs were commonly used.

160 *bull or bear*: bull-baiting and bear-baiting, further sports involving dogs.

161 *Moll Cutpurse*: an alias of Mary Frith (*c.*1584–1659), a celebrated transvestite and petty criminal in the London underworld. She was the heroine of *The Roaring Girl* (1611), a comedy co-written by Dekker; Cuddy may be referring to its alternative title, *Moll Cutpurse*, rather than the leading character.

165 *staved off*: beaten away with a stave; used especially of dogs in bear-baiting.

167 *wheel*: a small treadmill for a dog, used to turn a roasting spit in a large kitchen.

169 *lick . . . toes*: lick the grease of the roast meat off his paws for food.

172 *coats*: skirts.

181 *There . . . countenance*: the Dog may mean that he will worm his way ('shug') into a corrupt aristocrat's patronage ('countenance'), or that he may enter that person's body (compare lines 187–90), possessing him, and so literally acquire his countenance (i.e. face).

182 *Briarean*: Briareus was a hundred-handed giant in classical mythology.

footcloth-strider: a person whose horse wears an ornamental cloth over its back, a mark of high estate.

185 *the dragon's tail*: in the Bible, the dragon's tail pulls down a third of the stars from the heavens (Revelation 12: 3–4).

190 *atom*: minuscule.

192 *go in procession*: formally walk around the parish boundaries in the ceremony of 'beating the bounds' to establish their location in local memory.

195 *Thieving Lane*: modern Bow Street in London; the route along which thieves were taken to prison.

197 *stairs*: in London, steps down to landing stages on the River Thames, from which one could take a boat.

5.3.3 *at height already*: they are already grieving to the utmost limit of their endurance; it will be too upsetting actually to see the execution.

37–8 *cast . . . farrowed*: gave birth to a litter of piglets a day early.

39 *Bartholomew Fair*: an annual fair held in Smithfield from 24 August, St Bartholomew's Day, at which pork was customarily sold.

59 *sunk . . . wants*: gone bankrupt.

118 *them*: those who gave Frank bad counsel.

153 *but . . . passed*: except for the fact that I have given my promise.

159 *a thousand marks*: £666 13*s*. 8*d*. (a mark was two-thirds of a pound).

discharge: pay.

EPILOGUE

The function of the epilogue is, as always, to solicit applause. Here the actor does it in character, figuring the applause as a testimonial that will help Winifred secure a second husband. It is possible that the epilogue, like the prologue, was not part of the play as originally staged in 1621.

ADDITIONAL PASSAGES

2.2 *A devil*: in fact the merry devil of Edmonton was not a devil at all but a magician (see note on 3.1.145).

5–8 *But . . . season*: the prologue was written for a revival of the play in the 1630s.

The English Traveller

PROLOGUE

4 *bombast*: pad. (Bombast was cotton-wool stuffing, used in clothing to disguise a wearer's scrawny appearance.)

6–8 *Nor . . . self-will*: the playwright has deliberately omitted these elements: he is skilful enough to have included them had he wished.

1.1.8 *wandering*: moving through the heavens (making them, in more precise astronomical terms, planets rather than stars).

10 *to seek*: out of his depth, 'all at sea'.

12 *both th' Indies*: the East and West Indies.

24 *Mark*: observations.

40 *Small doings*: (*a*) few events; (*b*) not much sex.

42 *January . . . May*: a proverbial periphrasis for an old husband and a young wife (Tilley M.768).

60 *government*: decorous behaviour and habits, self-control.

72 *approves*: proves.

72–8 *This . . . deserve it*: Dalavill says that, to be loved by Wincott, Young Geraldine must be virtuous ('nobly propertied'); Young Geraldine modestly ascribes the virtue to Wincott's love rather than his own deserts.

98–9 *That . . . wife*: because she is so much younger than him, Wincott's wife is a surrogate child: she will outlive him and inherit his property.

115 *that great pyramis*: an obelisk, approximately 48 metres high, brought from Africa to Rome by Julius Caesar, and newly erected in the churchyard of St Peter's in 1586.

120 *Pantheon*: a domed temple in Rome, built by the Emperor Hadrian; later used as a church.

Capitol: the religious centre of ancient Rome, at the top of the Capitoline hill.

133 *the Empire*: the Holy Roman Empire, occupying most of central Europe between France and Poland.

136 *censure*: judgement, appraisal (without pejorative intent).

136–7 *my travel . . . language*: his purpose in travelling was to learn foreign languages.

143 *loath*: reluctant to.

160–1 *Greek . . . Turkish slavery*: Greece was ruled by the Ottoman Empire in the seventeenth century.

163 *change*: sexual variety. Perhaps the reference is to the Turkish harem.

165 *a strain . . . both*: combines the sexual characteristics of the French and Spanish.

192 *jack*: (*a*) mechanism for turning a cooking spit; (*b*) animated figure which strikes a clock bell.

1.2.1 *Corydon*: rustic; a typical name for a shepherd in Renaissance pastoral.

6 *anno tertio*: third year (Latin); the form used in legal language for a monarch's regnal year.

13 *Agreeing with*: suitable for.

20 *tiltyard*: the arena for chivalric jousts, an aristocratic martial display requiring horses bred for speed and manoeuvrability rather than the carthorse's physical strength.

Prank it: devote yourself to high living.

24 *lean Lent*: Lent was a time of fasting and self-denial.

27 *fly*: disappear.

40 *oves and boves*: sheep and oxen (from Psalm 8: 9); each of the Latin words has two syllables.

46 *stiletto*: a short, pointed dagger, associated with Italy and so considered genteel.

50 *musk-cat*: musk is secreted by a gland near the musk-cat's anus, so Robin is suggesting that, for all his perfumed sophistication, Reignald is no less filthy than he.

51 *cheese and onions*: smelly country fare.

61 *keep*: stay in.

68 *steward*: the chief servant of the household.

77 *widgeon*: a wild duck, commonly used as a byword for a fool.

84 *stock*: remaining money.

86 *butcher's meat*: heavy red meat such as beef, mutton, or lamb, considered plebeian food.

148 *All's one*: it doesn't matter.

149 *Or*: whether.

164 *precise*: morally fastidious.

195 *made . . . books*: Young Lionel has bought Scapha's clothes on credit; mercers' books were records of customers' debts.

216 *judged . . . stake*: condemned her to be burnt at the stake as a heretic.

227 *the bar*: where convicted prisoners stood in court to receive sentence; a metaphor, not a stage property.

228 *How, man, how?*: Rioter assumes that Young Lionel is about to ask Scapha to lift her skirts.

234 *cast*: second-hand, discarded, worn-out.

2.1.27 *usurious*: abundant.

34–5 *water tankards*: large tub-like vessels in which water was delivered in bulk.

35 *cocks*: the spouts of a public drinking fountain.

35–6 *like . . . day*: on coronation days, the conduits (public drinking fountains) in London usually ran with wine rather than water.

50 *soul*: spongy flesh around the lungs.

54 *stomach*: (*a*) fighting spirit; (*b*) hungry appetite: Roger's entire story is an extended play of double meanings, describing the preparation and consumption of a meal as if it were a brawl.

65–6 *pinioned . . . felons*: trussed them up like criminals about to be hanged.

66 *cut . . . heels*: (*a*) disgraced them by removing their spurs, signs of knighthood; (*b*) cut off the spurs of the cocks, ready for cooking.

69 *shrewd turn*: misfortune, punning on the birds turning on the spit as they are roasted.

72 *swallow . . . digested*: tolerate an insult (rather than retaliate).

77 *healthing*: drinking healths.

78 *by the belly*: regularly on demand.

78–9 *beggars . . . gate*: beggars would congregate at the gate of a wealthy household to be given the table leavings.

79 *daffodil*: Roger's alliterative choice of flower perhaps hints at narcissism in Lionel Junior: in classical mythology, the beautiful youth Narcissus was turned into a daffodil.

86 *ditches*: trenches.

88 *of their wings . . . fly*: were forced to relinquish their wings; the odd sentence construction is for the sake of an obvious secondary meaning.

100–1 *incident To*: commonly found in.

115 *Possess . . . novel*: tell us the news.

143 *discover*: keep lookout from the crow's nest.

145 *towards*: coming; heading in the direction of the 'ship'.

158 *Arion*: in classical mythology, a musician who threw himself into the sea to escape pirates, and was carried to safety by a dolphin.

163 *atone*: pacify.

207 *society*: companionship.

218 *he*: a generic person; does not refer to Wincott.

256 *crazed*: worn-out (literally, covered with cracks).

258 *be . . . life*: are still alive after Wincott's death.

2.2.10 *Metamorphoses*: a long Latin poem retelling stories of bodily transformation from classical mythology. For Ovid, see note on *Arden* 1.60.

18 *stiff*: erect, like both a soldier at attention and a tumescent penis.

22 *I'll . . . bottom*: pull you down, (*a*) as a drowning man does to a person trying to save him, and (*b*) as an amorous man does to a woman he wants to have sex with. In reality, however, Rioter falls in a drunken stupor.

24 *The Spaniard . . . sail*: England's primarily naval war with Spain formally began in 1625 (and lasted until 1630), but there were intermittent hostilities before that.

97 *Mercury*: messenger of the classical gods, known as a cunning trickster.

103 *lie*: be imprisoned.

137 S.D. *aloud*: loudly.

150 *hammer*: door-knocker.

3.1.12–13 *benefit Of*: a profit from.

18 *break their day*: fail to repay a loan on the due date.

23 *principale . . . use*: respectively, the sum originally lent and the interest paid on it.

55 *friend*: lover.

56 *Whether*: whichever.

117–18 *palpable . . . note*: obvious, clearly discernible.

145 *yonder place*: heaven.

152 *eminent*: noteworthy, notorious. Some other editors modernize to 'imminent', so that Old Geraldine emphasizes the immediacy rather than the scale of the moral disaster he suspects.

161–2 *take . . . forehead*: in seventeenth-century iconography, Occasion (opportunity) was represented as a figure, usually female, with a long forelock, but bald at the back of her head. The implication was that action should be taken at the right moment: it was easy to catch Occasion by the forelock, when coming towards her, but impossible to do so from behind, after the right time had passed.

168 *curious*: fastidiously discriminating.

169 *a . . . competent*: adequate financial means.

218 *unmatched yoke*: joining (in marriage) of a dissimilar pair.

224 *mirror*: model, paragon, exemplar.

227 *Cato*: the Roman statesman Cato the Elder (234–149 BC), a byword for stringent moral probity.

3.2.17 *cast*: dismissed, sacked.

46 *cancelled*: discharged.

47 *stay*: wait.

51 *cleave*: cling.

70 *main*: principal.

101 *country*: location.

102 *to seek*: lacking.

3.3.30 *term*: see note on *Arden* 1.51.

78 *keeps . . . common*: is sharing Mrs Wincott with her husband.

to blame: blameworthy.

80 *second self*: implying absolute trustworthiness.

89 *Drink that*: he gives her not wine but a *pourboire*, a gratuity to a servant or other inferior (here, to pay her off).

134 *open your mouth*: the pot has a lid which is raised to drink from it.

150 *of . . . counsel*: privy to his secrets.

167 *oblivious*: forgetful.

4.1.12 *alchemy*: alchemists claimed to be able to turn base metals into gold; but in practice their efforts were a confidence trick which produced only imitation gold, not the real thing.

32 *disable your estate*: imply that you are in financial difficulties.

33 *As far . . . sell*: he no more thinks of buying than you do of selling.

43 *make . . . quadrangle*: turn a pitched frontage into a square one like Ricott's.

44 *just*: exactly.

48 *Great Alexander*: King of Macedon (356–323 BC), who established an empire stretching from Greece and Egypt as far as India.

Agathocles: Ruler of Syracuse (317–289 BC), who brought Sicily under Greek control.

49 *Caesar*: Julius Caesar (100–44 BC), conqueror of Gaul (modern France).

63–4 *without . . . mainprize*: the person to be arrested by this warrant may not be released on bail.

94 *his inheritance*: the emotional associations of inherited property were stronger in the seventeenth century than today: to sell your patrimony was also to give up all that was left of your dead father.

103–4 *you may . . . sergeants*: Reignald suggests that Old Lionel may eventually occupy the property himself, and that its grandeur will befit a hypothetical future appointment as Sheriff (the principal legal officer of an English county); Reignald himself hopes to be one of the Sheriff's officers (sergeants). The posts outside the Sheriff's house were used to display public notices.

109 *bay windows*: Q includes a marginal stage direction, '*Bayes*'; its meaning is obscure.

4.2.5 *no . . . stirring*: anyone not in bed by this time must be up to no good.

9 *Qui va la?*: who goes there? (French)

11 *word*: password.

13–14 *you . . . corporal*: Roger is pretending to be a sentry, who would refer a suspicious passer-by to the corporal in charge.

20 *deposed*: sworn to.

4.3.17 *give us leave*: take yourself off.

93 *pallet*: this may refer to the table; the scene's opening stage direction makes no provision for a couch or daybed.

103–4 *And the . . . lent out*: because he has Mrs Wincott's agreement that they will marry when she is widowed, Young Geraldine regards her as 'on loan' to her present husband. During the period of the 'loan', he can only look at her in bed; in time, when she is his wife, he will be able to do more than that (i.e. enjoy the 'fruition' of her beauty).

132–3 *serpent . . . Circe*: Geraldine compares Dalavill to the serpent which tempted Eve and caused the fall of man in the biblical creation myth (Genesis 3) and to Sinon, who betrayed Troy in classical legend, and Mrs Wincott to the crocodile, notorious for its insincere tears, and to Circe, the enchantress of classical mythology who turned men into beasts and who was a byword for the dangers of women's sexual power over men.

139 *a base hangman*: public executioner was the most despised of all jobs.

146 *Damn on*: continue sinning (and thereby damning yourselves).

148 *Ossa . . . Pelion*: mountains in Greece piled on one another by the giants of classical mythology in an effort to reach heaven. Here their combined weight will press Dalavill and Mrs Wincott in the opposite direction.

4.5.41 *Orlando*: an alternative name for the French hero Roland, hero of the twelfth-century poem the *Chanson de Roland*, who died at Roncevaux sounding his horn for assistance.

4.6.72–3 *laid rods in piss*: prepared an unpleasant retribution; literally, put a bundle of twigs in an astringent liquid to harden them up prior to thrashing somebody with them.

90 *roaring lads*: see note on *The Witch of Edmonton* 1.2.76.

208 S.D. *he gets up*: Reignald climbs up the frame of the door representing Old Lionel's house and stands on the section of the stage balcony above it. When he comes back down, he uses the normal exit and entry points on the balcony and main stage.

244 *come . . . ropes*: 'go hang yourselves!' (A condemned man would climb a ladder by the gallows and be pushed off with the noose around his neck.) The ropes to which Reignald refers are the cords they have brought to tie him up.

296 *Fortune playhouse*: a theatre in north London, with an image of the allegorical figure of Fortune above the entrance. It burned down in 1621 and was rebuilt in 1623, the year before *The English Traveller* was written. The Palsgrave's Men, who played at the Fortune, were commercial

336

competitors of Heywood's company, but never fully recovered from the losses they incurred in the fire.

5.1.41 *viperous brood*: vipers were thought to kill their mother in the act of being born, and so were a byword for treacherous ingratitude.

117 *Sirens*: in classical mythology, mermaids whose song led mariners astray.

149 *Medusa*: the snake-haired Gorgon of classical mythology.

153 *He*: God.

210 *beneath the moon*: in Renaissance cosmology, the moon marked the boundary between the mutable universe (beneath it, including the Earth) and the fixed (above it). Compare note on *Woman* 13.63.

212 *misfare*: 'go the wrong way' (here used as a euphemism for dying).

DEDICATION AND ADDRESS TO THE READER

EPISTLE

1 *Sir Henry Appleton*: an Essex landowner, knighted in 1613, whose wife came from Lincolnshire (as did Heywood).

10 *Sir William Elwes*: a Lincolnshire gentleman, knighted in 1617.

14 *Laelius*: Caius Laelius Sapiens, a Roman politician of the second century BC, celebrated in Cicero's *De amicitia* as a lover of literature.

Scipio: Scipio Africanus the Younger (*c*.185–132 BC), who also appears in *De amicitia*, a friend of the poet Lucilius and the playwright Terence.

Maecenas: a Roman patron of the arts (died 8 BC).

15 *Augustus Caesar*: the first Roman Emperor (born 63 BC, reigned 27 BC–AD 14), patron of the poets Virgil and Horace.

17–20 *Inspice . . . est*: 'Consider the cost of your own games, Augustus: you will read of many expensive things like this. You have yourself seen these things and presented them to other spectators, so benevolent is your majesty everywhere.' (Ovid, *Tristia* 2.509–12) At this point in the poem, Ovid is pointing out that even indecent plays are considered socially acceptable by the Roman elite.

23 *Histriomastix*: a controversial antitheatrical tract of 1633, which inadvertently insulted Queen Henrietta Maria, the patron of Heywood's acting company and herself an enthusiastic performer in court drama, when it declared actresses to be whores; the author, William Prynne, was mutilated and imprisoned.

24 *Minerva assistente*: with the aid of the goddess of wisdom.

23–4 *I hope . . . satisfaction*: Heywood had published a pro-theatrical treatise, *An Apology for Actors*, in 1612, but he wrote no similar work in rebuttal to *Histriomastix*.

TO THE READER

6 *filius populi*: a child of the people (rather than of any particular father); an orphan.

8 *Works . . . others'*: Ben Jonson had included his plays in the collected edition of his *Works* in 1616; the ensuing jibes about his confusing work with play had a long shelf life.

GLOSSARY

a (*pronoun*) the unstressed form of 'he'
abject degraded person, outcast
acquittance document confirming that a debt has been repaid
adamant a magnetic stone thought to be the hardest substance in nature
alderman one of the twelve senior officers in London's local government
alfere ensign, standard-bearer
aloes a fragrant resin used in perfume
amain violently, forcefully
ambergris a waxy substance used in perfume
an if
anatomy skeleton
angel gold coin worth ten shillings
Apollo classical god of music
applausive agreeable
approve prove
aqua-vitae strong alcoholic liquor
arming puppy lapdog
arraign indict
artificer craftsman
asperse slander, defame
attach arrest
avaunt go away (*imperative*)
aye ever
back-friend false friend, secret enemy
baggage worthless woman
bait stop at an inn
baleful harmful
balk shun
ban (*v.*) curse
bandog mastiff, ferocious guard-dog
basilisk mythical reptile, fatal even to look at
bead-roll catalogue of names
beadsman humble servant
beard (*v.*) offensively confront
bedeem portend
Bedlam madhouse
beeves oxen
behoveful suitable, worthy, appropriate

beldam ugly old woman
bestead placed by circumstances
betimes early
bewray reveal, betray
bewrayed covered in filth
bill long-handled weapon combining axe and spearhead
billet thick piece of firewood
binal double, twofold
bird-bolt arrow used to shoot birds
blab betray by talking
blur smear with infamy
bodkin pin used to fasten hair
bootless useless, pointless
Bordeaux red wine from southern France
botcher clothes-mender
bottle of hay small haystack
brabble brawl about something trivial
brake (*v.*) broke; (*n.*) clump of bushes
branched embroidered
brokage trade
broker dealer in second-hand clothes
bruit (*n.*) noise, rumour; (*v.*) report in common gossip
buckler (*v.*) defend; (*n.*) a small shield
bulch bull-calf; used as a term of endearment
but only
buttery hatch a half-door through which provisions and liquor are served
by-chamber side-chamber
canary sweet wine from the Canary Islands
caper dance in a leaping, frolicsome way
capon castrated cockerel
carl low-born churl
caroche stately coach
cassia a cinnamon-based perfume
catechize interrogate
cates food
cavil find fault
challenge claim

chafe fret

chandler maker or seller of candles

chary punctiliously cautious

check strike, retard, restrain

cheerly blithely

Cheshunt Hertfordshire town four miles from Edmonton

chid rebuked

choleric prone to anger

civet oily animal secretion used in perfume

clew ball of twine

clip (n.) embrace

clog encumbrance, impediment

clown rustic, bumpkin

cock-boat small ship's boat

cock-shut light twilight

coil tumult, trouble, disturbance

coistrel, coisterel knave

complot conspiracy

composition agreement

con learn

consort harmony

contraction contractual dealing

copesmate sexual partner

costard head

counterfeit reproduced image

countervail equal

cowl-staff pole used for carrying heavy burdens

coxcomb (n.) fool; (v.) make a fool of

cozen deceive, defraud

crash (n.) a bout of revelry

credit reputation, good name

crotchet whimsical device

cross coin of small value

cross-point a dance step in which the legs are repeatedly crossed and uncrossed while leaping in the air

cross-tide a tide which runs across the direction of another

crown coin worth five shillings (25p)

cry quittance get even

Cupid classical god of love

curl-pate curly-haired one (term of endearment)

curry-comb comb used to rub down a horse

cutter cut-throat

dag handgun

dam confine

damosella pretty girl

dapple horse

denier a paltry coin; a tiny sum of money

Destinies the three goddesses of fate in classical mythology

Diana classical goddess of chastity

dogged currishly awkward or malicious

dog-pig roasted male pig

doit coin worth half a farthing; a trifling amount

Dominus factotum control freak (literally 'Lord do-everything', Latin)

dor buzzing insect

doublet buttoned outer garment worn on the torso

dower dowry, the money or property a wife brings with her in marriage

down upland pasture

drab (v.) use prostitutes

drift objective

dry-fat a large barrel

dudder shudder

dumb show mimed performance

dun dark brown

durst dared

ear (v.) till, plough

engross monopolize

entired exclusively attached

erst originally, at first

exclaim on rail against

extirpen root out

extremely harshly

facinorous atrocious, infamous

fain eagerly

falchion curved sword

fame reputation

fillip blow, buffet

firk beat

flam off deceive with a false tale

flaw gust of wind

flight-shot the maximum range of a bow and arrow

foot-boy page

fore-gallant principal morris dancer

forlorn totally lost

forslow idly neglect

forspeak bewitch

foster forester, gamekeeper

fowling-piece gun for shooting birds

fray affray

frets the divisions on the fingerboard of a stringed instrument

front (*v.*) confront

froward perverse, refractory

fumble with interfere with sexually, 'grope'

galled chafed, wounded

Gammer old woman

gentle (*a.*) well-born; (*n.*) gentleman or gentlewoman

giglot loose woman

gittern stringed instrument like a guitar

glaive spear, lance

gloze speciously flatter

Godamercies an exclamation of applause ('well done')

Goodman 'Mister'; used for persons of lower rank

gossip familiar companion

grange isolated country house

grazier one who grazes cattle for a living

groom inferior fellow

guardant guardian

guise characteristic or fashionable behaviour

gullery deception

gyved shackled at the ankles

hackney horse

halberds spear-like weapons with axe heads, carried by officers

hale pull forcibly, drag

hallow shout, holler

handsel auspiciously inaugurate

hangings painted cloths or tapestries hung to cover the walls of a room

haply perhaps

hard shift extreme effort

havoc (*v.*) squander

hay country dance in which two lines of dancers move in opposite directions, interlacing with each other

hedge (*v.*) block

hie hurry

High Germany central Europe (including modern Switzerland and Austria)

high water high tide

hind servant

hire (*n.*) wages, appropriate reward, just deserts

hist listen

hock cut the hamstring of an animal or person

honest chaste

horse-boy stable-boy

horse-trick an amorous dance step

hose outer garment for the legs

house noble family

hoy small sailing ship used for short voyages

husbandry farming, agriculture

Hymen classical god of marriage

ill-thewed evil-natured

impetrate procure by entreaty

ingle bosom friend

inly inwardly

interrogatory formal legal examination

intitle grant legal possession of something (e.g. land)

ireful angry

jade inferior horse

jet (*v.*) swagger, strut

jocund cheerful

Jove ruler of the classical gods

Justice judge, magistrate

keep dwell

keeper jailer

kickshaws fancy food

lading ship's cargo

lath thin, flat stick of wood

leese lose

letters patent open letter from the crown conferring a right on the recipient

link torch

lo see (*imperative*)

long of on account of

Low Countries Belgium and the Netherlands

lubric lubricious, wanton

lurdan generalized term of abuse implying loutish idleness

luxurious lecherous

main-top the crow's nest of a ship

make away murder

341

makebate breeder of discord

mammon money

mandate royal command

mange skin disease in furry animals

masque court entertainment combining drama, dance, music, song, and spectacle

maugre despite

maw stomach

maze state of amazement

measure a stately dance

mechal adulterous

meed reward

megrim headache, migraine

'mends amends

mercer cloth merchant

merlin a species of hunting bird

mich sneak; feign poverty

mirror example fit for emulation

misevent unwelcome, unpleasant event

mithridate universal antidote for poison

mittimus warrant to imprison someone

morris morris dance

muscado weapon, probably a musket

Muse one of the nine classical goddesses who patronized the arts; figurative term for a source of poetic inspiration

naught naughty

Neptune classical god of the sea

Nestor Greek hero who was a byword for longevity

neuf fist

Newgate a London prison

nice finicky, fastidious

nigh near

ningle bosom friend (sometimes with homosexual undertones)

o'erpry spy on

of from

on of

ordinary eating-house

orisons prayers

outmost utmost

overlade overburden

overplus surplus

oversway master, dominate

overthrow defeat

oyster-boat small shallow-water vessel

painting-table board on which a picture is painted

pantofles overshoes, galoshes

paps breasts

Paris Garden location of the bear-baiting house in Southwark

passenger traveller

pater father (Latin)

pater noster the Lord's prayer (Latin)

pathaire passionate outburst

patrimony legacy left by a father to his son

pawn (n.) pledge

peach (v.) inform against

physic (n.) medicine; (v.) administer medical treatment

piece gun

pinnace small, two-masted ship

planchers floorboards

plash splash

plate domestic utensils made of gold or silver

plume pluck a bird's feathers

pocket up put up with, tolerate

policy deceitful cunning

portion marriage portion, dowry

post ride swiftly

pottle two quarts, half a gallon

pox syphilis; also used as an imprecation

practic knowledge acquired from experience

precisian a person who is over-rigid in observing rules

prefer promote

prentice apprentice

press crowd

pressing-iron used by tailors to smooth cloth

privy secret

prospect view of a landscape

purblind utterly blind

pyramis pyramid

quarterage quarterly payment

quean strumpet

quite utterly

quittance repay

quondam former (Latin)

rapt enraptured

rate (*v.*) rebuke, berate

ratsbane arsenic, a common household rat poison

ravelin outermost fortification

rebato wire wire used to support a ruff

receipt recipe; medicinal cure

report gossip

ribald (*n.*) low-born rascal

ris risen

rivelled wrinkled

roan horse

Rochester a town in Kent, between London and Faversham

roisting riotous revelry

rot-gut adulterated liquor

round a dance with circular motion

rub in a card game, to have a hand all of the same suit

runlet cask

russet coarse, homespun woollen cloth, associated with rusticity

ruth pity

sack white wine imported from Spain or the Canary Islands

Savoy a duchy in northern Italy

'sblood by God's blood; an especially offensive oath

scape escape

scarf (*v.*) cover

sconce fort

semitune semitone

sensible sentient

sergeant court official responsible for executing summonses

sessions a judicial sitting

several separate

'sfoot an oath ('by God's foot')

shilling silver coin worth one-twentieth of a pound

shrievalty a sheriff's period in office

silly innocent

sink cesspool

Sion the hill on which Jerusalem stands

sith since

Sittingbourne a town in Kent, east of Faversham

'size assize

snuff the liquid left in the bottom of a cup after drinking

sound swoon

speck fat meat

speed fare

sprite soul, spirit

spurn kick; refuse

starven starved

stay wait

stews brothel

stigmatic marked with infamy

still always

stock the portion of a pack of cards which has not been dealt

stout proud, haughty

straightways at once, immediately

strait tight

strong water an alcoholic beverage

'stroy destroy

sullen dull-coloured, gloomy

swart black, swarthy

tables backgammon

tabor small drum

tedious long

temper (*v.*) mix

tender (*v.*) give, proffer

term period

tester (1) bed-canopy; (2) coin worth sixpence

theoric theoretical knowledge

thrall enslave

throughly absolutely, through and through

tissue rich cloth often interwoven with gold or silver

tother the other

to-torn ragged

touse handle roughly

trace (*v.*) dance

train lure

transmarine foreigner

traverse (*v.*) dance with rhythmic movement of the feet

trench (*v.*) cut

trencher platter

Tritons lesser sea-gods in classical mythology

trot (*n.*) crone

troth in truth (asseveration)

trug prostitute

trull prostitute, whore

trundle-tail a low-bred dog with a curly tail

turtle turtle-dove
twelvemonth year
twine (*n.*) embrace
Tyburn site of the London gallows
unhallowed wicked, unholy
unthrift wastrel
use interest on a loan
use-man moneylender
victualler purveyor of food
vied-ruff a card game
wain large cart
watchet light blue
water-dog hunting dog trained to
  retrieve wildfowl
wax grow, increase in substance
well-hatched sumptuously inlaid with
  precious metal
Westminster Hall location of
  London's law courts

whig whey
whistly quietly
white-livered cowardly
wicket a small door set in a larger gate
winding sheet used to wrap a corpse
  before burial
wink close one's eyes, blink
wit intelligence, shrewdness
witch (*v.*) bewitch
wonnot won't
worsted woollen
wot know
woundy extremely
wrack destruction, ruin
wreak vindictive attack
wrest force; twist out of shape
writhen twisted, deformed
zounds by God's wounds; one of the
  most offensive Elizabethan oaths

ALEXANDER POPE	Selected Poetry
ANN RADCLIFFE	The Italian The Mysteries of Udolpho The Romance of the Forest A Sicilian Romance
CLARA REEVE	The Old English Baron
SAMUEL RICHARDSON	Pamela
RICHARD BRINSLEY SHERIDAN	The School for Scandal and Other Plays
TOBIAS SMOLLETT	The Adventures of Roderick Random The Expedition of Humphry Clinker
LAURENCE STERNE	The Life and Opinions of Tristram Shandy, Gentleman A Sentimental Journey
JONATHAN SWIFT	Gulliver's Travels Major Works A Tale of a Tub and Other Works
JOHN VANBRUGH	The Relapse and Other Plays
HORACE WALPOLE	The Castle of Otranto
MARY WOLLSTONECRAFT	Mary and The Wrongs of Woman A Vindication of the Rights of Woman

Late Victorian Gothic Tales

JANE AUSTEN

Emma
Mansfield Park
Persuasion
Pride and Prejudice
Selected Letters
Sense and Sensibility

MRS BEETON

Book of Household Management

MARY ELIZABETH
BRADDON

Lady Audley's Secret

ANNE BRONTË

The Tenant of Wildfell Hall

CHARLOTTE BRONTË

Jane Eyre
Shirley
Villette

EMILY BRONTË

Wuthering Heights

ROBERT BROWNING

The Major Works

JOHN CLARE

The Major Works

SAMUEL TAYLOR
COLERIDGE

The Major Works

WILKIE COLLINS

The Moonstone
No Name
The Woman in White

CHARLES DARWIN

The Origin of Species

THOMAS DE QUINCEY

The Confessions of an English
    Opium-Eater
On Murder

CHARLES DICKENS

The Adventures of Oliver Twist
Barnaby Rudge
Bleak House
David Copperfield
Great Expectations
Nicholas Nickleby
The Old Curiosity Shop
Our Mutual Friend
The Pickwick Papers